PENGUIN BOOKS
RAJASTHAN: AN ORAL HISTORY

Rustom Bharucha is an independent writer, theatre director, and cultural critic, based in Kolkata. A leading theorist of interculturalism and the impact of globalization on local and indigenous cultures, he is the author of several books including *Theatre and the World*, *The Question of Faith*, *In the Name of the Secular*, and *The Politics of Cultural Practice*.

RAJASTHAN

AN ORAL HISTORY

Conversations With Komal Kothari

Rustom Bharucha

PENGUIN BOOKS

PENGUIN BOOKS
Published by the Penguin Group
Penguin Books India Pvt. Ltd, 11 Community Centre, Panchsheel Park, New Delhi 110 017, India
Penguin Group (USA) Inc., 375 Hudson Street, New York, New York 10014, USA
Penguin Group (Canada), 90 Eglinton Avenue East, Suite 700, Toronto, Ontario, M4P 2Y3, Canada (a division of Pearson Penguin Canada Inc.)
Penguin Books Ltd, 80 Strand, London WC2R 0RL, England
Penguin Ireland, 25 St Stephen's Green, Dublin 2, Ireland (a division of Penguin Books Ltd)
Penguin Group (Australia), 250 Camberwell Road, Camberwell, Victoria 3124, Australia (a division of Pearson Australia Group Pty Ltd)
Penguin Group (NZ), 67 Apollo Drive, Rosedale, North Shore 0632, New Zealand (a division of Pearson New Zealand Ltd)
Penguin Group (South Africa) (Pty) Ltd, 24 Sturdee Avenue, Rosebank, Johannesburg 2196, South Africa

Penguin Books Ltd, Registered Offices: 80 Strand, London WC2R 0RL, England

First published by Penguin Books India 2003

12 11 10 9 8 7

ISBN 9780143029595

Typeset in Sabon Book by Eleven Arts, New Delhi
Printed at Repro India Ltd., Navi Mumbai

CONTENTS

ACKNOWLEDGEMENTS

This book is the outcome of many hours of conversation with Komal Kothari over a two-year period. I am indebted, therefore, to him, for giving me so much of his time, attention, care, and above all, the generosity of his knowledge. To his wife, Indira-ji, and other members of the Kothari household, I remain grateful for their warm hospitality in Paota, Jodhpur, the site of my research, which became a second home. To the dedicated staff of the Rupayan Sansthan, administered by Kuldeep Kothari, I extend my gratitude for their sincere support through the entire documentation process.

The first reader of this book was Rowena Hill, who responded meticulously, yet empathetically, to the manuscript, as it was in the process of being transcribed. Marian Pastor Roces and Judy Freya Sibayan also contributed to the conceptualization of the narrative, when I was not sure how to inscribe myself in it. Ira Sisodia translated Rajasthani songs and other minutiae of local knowledge, provided in part by the eminent writer and folk archivist, Vijay Dan Detha, the co-founder of Rupayan Sansthan. Manohar Lalas also made some useful last-minute corrections in the manuscript.

During the final stages of the book, Shubha Chaudhuri provided invaluable help not only as the diacritics consultant, but also as a commentator on tricky questions relating to Rajasthani folklore and ethnomusicology. Her capacity to share her research with a total absence of territoriality made her a very special colleague. For the overall editing of the book, I remain grateful to Kamini Mahadevan of Penguin Books India for her solid support through the publishing process.

Alok Rai also provided pithy comments that contributed positively to the rewriting of the book.

As a former recipient of the Nehru Fellowship, Komal Kothari would like to acknowledge the research facilitated by this grant, which was communicated to me in the course of writing this book. Both of us are grateful to the office of the Sangeet Natak Akademi for promptly processing a grant that facilitated the recording of our conversations. A wide selection of this recording is now available in the archives of the Akademi for future reference. Excerpts from one of Komal Kothari's essays on Rajasthani folk music have been included in the Appendix with the kind permission of the American Institute of Indian Studies. I also wish to acknowledge the professionalism of the ARCE library in Gurgaon, which enabled me to access a wide spectrum of research materials.

For suggestions and contributions to the visual inputs of the book, I wish to thank Daniel Neuman; the *paṛ* painter Rajendra Joshi; and Kuldeep Kothari, who has photographed the entire research process with involvement and care. The Prince Claus Fund for Culture and Development has also provided a generous grant to Rupayan Sansthan for the production of a CD that can enhance the listening pleasure of this book through diverse musical selections from Rajasthan.

While writing the book, I became only too aware that Komal Kothari has friends scattered in different parts of the world, ranging from the desert musicians and nomadic communities of Rajasthan to ethnomusicologists and folklorists based in some of the leading institutions and universities of the world. I recall one friend in particular, the Scandinavian musicologist Vibeke Homaa, who chose to spend precious time with Komal Kothari and his family in Jodhpur, shortly after she was diagnosed with terminal brain cancer. I wish Vibeke were alive to read the book, but her spirit and courage have inspired me to recognize the privilege of writing as a labour of love.

My own friends have continued to be a source of support, primarily Rajeev and Tani Bhargava, whose residence in Delhi became a very comforting *dharamshala* on my frequent trips from Calcutta to Jodhpur. It is only appropriate that I should write these acknowledgements in their home.

New Delhi
December 2002.

NOTE ON DIACRITICS

Steeped in a highly localized and indigenous vocabulary, this book uses diacritics to inflect numerous Rajasthani and Hindi words, some of which are not likely to be found in standard dictionaries. Without diacritics, for instance, it would be difficult to distinguish between 'sand' and '*sānḍ*' (a female camel); the brass plate (*thāḷi*) and the ethno-geographic land category (*thaḷi*), and so on.

In certain contexts, diacritics have been eliminated altogether. For example, there are no diacritics for place names (which have been rendered by census spellings); nor have they been used for familiar texts in Indian literature like the *Ramayana* and the *Mahabharata*, or common categories like Brahman and Bania. Frequently used words in the book like the names of musician castes, notably the Langas and Manganiyars, and proper names like Pabuji and Ramdev have also been represented without diacritics.

Diacritics have primarily been used to indicate vowel length as in the long 'ā' (*jajmān*), 'ū' (*rūp*), and 'ī' (*khīr*), which could also have been rendered with a double 'a', 'o', and e', respectively. To differentiate between consonants, 'ṭ', 'ḍ', 'ṇ', and 'ḷ' have been retroflexed as in '*ṭānkā*', '*ḍhol*', '*surṇāī*', and '*gāḷī*'. 'Ṛ' has also been used in words like '*jhāṛu*', where 'ḍ' is not appropriate, and 'n' has been used to indicate nasalization as in '*gehun*'.

For a quick reference, a comprehensive list of words with diacritics has been included in the Glossary to the book.

NOTE ON CD

This book can be read in its own right without being supplemented by musical resources. However, readers have the option to enhance their awareness of Rajasthan's diverse musical traditions by listening to a specially designed CD, *Rajasthan: A Musical Journey*, which has been drawn from the archives of Rupayan Sansthan.

In this journey, there are excerpts from three different versions of the Pabuji epic, drawing on the acoustic and rhythmic differences of three instruments—the *rāvanhatthā*, the *māṭā*, and the *gujari*. In addition to landmarks in the Rajasthani folk song repertoire—*Gorbandh*, *Hicaki*, *Kurjan*, and *Nimbuḍā*—the musical selections are punctuated with brief snatches of oral genealogy and panegyric verses. Along with group singing, there are striking examples of solo renditions by women singers, ranging from the quasi-classical style of Allah Jilahi Bai and the robust Manganiyar singing of Rukma, punctuated by the *ḍhol*, to the unaccompanied voices of nomadic Kālbeliā women singing in the wilderness of the desert.

Rajasthan: A Musical Journey can be ordered directly from Rupayan Sansthan, B/2 Road, Paota, Jodhpur-342010. E-mail: rajfolk_jp1@sancharnet.in

INTRODUCTION

LISTENING TO KOMALDA

Once upon a time, there was a wise old man who lived in Jodhpur, who could talk about everything under the sun. From morning till night he talked, pushing the seconds into minutes into hours into days into months into years, never stopping to take stock of what he was talking about—land, water, agriculture, livestock, musical instruments, oral epics, folk songs, genealogies, rituals, trances, even contemporary exotica like intellectual property rights. There was nothing that he couldn't talk about, this old man from Rajasthan. Gradually, it became clear to everyone around him that he was no longer just talking, but an oral epic was taking shape through him.

This folklore is fictional, but it conveys some of the aura surrounding Komal Kothari (or Komalda, as he is affectionately called by his younger colleagues and friends). As much as one needs to resist this aura for its obvious sentimentality and deference to the cult of omniscience, it cannot be denied completely. Let us face it: there *is* a certain magic in Komalda's mode of thinking, without which I probably would not have been inspired to write this book. In the intricate web of his connections, spanning the cultural geography of Rajasthan, he moves in and out of several contexts, shifting tracks, going off on tangents, making intuitive leaps, but never quite losing the thread in the labyrinth of his mind.

'Is this a peculiarly "*Indian* way of thinking?"' as A.K. Ramanujan once teased out the interpretive possibilities of a famous question.[1] Without embracing the cultural essentialism of what 'Indian' could possibly mean, I would acknowledge that this garrulous, circumlocutory, yet deeply interconnected thinking is not easily encountered anywhere else outside of India. The *thinking* is perhaps more important than the thought itself. When a particular session with Komalda runs its course, one is never left with any conclusive argument or insight, still less a thesis. But one thing is clear: something has been learned along the way.

For more than two years, I have attempted to record Komalda's intimate knowledge of Rajasthan through extended conversations and dialogue. In the process, I have learned that he is neither a seer in the traditional mode, nor a scholar in the academic sense. Whatever he has learned about and contributed to the folk culture of Rajasthan has been, for the most part, orally transmitted. In this context, he is not merely knowledgeable about oral history; in a sense, he *embodies* this history through his almost ceaseless capacity to talk. '*Mere liye bak-bak karne me kuch dikkat nahin hai* (I don't have any problem chattering),' as he once put it with self-deprecatory humour.

When I decided to write this book, I knew that I had to *listen* to Komalda very carefully. In fact, for a long time, I resisted the demands of authorship by saying, 'I'm not writing this book, I'm listening to it.' Today I realize that this was a bit disingenuous, because between listening and writing, there are many other processes and mediations of reading, analysis, and research. It could also be argued that there is a listening-in-writing, and a writing-in-listening, which the interstices of this book will hopefully reveal, in the counterpoint of Komalda's voice and mine. For the moment, it would be useful to ask, 'How did it all begin?'

I first met Komalda in his home-town of Jodhpur in 1986, when I came under the spell of his oral history. Somewhere in these epic ramblings I knew that there was a narrative and something needed to be done about it. But apart from internalizing this very strong memory of our first meeting, my world of theatre and intercultural research was far removed from the material and cultural specificities of Rajasthan. Nothing materialized till sixteen years later when I happened to meet Komalda quite by chance at a conference in Delhi on documentation, which I had reluctantly attended. 'Reluctantly' because documentation seems to be a very dreary and technical subject, until you get involved in its experiments and the debates relating to the ethics of mechanical reproduction in the age of globalization.

At this conference, Komalda held my attention with down-to-earth observations on the intellectual property rights of folklore, in which his own organization Rupayan Sansthan has been directly implicated. I will leave you to read the details of this surreal controversy in which a fragment of a Rajasthani folk song was used for the television commercial of an American insurance corporation.[2] But, for the moment, let me say that something was sparked in me as a cultural critic, as I heard Komalda talk about intellectual property rights. I realized that it was time for an update, not just on the globalization of folklore, but on where Komalda himself stands in relation to traditional communities in Rajasthan today.

'Communities': I have in mind here the intense debates among intellectuals and activists in post-Ayodhya India around the 'narrative of community', whose opposition to the state has invariably been pitched around an anti-modernist agenda.[3] This is not the place to substantiate the tired polarities of this debate, but it doesn't help that the upholders of 'community' continue to be steeped in highly secularized, cosmopolitan, globalized locations, whose benefits of modernity—notably, the conceptual apparatus to critique it—are rarely acknowledged. Nor is it particularly convincing that communitarian theorists should flaunt the pluralist principles of traditional belief-systems, without subjecting the patriarchy of communities to critical scrutiny.[4] Conversely, the disdain of die-hard secularists for any mode of knowledge that cannot be rationalized within the paradigms of an enlightened modernity continues to suffer from its own blind spots.[5]

Komalda, I should emphasize, is not part of this theoretical debate. However, this book can be read as providing a certain body of *evidence* in relation to the lives and indigenous knowledge systems of traditional communities in Rajasthan today, against which theoretical constructs of 'community' in the communitarian/secularist debate can be measured. I should add that Komalda's interactions with traditional musician communities like the Langas and Manganiyars have been sustained over forty years of active fieldwork—a fieldwork that has not, for the most part, been written up as ethnography. Having made this point, it is equally necessary not to equate his intervention with that of a son-of-the-soil nativist. While opening himself to non-modern belief-systems, Komalda never uses them to deny his own modernity or what could be described as his 'vernacular cosmopolitanism.'[6]

In this regard, it is worth remembering that if he is identified with the so-called 'region' of Rajasthan, he has also been largely responsible for both the nationalization and internationalization of Rajasthani folk music. The traditional caste musicians like the Langas and the Manganiyars, who continue to live outside of modernity within their own social and legal systems, arguably inimical to the tenets of the Indian Constitution, are also among the most widely travelled of jet-setting international performers. To what extent this travel actually affects the inner lives of their communities will be examined later in the book.[7] But so far as Komalda is concerned, I would stress his affinities to both 'home' and 'the world', which are not so much oppositional categories as they are shifting relations in the same continuum.

An irony is worth dwelling on here. On the one hand, Komalda has fed the research of more international scholars dealing with Rajasthan than almost any other academic in the field. Indeed, it is almost mandatory that whether the research is on oral epics or on religion or on puppetry or on pottery or on architecture that 'Komal Kothari' will be cited not necessarily with any of his publications, which are remarkably few, but through 'personal correspondence'. And yet, while verifying, authenticating, correcting, and contributing to the research of others, he himself has not been researched. This is a classic instance, I would say, in the larger fields of folklore, ethnomusicology, and anthropology, of the 'native informant' being taken for granted.

Here, of course, one could reverse the question: Why has Komalda allowed himself to play the role of the 'informant', which could more euphemistically be rendered as 'guide', 'advisor', or 'expert', without taking on the risks of authorship? I think this question is vital for the contextualization of my own authorship of his work. So, in the spirit of oral narratives, where formalities can be dislodged by all kinds of interruption, I put Komalda that question now:

Komalda, why do you talk so much about Rajasthan? You don't write as much as you talk. Why is this?

Earlier I used to write quite often. But slowly, what happened was that I started to gather material on Rajasthan, and most of this material came from oral sources. Of course, I continued to read, but this reading only compelled me to go deeper and deeper into collecting material from the people directly. At all points I felt that I had to know more, and as long as I didn't know any subject adequately, it was difficult for me to write. Slowly a situation emerged in which I found it impossible to write, because I realized only too clearly that I didn't know enough about this or that phenomenon. What I felt was that my area of darkness increased as I learned more about anything. And this convinced me that I should not write.

There was another problem. When I read serious books on history, anthropology, and the methodology of different disciplines, I was afraid of all those quotations and references. And since I was working in so many different areas and on so many subjects, it became even more difficult to get material relevant from the scholarly, academic point of view. One problem that loomed before me was history, because whether I was talking about the singing of the Langas or Manganiyars, or folk instruments like the 'kamāychā' or the 'rāvanhatthā', I would invariably be asked about their individual histories.

Now, history is not my discipline. And the history of music is particularly difficult because you have to address so many technical things—how do the strings of a particular instrument sound? How are the notes produced? What are their vibrations? There are any number of details that need to be taken into account. So I decided not to enter the field of history at all. I would continue to read history, but I would never use the discipline as such for the presentation of my views.

Many years ago I spent some time in the company of Milton

Singer in Chicago. We talked about many things, traditional instruments and the devotional music traditions of India, and so on. At one point he raised a few questions about a particular instrument: 'How old is it? When did it come into existence?' I told him, 'This is one of my biggest worries. I don't want to answer such questions because I can never be sure of the answer.'

Obviously, there is a fear of history at work here, which is all the more moving for me (as the author of this book) as I confront the profound humility of my subject. Komalda claims that he needs to 'know' more before he can write. At first glance, this is surely ironic because the popular conception of Komalda is that he knows almost everything that needs to be known about Rajasthan. However, what will become evident in the course of this book is the very imperfection and fragility of his knowledge—a knowledge that becomes all the more precious because its nuggets of wisdom are so few, yet resonant. Needless to say, in his rambling discourse, there are almost no dates, the facts are occasionally imprecise even as they are presented with an aura of third-person omniscience, and they are not theoretically imbued with Clifford Geertz's now axiomatic principle that 'cultural facts are always already interpretations'.[8]

Obviously, if we go by the rules of theoretical correctness today, a lot of Komalda's narrative would not pass as history. However, my own reading is that Komalda is entrapped by a particular idea of history, culled to a large extent from his early reading of D.D. Kosambi (1956), among other historians, to whose exacting standards of material analysis the self-estimation of his work doesn't measure up. The point is that it *cannot* measure up because Kosambi's idea of history, for instance, is itself enmeshed within a particular terminology, tradition, training, and intellectual rigor that are inseparable from a particular Marxist reading of the means and modes of cultural production. Without undermining the exemplary clarity of this model, the point is that there are other readings and writings of history that need to be taken into account, which Komalda does not consider. In fact, he seems oblivious of the more recent experiments in the (re)writing of history, incorporating fragments, orality, reflexivity, and an almost mandatory inscription of the very limits of writing on the borders of different disciplines.[9] It is one such experiment in writing, framing, and questioning 'oral history' that constitutes the multi-layered agenda of this book.

Stages of Listening

Let me now focus on the central act of listening that underlies this book, without which it could not have been written. I would stress the 'act' of listening, because listening is no mere reflex, or passive state of aural reception. Listening is active. Listening is embodied. And above all, listening is a communicative energy.

My work in theatre over the years, particularly in intercultural projects where I have worked in languages that I don't know, has given me some preparation in the act of listening.[10] Let me share one such experiment with a group of young student actors in the village of Heggodu in Karnataka, where I was conducting a class on 'listening'. Actors can be notoriously lazy when it comes to opening their ears. While improvising movements to the sounds of a flute, and exploring physical reflexes to the rhythm of wooden clappers, I realized that these exercises were merely pretexts for listening. They were not helping the actors to *listen*. Finally, with some exasperation, I opted for a minimal experiment, as I realized that the actors were oblivious even to the night sounds of the countryside, punctuated by the drone of crickets.

The actors stood on stage, while one of them walked out of the theatre singing a Kannada folk song at the top of his voice. He continued to sing this song as he walked out of the theatre, down the village road, into the wilderness of the countryside, and after twenty minutes or so, he came back, retracing his steps, while continuing to sing the song at the same volume. The other actors simply had to listen to the rise and fall and sudden disappearance of the voice, followed by its steadily amplifying crescendo. I don't wish to mystify this experience, but during this process of listening, the very bodies of the actors were transformed. Listening had energized their inner beings.

While this description is something of a detour in my reflection on ethnography, I think it helps the reader of this book to know 'where I'm coming from.' I'm not a trained anthropologist or folklorist, but I have some knowledge of performance, without which it is not really possible to understand what goes on between two men facing each other—one talking, the other listening—with a microphone recording their conversation, positioned between them. Of course, the 'language' of theatre is synaesthetic, involving multiple components of gesture, movement, expression, rhythm, silence, and so on. In the predominantly verbal communication that I had with Komalda, there was almost no visual intervention through the insertion of video recordings or photographs. It was talk, talk, talk, and I daresay, listen, listen, listen.

When does listening become a performative act? There is a growing literature on performance analysis in relation to folklore, in which 'performance' is now viewed beyond the strictures and conventions of theatre to include 'practically any kind of human activity', where something is done 'for a reason, with an intention.'[11] In this context, 'informal conversations, interviews, and recording sessions' *staged* 'especially for the scholar', are viewed as 'performances'.[12] But doesn't this make 'performance' almost indistinguishable from 'context'? As Stuart Blackburn spells out the difference succinctly: 'Context is the sum total of factors from both the cultural and the more immediate situations that impinge upon an oral presentation. Performance, on the other hand, is the delivery and stylization of a story within a context; it tells not "what" but "how."... Performance, in other words, is what happens to a text in a context.'[13]

The challenge is to figure out the precise nature of this 'happening', particularly when its 'delivery' and 'stylization' are not very far removed from conversations in everyday life. This is one of the most difficult tasks that I've faced in 'inscribing', 'transcribing', and 'describing' Komalda's discourse and subsequent transformation into a narrative.[14] When I talk to him early in the morning over a cup of tea, for instance, I am aware that the tone and drift of his conversation are more fluid than what comes through in our recorded sessions. For a start, while sipping his tea, he is also peeling vegetables—mounds of *barbaṭi*, *guārphali*, *methi* that feed the eighteen members of the Kothari household. Certainly, there is a shift in 'context' as we move from conversation to recorded session, but this shift, I would argue, is so slight that I never consciously felt that we were engaged in a 'performance' at all.

However, the point is that even the slightest shift through the insertion of a seemingly innocent technological device like the microphone alters the intentionality of a 'conversation'. In essence, the conversation is no longer entirely a conversation and 'the field' has been enunciated in a different way. What is 'the field' of this book? One could say, 'Rajasthan.' But this 'Rajasthan' is twice mediated—once, through the presence of Komal Kothari, who unselfconsciously has his own priorities and biases in viewing his home-state. In this regard, he has no difficulties in marginalizing the over-represented Rajput hagiography surrounding royal families and warriors. The Langas and Manganiyars, Bhāmbhis and Meghwāls, among other communities from the downtrodden sections of society, matter a lot more to him than Rajputs and the royal family. Inevitably, in this book, you will not find descriptions of palaces and forts, still less any reference to the Palace on Wheels, among other attractions of five-star Rajasthani tourist exotica. Despite its epic span of diverse subjects and references, 'the field' of Rajasthan presented in this book is decisively selective and interconnected.

The second mediation in representing 'the field' is technological. As a 'listener', I opt to hear Komalda talk not 'in the field', but within the familiar, yet anonymous confines of the recording studio in his own research institute, Rupayan Sansthan. Far away from the ramparts of Jaisalmer Fort or the desolate beauty of the desert, the site of our conversations is positively hermetic, devoid of 'local colour'. Nor are they free of the pressure of time to which suburban life in Jodhpur seems quite oblivious. For all their informality, our recordings were determined to a large extent by the duration of the tapes, which curiously seemed to coincide with Komalda's capacity to speak impromptu for around seventy-four minutes (the average length of a digital mini-disc). What, it could be asked, was 'impromptu' about these seventy-four-minute sessions confined within a recording studio?

For a start, I would say that no session was ever conceptualized in advance. There was never a prior 'script' spelling out where 'we wanted the session to go.' Significantly, there were no notes, reference books, or other mnemonic aids used by Komalda while he talked. If he had a memory lapse about a particular fact or name, we had to accept this as part of the 'performance'. At no point did I feel that he was trying to be somewhat more 'academic' for the sake of the recording. Indeed, as I retrospect on the approximately thirty hours of recording that we have made, I realize that at no point did Komalda cite a theoretical or scholarly reference, or quote from a particular book. Unabashedly, he presented his understanding of 'folklore' without 'folkoristics', which would seem to be anathema to most folklorists today.[15] If there is a 'fokloristic' dimension that is latent in Komalda's discourse, as I believe there is, it is clearly devoid of any technical jargon relating to the difference between 'variants' and 'versions', 'countertexts' and 'metatexts', still less, more formidable categories like 'cross-genre isomorphisms'. Even the banalities of the Stith-Thompson indexing system, or the very familiar categories of A.K. Ramanujan's *ākam* and *pūram* distinctions, were never once invoked in the course of his discourse.

In this resolute absence of folkloristic terminology, I was compelled to ask Komalda at one point: 'Is what you do folklore?' He responded vaguely: 'Yes, you could say so.' Next question: 'Do you know anyone else who does folklore like you?' He was silent for a moment, and then with a touch of embarrassment, mumbled, 'No, I haven't come across such a person.'

At one level, it could be argued that it is precisely this absence of folkloristic terminology and rhetoric that enabled me—a non-folklorist— to listen to him for hours on end. But did this lessen the challenge of transcribing what he had to say? Hardly. What emerged from the first typed transcripts of the recordings was a totally ungrammatical gibberish that was a linguistic nightmare. I had wanted a verbatim account of Komalda's discourse, which was provided by a stenographer with admittedly meticulous copying abilities, but no comprehension of what had been said. Stenographic copying, as became only too evident from the gibberish, does not result in a transcription.

As I entered the process of transcription myself, I had no other choice but to listen to all the tapes over and over again in an uneasy, yet heightened solitude. Now, Komalda was no longer physically present as he had become a disembodied voice, which I could control by 'rewinding', 'fast-forwarding', and even making it 'pause' when it got on my nerves. With the memory of our actual conversation at the back of my mind, I began to 'write over' the gibberish in order to make sense of it. Slowly, with the insertion of grammar, the reordering of sentences and phrases, the deletion of redundancies, and many torturous alterations, the transcripts began to make sense even if they did not breathe with a life of their own.

If in the first round of recording, I hardly took notes at all, concentrating totally on the act of listening, in the second round of listening, I found myself taking notes furiously. Along with 'writing over' the transcripts-in-the-making, I was also 'writing *down*' all kinds of confused queries for Komalda's clarification. Clearly, the intensity of listening was giving way to the struggle to clarify meanings and, inevitably, to interpret what seemed to be a relentlessly 'objective' text, heavy in empirical observation and extremely thin in description.

The dilemma of transcription has been well documented by anthropologists and folklorists. For example, from James Clifford's impeccable 'Notes on (Field)notes', one is more than adequately prepared, at a theoretical level, not to be falsely reassured by a transcription's capacities to appear 'innocent', as if it were a mere matter of 'copying', with minimal 'transformation'.[16] As Clifford astutely emphasizes, a transcription's 'ethically superior and nonauthoritative' aura may have 'the political effect of making canonical what is simply one telling of a myth or item of culture lore.'[17] This was precisely the problem that I faced in the early stages of my own transcription process, because, against my will, Komalda was coming across as 'canonical', the Voice of Rajasthan itself, droning on and on with an omniscient, detached, colourless, grass-root form of punditry.

Can I deny that the banality of these early transcripts was oppressive? But they were also deeply troubling because this is not how I *remembered* listening to him in person, or for that matter, listening to him on tape. In person and on tape, his 'objectivity', I would argue, is invariably counterpointed by a sense of exploration, as his voice searches for the right word or term, even as he is aware of it. But this search for the word doesn't come through in the written text, nor the timbre of the voice, nor the circuitous deviations of his mind.

Needless to say, I was terribly depressed by my efforts. But as much as I was deflated by what I had written *down* and written *over*, I was equally resistant to writing *up* the transcripts to make them more 'immediate'. Of course, they had to 'work' as texts—in other words, they had to be as intelligible and vivid as possible, but I was not going to dress them up. In other words, even as I had no other option but to accept that I was writing Komalda's text and altering it in the process—now it was no longer possible to resist authorship—I was not going to make its 'thin' description 'thick.' If his discourse is devoid of adjectives—and Komalda has acknowledged to me that he hates adjectives—then I was not going to add them to colour the text. If his episodes on different aspects of cultural life in Rajasthan didn't have a strong 'sense of an ending', I was not going to provide an appropriate climax or tricky closure. If his narration of the story of *Pabuji* was skeletal, with large gaps and holes, I was not going to cover them up. Rather, I was going to expose them through notes and commentary.

Why, it could be asked, does the transition between the spoken word and the written text pose specific problems in the case of Komalda? I would speculate on three possible reasons.

1. Contrary to what his numerous admirers and listeners may assume, Komalda is not a story-teller. This doesn't mean that he doesn't tell stories, but he tells stories more often than not to substantiate contexts. There are numerous examples in this book where it will be clear to the reader that the context is invariably more important to Komalda than the text. I will give you one example—*Hīr Rānjhā*, which is by Komalda's own admission an extraordinary romantic epic, suffused with Sufi sentiments and philosophy. When he first brought this up, I thought, 'Ah, now he's going to talk about *Hīr Rānjhā*.' And within five minutes, the text was forgotten and Komalda was expounding on foot-and-mouth disease, to which a ritualistic reading of *Hīr Rānjhā* is linked, particularly among those tribal communities in the desert whose animals are afflicted during the epidemic.

Now, at one level, it could be argued that this insertion of 'foot-and-mouth disease' is just fantastic. But Komalda is not interested in shock tactics—he is merely stating 'facts', as he has imbibed them. And while these 'facts' can be startling in their first utterance, they cease to be so as they get expounded through many pedestrian details.

In other words, one problem in transcribing Komalda's discourse concerns its overwhelming 'facticity', which overrides other investigations relating to poetry, fiction, and even song. Tellingly, for a man who is widely regarded as one of the leading authorities on Rajasthani folk music, Komalda, by his own admission, cannot sing. We are not dealing, I should emphasize, with an epic bard here, even though the folklore around Komalda may contribute to this image.

2. Earlier, I had said that Komalda doesn't like adjectives, but he loves nouns. And most of all, I would say that he loves nomenclature—clusters of categories around land, water, livestock, ownership patterns, and so on. Is this passion for categories yet another sign of Komalda's 'Indian' way of thinking? Nothing I have written in this book can quite capture the relish with which he articulates words that would seem to come from another time, but which are still used by traditional communities in the desert. When Komalda invokes ethno-geographic categories of land like *swāḷakh* or *dhāṭ* or *thaḷi* or *tālāb kā peṭā*, there is such a resonance in these words. But when they get transcribed on to the printed page, without much description beyond a cursory line or two of their predominant features, they come out sounding like 'ethno-geographic categories', which is precisely what they are at one level, but they are so much more than that. Sadly, what is conveyed through the voice is not always translatable in the written word.

3. This brings us to the tricky and indeed intransigent problem of translation. James Clifford has rightly emphasized that 'transcription always raises questions about *translation*', calling attention to Talal Asad's valuable perspective on 'unequal languages', which are subsumed within the larger inequities of global politics.[18] I have engaged with Asad's position in my own inter/intra-cultural theatrical experiments with European texts in 'Third World' cultural and political contexts.[19] In this book, I have had to face the problem of power in language at a more localized level, as I have been compelled to translate Komalda's English into my own. Clearly, the 'Indianness' in our different uses of and exposures to English has very different contexts and social backgrounds.

Nonetheless, almost all our recordings were conducted in English, because this is the language that that we share and it is also the language I happen to write in. Moreover, English is the language that Komalda has used extensively not only in his dialogues and lectures in numerous international forums and festivals, but in his interactions with folklorists from the southern states of India. Significantly, Komalda used Hindi as a language of 'explication' when he corrected my transcription with detailed clarifications of words and terms. At one point, I felt that it would be interesting to switch between languages, but what emerged in the hybrid text was an unconscious caricature of Hinglish, with which both Komalda and I were uncomfortable.

In the final analysis, I think there was no other choice for me but to accept the different contexts and intellectual constituencies of Indian English, which I have attempted to highlight through the juxtaposition of two texts in this book—Komalda's narrative and my commentary. While it could be argued that both these texts are ultimately stamped by my own authorial voice, I have tried to counterpoint them, attempting to resist the 'rhetorical fusion of viewpoints' which is so apparent in classical models of ethnography.[20]

Resisting yet 'another harmony',[21] one positive factor that has contributed to the contrapuntal narrative of the book is disagreement. It will become very clear to the reader that I am troubled, for example, by Komalda's folkloric perspective on sati, and that there is much more that needs to be said on, say, the Ismaili connections of medieval religious sects than his own comments provide. So, in those places where I have felt that the gaps in his narrative needed to be filled with other critical and theoretical perspectives, I have done so by incorporating them within my own comments. Not surprisingly, the reader will find that my comments tend to dilate when I disagree with Komalda, or perhaps, when I am in a position to disagree with him.

If disagreement catalyzes comment, a shared cognizance of a particular area of research can stimulate dialogue. Tellingly, in the last two chapters of the book, which deal with the nationalization and internationalization of Rajasthani folk music in relation to 'festival culture', intellectual property rights, and the cassette industry, Komalda and I meet on a shared ground of common concerns. This context is familiar territory for me as a cultural critic, and therefore it became possible for me to intervene directly in his discourse in a dialogic mode rather than through critical commentary.

In short, I have tried to explore different modes of narration in this book, to keep its reflexive dimensions alive. There are also copious notes at the back of the book, which I have reserved for those citations and scholarly inputs that can help to situate Komalda's non-academic discourse within a larger framework of theoretical affiliations and critical debates circulating around the field of 'Rajasthan'. I should add that some of these notes use a technical language that may not be readily accessible to non-specialists in the field. For the larger narrative of the book itself, however, I have adopted a more conversational tone in order to reach a potentially wider readership, keeping in mind Komalda's own capacity to speak to just about anyone, independently of his or her expertise.

For a long time, I should confide to the reader, this was not going to be a book. I even speculated on the advantages of *not* attempting any transcription in words, resorting instead to an editing of the existing audio-tapes, so that the 'oral history' could remain 'oral/aural'. In a more virtual mode, I began to think about 'hypertexts' and the interactive computerized technologies of CD-Roms. However, not only am I incompetent to control this technology, but I'm not sure that it's entirely appropriate for the oral mode of narration. Cybertexts function with notions of multiple linkages, randomness, and selective inattention, which are very different from the kind of face-to-face, person-to-person intimacy that is so much part of Komalda's discontinuous continuity. Finally, I have come around to accepting the limitations of the written word, but also its possibilities of being strategized—and questioned— within the very constraints of a particular narrative.

Was I the only listener of this book while it was being written? I'm happy to say 'no'. As the transcripts got written and re-written, edited and re-edited, contextualized and re-contextualized, they began to mutate and acquire their own shapes. Naturally, I wanted Komalda to read these new versions based on his earlier comments, but, as many of his close friends know, Komalda is not much of a reader. I had no other option, therefore, but to sit with him, and read sections of the text, line by line, word by word. Here I found Komalda becoming the listener, the *hunkārio*, the epic respondent, the one who echoes the last words of every line in an epic performance, occasionally interjecting a comment. Komalda was 'listening to Komalda'.

1

THE PAST IN THE PRESENT

We begin with memory, and more specifically, with the mnemonic devices and learning processes that are nurtured in childhood. Nostalgia, I should emphasize, is not Komalda's concern here, but as I urge him to reflect on the intricate links between memory, folklore and oral history, he begins of his own accord to draw on very specific games that he played as a child. As I listen to him, I realize how casually he prepares the ground for the insights that follow on the transmission of fairy-tales; orality and literacy; and larger speculations on time, genealogy, and 'cultural memory', in which the identities of specific communities are grounded.

This chapter begins very much at home, within the cultural moorings of Komalda's own Oswāl Jain family, but it ends with oral genealogies of tribal communities in Rajasthan. As always the span of Komalda's connections is wide and socially differentiated, even as the contexts of individual cultures are respected and held within the shifting contours of his memory.

Memory

Looking back on my childhood, I remember a 'memory game' that I used to play when I was around five or six years old. By this time I had already begun to write. Someone in the family would place a lot of things on a table—all kinds of household items, like matchboxes, playing cards, utensils, and so on. After we had looked at these objects for a few minutes, they would be concealed under a bed sheet, and then as many of the objects as we could remember had to be written down. The one who remembered the largest number of objects would win. As I recall this game today, I realize that we would remember the objects best by placing them in different categories. So, for instance, the *chimṭā* (tongs), the *kaṭori* (bowl), and the *thāḷi* (plate) would be identified with 'the kitchen'. Even today, when you think of all the intricate memory games that continue to be played all over India, during rituals and festivals, you will find that they are invariably built around the principle of categorizing objects in specific ways.

We used to play this memory game while I was still living in the village of Kapasan, before my family moved to Jodhpur. Here in Kapasan I also remember playing *gulli ḍanḍā*—one of the most popular children's games in India, which is played with any number of variations in different regions. At the heart of gulli ḍanḍā, I would say, are very intricate calculations which are made on the basis of how far you can throw a stick—the calculations are so minute that at times you have to measure distances in fractions. As a matter of fact, I was very good at fractions and all kinds of problems in arithmetic, as a student at the Sumer School in Jodhpur in my early years.

I still remember Parashuramji, our arithmetic teacher, who would come into class and promptly start writing questions on the blackboard very quickly and in beautiful handwriting. As students we had to work out the answers in our heads and write them down, before Parashuramji would wipe the questions off the board. And then, he would begin his interrogation. While I and my nephew Swatantra, who was the same age as me, invariably scored full marks, many of our classmates would be in trouble. The problem was that Parashuramji had a peculiar way of punishing them. If, for instance, a boy had only got twenty sums correct out of forty, he would expect Swatantra and myself to actually slap the boy twenty times, once for each wrong answer. Naturally, we felt awkward and also a bit scared, because some of the boys were a lot bigger than us, and they could easily fix us after class. So we decided to slap them very lightly.

But Parashuramji would have none of this and would then proceed to demonstrate how they should be slapped by slapping us!

Numbers played a very important role in my childhood education, and when I look back on it I realize that we learnt our tables by chanting them in unison on a single note. Mind you, we didn't study tables, as is the normal custom today, from two times two up to twelve. We knew our tables all the way to hundred—and not just the prime numbers, but fractions as well. So we could calculate tables on the basis of one and one fourth, two and a half, one and three quarters, and so on. All these tables had to be recited. Invariably, they were conducted by one guruji, who would sit in the classroom of our *poshāl* (elementary school) and make us learn these tables by heart. As the tables got more intricate, we used to explore different pitches; the brighter the student, and the more he wanted to impress the teacher, the higher the pitch he would use and the more accelerated the pace of his rendition. But the basic principle that I would like to stress here is that if you have to learn anything by rote, then you have to *chant* your text. Then only will it enter your deeper memory register.

Each culture has different ways of calculating numbers—for example, we can calculate in fours, using the thumb to count the divisions on the insides of our four fingers in consecutive order—one two three four/five six seven eight/ . . . all the way to sixteen. Sometimes we calculate on the basis of three—one two three/four five six/seven eight nine, and this kind of counting invariably ends on fifteen. Of course, we also count in the 'western' way in which each number is an independent unit—one, two, three, four . . . all the way to ten. That's the cut-off point. The intricacy of calculation depends to a large extent on the basic unit of calculations—is it three or four or five? Earlier, when there were sixteen annas to a rupee, for instance, most calculations were based on the unit of four. Sometimes, while working with nomadic communities, like the Kālbeliā, for instance, we found that the basic unit of their calculations is eight—never nine or ten. And the amazing thing is that they can calculate up to thousands on the basis of the numeral eight.

It's strange how we remember certain things from our childhood, and at the same time, we forget so much. For instance, while I can still chant some of the tables that I learned in school, I have a hard time remembering nursery rhymes. In fact, I cannot recite *dohās* (couplets) that I knew by heart when I was around twelve years old. My friend Vijay Dan [Detha], on the other hand, can actually talk through poetry. At one time I could have recited for hours and hours on end *chhand alankār* in Hindi, the rules of prosody and rhetorical embellishments—I could have differentiated between different *chhand* like *savaiyā*, *muktādām*, *harigitikā*, and so on. Today, with difficulty, I might be able to recite one or two dohās, but otherwise, my memory has failed me. Even folk songs I am not able to sing freely. Of course, as soon as a song is sung, I can recognize it; I know how it will proceed melodically, rhythmically, and so on. What I have discovered is that memory operates in different ways, and these differences are linked to specific genres.

Remembering Stories

Let us turn to stories in this regard. I remember one particular story that my maternal aunt used to tell me as a child. There must have been around five to six children around me at that time, including my younger brother Keshav, who is just sixteen months younger than I am. We would all demand that our aunt tell us the story of Chiḍa-Chiḍi.[1] And what was the story? It had something to do with a pair of birds who would swing on a string suspended on a well's pulley. One day, this string broke, and the birds fell into the well. I remember what a strong impression this story made on me as a child—but, though it was deeply imprinted somewhere in my memory, for the longest time I couldn't remember it at all. When I started to work on folk stories, then I tried with great difficulty to recall this story and, suddenly, it came alive vividly. At that very moment, I realized that when Chiḍa-Chiḍi fell into the well, they didn't die as I had imagined earlier; rather, they flew out of the well into the sky. What a relief that moment was for me, because I realized that the birds were alive.

The question, however, that needs to be asked is why my aunt, who must have told us that story over and over again, never told us that the birds flew away. As I understand it today, I would say that we, as listeners, have to realize that the birds flew away. The teller of the tale, in this case my aunt, is not meant to give us the meaning of the story. This I would regard as a very important clue. When we started collecting children's stories, particularly those told to under seven-year-olds, we discovered that in no folk story whatsoever is anything like a moral or a maxim added to the story itself. Folk stories were never meant as teaching aids, which is how they are being used these days. Basically, I would say they were taken to be some sort of realization—but you must be prepared to 'realize' your answers, not necessarily when you hear the story for the first time but at any point in your life.

Nowadays we find that children are taught the moral of a particular tale. This was not the case in the earlier practice of story telling, as I experienced it. In contemporary situations, children are told stories, and are then expected to tell the stories back to the adults in their family during breakfast or whenever. They are quizzed—what did the lion do? What did the rabbit do? And what happened at the end of the story? As the child rattles off the answers, we feel pleased that something has been learned. Story-telling today has a function, which was not the customary practice in earlier times.

One reason for this is that the stories we heard in our childhood were not necessarily shared with anybody else. So, while I remember hearing Chiḍa-Chiḍi from my aunt, I don't have any recollection myself of telling this story to any of my friends. In other words, I didn't become the carrier of this particular story—it lay deep in my memory for many years, but it was never shared as I am sharing it with you now, or as I have reminisced about it in recent years with many people in different forums. Now, as I have become the carrier of the tale, I realize that there is a certain 'format' in the telling of children's stories. Invariably, they are told by an adult to a child, never by a child to another child. This is one reason why we, as children, never felt the need to tell stories beyond listening to them.

Modalities of Remembering

The origins of stories are mysterious, but not unknown. When we started collecting folk stories in Borunda, we would begin by asking people if they remembered any story from their childhood. And, almost unfailingly, the answer would be an emphatic 'no'. But when we would persist, sometimes for as long as a month, 'When you were put to sleep, surely someone must have told you a story?', most people would remember being threatened with a slap: 'Go to sleep, or else . . .' But then, gradually, the stories would begin to emerge.

Take my elder brother, for example, who came to visit me in Jodhpur shortly before he died at seventy-three. I remember asking him if he remembered anyone telling him a story when he was a child. At first he said, 'Nobody used to tell stories in the family.' So, for the next three to four days, whenever I saw him at breakfast or dinner or tea, I would repeat my question. Finally, one morning he told me that he did remember something, but it was only one line from a story he otherwise no longer remembered. Then I asked him: 'Can you remember who told you the story?' Very vaguely he recalled the name of Heera Bai, who worked as a maidservant in our family; he thought she had told him the story. I asked him further: 'Can you remember who else in the family was around you at that time?' He recalled the company of my two older sisters, Deep Kunwar and Tej Kunwar—Heera Bai would tell the story to these three children, when they would be snuggling under their *rajāis* (quilts) on winter nights. 'Can you remember,' I asked, 'where our family was living at that time?' 'Parbatsar,' he recalled. And sure enough, as my mother confirmed for me, my brother must have been around five years old when our family was in Parbatsar, and Deep Kunwar and Tej Kunwar were already born at that time. My mother also recalled Heera Bai, a widow from the Sādh community who must have been around thirty-five to forty years old.

Now, if we take into account all these facts, it is not difficult to confirm the age of the story in question. If a seventy-three-year-old man is recalling a story that was told to him when he was five years old, and the woman telling him the story was around thirty-five to forty years, then, historically, this tale must go back at least one hundred years. I, too, heard this story during my own childhood, and it continues to be heard in any number of versions, in practically every part of Rajasthan, from Alwar to Udaipur to Banswara. The story lives on.

If you had to ask me to tell you the story right now, I wouldn't be able to give you anything more than the bare facts. There is this child who wants to see his *nāni* (maternal grandmother). On the way to her house, he meets a lion, a wolf, and a dog, who want to eat him. Each time the boy says, 'I'm very lean and thin. Let me go to my nāni's house, where I'll fatten myself up by eating a lot, and then when I come back, there will be more of me to eat.' When he does come back, however, he gets inside a drum, which rolls him safely all the way back home. *Chal meri ḍholki ḍhamāk-a-dhām*—that's the central line of the story that my elder brother had remembered from the forgotten story told to him as a child by Heera Bai.

Now, it's strange how, even as you ask me to tell you the story right now, this line acts as a kind of memory cue—the details of the story I cannot give you, but the substance I remember. What we have discovered from our research on stories is not only that people *do* remember at least one story, even after claiming that they don't remember any; we have also found that most of the stories told to children at a very early age are animal tales. The religious and mythical stories from the Ramayana and the Mahabharata follow somewhat later.

If, as I mentioned earlier, children are not the carriers of tales, then how do these stories get around? In almost any given context in Rajasthani society, we have found in our research that it is not necessarily the mother who tells stories to her children; even the grandmother is not the carrier of tales, as is often believed, especially if her husband is still alive. Most of the time we have found that it is widows living and working in families as domestic helpers who are the key story-tellers. It is these widows who bathe the children, send them to school and attend to all the odd jobs at home; it is they who clean the kitchen, wash the utensils, and tell children stories when they go to bed. Once we were able to identify the widow as the carrier of tales, our methodology for collecting stories was greatly facilitated. We only had to identify the widows in any particular village to acquire stories to add to our collection.

I would not underestimate the role of memory in the telling—and re-telling—of any story. At one level, if I happen to be a good speaker and have a certain command of the language and the form of the story that I am narrating, I might be able to remember a story more effectively. As I told you earlier, I don't have this capacity to remember. But this also makes me think about how important it is to forget. If you do not have the capacity to forget, your life could become very complex. Indeed, there are a lot of things related to the family, all kinds of social tensions, which have to be forgotten. Else this cluster of problems would make it very difficult for us to live. So, in any given society we need to ask what things are retained in one's memory, and which ones get released. What are the processes of remembering and forgetting? Here the reality is that I am talking to you about memory, by using my memory, and my memory is fading.

* * *

Listening to Komalda acknowledge his failing memory, even while witnessing it come alive, is a leitmotif that runs through this book. Whether one is dealing with a children's story like 'Chiḍa-Chiḍi' or an oral epic like 'Pabuji' (Chapter 4), memory lies at the core of any narrative. However, there are different modalities, structures and forms of remembering, which will become only too evident when we deal with women's songs. Here we will note how a song can never be sung the same way twice even by the same women. More mysteriously, the same song can be sung collectively by all the women, even by those who may never have heard it before. How is this possible? How does one remember a song that is not consciously part of one's memory? These are some of the enigmas of folklore.

I would like to return now to one little clue that Komalda acknowledges while recalling the 'memory game' he used to play as a child in Kapasan: the fact that he could write *by this time. How is memory affected by the act of writing? This brings us to the time-tested, yet unresolved problem of relating orality to literacy. Listen now to Komalda tease out the contradictions of this relationship through one direct encounter with traditional musicians.*

Orality and Literacy

In the 1950s, I used to transcribe songs dictated by a few Langa musicians living and working in the Jodhpur area. All of them were illiterate. Later we thought that if they could join adult education classes they would be able to read and write, and this would make it easier for us to collect songs written by them. But this is not how it turned out. We found that when Lakha, one of our chief musicians, learned how to read and write, he needed to consult his diary before he could begin to sing any song. To this day he continues to do this, but the rest of the singers, who are illiterate, don't have to touch a book and they will be able to render hundreds of songs.

So literacy raises a lot of complex questions relating to memory. On the one hand, you can fall back on the written word when your memory fails, but in those contexts where the written word is not available, then the brain itself develops a capacity to memorize—there is simply no other option. What we find is that, when folk musicians become literate, the text of their songs diminishes—it gets squeezed and squeezed in relation to its early size. Or else, through frequent performances of the same song, there is a new learning by rote. On the other hand, the nomadic Kālbeliā women who are illiterate can sing songs with thirty or forty or fifty lines with no memory lapses whatsoever, even though the order of the lines in the song remains totally fluid.

The larger problem we are talking about is the difference between the oral word and the written script. Even today, in some rural areas, writing is often regarded as some kind of magic. After all, how does one account for the fact that twenty people looking at some black scribbles on a page can read the same thing? Ironically, even when we try to involve villagers in adult education movements, we continue to play on their fears—'if you don't know how to read, someone can cheat you of your land or your property, you should know what you're signing', and so on. Isn't this how we promote literacy campaigns? Today, even the very act of signing anything continues to be a source of fear for most neo-literate villagers.

How has this condition existed for so long? The truth is that low-caste people have been prevented from becoming literate in our society. Traditionally, there have been two sectors in Indian society that have pursued literacy—the Brahman communities, with all their religious and astrological practices, the reading of almanacs, and so on; and the trading communities, whose priorities are more utilitarian, connected with the day-to-day activities of buying and selling, the calculation of grains and transportation costs. Unlike the literary and learned Sanskrit traditions, both oral and written, monopolized by Brahmans, the Bania tradition, which is known as Kātantra, is predominantly spoken and functional and has nothing to do with Sanskrit learning.

There's a popular story in Rajasthan that highlights the material priorities of literacy in the trading communities. A peasant goes to a Bania merchant from whom he has taken a loan. The pen wedged on top of one of the Bania's ears falls down—this is where they normally keep their pens. The peasant picks up the pen and returns it to the Bania saying, 'Here, take your *chhuri* (knife).' 'Why *chhuri*?' asks the Bania, 'it's only a pen.' Then the peasant says, '*Āp ki chhuri hi mere gale pe phiri thi*' (Your knife has cut my neck).'

To get back to memory, I would say that with the rise of literacy, new support systems have emerged to facilitate the memory of oral traditions in folklore. There are a lot of things that we may not be able to remember, but all we have to do is to consult a book or a reference library, and more recently, a web-site. In this regard, I think it's important to keep in mind that folklore is always contemporary, even when it deals with cultures and communities who continue to live outside of modernity. If the past continues to have any meaning in society, it survives; otherwise, it disappears, not unlike a ripple on the surface of a lake, which breaks sooner or later.

Obviously there's a lot more to be said about orality and literacy than this fragment suggests. A.K.Ramanujan, for instance, in his classic essay on 'Who needs folklore?'(1999) calls our attention to the 'interpenetration' of orality and literacy, and not just their 'opposition'.[2] *Emphasizing that the 'classical, the written and the fixed' are not necessarily yoked together, Ramanujan provides numerous examples to subvert stock associations that the 'folk' tradition is necessarily oral and fluid. The Vedas, for instance, are fixed, but were not written down until two hundred years ago, following centuries of oral transmission—a transmission that testifies to the phenomenon of 'oral literacy', as Narayana Rao has termed it.*[3]

On the other hand, folktales transmitted orally with numerous variations may have fixed motifs embedded in their structures, not unlike refrains in folksongs, which never change. These fixed motifs in turn may be linked to written versions of the tale, which may have precipitated their oral renditions in the first place. So it's deceptive to assume that an oral tradition necessarily precedes a written one, because their relationship is a lot more volatile and multivalent. Indeed, 'different genres', according to Ramanujan, contain 'different proportions' of what remains 'fixed' in any oral rendition—the order of words and phrases in a proverb, for instance, is set and repeated verbatim. In a joke, however, almost everything can be improvised apart from the punchline.[4]

The relationship of the oral tradition to classical epics, notably the 'Ramayana', will be dealt with more extensively in the chapter on 'Pabuji'. For the most part, however, Komalda does not specifically address any written text in the course of his reflections on orality in order to problematize its vagaries. Instead of texts, Komalda addresses larger contexts of time and genealogy without which specific utterances of memory would be meaningless.

* * *

Time

In the rural areas of Rajasthan, when you ask someone, 'What is your age?', you are not likely to get a clear answer. But it is more likely that you will be told that in such-and-such *kāl*, or more precisely, drought year, I was three years old, ten years old, and so on. *Chhapannā, Chhabbīsā, Behtarā*: these are very well-known time-markers of particular famines. So people will talk about their age only from the point of view of these acute famines. This is their way of measuring the past.

In everyday life, we find that most people can go back to three generations in their families: father, grandfather, great-grandfather. Beyond that, a person generally does not know anything about his past. Of course, if he makes the attempt, there are always sources that can verify the past beyond three generations. What happens is that while a person may know his father's activities intimately and his grandfather's slightly less so, a few things from his great grandfather's life as well will somehow reach his ears.

Let me tell you a story in this regard about my own family, which I heard from my grandmother when I was a child. My great-grandfather was the Diwan of Ratlam state. In this state, there was a king who was old and had two sons—the older son who was his rightful heir and a younger one. My great-grandfather conspired with the younger son to get his brother sent away to a distant place, during which time the younger son poisoned his father, captured the fort of Ratlam, and declared himself king. Now this was the British period when it was not possible to say, 'The king is dead, long live the king.' Rather, the king is dead, and now the kingdom will have to revert to the emperor, who in turn will appoint a political agent to look after the kingdom. Such was the case with all princely states like Ratlam. Here too the younger son could not be recognized immediately as king; it was not an automatic process. To facilitate his appointment, my great-grandfather played a critical role, and somehow or the other, perhaps by bribing the British officers, he managed to get the younger son declared king. By this time the older brother had taken shelter in Jaipur, where another branch of the family developed, while my great-grandfather became the Diwan of the new king in Ratlam.

Today, I can view this episode from the past only in the larger context of a conspiracy. But for my grandmother, it was no conspiracy. On the contrary, she had deep regard for the intelligence of my great-grandfather and the details by which he managed the coup so effectively. I still remember one detail—a locked door, which would have prevented the old king from being killed, had my great-grandfather not arranged for an elephant to break the door down. Many such sensational details were part of the story that I heard from my grandmother. Later, it appears, after becoming the Diwan of the new king, my great-grandfather was accused of embezzlement. This must have been around the 1880s. He was put in jail for eighteen years, during which time his case was taken up by the Privy Council in London. He won the case and received an enormous monetary compensation, Rs 1 lakh for each year of imprisonment, which was a fortune at that time. So this is how the story has come down to me from three generations ago.

Let us examine a different story now, involving a low-caste community. This story comes from a low-caste Bhāmbhi boy in the village of Borunda, who looks back three generations to his great-grandfather, who worked as a *kāsid* (postman) in that same village. Every day this man would go to Jaitaran, which is almost twenty-one miles away from Borunda. He would get up early in the morning, walk those twenty-one miles, collect the *ḍāk* (post), and come back in the evening to Borunda. He did this for twenty years with no payment whatsoever. All Bhāmbhi families were expected to provide at least one person to serve the *jāgirdār* (feudal lord) of the village, thereby enabling the other family members to be free to earn their living. So in this way the Bhāmbhi great-grandfather's services had been indentured to the jāgirdār. Naturally, we were sympathetic when we heard this story—twenty years of work, and no payment. Those were hard times. But on hearing us talk this way, the boy got angry: 'What are you talking about? Why don't you see that my great-grandfather was capable of walking forty-two miles every day? Don't you see what strength he possessed? Why are you talking about money?'

On hearing this response, it struck me afresh that there is more than one way of looking at things. How do you put elements of the past together, and where do you put them? In what frame of reference? Whose frame of reference?

Genealogy

Now these are merely individual recollections of the past. What happens when you deal with larger groups and their modes of remembering the past? Take the genealogists from musician groups like the Langas, Manganiyars, and the scheduled castes. These genealogists can easily go back fourteen to eighteen generations. And they can recall all kinds of details—for instance, so-and-so's great-great-great-grandfather had four sons; from the older son, this family emerged, from the younger son, another branch of the family grew, and so on. Most people think that Langas and Manganiyars survive only as singers of folk songs, but they don't know that these traditional musicians also earn their living by maintaining the genealogy of their patrons (*jajmāns*).

Indeed, the genealogical record of the Langas and Manganiyars, which is entirely oral, is often regarded as definitive. In controversial decisions regarding whether or not a marriage can take place across two sub-castes, it is their sources that are ultimately relied upon. Yet another way by which the Manganiyars preserve the genealogy of their patrons is in the form of a panegyric called the *shubhrāj*, in which the well-being of the jajmān family is ensured by poetic references to all the people in its ancestry. This is yet another way of remembering family histories across generations. I will have a lot more to say about these practices in Chapter 10, where I elaborate on the caste affiliations and social institutions of the Langas and Manganiyars.

Apart from the traditional musicians, there is another kind of genealogist—the *Bhāṭ*—who keeps a record of all the births in the male line of individual families. Actually there are two kinds of *bhāṭ*—the *Mukhbanchā Bhāṭ*, who relies entirely on his memory for his oral recitation, and the *Pothibānchā Bhāṭ*, who has meticulous written records to fall back on. Both these *bhāṭs* visit homes on an average of once every three years, generally on occasions like marriage, childbirth, or any festival. By contrast, the *panḍā* (priest), who also keeps records of all the deaths in individual families, both in the male and female lines, is generally consulted in holy places like Hardwar, where people go for death ceremonies, the immersion of the ashes, and other related rituals. At such places, the two essential questions that are asked of any *yātrī* (pilgrim) are: *Kis gaon ke ho? Āpkā jāt kyā hai*? (Where are you from? And to which caste do you belong?) What is amazing about this genealogical system is its quick retrieval of information. This has yet to be studied adequately. While the written records of the panḍās in Devanāgari script go back more than twenty generations, the Pothibānchā Bhāṭs are also literate, but they use an invented script for their records that is impossible for others to read.

Now, how does genealogy affect the ways in which people are addressed in specific families? My great-grandfather was Jawahar Chand. He had one son called Khuman Singh. Khuman Singh had two sons—Dulah Singh and Berisal Singh. Dulah Singh had four sons, and Berisal Singh had eight sons. Now all male members in the family are identified by the suffix 'ot', which means 'son of'. So I am Berisālot, but since my father Berisal was the son of Khuman, we (I and my seven brothers) can also be identified as Khumānot. My cousin on the other hand, Daulat Singh, was the son of Dulah Singh, so he can be called Daulat Singh Dulahot, but since Dulah Singh was also the son of Khuman Singh, he too can be addressed as Khumānot, like myself and my brothers. So, you see how at some levels the genealogical names separate, only to meet up again.

Another vital aspect of genealogy concerns the husband-wife relationship. I am an Oswāl—this can be regarded as my jāt (caste)—but my sub-caste (*sakh*) is Dugar. Koṭhāri is only a title—originally it referred to people who looked after the army stores (*koṭhār*). Now, the point is that I can only marry within the Oswāl caste, but I cannot marry another Dugar. Likewise, since my wife's sub-caste is Bordiā, my children can marry neither into the Dugar nor into the Bordiā sub-caste groups. Likewise, since my mother was a Kānkariā Bhandāri, none of my children can be married into that group. I can even go so far back as my great-grandmother who was from the Mohnot Mehta sub-caste group. So even to this day no one from my family can marry into this group.

Now, all these rules are there for a very simple reason, and that is to define the areas of incest, so that they can be avoided. In different groups we encounter different incest rules. Once you know the rules that apply to your family, then it becomes possible to determine into which families you can be married, and with which families marriage is prohibited. In this way, entire genealogies of families have been determined over the years.

The Story of Puniā

There are oral genealogists from low-caste and tribal communities as well. But their recitation of the past draws primarily on mythical references. For instance, they will talk about how the sun and moon were born, how the sea emerged, how agriculture came into existence, and so on. The recitation of the Bhil and Garāsiā genealogists, for instance, is very like the Puranas. In the Puranas, there are primarily five divisions—*sarg, pratisarg, kalpa, manvantara, and pralaya*.[5] It is only with *manvantara* that human beings come into existence; it is from this point in time that genealogy begins. The earlier parts of the life-cycle deal with the evolution of nature.

Significantly, most of the low-caste genealogists, who also function as Mukhbanchā Bhāṭs, are from the acrobat communities, such as the Naṭ, the Rājnaṭ, and the Bādi. These acrobats recite the genealogies of low-caste communities like the Meghwāls, who are associated with leather-related occupations and weaving. While the Bādis operate in the western desert zone, the Naṭs function in other parts of the state, rather like the itinerant *kaṭhputli* (puppetry) groups, who are known as Baḷāion ke Naṭ, in the area of Nagaur from which they originate. However, this is not how the puppeteers identify themselves in other parts of Rajasthan and the rest of India, where they present themselves as Bhāṭs. They have double identities, as we shall examine later in the book. (See Chapter 9)

What is important to stress is that the upholding of genealogy is perhaps stronger in the low-caste groups than in the upper castes. For example, if a Bhāṭ had to enter the home of an untouchable, say, a Bhāmbhi's home, then if there is one cot in this home, then the Bhāṭ will sleep on that; if there is one *roṭi* available in this home, then it will be eaten by the Bhāṭ. The Bhāṭs charge the lower castes large sums of money to maintain their genealogy, and their poor patrons have no other option but to pay through their noses. The irony, of course, is that the Bhāṭs themselves are from the lower caste. But, as is well known, even among the lower castes, there is a hierarchy.

So, for example, between handling the carcass of an animal, skinning it, tanning it, and making a shoe out of the leather, there are levels of respectability. The *mochi* (cobbler) would be of a higher status than the *rangāi*, who is responsible for the tanning of the leather, and so on. At times there are contradictions within the caste hierarchy. From an upper-caste perspective, the *dhobi* (washerman), for instance, is not considered untouchable, but for the untouchables themselves, he is untouchable. Likewise, there are hierarchies among the lower castes as to who provides the genealogies for whom.

When you listen to these genealogies, you are forced to confront the fact that low-caste people in India have been denied basic human rights for centuries. If we compare their situation to what we see in the great Hindu myths of the country, can we expect low-caste people to survive on them—on the myths of the *savarṇa*, the upper castes? We know that no society can survive without its myths. Indeed, I would go to the extent of saying that no caste can be fully acknowledged without a genealogy. So what are the myths of the low-caste communities? Where can we find these myths? I would say that it is in the genealogical records of the Mukhbanchā Bhāṭs that we come across the stories of their origins, which enable us to understand how they have survived as groups and from where they have derived their strength.

Let me at this point share a story with you that will give you a more concrete idea of the oral genealogy of low-caste groups.[6] Many years ago, on one of my field-trips, I and my colleagues were passing through Pipalia village near Chhoti Sadari in Mewar. I think we must have arrived around 8.30 in the morning in this village where we saw 400–500 people sitting in one place listening to two genealogists, Mukhbanchā Bhāṭs, who were reciting a story with intricate rhythms patterns beaten on the *ḍhol* (drum) with sticks, on both sides. We noticed that these Bhāṭs had arranged a lot of things around them for an acrobatic performance—ropes and bamboo structures and poles. But now they were reciting the genealogy of a particular community called the Raut, as we came to know from listening to the narrative. The acrobatic stunts would follow after the genealogical record was completed.

During this narrative, there were a number of stories told relating to the ancestry of the Raut community. One story was particularly interesting. It concerned a man called Puniā. Before his time, it appears that no agriculture was practised. Of his own accord, Puniā decided to grow some *makkā* (maize). From where he learned to do this, one doesn't know, but he sowed the field and the makkā grew well. Finally, when the crop was ready and he was preparing for the harvest, the Sun and the Moon arrived. Both these gods told Puniā, 'Without us, could you have grown your crop?' He said, 'No, it would have been impossible. It's because of the rays of the sun that I got light, and because of the moon that my crops could sleep in the cool of the night. So without your help, I could have done nothing.' Then the gods said, 'Why don't you give us our share?' So he said, 'Certainly, not just my share, but whatever I've got, you can take it.' Promptly the Sun and the Moon moved into the fields, but they had never seen such plants growing in their lives. Now, makkā grows on the stem of the plant, on the top of which are some flowery tendrils, which look very beautiful. So the Sun and the Moon decided to take the top part of the plant and leave the rest for Puniā. Inevitably, the top part amounted to nothing, while the stem of the plant on which the makkā grows yielded a rich harvest.

Next year, Puniā decided to grow another crop. And this time he decided to grow *jawār* (sorghum). So he ploughed the field, planted the seeds, and again, the crop was wonderful. Once again, when it was time for the harvest, the Sun and Moon arrived, and repeated what they had said earlier: 'Without us, would you have been able to grow your crop?' And he said, 'No, not without you.' 'Our share?' said the gods. And Puniā said, 'Take whatever you want.' Since the last time they had taken the upper part of the plant which had resulted in nothing, this time the gods decided to take the lower part. Puniā agreed. Since jawār grows on top, Puniā was lucky once again, because he got a rich harvest, while the gods were left with nothing but straw.

Now, after this story was told, one of the Mukhbanchā Bhāṭs raised an open question to the hundreds of people sitting in front of him: 'You've all heard the story, what do you think about it? Can you identify the Sun and the Moon?' And four to five hundred people, almost in one voice, shouted in unison: 'Chandravanshi, Suryavanshi.' Now, these are the names of the feudal lords from the Rajput community.[7] From this response it became very clear to me how genealogical records contain information not only about how a particular community sees itself, but how it sees other communities, particularly from the dominant section of society. This particular genealogical account is not merely a record; it is also a satirical comment on the exploitation of the upper castes, who are ignorant of the most basic realities of life. And yet, they continue to deny people their means of livelihood.

Another story narrated by the Bhāṭs involved the building of a temple for the mother goddess by the Raut community. The temple was built, everything was fine, it was beautifully constructed, but there was one slight problem. In every temple there is a *kalash* (rounded pinnacle) that is placed on top of the *shikhar* (tower, dome).

Now, the kalash of this particular temple was made out of gold, and it was very heavy. Many men tried to lift it, but failed to do so. Finally, the elders in the Raut community decided that only a virgin girl would be able to lift the kalash. So, any number of girls tried to lift the kalash, from the Brahman, Rajput, and Bania communities, but it didn't budge. Finally, a girl from the Raut community came and touched it, and the kalash was easily lifted and put on top of the temple. Once again it is obvious that this story comments on other groups, in this particular case the alleged purity of upper-caste women. It reveals what the Raut have to say not only about their own genealogical record, but about those groups which are more privileged than their own.

Listening to Komalda tell these stories makes me realize the many ways in which 'history' is shaped and remembered. Not history in the formal sense of 'itihasa', but more in the Puranic sense of an old story—'bahut purāni bāt hai'—in which people's values and beliefs are vividly set forth. We have here an instance of how history can be performed—*not just through oral narration, whose specific resonances Komalda doesn't spell out but which he suggests through the rhythmic beats of the drum and the cries of a very interactive audience. Let us also not forget that this 'history' is followed by acrobatic stunts of which, sadly, we don't have a description. So we have to imagine the 'gulach khānā' (somersaults), 'rasi pe chaḍhnā' (tightrope walking), 'gol gol ghumnā' (whirling on a pole suspended in the air), demonstrated by the 'Mukhbanchā Bhāṭs'. These recorders of the past are also the entertainers of the community. Oral genealogy and gymnastics share the same ground.*

While the stories of the Raut community are legendary, the response to the story of Puniā—a collective vocal one, as Komalda affirms—makes it clear that it has been comprehended not just dialogically, but critically. Genealogy is received by the people not merely as a ritualistic record of the past, but rather, as a reaffirmation of the present. In this sense, it highlights the political awareness that the 'Chandravanshis' and 'Suryavanshis' of this world are still around. Countering the ecological mystique that is built into the mythic personae of the Moon (Chandra) and Sun (Surya), at least in certain brands of contemporary holistic thinking, these gods are divested of their sanctity. More critically, they are shown to be ignorant of two of the most basic 'staple-food' categories of Rajasthan—'makkā' (maize) and 'jawār'(sorghum)—on which Komalda will dwell at length in the next chapter.

2

LAND

At a time when the concept of 'land', particularly in urban and metropolitan contexts, has been reduced to 'real estate'—homogenized and neutered of almost any nuance or gradation of meaning—this chapter on indigenous land categories in Rajasthan offers a necessary counter-perspective. Here we do not find the xenophobic strains of patriotism embedded in notions of land as national and regional territory, even though there are codes of owernship written into the indigenous nomenclature of land that can be divisive in their own right. Nor are we dealing here with the innate romanticism that is symptomatic of those ecological theories where land is inseparable from the nurturing of Nature and the mythical sustenance of Mother Earth. There is very little mystification in what Komalda has to say about land—in fact, the problem could be that his nomenclature is a little too concrete without adequate description or symbology.

As I listen to him, I am often lost in the thicket of his words. Indeed, this land-vocabulary is not likely to be found in any Rajasthani or Hindi dictionary, because it comes from local communities whose languages (and knowledge-systems) have not been adequately addressed, even at 'subaltern' or 'developmental' levels. By focusing on land in the early part of the book, I trust that the connections that follow in the remaining chapters, such as the relationship of geography to oral epics, will become more vivid.

Nomenclature

In the early days, when we used to go into the interior of Rajasthan, there were no roads. I still remember asking villagers, 'How do we get to such-and-such village?' And they would say, 'Go straight ahead and you will pass *thaḷi*, then you will come across *dhāṭ*, and from dhāṭ, you will once again re-enter thaḷi, and further ahead, you will come across Harsani, the village you're looking for.' Even today when I go to the village of Borunda, where I am very well known, and I ask some people for the whereabouts of my friend Vijay Dan, someone might say, 'I saw him in *fānglā*.' Another person might say, 'No, he was in *dhāṭi*', and still others might use words like thaḷi or *bēr*, and so on. Now, all these words refer to actual divisions of land within and across the villages of Rajasthan. We could describe them as ethno-geographic categories, which reveal the people's understanding of land.

So, for instance, when 'thaḷi' is used, it refers to an area in the village that is sandy, with a lot of dunes, while 'bēr' is used to describe rich agricultural land. Some fields that have been cultivated for hundreds of years actually have proper names, but most fields are identified according to their specific soil composition. *Kankreṭi* land, for instance, will contain small pebbles, while *magreṭi* land would suggest that the soil is at once sandy and stony. Like this we have so many words denoting the quality of the land and its productive capacities—thaḷi, bēr, *relā, sar, dhorā, tālāb kā peṭā*. It goes on and on.

a. *dēr*

When we try to name different types of land in Rajasthan, it's not just the soil that is taken into account, but also the direction and flow of water on this land. For instance, if a field is described as dēr, this means that it's in a low-lying area, so that when it rains, the water remains there for two to three months, between July to September. By the middle of October, after the water seeps into the ground, it is time for the field to be ploughed, after which only three crops can be sown—*gehun* (wheat), *sarson* (mustard), and *chanā* (gram). At this stage, the normal practice is to run a very heavy log of wood attached to a tractor—earlier it used to be a pair of bullocks—over the furrows in the field, so that the humidity is retained in the earth itself. This practice is called *sanwār denā*. The crop that follows this sowing process achieves full seed-to-seed cycle in ninety days, and it is achieved without any irrigation at all. This type of cultivation, which is known as *sevaj* in the Marwar region and *sīrmā* in the south of Rajasthan, yields a full crop without irrigation. Significantly, it will reject any kind of pesticide or chemical fertilizer.

b. *sar*

There is another kind of land called sar, which draws on rain-water coming not from any one particular source, but from the entire catchment area covering a number of villages. This water collects in the form of small rivulets, and as it flows faster and faster, without cutting the ground, it eventually settles at a particular point within a depression in the land. Rich in manure, the soil of sar is rich and black, but very hard—literally, hard for the plough to break. In earlier times, the jāgirdārs or landlords would give this land to ordinary people in order to punish them. Today, however, with the widespread use of the tractor, sar can be easily ploughed and it is regarded as rich agricultural land.

c. *bēr*

There is another kind of land called bēr, which is also enriched by a vast quantity of water which, as we say in Rajasthani, 'moves very sleepily' (*sote huey behnā*). At times this water rises at least six inches to two feet above the ground, never eroding any of the topsoil. But in the process of moving very slowly over the earth, it deposits large amounts of clay and manure, which it collects along the way and spreads over a very large area. Bēr always consists of many hectares of ground, and it is another form of rich agricultural land. On this land, you can practise almost any type of cultivation, and if you have the appropriate irrigation facilities, you can grow any type of crop. Without irrigation, however, this land produces *bājrā* (pearl millet) and *mung* (lentil) during the *kharif* or monsoon crop. Like bēr, relā refers to the land that emerges out of the deposits of evenly flowing water that does not cut into the earth. Unlike bēr, relā does not leave behind banks of accumulated soil.

Identifying Land

a. *Crop patterns*

I mention these details surrounding different types of land like bēr, sar, dēr, relā to point out how the villagers of Rajasthan are capable of identifying different kinds of land with specific names. Another source of identification is the different crop patterns available for different types of land. Unlike bēr, thaḷi, for instance, is sandy, and yet it is possible to grow bājrā and *moṭh* (pulse) on this land. Other types of land like dhorā or tālāb kā peṭā are specifically used for the *rabi* or winter crop.

At times, the nomenclature of land suggests different things in different parts of the state. For example, in our region in Marwar, *usar* suggests a non-cultivable land, but in other regions of Rajasthan I have found that it can connote land which is cultivable but only after a considerable amount of work has been put into it. In these regions, usar has some economic value, quite unlike in my part of Rajasthan, where it is agriculturally non-productive. Some categories of land, however, like dēr, sar, bēr, have identical meanings in different parts of of Rajasthan.

b. *Language*

Land is also identified in relation to the local languages spoken by people in particular areas. In the early days of our research, it was not uncommon for us to come across people who spoke swāḷakhi or dhāṭi or khaḍāli from Swāḷakh, Dhāṭ, and Khaḍāl, respectively. Of course, these were highly localized languages extending to merely 100–150 villages, but they existed nonetheless. We also discovered that the names of many dominant groups were linked to the areas in which they live. In Soḍhaṇ, the Soḍhā are the ruling group; the Shekhāwaṭs live in Shekhāwaṭi; and the Hādā have ruled in Hāḍoti for generations. Even a very common name like Mewar, for instance, can be viewed as an ethno-geographic category. If you go to the Udaipur region and ask the local people there, 'Where is Mewar?', some of them at least are likely to say, 'Udaipur is not part of Mewar. This region can be found about twenty kilometres outside of Udaipur, extending all the way to Kapasan.'

c. *Animals*

The nomenclature of different types of land has also contributed to the naming of special breeds of animals. For example, it's a well-known fact that the camels from the Jaisalmer region are a very fine breed, but nobody identifies them with Jaisalmer as such; they are called Khaḍāli after Khaḍāl, where they are bred for riding purposes. Likewise, one of the best breeds of bullocks in India is named as Nāgauri from Swāḷakh, a cluster of 136 villages in the Nāgaur district. So renowned are the breeds from Swāḷakh that a bullock from this area would sell for as much as Rs 25,000, which is almost the same price that one pays for a used tractor. On the other hand, a bullock from Merta, which is merely twenty kilometres away from Swāḷakh, would sell for merely Rs 5,000. All these identifications of livestock are well known to the people at large.

Indeed, so important is the ownership of livestock, particularly in the cattle-breeding areas, that there are actual names for persons who own a specific number of animals. Bāghelā, for instance, refers to a person who owns more than 400 cows; Varag refers to one who owns more than 100 camels; Chhāng is used to describe those who own more than 200 sheep or goats. What needs to be kept in mind about the cattle is that they are non-stable-bound, and therefore, they graze over large areas. Here again we come across specific ethno-geographic names for specific grazing grounds, such as the Pali area, which is known for a particular variety of grass called *sevaṇ*. This grass can grow to the height of a camel, almost seven to eight feet; it is nurtured by rainfall that averages three to five inches. The protein and food content of this grass is one of the richest in the world.

Now, when we went out to study different kinds of land in Rajasthan, we encountered knowledge systems that were linked to the different kinds of land divisions that I have been discussing so far. We found that the peasant communities, who have been working on the land for generations, were most keenly knowledgeable about these divisions. They were able to identify the number of *bighas* of land that could be described as bēr, or sar, or kankreṭi, or magreṭi, or thaḷi, and so on. So, on the basis of their knowledge, we were able to map the different kinds of land within a particular terrain.

Simultaneously, we listed the different castes of people living on different kinds of land in specific areas. We covered a wide cross-section of communities like Jāt, Gujar, Rajput, down to low-caste Meghwāl families. And what we discovered, when putting our research together on land and caste, was that almost 80 per cent of the agriculturally rich land was owned by hardly 20 per cent of the people from rich peasant communities, while 20 per cent of the less cultivable land was owned by other communities. This observation compelled us to open up the ownership patterns built into different types of land.

Ownership of Land

Before Independence, Rajasthan was divided into princely states, which were governed by royal families through jāgirdārs, who administered a large percentage of the land. Basically there were two types of land that were designated according to administrative and revenue categories—*khālsā* land included those areas where the revenue was collected directly by the king, while in *jāgiri* land, it was the jāgirdārs or feudal lords who had the right to collect revenue. Before Independence, farmers had no ownership rights on land, which was distributed to the farmers by the jāgirdārs themselves on a yearly basis. After Independence, however, certain land rights were given to farmers, but on the basis of some proof that the farmers had to submit on a three-year basis to local government bodies that the land in question was being cultivated. Once confirmed, the farmer had the freedom to sell the land, mortgage it, get a bank loan on it, pass on its inheritance rights, among other official transactions. However, even as this *khatedāri* land was regarded as some kind of property, its ultimate ownership remained with the state and not with the farmers.

At this point, we need to speak a little more about the official categories and criteria by which land is defined in Rajasthan from the point of view of revenue collection. Any village is determined by a boundary, within which there are land classifications on the basis of irrigated (*sinchit*) and non-irrigated (*asinichit*) land. The latter includes *bārāni ekam* where very little agriculture is possible, while *bārāni doyam* would indicate land with possibilities of a monsoon crop. Likewise, *mumkin kāsht* is land where agriculture is possible, while *gērmumkin kāsht* refers to land on which agriculture is not possible. Within the category of irrigated (sinchit) land, there are divisions like *chāhi*, which refers to land irrigated by wells, while *pīval* draws on other water sourcers like rivers, lakes, and canals.

If one had to examine the land map that is always available with the *paṭwārī* (registrar of revenue and land accounts) in any village, it would be possible to see which specific areas have been marked out for agriculture, and which are considered to be habitable (*ābādi*). There are also other distinctions like *janglāyat*, which is forest land; *gochar*, land specified for grazing purposes; and *sivāychak*, land owned by the government. Finally, there is land that is marked for social institutions like schools or *dharamshālās* (rest-houses), and government offices. These institutions are generally built on *paḍat*—land specifically not under cultivation. If we had to study the paṭwāri's registers over a period of time, we would be able to gauge the exact number of years that particular areas of land have been marked for cultivation or habitation. Some agricultural lands could go back hundreds of years, while others have been designated as such only twenty or thirty years ago. Studying these records also enables us to understand how particular land patterns have been manipulated in the name of land reform and public utility.

Common Land

This brings us to the very large issue concerning common land. In Rajasthan, particularly in the desert zone in the western part of the state, I would say that the very life-line of poor people depends on this particular kind of land. We have two words for this land—*oran* and *ān*. Oran refers to a defined area that is generally named after some god or goddess or saint, in whose honour there is a shrine within the precincts of the land. Within the boundaries of the oran, it is prohibited to cut any tree or to take away any foliage for private use. It is believed that any transgression in this matter is likely to be punished by the gods—one could go blind, or meet with an accident, or die. The consequences are very serious.

In almost any village in western Rajasthan, there will be some sort of an oran in which the trees and vegetation are protected. In fact, orans have been recorded in the earliest revenue records, where specific areas of land were designated under this category. But later, the land designated under oran was replaced by sivāychak—in other words, land that could be allotted by the government for any use. What becomes evident from later revenue records is that encroachments have been made on common land under the guise of registering some charitable or religious trust or some such enterprise.

There are other kinds of violations that have taken place on lands designated as ān, which are grasslands where the cattle are free to graze but from which no tree can be cut. Significantly, the recent nuclear tests conducted in Pokaran, Rajasthan, took place on land that is designated as ān, where there were relatively few people that needed to be evacuated. In fact, if you examine the sites of atomic tests almost anywhere in the world, you will find that they invariably take place on some kind of common land, and in this regard, Pokaran was no exception.

If we examine the soil in most āns and orans (or *vanis*, as they are called in other parts of Rajasthan, outside of the western desert zone), we find that the ground has developed a very solid crust. This is because of the weight of the hooves of the cattle, which graze in these areas in large number. So when seeds from the trees fall on this ground, they do not germinate because the hard crust of the earth cannot be easily penetrated. As a result, the local varieties of trees that you find in these groves are very old—generally *khejṛā*, *kēr*, and *ber*. However, there are other areas in the Aravalli hills, for instance, where you will find a more diverse range of flora and fauna. Some of these plants are hundreds of years old; they are an ecological treasure trove of the past.

As I said earlier, these common lands represented by the oran, the vani, and the ān constitute the very life-line of poor people, who graze their cattle in their precincts. However, with the new encroachments, including those by the government, which has constructed *manḍīs* (agricultural markets) in these areas, and with the manipulation of revenue records, where *orans* are now being allotted to specific owners, we are seeing the privatization of property making inroads into common land. And, in this sense, the situation is not very different from the growing private enterprises surrounding water, which we will discuss in the next chapter. In both cases, a common resource of the people is being appropriated, and the legalities surrounding this predicament are tricky.

As I listen to Komalda drone on about 'land' in all its intricate details relating to soil composition, the flow of water, revenue categories, irrigation, livestock, I cannot deny that my metropolitan ignorance is deeply challenged. Even when the 'oran' comes up in our discussion through my specific interest in 'sacred groves', I realize to my embarrassment how 'metaphoric' my undertanding of ecology is, fed more through theory than fact. In fact, when I eventually got to see an 'oran', stretching for miles around Pabuji's 'mandir' (temple) in Kolu, Rajasthan, I realized what Komalda meant by a 'life-line'. This 'oran' was no 'grove' but a vast stretch of seemingly desolate forest land dotted with shrubs and trees. While 'orans' are being encroached upon, and their ecology needs nourishment, they still provide a necessary space to counter the systematic reduction of land into industry and commerce.

Perhaps at no point was Komalda's discourse more disturbingly punctured by contemporary reality than through his passing reference to Pokaran.[1] I should add that this was not made for dramatic effect. The use of common land for nuclear tests was just another 'fact' stated by Komalda. He did not elaborate on it to 'prove a point', nor did he use it to rail against the possibilities of ecocide, as the very real impact of the nuclear tests is beginning to show in the depleting health conditions of the people surviving in Pokaran today. I indicate these facts to state that while Komalda may not be an 'activist' in the conventional sense of the word, he is nonetheless aware of how people's knowledge-systems are being destroyed in our contemporary world.

Let us now shift the focus on land by drawing on Komalda's larger understanding of a people's geography. I had expected such a geography to be grounded in material and geological realities, but I could not have anticipated its illumination through 'staple foods', as Komalda describes in the following section.

Staple Food Categories

When people think of 'Rajasthan', they generally think of one state that is located within specific geographical boundaries. But the truth is that this state is of very recent origin, both at the political and the topographical levels.[2] Prior to independence in 1947, Rajasthan was actually a cluster of nineteen princely states—Mewar, Marwar, Jaipur, Bharatpur, and so on. After independence these states became districts. So today we talk about Jaisalmer district, Barmer district, Jaipur district, and so on. Actually these districts are merely the geographical divisions of the state from the point of view of administration, or revenue collection, or law and order maintenance; they have not been determined on social or cultural grounds.

Let us try, therefore, to think differently about a people's geography, at ethno-geographic levels, because the conventional notions of geography don't always apply to the context of Rajasthan, particularly to its folk and rural cultures. What mattered to us from the very beginnings of our research was the intimate ways in which people identified the geography of their own locations in relation to what they eat. This insight led us to divide Rajasthan into three zones—the bājrā zone, the jawār zone, and the makkā zone. When we started talking about these three zones, we found that people knew exactly what we were talking about. For us these zones became alternative regional divisions for the entire state.

Geographically, it became important to consider that wherever bājrā or jawār or makkā are grown, it depends on three factors—the weather, soil, and rainfall. Apart from determining the topography and physical features of a particular region, the weather, soil and rainfall also determine the botanical growth in that area. The trees and vegetation in turn provide the basic materials for the construction of people's homes. If we examine the huts in the villages of Rajasthan, we find that they are so economically constructed. About 80 per cent of the material used in these dwellings come from indigenous resources—mud, grass, bamboo, *gobar* (cow-dung), local plants, fibres, and scrub. So we have come to realize how even rural architecture depends on specific local conditions of the weather, soil, and rainfall, which in turn determine the availability of certain botanical resources, which are then used in the construction of homes. This gave us a huge clue to understanding how people live.

To get back to the bājrā, jawār, and makkā zones, these are not so much agricultural categories as they are 'staple food' categories. By and large, the staple diet of the people in Rajasthan will consist of these three grains. More specifically, rural communities will eat only one of these grains as part of their daily diet; they would be almost ignorant of the other two. In other words, the consumption of these grains is very region-specific—in Mewar, people tend to eat makkā; in Marwar, bājrā; in Kota, jawār, and so on. A villager from the Mewar region may never have tasted a *chapāti* made of jawār or bājrā. Such is the regional specificity of food cultures in Rajasthan.

Rice, as such, is not a staple food in Rajasthan, even though a very fine quality of rice is produced in the Banswara-Dungarpur area. As for wheat, it is associated with modernity. At political, economic, and scientific levels, we have forced people to consume wheat. Right from the 'Grow More Food' national campaign in the 1950s onwards to the present day. Crores of rupees have been spent on wheat cultivation. In the process, wheat has acquired a prestige value. You see, there is a hierarchy, even among grains. Ironically, the *chhoṭā anāj* (small grains)—bājrā, makkā, and jawār—have become costlier than the regular anāj like wheat. The poor man's food is now being eaten by the rich. Consumption patterns are in the process of changing, as there is a new *shaukh* (taste) among the elite classes for experimenting with different kinds of 'health food', 'ethnic cuisine', and so on. There is also a resurgence of interest in indigenous food preparations in the numerous 'Rajasthan food festivals' that are now being promoted by five-star hotels. At one level, therefore, we are seeing a certain kind of reversal of hierarchy in traditional food practices, as these indigenous grains are being integrated in cosmopolitan cusines.

Cooking Practices

When we started our research on food, we found that roṭi was not eaten widely. In fact, it was not eaten at all. Almost always we found that it was boiled grain that constituted the staple diet of ordinary people. This led us to think about the traditional generic modes of preparing food. Broadly there are two distinct categories: *ākhā*, which incorporates all techniques relating to pounding and grinding; and *chokhā*, which includes all forms of boiling and steaming practices.

There are even more minute discriminations. When the grain is raw and the seed is not yet full, for instance, we call it *dūdhiā* ('milky').

The full seed preparation, boiled (but without the water thrown away), is called *gūgri*. When the grain is pounded in the *okhli* (grinding stone) with a pestle, and subsequently cooked, it is called *khīch*. When the grain is split into very fine particles, then the food preparation is called *ghāṭ*. This food can be eaten sweetened, salted, chilli-hot, any way you like. *Āṭā* (flour) mixed with the buttermilk (*chhāch*) made from curds is known as *rāb*. Keep in mind that these words, like gūgri, rāb, khīch, are generic terms that can be applied to the preparation of bājrā or makkā or jawār.

Now there are other possible developments. Some of these grains pop, others don't. The ones that pop—bājrā, for instance—have no further edible substances that can emerge after they have popped. But those grains that do not pop can provide new material for different kinds of cooking preparations. Chanā, for instance, becomes *bhungrā*, which in turn provides the raw material for the preparation of *sattu*, a dough made out of gram, which is widely eaten by labourers in many parts of India.

While researching these indigenous food preparations thirty to forty years ago, we found that in the rural areas, particularly in tribal regions, no iron or metal utensils were used for cooking. Only pots made out of clay were used. We also discovered that fried food was prepared in cauldrons (*kaṛhāi*) that were used specifically for community feasts. But everyday food was not fried. Nor was it baked. We came to the conclusion that people's staple food consisted neither of roṭi or chapāti, but was more like the preparations described earlier—rāb, khīch, and ghāṭ.

Roṭi became a staple food only after the advent of the flour mills in Rajasthan. This would be in the first decades of the last century. Earlier you had to produce flour by using the *ghaṭṭi*, the grindstone, or else the full grain had to be pounded by hand. This was the practice in the village of Borunda right up to 1954, where the grinding of grain by hand would begin at four in the morning. Today much has changed, not only in the technologies for grinding and pounding grain, but also in basic consumption patterns. The reality is that certain food substances are no longer available, not merely for human beings, but for animals as well.

Even today in Borunda, people who are around sixty-seventy years old, remember how during the rains, it was common to see *kuri* growing profusely in the fields. This wild grass was used to feed the cattle in a big way. Today we do not have a single kuri plant in Borunda. This brings us to the important area of seeds and natural, non-irrigated food resources—the early knowledge-systems associated with them and their gradual disappearance today.

Seeds

Certain types of seeds grow naturally. They are not sown by people. They are gathered and used for different food preparations. We have been able to identify forty such natural seeds that contribute to a staple-food diet. At times the seeds are to be found growing in particular fields—for example, *malichā* grows exclusively in wheat fields. Earlier the owners of these fields would sell the wheat, but they would hold on to the malichā, which was part of their staple diet. This fact led us to an important understanding of the relationship between seeds and food cultures.

Natural seeds like kuri, *kāngni*, *barṭi* can last for many years without losing their generative capacities. When the rains come, they can grow and complete the seed-to-seed cycle. This is not the case with cultured seeds—if these seeds are not properly sown and just lie scattered on the ground, they are not likely to yield any crop. Even if they do grow, what is likely to emerge is a beautiful plant—perhaps very tall and strong—but it will not complete the seed-to-seed cycle. The plant will grow, but there will be no seed in it. Such a plant is called *adak*.

From our fieldwork we have learned that the people who are most dependent on natural seeds for their daily food are low-caste and tribal communities. The major nutritional content of their food comes from these seeds. Significantly, these natural seeds and plants can grow only in those areas where the soil cover on the earth is not more than 4–5 *angul* (a finger measurement). In Banswara, for example, which has the richest agriculture from this point of view, we have the largest number of natural seeds. One should also acknowledge that, apart from the low-caste and tribal communities, there are also a few upper-caste communities, particularly in the foothills of Mount Abu, who use 'natural' foods in their staple diet. But what needs to be emphasized here is that these indigenous foods have a religious significance, in so far as they are eaten as ritual food during *vrats* (religious fasts) and for other ceremonial occasions. In this sense, they have a different function from the regular consumption of natural seeds by low-caste and tribal communities.

Today, seeds are becoming yet another commodity. Kāngni, for instance, is now being cultivated for use in products like biscuits. Seeds have acquired a commercial value. They are being used for fodder as well. The harvesting and sowing systems have changed. The seed-to-seed cycle has been disrupted. Therefore, we can no longer predict the potency of 'natural seeds'. What is 'natural' and what is 'produced', has become difficult to differentiate. Moreover, if the seeds fail to germinate, we realize that there may be nothing to fall back on.

Just think: It took centuries for different graftings of bājrā and wheat to cross geographical borders all the way from Egypt across Afghanistan to India. It was a long process of cross-fertilization and transference. But none of this materialized before the fourth century BC. So what were people eating before that? Through archaeological findings and other sources, we realize that they were dependent largely on natural seeds, which had the capacity to re-germinate. Today there is a rapid decline in the number of different seeds in Rajasthan, as in all parts of India. And this is a matter of grave concern.

Without using a technical language, Komalda is echoing here some of the positions upheld by environmental activists in relation to the manufacture and marketing of seeds. As always, there is no polemic—for instance, against global transnational companies like Monsanto and their tie-ups with Indian manufacturers producing hybrid seeds. Nor does Komalda equate the trading of seeds with the dubious patenting policies of global bodies like GATT, TRIPs, and the WTO.[3] *Within his broader perspective, however, he does imply:*

a. The perils of monoculture through the gradual disappearance of varieties of seeds.

b. The shift from seed as food and fodder to its more commercial use as a constituent in the manufacture of new products, like biscuits.

c. *The increasingly tricky differentiation between what is 'natural' and what is 'produced'.*
d. *The devastation resulting from not being able to renew a process of agriculture when an experiment with fertilizer-enriched seeds fails.*

While Komalda does not adopt an overtly anti-globalization stance, he is aware of the terrible costs being inflicted on local cultures through the commercialization of a fundamental resource: seeds. Along with this commercialization, there is also the actual destruction of flora and fauna through the widespread cancerous growth of imported shrubs and plants, notably the vilāyatī bambūl (prosopis juliflora): *a 'foreign' shrub that is marked by villagers as* 'angrejī'.

Preservation

Let us turn to the preservation of foods. Rajasthan, especially the desert region, has one advantage: it is hot, but there is very little humidity. Humidity is more harmful for preservation than heat. No wonder the Jain *munis* (seers) created a temple in Jaisalmer Fort where they used to preserve their manuscripts. These manuscripts go back 2,000 years, if not more. Had the audio and video cassettes stored in the Rupayan Sansthan archives in Rajasthan been located in Kolkata or Mumbai, they would have become manure by now. However, almost everything that we have recorded, from even forty years ago, still remains in more or less good condition. Not that we worked at preserving our material, we simply didn't have to face the problem of humidity.

Now, for different substances, there are different types of preservation. Take milk, for instance. One biological fact that we learned about camels is that the she-camel (*sānḍ*), while giving birth, produces practically ten-fifteen kilogrammes of milk. If this quantity of milk were to be given to her calf, it would die. Not only do the camel-herding community of the Rāikā consume this excess milk, they also distribute it to people in the village. It's very good milk—health-wise as well, it is nutritious. Unfortunately, apart from the

Rāikā, other communities in Rajasthan are prejudiced against drinking camel-milk. The basic problem is that this milk goes sour in a short time, so it cannot be preserved.

Camel-milk is always consumed as milk; it is not converted into *dahi* (curds) or cheese. If this milk could be made into dahi, it could be preserved for two-three days. If it could be made into *mākhaṇ* (butter), it could be preserved for fifteen to twenty days, and after that, it could be converted into *ghee* (clarified butter), which could be stored for at least six to eight months. This entire process of transforming milk into ghee is one of the most widely practised forms of food preservation in India. But the point is that camel-milk is not preserved in this particular way, quite unlike in Arab countries where cheese is made from camel's milk.

Moving on to other areas of preservation in food culture, we find that the granaries in rural areas are invariably made out of clay. This clay, however, is specially treated with horse-dung (*ghoṛe kī līd*) and donkey dung (*gadhe kī līd*). Note that there are distinct names for the dung (*līd*) of different animals—*mīngṇi* for goats and sheep, *mīngṇā* for camels, and gobar for cows. The point is that horse and donkey dung serves as an effective preventive against humidity. Used in the construction of clay pots, which are stored in granaries (*koṭhi*), it ensures the freshness and quality of the grain.

Today, if you wish to purchase half a kilogramme of wheat or any other kind of grain, you can go to the market and buy it. But earlier, people had to store grain for the whole year. As far as my own family is concerned—I am now over seventy-five years old—my wife and I prefer to buy a year's supply of wheat or *dal* during the harvest season. Whether it is *mūng kī dāl* or *uṛad kī dāl*, we purchase an entire stock for household use. We do this for many reasons.

Firstly, we know that it is a new crop. We can afford to be selective. Then the advantage is that the crop of our choice comes from one field. Today, if there are 200 farmers in a particular region, all their supply of wheat and dal will be assembled in the market, where the grains will be mixed together and then sold. Taste-wise as well, it is best to know what you are eating. For instance, in our home, we use *bājyā gehun* (red wheat). This wheat is non-irrigated, and therefore, it will resist any kind of pesticide or chemical fertilizer. If these things are added, the wheat will not grow. The chapāti made from this gehun will always be smooth; it will never become rubbery like the chapāti made out of *maida* (finely ground white flour). So, as far as food content, taste, and health are concerned, these *desi* grains and foods are what we prefer—like *sāṭhi makki*, the corn that takes sixty days to grow, and *mathāṇīa mirch*, the red-hot chillies from Mathania.

Even today these kinds of things grow on many small farms and land-holdings in India, not because the farmers don't want to grow other cash crops, but because that is all that grows in their fields. And yet, even though these 'natural' foods are available, my own sons will promptly go to the market and buy a packet of ready-made āṭā (flour), instead of getting the wheat, cleaning it, and getting it ground in the chakki. They will do the same for *jīrā* (cumin) or chillies, or whatever. This 'ready-made' culture I find impossible to accept.

At this point I cannot help reminding Komalda that if he is able to store up on provisions over the year, that's because he can afford to do so. Inevitably, there is yet another condition for food preservation that needs to be taken into account—the economic entitlement to food and the availability of space. Komalda readily accepts these facts which cannot be separated from the larger benefits of social privilege. 'What about those people who don't have space or money, or who are constantly on the move?' I ask. It is at this point that Komalda makes one of his numerous intuitive connections by bringing into the discussion the larger phenomenon of nomadism.

Nomadism

Nomads are 'wanderers' (the Hindi word is '*ghummakaṛ*'). As their very existence demands, they have to travel light. They can keep nothing stored with them apart from the most basic needs. So nomads represent a 'throw-away culture'.

There are approximately eighty different types of nomads in Rajasthan. Under the generic category of Jogi, who provide different technical services, we have different nomadic groups like the Kālbeliā, the Ghaṭṭiwāl, the Bānsdewāl, the Kuchbandiyā, the Gaḍolia Luhār, and so on. Under the category of the Banjārā, who are involved in the transportation of trading items like salt and red oxide, we have groups like the Bāmaṇia Bhāṭ, the Bāldiyā Bhāṭ, and the Gāvariā.

It is important to distinguish the nomadism described above from the pastoral nomadism of the Rāikā community. These herdsmen are concerned primarily with finding grazing grounds and adequate drinking water for their cattle, goats, sheep, or camels. Moving from one grazing ground to another, they eventually return to their homes before the rains. These nomads are driven by the needs of their livestock (on which their own livelihood depends) rather than by any service rendered to the community. They are the strongest devotees of the god Pabuji, on whom I will have more to say in Chapter 4.

Dependent on hunting and food-gathering practices, the nomads collect grain and food from village to village. They also have certain rights to collect residual grain after the harvest season, which may last them for a week or so. Mostly they depend on hunting, which they carry out with the aid of dogs, primarily the *lavāri*, a particular breed of hound. Almost 90 per cent of these groups consume carnivorous animals. The jackal is one of their ritual foods, eaten during marriage, childbirth, or any other auspicious occasion. They are also known to consume fox and wild cat, even though they do not talk about these things. Along with carnivorous animals, they also consume herbivorous ones like the rabbit and deer.

It is important to differentiate nomads from beggars, those vagrants who can be found begging for a livelihood in bus and railway stations and on the streets. Nomads are not beggars: they provide certain types of services for which society is obliged to provide them with food. The services are primarily of a technical nature, which are not otherwise available in the villages. But the Jogis also perform other functions that combine ritualistic services and other kinds of indigenous expertise. So, at one level, for example, the Kālbeliās are recognized as snake-charmers, but let us be clear as to what snake-charming means. The snake is regarded by many communities in rural Rajasthan as the embodiment of God, and the Kālbeliā are regarded as the priests of the snake. They carry their makeshift snake shrines to local neighbourhoods, where they play on the gourd-pipe (*pungi* or *bīn*), while offerings of milk and donations are made by individual families. This ritual is not for entertainment purposes.

But only 5 per cent of the Kālbeliā are involved in this snake-worship.

There are other kinds of services provided by both the Hindu Jogis who sing for the Mīnā, and the Muslim Jogis who sing for the Meo. Unlike the Langa and Manganiyar musicians, who earn their living as genealogists apart from their singing assignments, the Jogis have a very different relationship with the Meo and Mīnā farming communities. In exchange for specific functions, they receive donations of agricultural produce from the lands belonging to these communities. What are these functions by which the Jogis serve their patrons? I was curious to know. I remember asking them, 'Do you sing for your patrons during the wedding and death ceremonies conducted in their homes?' And they said, 'Yes, we do get paid for singing, but there's a limited obligation (*nēg*) on the part of our patrons to pay for these services.' Then they revealed to me that they are essentially paid for protecting the fields of their patrons from the encroachment of certain insects, which have the capacity to destroy crops. So I asked them, 'How do you protect the fields?' And this is how they—both the Hindu and the Muslim Jogis—put it: 'We receive the *ishṭ* (blessing) of Lord Bhairav. And it is because of this power that the farmers pay us.'

When I heard them talking like this, I suddenly remembered from my childhood how Jogis were believed to have powers by which they could get rid of locusts whenever they would attack any village. In every village, there would be a few Jogi families, and I remember being told how a Jogi would simply have to catch a single locust and hold it in his hand, while walking out of the village, and the entire flock of locusts would follow him. There are other such folk myths that have gone around Rajasthan.

I remember how on my first meeting with them they had given me as many as twenty names of deadly insects that could destroy entire fields. Today I remember only a few of them like *bahbal*, *kasāri*, and *ginḍolā*. The Jogis claimed that in a violent attack of these insects, entire acres of land could be destroyed within hours. I learned that all the insects over which the Jogis had power were winged insects, which could multiply very rapidly, at times in millions.

I was impressed by their minute knowledge of the life-cycle of particular insects, and of those specific stages in the cycle when an insect was in a position to destroy a field. They were also aware of those stages where it was not possible for an insect to attack—for example, if the seeds in a field had already sprouted, then that meant that the ginḍolā was not capable of attacking the crop. How exactly their techniques of destroying the insects were implemented I cannot be sure, but I realized that they did have an entomological knowledge that was passed from generation to generation—a knowledge that the farmers clearly do not possess. And it is for this reason that the Jogis continue to be patronized by the farmers for protecting their fields.

The rest of the Jogi community is occupied in different technical activities—for example, the repair of a particular part of the pit-loom known as *rās*, which is made out of bamboo. Earlier every village had about five to six pit-looms for the weaving of cloth. The Kālbeliā would move from village to village, repair the rās, construct new ones, and proceed to other villages. A single village would not be able to provide them with adequate work, while others might not need their services. So they had to be constantly on the move. Even today, despite the emergence of new technologies, the pit-loom continues to be used for the weaving of cloth of narrow width—for instance, the cloth used for tying turbans (*sāfā*).

Other nomadic groups like the Ghaṭṭiwāl are known for their services relating to the repair and maintenance of the chakki or stone mill. They wander the streets with familiar street-cries: '*Ghaṭṭi tachālo, ghaṭṭi tachālo*.' Then there is the group called Singiwāl, who travel all the way to the foothills of Himachal Pradesh and beyond, to Assam and Meghalaya as well. These people are medicinemen who cure all kinds of illnesses, aches and pains, by the sucking of blood. The blood is generally sucked through a particular kind of deer-horn, which is used to make an incision in the affected area of the body. The Singiwāl also collect *kasturi* (musk) from the *hiran* (deer) and black buck; this is used for all kinds of medicinal and cosmetic purposes. Likewise, there are the Kuchbandiyā, who make different kinds of brushes used in the handloom industries and by goldsmiths, painters, and household workers as well. In contrast, the Gaḍolia Luhār are known for their services as ironsmiths. Out of a hundred villages, not more than three or four villages will have a local ironsmith. So the services of the Gaḍolia Luhār come in handy.

From all these examples it becomes clear that nomadism is not some historical residue of the past, but a continuing phenomenon of the present. Even today nomadism continues in contemporary life in different guises—for example, if you take the case of the medical representative who moves from one small town to another, carrying a particular kind of bag, adopting a specific type of mannerism, perhaps he can be regarded as a contemporary nomad. Each society creates its own nomads.

Taken out of context, Komalda's final statement—'each society creates its own nomads'—could almost play into contemporary postmodern theories relating to migrancy in which the 'nomad' is an iconoclastic figure rejecting permanent and established structures. Within the jargon of postmodernism, this figure embodies the 'in-between' state of liminality, neither here nor there. Needless to say, this context is far removed from the communitarian bases of nomadism in the rural areas and desert of Rajasthan, where the act of wandering from place to place is a way of life for entire communities. The mobile 'throw-away' culture represented here is not a protest against consumerism, but the very source of subsistence and survival.

While Komalda connects nomadism and different modes of food preservation, it should be clear to the reader by now that his narrative never unfolds in a linear mode. Invariably, he gets side-tracked into dwelling on some material reality that he encounters along the way, and in the process, the conceptual component of the connection becomes far less important than what it is capable of triggering by way of exposing some new content of a particular phenomenon. As a listener, I've learned to accept the way his peripatetic mind works, and instead of insisting that he 'keep on track', I encourage the digression, which then contributes to the narrative in its own right.

In this particular transition between 'food preservation' and 'nomadism', Komalda had emphasized while reflecting on the preservative possibilities of milk that he had never studied the problem of 'milk preservation' as such. It had come up while he was researching camels, and this observation inevitably led to his elaboration on the connections between camel-culture and the nomadic practices of their herders. Here then are his observations on Rajasthan's most ubiquitous animal—the camel—and the communities whose livelihood depends on its economy. An underlying theme of this section concerns the intimate relationship that exists between animals and their herdsmen, a relationship that extends beyond camels to cattle, on which Komalda has a few personal observations as well.

Camel Culture

While working on camels, we were inevitably interacting with the Rāikā community of camel-herders. Rāikā or Rabāri are the generic names for camel-herders in Rajasthan. Among the Rāikā, there are two broad divisions—the Chāvanḍiā, who also deal with sheep, and the Māru, who deal exclusively with camels. The honorific name for the camel-herders is Devāsi, the pejorative name is Bhūt (literally, 'ghost').

Each group in Rajasthan has at least three names. For example, people will refer to my community as Oswāl. In my presence, I would be addressed respectfully as Mahajan. In my absence, I would be called Bania. And if I were abused, I would be called Kirad or Lerh. Likewise, Rajput is the common name for a well-known group of people from Rajasthan—Sardār or Thākur would be their honorific name, and Khilā would be the abusive name. This multiple naming system applies to all the communities in Rajasthan.

So, as I was saying, we were working with the Rāikās or camel-herders. We were recording their songs and, inevitably, we learned about their work and interaction with camels. Like the *gwālā* or cow-herder, the camel-herders travel long distances with their camels—literally hundrerds of camels in each pack. And it is remarkable to see how the herders can control the movement of these camels with particular cries and sounds. They can, for instance, instruct the camels to go right or left, to stop, to graze in a particular place, not to graze in a particular place, to keep moving, and so on. It is also very interesting to observe how the camels themselves interrelate, particularly through a practice which is popularly called *bālgiri*. This takes place early in the morning when the older camels have to go out for grazing, while the younger calves remain behind. With my own eyes I have seen how the older camels separate themselves from the larger flock, while making loud braying sounds rhythmically. Rather like grain passing through a sieve, the older camels separate themselves from the calves, which remain behind, standing motionless in one spot.

Like the camels and their herders, the relationship between cattle and their cowherds (gwālā) is very intimate. How closely the cattle respond to the calls of the gwālā. Even if they haven't drunk any water for days on end, and they finally arrive at some well or tank, the gwālā only has to give one particular call and all the cows will drink in an orderly fashion. They literally take it in turns to drink and share the water. Likewise, the gwālā only has to utter one sound for all of them to stop, and they will stand rock-like. I tell you, nothing will budge them. And if there's an emergency situation, then one call is sufficient for them to charge in one direction.

Let me share a funny incident in this regard. We were assisting the film-maker Mani Kaul on a documentary which he was shooting in Rajasthan. Mani wanted to explore why people continue to live in the desert with all its difficulties and inconveniences—why don't they migrate to more habitable places? I remember one sequence where we were trying to shoot a herd of cows drinking water at the *bēri* (a shallow well). We asked the gwālā to enact a sort of fight with the people around him, assuming that he would be able to control the cows when they charged. So, as instructed, he gave a call, but the cows looked here and there, very distractedly, almost as if they were wondering why the call was made. The second time he made the call, they didn't attack the local people as we had expected; rather, they attacked the camera crew. Everybody had to run helter-skelter, but once again, at the sound of the gwālā's call, all the cows stopped dead in their tracks and calmed down. This is an experience that I cannot forget.

I'll share another experience that can reveal the close relationship between the cattle and their herders. In 1979 there was acute famine in Rajasthan, and in Borunda, where we have some lush green agricultural fields, there were some 25,000 cows from the desert zone trying to enter the village. Mind you, there were only seven to eight herdsmen handling all these cows. So we requested these men not to allow their animals to graze in our fields because they would destroy our crops. However, we suggested another grassland owned by the government where the cattle could graze. I tell you, it was simply unbelievable to see these men with a single *lāṭhi* (stick) in their hand guiding the cows in a single line past our agricultural fields to the government plot. These animals had not drunk water for days on end, they hadn't eaten adequately for almost a month, and yet they did not stop till they arrived at their destination. We offered the herdsmen truckloads of wheat husk as fodder, but they told us that their animals could not eat any form of cut grass; they could only graze in the fields.

To get back to camels, there are different breeds of camels that are reared in different regions of Rajasthan. In the Khadāḷ region, for instance, in the Jaisalmer area, which I referred to earlier, the camels are bred for riding purposes. Like Khadāḷ, Chitrāng is an ethnogeographic category, referring to an area situated near the Nachna region. It's interesting, but if you go to Chitrāng and ask a camel-herder, 'How many camels do you own?' he might say, 'Two hundred camels.' Then if you ask him if he has ever seen all his camels, he will say, 'No, I've seen only a few of them, but I know that I own two hundred.' How is this possible? You find out by walking with him for about two to four kilometres. He will point out all the hoof-prints of the camels, and from these alone he will be able to confirm that his animals have gone grazing in the desert. In the Nachna region of Rajasthan, even today, if a herder wants to sell some of his camels, all he does is to identify the hoof-prints of his animals, and it is on this basis alone that the deal is made. The word '*pāgi*', for instance, refers to local experts who are capable of deciphering the hoof-prints not only of camels, but the footprints of humans as well.

There are large problems, however, being faced by camel herders and traders today. Most important, the camel population is decreasing in Rajasthan. At one time, camels were important for ground transportation. Today this is no longer the case. Secondly, camel herds need large grazing areas, which are no longer readily available. Third, the price of camels has gone down to as little as Rs 4,000. By contrast, the price of cows is more competitive, in so far as it varies according to the quantity of milk produced by the cow. If it gives one kilogramme of milk, then the cow costs Rs 1,000; if two, then Rs 2,000.

Yet another reason for the economic duress of camel-culture has to do with the fact that camel meat is not eaten widely in India, except during celebrations of Eid in a few areas. Likewise, the possibilities of curing and preparing camel-skin to make products like perfume (*itr*) and oil bottles and containers have not been developed, unlike in the Arab countries where camel-skin has an economic value. In earlier days, large containers called *kūḍā*, which could store large quantities of ghee and oil, were made of camel hide. Even though a kūḍā could store as much as 100–200 kilogrammes of oil, its own weight was exceptionally slight. Sadly, these objects are no longer used, even though perfume bottles from Ujjain and Indore are still locally manufactured. Unless there are major changes in the ways in which the camel is perceived as a source of production in Rajasthan, its status can only decline.

In describing the intimate relation between animals and their keepers, Komalda calls attention to a living tradition of animal husbandry that continues to be practised by traditional herding communities in Rajasthan. Let us end this chapter with one particular instance in which animals are cared for during periods of crisis. I refer to the 'foot-and-mouth disease', which I had brought up in the introduction—a disease that has not been eliminated in the modern world despite all the progress in veterinary science and epidemiology. Indeed, the recent outbreaks of foot-and-mouth disease in the so-called 'developed' world have been particularly harsh reminders of the brutality underlying the farming industry. Through new breeding techniques, animal populations have multiplied. Through non-vegetarian inputs in newly manufactured, enzyme-enriched fodder, they have been subjected to post-technological diseases, like 'mad cow disease'. And yet, with the continued outbreak of older diseases like 'foot-and-mouth', it is significant that there is no vaccine that can prevent the animals from dying. The only 'solution' would seem to be the mass slaughter of diseased (and potentially diseased) animals, all in the name of preventing the contamination from spreading further.

Listen now to a very different perspective on how traditional cattle-herding communities in Rajasthan deal with this crisis not just at a ritualistic level, but through grassroot quarantine practices that prevent the spread of the disease at very human and concrete levels of resistance.

Hīr Rānjhā and Foot-and-mouth Disease

Let me talk a little bit about *Hīr Rānjhā*. Sung in the Alwar-Bharatpur region to the accompaniment of the *jogīā sārangi* (bowed stringed instrument), it is known primarily as a romantic tale composed by Waris Shah, who took the story-line of a long lay from Punjab, adapting it within the Sufi philosophical tradition. Now what we find is that *Hīr Rānjhā* is sung in those rural areas that are prone to cattle epidemics, more specifically to the foot-and-mouth disease that affects cattle. Whenever such disease is rampant, *Hīr Rānjhā* is sung, and the local people say, 'We are doing the *paṭh* (religious reading) of *Hīr Rānjhā*.' Just as there are readings of the Gita and the Ramayana, in the same way there are readings of *Hīr Rānjhā*. In the course of this reading, it becomes a religious text.

Now, who is Rānjhā? He is identified as a *mahiwāl*, which originates from the Sanskrit word *mahishpāl*—a buffalo-keeper (*bhains-pālak*), as he is known in everyday life. In this role Rānjhā is identified as a god who can effectively counter any cattle epidemic, particularly the disease concentrated in the *khur*, literally the cleft in the hooves of the animals. Formerly, Rānjhā was effective only with the buffalo, but gradually his power extended to the cow as well, the animal most closely identified with Krishna. And yet, in Krishna's own territory, in Mathura, Govardhan, and the entire Braj area, whenever cows and buffaloes face any epidemic in this area, it is Rānjhā who is invoked to solve the problem and not Krishna.

Of course, it could be argued that it is not *Hīr Rānjhā* itself that is instrumental in preventing the disease, but any number of preventive rituals surrounding the singing of the epic. Very often, we focus exclusively on the musical and literary aspects of any epic poem, without taking into account the social activities and material practices adopted by a particular community in their everyday life. In any crisis of foot-and-mouth disease, there are particular *niyam* (rules) that have to be followed by the community during this time. The most important rule is that all the affected animals have to be isolated—

they cannot be taken out of the infected area, nor can any animals be admitted into this area. There is total quarantine. No migration of animals to the surrounding areas is permitted. Secondly, no smoke should filter out of the household fire into the neighbourhood—it is believed that the disease spreads through *dhuān* (smoke). There are also restrictions on cooking fried food. Also, another preventive practice is the addition of alum to the fodder of the cattle, and potassium permanganate to all drinking water. All these actions are part of a larger vigilance upheld by the entire community to prevent the foot-and-mouth disease from spreading.

Till the disease passes away, a certain discipline has to be maintained in the community. The singing of *Hīr Rānjhā* merely consolidates all these preventive rituals at a psychological level, and therefore, people come to believe that it is directly responsible for eliminating the disease. Interestingly, on a trip to Islamabad in Pakistan some years ago, I told my colleagues there that *Hīr Rānjhā* is sung in order to heal cattle diseases; it is not just a romantic tale. They all laughed and said, 'You say such funny things.' So I requested them to get any person from the rural area of the Doab region who could sing *Hīr Rānjhā*. Next day a group of villagers arrived, and sure enough, they sang *Hīr Rānjhā* to the accompaniment of the *algojā* (double-flute) and it was the same composition by Waris Shah. Then I asked them: 'If your buffaloes and cows fall ill, do you sing *Hīr Rānjhā*?' And they said, 'Yes, but not this *Hīr Rānjhā*, we have another version.' And they sang that as well.

At first glance, this would seem like a typically folkloric fragment, for which Komalda could be critiqued by more theoretical interlocutors for not 'taking the folksiness out of our perception of folk traditions.'[4] *But the point is: Can there be any unilateral consensus on 'our' perception of folk traditions outside of sharply differentiated social and cultural contexts? Clearly, for Komalda, the correspondence of* 'Hīr Rānjhā' *with foot-and-mouth disease is not some kind of folk antidote, a premodern magical healing system. Significantly, he doesn't mystify the text of* 'Hīr Rānjhā' *itself as possessing a redemptive or exorcist ritual power; rather, in a pragmatic mode, he spells out a few concrete measures adopted by local communities to prevent the spread of the disease. These measures are a necessary supplement to the transformation of the text into a religious reading ('pāṭh').*

For my own part, I would seize the word 'discipline' which Komalda emphasizes—the 'discipline' which has to be sustained by people through the entire period in which their animals are afflicted by the disease. Eliding its Foucaultian associations, 'discipline' in this particular context connotes a means of coping with tragedy. It suggests practicality and presence of mind. While it does not offer a solution to the epidemic itself, the 'discipline' provides a ritualized mode of community self-preservation. Why the text in question should be 'Hīr Rānjhā', *despite Rānjhā's association as a buffalo-keeper, is something that Komalda does not elaborate on. And in this instance, as in in so many other examples in this book, it becomes clear that texts in his understanding of folklore are* pretexts *for a wide spectrum of social and community-related actions.*

As we come to the end of this chapter, it becomes clear that we have travelled through some very down-to-earth ethno-geographic considerations of land and geography, but the primary problem concerns the shrinking of common land, intensified by new modes of privatization. Unless land is protected, we are likely to see a marked decrease in the availability of land for grazing purposes, particularly during drought and famine. To address these problems, let us turn now to Rajasthan's most precious natural resource—water.

3

WATER

Drought: This could be one of the most harrowing associations of Rajasthan in public consciousness. Even in the conditioned amnesia of metropolitan India, where there is growing immunity to all kinds of suffering and violence, the calamitous effects of drought are hard to ignore. Not 'everybody love a good drought', as a cynical title of a popular book on the subject goes.[1] *Needless to say, when I brought up the subject of 'water' with Komalda, I was actually thinking about 'drought'. That seemed to be the 'real issue' of the session I had in mind.*

Typically, Komalda did not begin with the conditions of drought; rather, very slowly and with sustained calm, he began to prepare a context around water—its preservation in the rural areas of Rajasthan, its modes of ownership, the consequences of irrigation, and so on. This material history offers very ordinary, yet critical observations, relating to the ways in which local communities in the desert region of Rajasthan have coped over the years with the scarcity of water. This is not a problem, so much as it is a condition of their lives. However, it is becoming a crisis of staggering proportions as the traditional mechanisms of water conservation are breaking down. Listen now to Komalda on the subject of water. Neither a technician nor an NGO activist, he presents his facts differently.

The Elements

I began to think about water while I was working on the problem of *panchatatva*—the five elements: fire, earth, sky, wind, and water. I was exploring these elements from my own point of view, not from any philosophical or metaphysical perspective. What concerned me is how people view these elements and what they have to say about them. I wanted to know what kind of insights could emerge from their day-to-day experience of these *tatvas* (elements). This was my quest. So throughout my research I focused on what people had to say about the elements and not what has been written about them in Sanskrit treatises.

I will give you one example of what I learned. On getting to know some singers of devotional music from the Bavari tribe, I asked one of the musicians: 'What is *ākāsh* (the sky)? How do you explain it?' And he said: 'Have you ever seen a *ghaṛā* (earthen pot)? Move your hand inside it, but don't touch its periphery. That is ākāsh.' A space with no boundaries.

I had another insight into the elements. This came while I was working on rural gods and goddesses. Not far from Udaipur I came across an abandoned temple. There are many such abandoned temples in Rajasthan with no priest, no deity, no ceremonies, no *jāgraṇ* (all-night singing sessions of devotional songs).[2] Some temples are abandoned if their inaugural rituals have not been completed. Others get de-sanctified even after all their rituals have been performed. Here in this abandoned temple near Udaipur I came across a sadhu. As we got talking, I asked him: 'How do you explain the phenomenon of *bhūt* (ghosts)?' He said: 'Everything is bhūt that does not have the element of earth.'

Along with these local explanations of the tatvas, I was also concerned with a larger problem: the state versus panchatatva. What kind of control does the state have over the elements? If we take *vāyu* (the wind), we realize that no king or emperor can control its force or direction. No human agency can govern the wind. But if you take *bhūmi* (the earth), then we find that there is much for the state to do in terms of land laws, agricultural laws, revenue laws, distribution rights, and so on. As for water, more than any other element, it is essential for the very existence of human life. One may not have land for agriculture, one may have to labour in order to survive, but without water, it is impossible to live. So in trying to understand the role of the state so far as the elements are concerned, I began with a formal study of water. Can the state control water?

Sources of Water

In the late 1950s, when folk musicians used to come to my house, and I would go to their villages, one of the first questions that I remember asking them concerned the traditional sources of water in their villages, especially for drinking purposes. A number of things came to light.

In the desert zone there are traditional water sources known as *nāḍis*, small man-made village ponds with embankments wherein rainwater from the adjoining catchment area is stored.[3] Traditional nāḍis have survived for hundreds of years. But after Independence, whenever government agencies have made them, they have invariably dried up. The point is that the local knowledge of people is rarely taken into account. People know what goes into the construction of a successful nāḍi—they know, for instance, where it should be located, how deep into the earth one must dig, how to deal with the slope of a particular ground, how certain layers of earth need to be strengthened in order to prevent water-seepage. Local communities know these conditions very well. And therefore, they laugh when state departments attempt to build nāḍis of their own accord. They know that most of these nāḍis will never contain water.

Apart from the nāḍi, there are other traditional structures of water harvesting, such as the *ṭānkā*,[4] which is an underground tank drawing on rainwater either from the surrounding catchment area or from other artificially prepared storage spaces like rooftops. In addition to these sources which are largely dependent on the availability of run-off surface rainwater and the topography of the surrounding land, the desert region of Rajasthan is known for its numerous wells drawing on subterranean water channels. These wells, which have many different names depending on their type, can be found in the most remote of *ḍhāṇis* (settlements).

Among different kinds of step-wells there are the *bāvaḍi*, the *kunḍ*, and the *jhālrā*, which vary according to their depth, dimensions, and the positioning of the steps. The sources of water in these indigenous wells are sometimes minuscule. In the jhālrā, for instance, we find tiny drops of water emerging from all sides of the well. This is different from another kind of well, the *sīr*, in which continuous lines of water flow with the force of capillary action. There are different movements of the water depending on the dimensions, materials, and construction of the wells.

Practically all over Rajasthan I have also come across yet another kind of well that is called *sāgar ke kuey*. This source of subterranean water has a continuous flow—even as it draws on water as deep as 180–300 feet, the water table of the well itself is never more than three to four feet. You can actually go inside the well and stand in the water. At best it might come up only to your waist. The striking thing is that if you use an electric pump to draw the water, you can get as much as ten to eleven gallons of water per hour. But whatever the quantity or force of the water drawn, there is not a ripple on the surface of the water. Its flow is constant. Whether it is located in Jhunjhunu or Barmer or Jodhpur or Udaipur, moss or slime (*kāi*) never gathers within the sāgar ke kuey.

Ownership and Rights to Water

Apart from questioning people about the sources of water in their village, I always ask another question: Do you know who got the nāḍi dug in your village? From my sources of information, covering almost 300 villages in the desert zone, I have learned that none of the drinking water sources in rural areas has ever been constructed through the direct sponsorship or patronage of the jāgirdār or king. Invariably, it is an individual who has assumed this responsibility, a person with no state or official authority. Generally it is assumed that a bāvaḍi or step-well is built as a form of religious action, to ensure *punya* (merit). We can also assume that whenever a well is called *kuā* or *kohar* or *taḷā*, it is personally owned; the *sar* and *pīchka*, however, are owned and used by the entire village. In these indigenous wells in the rural areas of Rajasthan, there are local ownership patterns.

In urban areas, however, of the larger *jāgirs* (feudal principalities), one can find a few water bodies that are credited to a particular jāgirdār or king. For example, in Jodhpur we have a man-made lake Gulabsagar, which along with two temples—Nenibai ka Mandir and Ranchorji ka Mandir—were constructed by queens. But when we go into the details of these structures we find that they were made when these queens became widows. Here we have to understand the laws relating to primogeniture (*pāṭavi*) inheritance, where the property of the father goes exclusively to the eldest son and is not divided among the brothers, as in the *bhāi-bant* inheritance system.

In the pāṭavi system, we find that as soon as the king dies, his widowed queens are removed from the royal premises along with their servants. It is assumed that they pose a potential threat to the new king with their manipulations and conspiracies. Only if the new king sanctions it, can these ex-queens hold on to their property; they may however, be denied access to it. Now so far as moveable property (*chal-sampati*) is concerned, including ornaments and money, this could remain with the queens unless the king orders that it should be returned to the royal treasury. What we find is that when the queens became widows, they would often give their property to a Brahman—this form of donation is known as *udakanā*. It works on the premise that anything given as *dān* (gift) to a Brahman cannot be reclaimed by the king.[5] While the queen lived she had rights over this property, but on her death, it became the Brahman's property. We find that the patronage of many water bodies has come from such sources.

The other prominent donors were female dancers and singers who were adopted by the king and given the status of *pardāyat*, *pāswān*, and *bhagtan*. There were also women from prostitute musician groups like the *patar*. We find that these women financed the construction of quite a few temples and drinking water sources after the death of their respective masters. This does not mean that kings and jāgirdārs themselves did not finance drinking water sources, but the fact is that whenever they did, no one except the royal family had access to the water.

Balsamand in Jodhpur, for example, is a big lake, but during my childhood taking drinking water from there was totally prohibited. In fact, one could not go there because there were so many chowkidars guarding the place. The people could only take water from another lake, the Balsamand ka Bachia, the 'child of Balsamand'. Likewise, in Udaipur, the waters of the Fatehsagar and Swarupsagar could not be used for drinking purposes. Instead, they were used to feed the *phunwārā* (fountain) in the Saheliyon ki Badi gardens. Only the water from Pichhola Lake could be used at that time for drinking purposes. Did the royal family build this lake? No. It was the Naṭ, or acrobat community, which constructed Pichhola Lake, and it was through their patronage that the people of Udaipur had access to drinking water—indeed, their only source of drinking water till the 1950s.

The question of rights to water cannot be separated from the social hierarchies of Indian society, where we continue to face the problem of untouchability among diverse low-caste and tribal communities. Upper-caste communities in the desert region have direct access to the actual source of water at the well. Further away there is a *kunḍiā* (water-container) marked for the next caste group in the hierarchy. Further on, there will be another container, which will be used for drinking water for cattle and other animals. It is from this source that the scheduled castes used to take water. Though the situation may have changed slightly, the pattern continues. The very practice of drawing water from the well represents the hierarchies and disparities in our social structure. At times, each caste is allotted a particular time to draw water, with low-caste communities inevitably being permitted to draw the water last. This strong governance in the distribution of water reveals the actual functioning of caste in our society.

To get back to the question of 'Who owns water?', we need to examine the legality of the rights involved. In Jodhpur, for example, we have at least two important drinking water sources in the Kaylana Lake and the Balsamand Lake. There are also smaller sources like the Akheyraj-ji ka tālāb. Now, if we raise the legal issue of ownership, nobody can explain who owns these sources overall, which, in effect, means that no one knows who is responsible for their maintenance. So water belongs to the irrigation department, the land both under and surrounding the water belongs to the revenue department, the fish in the lakes belong to the fisheries department, the water for drinking purposes is controlled by the public health department, and so on. Even though these water sources fall within the boundaries of the municipality, the authorities don't know how to interrelate the different responsibilities upheld by these different departments.

Near the Jodhpur Fort is Ranisar Lake, which is owned by the royal family. In the late nineteenth century, the water of Jodhpur within the city limits used to come from the Padamsar Lake, which was common property. But nobody was allowed to take water from Ranisar. A few years ago, there was a problem. Both in Padamsar and Ranisar, it was discovered that the fish were dying because the oxygen content in the water was decreasing on account of accumulated dirt. The people argued that the Padamsar lake should be cleaned with government money and the Ranisar lake should be cleaned by the king, since he claimed to own this water source. The situation becomes more complicated when one realizes that the water comes first to Ranisar, and then to Padamsar. Whatever the direction of the water, I would say: forget about who owns and who doesn't own the lakes. The fact is that the government does not want to acknowledge that large water-bodies *cannot* be owned by individuals or trusts.

The same situation can be found in the village of Borunda, where at one time a particular nāḍi was used for drinking water for all the cattle. Now, who owns this nāḍi? Is the nāḍi owned by the panchayat? The answer is no. Is it owned by the irrigation department? No. By the revenue department? No. Owning the nāḍi or lake is not the only problem. The real problem is that the nāḍi and lake have to get water from the catchment area (*āgor*). If you destroy the catchment area, there is no water. So if ownership claims on nāḍis and lakes are made, then that ownership must extend to the maintenance of the catchment areas as well. Otherwise, our traditional water systems will continue to remain in dire straits.

Irrigation

Let us turn now to the vital relationship between water and irrigation, and its inevitable links with agriculture. During the colonial period, the British government put pressure on the kings of the Princely States to develop irrigation projects ostensibly for the welfare of local communities, but more concretely, for the generation of revenue from land and agriculture.[6] Inevitably, the rulers of local principalities resisted the colonial order because they believed that by submitting to the laws of irrigation commissions, the availability of water in the region could be controlled by the central authorities. Nonetheless, a number of irrigation projects were started around the first decades of the last century. Significantly, almost all these projects have become drinking water projects today. It has become very clear to me that so far as water is concerned, people have to create their own sources of survival, and they can do this most effectively by turning to traditional sources of water conservation and irrigation.

Among the most important traditional water-harvesting systems in Rajasthan is the *khaḍīn* system, which goes back to the fifteenth century, a technology attributed to the non-ritual practising Paliwal Brahman community of Jaisalmer.[7] Unbelievably, it is said that around a hundred years ago, Jaisalmer was actually exporting wheat to Punjab. And this was possible because of the khaḍīn system, which reveals a very deep understanding of topography, gravitational movement of water, water-harvesting, moisture conservation, drainage, desalination—all of which combine towards the most productive form of agriculture available in the desert region of Rajasthan. Basically, the water in the khaḍīn is drawn from a rocky and highland catchment area, from where it collects in a low-lying plain area surrounded by an earthen embankment (*bund*). This bund, which arrests the water in the khaḍīn area, has provisions for a spillway from which excess water can be removed; there is also a sluice from which all the water can be drained. The water in the khaḍīn is capable of being stored for two to three months after the monsoon season, following which it seeps into the ground and the sowing for the rabi (winter) crop begins. So rich is the damp soil of the khaḍīn area, containing all kinds of natural minerals and organic materials, that it is not necessary to use any fertilizer or additional irrigation.

Despite this striking instance of indigenous knowledge, one illusion needs to be cleared up: Not every person in a village has access to technical knowledge of this kind. Not everyone is an irrigation expert. People's knowledge is also the specialized knowledge of a few groups that pertains to the sustenance of the community at large.

This knowledge involves particular skills and modes of transmission. The community of the Satnāmi, for instance, specializes in digging wells; the Od, on the other hand, remove the surface earth for the construction of bunds and nāḍis. Such are the digging skills of these nomadic groups that they are capable of identifying each layer of earth and stone as they dig into the soil. In the construction of wells, they know which layers are prone to water-seepage, and which are resistant. I would regard these insights as part of the ethno-geological knowledge of the people.[8] This knowledge does not merely pertain to what lies in the depths of the earth; it also includes an awareness of the individual properties of stones and minerals.

To return to irrigation, I have found that whenever we track the water source of a particular lake, we invariably discover a chain of lakes. Water from rivulets enters the first lake, then overflows into the second, and then into the third, and so on. This chain of lakes gets entirely filled with water during the rains. What does this suggest? It suggests that no one has the right to stop the water at any one point. If there is any obstacle to the natural distribution of surface water, local communities have the right to intervene.

It is necessary to point out here that the river watershed is not the only source of natural irrigation in Rajasthan. Far less conspicuous, though more vital, are the rivulets which run anywhere between 10–100 kilometres, spreading out into the environs. This kind of rivulet water source (*balā*) may not contribute to the major river system, but it is the very life-line of Rajasthan. When all is said and done, what should not be forgotten is that the vast majority of small farmers and cultivators in Rajasthan continue to be totally dependent on the monsoons for agriculture, and not on schemes of irrigation. The need to strengthen the traditional sources of water-harvesting during the rainy season, therefore, remains more urgent than ever before.

One problem with the irrigation projects is that they invariably get diverted from their original goal. Recently a strong lobby has emerged in Rajasthan, which asserts that water should be used primarily for drinking purposes. Jodhpur is the first beneficiary of the recently completed Indira Gandhi Nahar Pariyojna Canal, more commonly referred to as the Rajasthan Canal, which has prioritized the availability of drinking water. The results of the Canal are mixed.

On the one hand, there is no dearth of drinking water in the town. The quality of the water is good. But there are other problems.[9] Whether you are dealing with Kolkata or Mumbai or Delhi or Jaipur or Jodhpur, the point is that cities and towns can never depend entirely on the water within their municipal limits. Invariably, they will draw on water from the rural areas, which means that they encroach on the water sources of rural people. Water scarcity is one of the main reasons why people migrate from the villages into the cities. But, as people become conscious of their rights to water, it will become impossible for government agencies to deprive them of their own resources.

Earlier, before the completion of the Rajasthan Canal project, we used to get our water from the wells of Ransi Gaon and Rampura. A lot of underground water from these villages was channelized for use in Jodhpur. This resulted in the total drying up of water sources in these rural areas. Today the water levels in Ransi Gaon and Rampura have gone down by nearly thirty to forty feet. Likewise, when the lake of Soorsagar was built, eighteen kilometres outside Jodhpur, it resulted in the desertification of villages in the neighboring areas. We have seen time and again that when tanks and canals are built in one area, neighboring desert villages don't get water, their wells dry up, there is a decrease in agricultural activity, and a corresponding increase in the migration of labour from the village to the city. In the process, entire villages are wiped out, resulting in a great deal of misery for people at large.

While acknowledging the crisis of water, there is a very peculiar situation in Rajasthan that needs to be acknowledged. Over the years we find that the population in the rural areas has either remained stable or has even increased in drought-ridden areas. If people have migrated from certain areas, other people have settled there. It is said that the Thar Desert is a very fragile zone. Fragile in the sense that it cannot sustain a large population of people, or larger numbers of cattle and sheep. But the reality is that this area has the highest concentration of human and animal life among the world's deserts. In almost thirty-eight of over fifty years of our independence, drought has taken place. Yet the cattle population in Rajasthan has increased by 23 per cent, the sheep and goat population by 27 per cent. Only the camel population has gone down, as I mentioned earlier. How do we account for this increase? It is hard to say.

Statistics are not Komalda's forte, but his basic perspective is on the mark. For instance, it is now widely accepted by activists and theorists in the field, even among a few supporters of the government's developmental agenda, that so-called 'successful' projects like the Rajasthan Canal project do not benefit those sections of rural society which are not located within its reach. Intensified agriculture has led to indiscriminate water extraction resulting in a lowering of the water table, which in turn has made the reality of drought even more irreversible.

From Milind Bokil's very useful analysis on 'Drought in Rajasthan' (2000), there are some statistics that are worth confronting.[10] *It appears that in a state where 60 per cent of the total land is in the desert region, 'the proportion of net sown area to total geographic area in 1995–6 was 46.91 per cent', which was higher than the national average of 43.26 per cent. The index of all crops in Rajasthan over the past twenty years has 'more than doubled'. More critically, 'the proportion of the net area irrigated to the net area sown' in 1995–6 was 31.56 per cent, which was substantially higher than seemingly more prosperous, drought-resistant states like Karnataka (22.09 per cent) and Maharashtra (14.33 per cent).*

Why then, as Bokil raises the pertinent question, does intensified growth of irrigation, ostensibly benefiting agriculture, not compensate for the deficiency in rainfall? Here he states the obvious fact emphasized by Komalda that the bulk of the cultivators are still entirely dependent on the 'vagaries of the monsoon'. But he also adds that the 'entitlement' to irrigation in Rajasthan has not been equitably distributed, and unless 'equity in irrigation becomes an essential element of policy and practice, agricultural intensification [can only continue to be] counterproductive' (p. 4172).

Here Bokil draws on Amartya Sen's seminal theory of 'entitlement', by which droughts and famines can be resisted. 'Starvation', as Sen has reminded us, 'is the characteristic of some people not having enough food to eat. It is not the characteristic of there not being enough food to eat.'[11] *While entitlements can be activated through various 'exchanges' based on trade, production, and labour, reinforced by government subsidies and employment schemes, Bokil rightly asks whether entitlements can be fully applied to water, which is better regarded as a 'natural resource' rather than as a 'commodity' (p. 4174). Today, of course, there is an aggressive attempt to commodify water in India through private enterprises, as is only too evident in the ubiquitous use of bottled mineral water during train and bus journeys.*

While avoiding a polemic on the subject, Komalda would concur with those activists that 'common' resources like land and water are best controlled by people rather than by governments. But he would extend the benefits of this control not only to human beings, but to animals as well, as he elaborates in the next section.

Water and Livestock: The Cattle Fairs

Rajasthan is said to be 'the only state in the country where the livestock population is more than the human population.'[12] *On the one hand, there is a substantial increase in the livestock population (with the exception of the camel population, which, as Komalda has pointed out earlier, is declining). But, on the other hand, thousands of cattle and other animals perish in the drought years, after having been abandoned by small cultivators migrating to other places for their own survival. It is obvious that a substantial percentage of the rural population in Rajasthan continues to rely on animal husbandry for its livelihood, even as the resources for grazing, fodder and drinking water for animals are shrinking.*

In no site is the omnipresence of animals more visible than in Rajasthan's ubiquitous cattle fairs, which have continued to exist through the worst years of drought precisely because of the availability of its most precious resource: water.

At Pushkar, where a large number of cows, bulls, horses, and camels are assembled together for the annual fair, the availability of drinking water becomes a prime consideration. Not only for the numerous buyers and sellers coming from different parts of Rajasthan and from many other states of India, but, more specifically, for the animals themselves. Such fairs are generally located near a river, lake or spring, where there is some natural source of water. Even though the Pushkar fair today is held near the man-made Pushkar Lake, which goes back only to the thirteenth century, the ancestry of Pushkar as a *tīrtha*, or place of pilgrimage, goes back to the ancient Budha Pushkar Lake. Invoking a Vedic ancestry, this lake is not fed by any river or stream, but rather by the water oozing from within the bed of the lake itself. Budha Pushkar is one of those tīrthas whose mythic significance is specifically related to the natural availability of water.

Likewise, there are numerous tīrthas all over India like Ban Ganga, where it is said Arjun shot his arrow into the earth and the water sprang out from there. There is Bhim Goda, where a spring is believed to have emerged at the exact place where the mighty Bhim thrust his knee against the ground. And, of course, there are numerous stories around the confluence of rivers, as in the meeting of Ganga and Jamuna in Prayag, and the meeting of Som and Māhi in the Dungarpur region, where the third river is invariably the hidden Saraswati.

For the cattle fair, an important criterion is not only the location of the land itself, but also the particular timing of the fair. The Pushkar fair, for example, always takes place in the month of Kartik during the Diwali season, while the Tilwara fair takes place after Holi. By the month of Kartik, the kharif (monsoon) crop is ready for harvesting—so this is a good time to hold a fair because the animals are not needed for ploughing the fields. It is possible to transport them to the site at Pushkar for the inevitable buying and selling of animals, which follows its own procedures of bargaining, registration, taxation, and transportation of the animals that are sold. The pricing of the animals itself will depend on land-related issues—for example, even if there has been a good rainfall in a particular year, but there is insufficient grass for grazing, then the cattle are likely to be priced at a lower rate. All these variable factors come into play at Pushkar itself.

The timing of the Tilwara fair, however, has a different logic, for which I would like to share a story. The Tilwara fair is held on the Luni riverbed near the town of Balotra. The Luni, it should be kept in mind, is not a perennial river; it rises only during the rainy season, and when there is no rain, as has been the case in the last few years, then the riverbed is dry. If you went to this area right now and dug a hundred feet into the ground, you would not find any water. However, in the month of Chaitra during which time the fair is held for a period of fifteen days, all you have to do is to dig barely six inches into the ground, and there is water. It is only because of this availability of water that it becomes possible to accommodate almost 20,000 people and around 50,000 horses, bullocks, and camels.

Now, from one point of view, this sudden availability of water is a kind of phenomenon; but I don't think that there is anything mysterious about it. We know for a fact that the Tilwara fair has been held during the month of Chaitra on the Luni riverbed for hundreds of years. Obviously, we need to study how the water level rises in the riverbed at this time.

I still remember how I visited this fair many years ago in the company of the photographer Raghubir Singh. We decided to move around the fair grounds through the night past camels, horses, bullocks, which surrounded us. Suddenly, at 2 a.m, we heard a loud gurgling sound approaching. I tell you, we were afraid. We thought that all the animals would start running here and there, and there would be a stampede. But the people who were sleeping in the area with their animals told us not to worry because nothing would happen. Like a tidal wave, the sound continued to draw closer and closer, and we could feel it crossing our path and fading into the distance.

What happened? There are two kinds of explanation—one, put forward by the people, was that the horses of the god Maldev were proceeding towards the residence of Rāni Bhaṭiyāṇi and the sound that we heard was merely their hooves while galloping.[13] We asked whether this would have any effect on the fair itself. Yes, we learned from some of the people—the prices of all the cattle would go up the next day. How was this possible? And that's when they came up with the saying, '*doodh uphanta hai, us tarah se yeh melā uphnegā*' (just as the milk froths, so will the mela).

Then we asked the people how many years they had been coming to the fair—some said twelve years, others fifteen. It was clear that they were familiar with the territory. We then wanted to know if this sound that we had heard was a regular feature of the fair, and someone said that, in the last ten years or so, he had heard it only three times. However, even if one accepts that this sound is not a regular feature, it is obvious that it is related to some geological change in the water level of the riverbed. And this needs to be studied scientifically. Unfortunately, a lot of such things in our society get taken for granted—people get used to the phenomena, and there's no urge to understand what they mean and why they happen. If we could be better aware of the ecological laws determining the availability of water in seemingly dry spaces like the Luni riverbed, this could be very useful for studying the social ecology of the fair itself.

From this story it becomes obvious that water is both a natural phenomenon linked to all kinds of meteorological and geological laws, which Komalda is calling our attention to, even though he is not in a position to provide a scientific explanation for their connections. But water also has other mythic significances, which I am curious to know more about as we enter the difficult and all-too-real phenomenon of drought.

In the following section, we move from a few critical observations on the bureaucracy surrounding the reality of drought and relief measures, to the sharing of some extraordinary stories, in which the resilience and survival of people in times of drought are recalled at the level of fable and song.

Drought

Drought is a continuing proposition in Rajasthan. People live with it. It is not something like an earthquake or a flash flood. It happens on a regular basis and people have learned to survive.

Yesterday it rained. If it hadn't rained for another ten days, then you would have seen long faces. So now people are happy, this was the first rain in the season, even though it is already August. Now the sowing can begin. But the farmers also need a second rainfall. And after that, they need no rain at all for the crops to grow well. Now that they have got the rain, they will need one more rainfall within 15–20 days or a month, and that will be sufficient for the seed-to-seed cycle. In Rajasthan we say that two and a half rains is all that we need: *ḍhāi barkhā*. With this amount of rain we have enough to eat, but one rainfall alone will pose a problem. Sometimes it may rain more than two and half times, or three times, and that is all right, but if suddenly in the last period, it just keeps on raining, well, in that case, everything will be destroyed.

In popular terminology, there are basically three kinds of drought—*akāl*, resulting from the shortage of grain; *jalkāl*, resulting from water scarcity; and *trikāl*, which involves the shortage of grain, fodder and water.[14] Coping with drought is not a new thing. By September-October in the month of Kartik, all paṭwārīs are expected to send in a report to the SDO (the Sub-Division Officer) and the Collector in their district. The local criterion for measuring drought is calculated according to the monetary unit of the anna in relation to the percentage of crop that has grown in a particular area. So, it is possible to speak of an *āṭh ānā* crop (8 anna crop), or a *bārā ānā* crop (12 anna crop), and so on. Drought is generally assumed when there is less than a 'two-anna crop' in a particular region. This system of calculation is called *ānāwari*.

From the district level, all the facts and figures are sent to the state government of Rajasthan, and finally, to the central government in Delhi, which officially declares the existence of drought (or famine) not earlier than mid-October through the Girdawari report. More often that not, this official confirmation of the drought is delayed, at times for months on end. By the time the government gets its act together and sends a team to assess the problem and to distribute relief measures—this could be around December or January of the following year—the people have already taken the necessary measures in order to survive.[15]

Inevitably, they resort to a number of survival strategies. Some people move out of the area altogether. Others get recruited as labourers particularly in the mining sectors, where there is ready employment in the quarries. Apart from migrating to less drought-hit areas, people fall back on their reserve food supplies and fodder for their livestock, if they have any. At times they resort to loans. Or seek help from the government-sponsored wage employment schemes.[16] If the situation worsens, then they have no other alternative but to leave their homes and go wherever water is available. Today there are new relief measures, new modes of transporting water. There are also new water resources through the installation of bore wells.

Most significantly, there are local initiatives for relief work, which have a tremendous outreach at a grassroot level. One Manganiyar musician, Gazi Khan, who plays the *khaṛtāl* (wooden clappers), has started his own institution called Pahchān (Recognition). Through donations and grants, he was able to supply water and fodder for livestock to different villages during the worst period of the drought in the year 2000. My foreign friends all over the world, who have worked in Rajasthan in one way or the other, also wanted to send donations when they heard about the drought. But basically, as a long-term measure to deal with droughts, what is urgently needed is not donations, but as I have emphasized earlier, the rejuvenation of traditional water-harvesting resources, which have been grossly neglected over the years.

The question is: Who should initiate the process of water management? Earlier this management was in the hands of villagers, who decided how the water should be distributed in their villages at a collective level. After 1947, however, they have become increasingly alienated from decisions concerning water management, assuming that the government has to provide people with water and maintain all the water bodies. Even the panchayats are not prepared to take on any responsibility for ensuring a just distribution of water from sources created by the government. So the government has to appoint different agencies to deal with the maintenance and repair of water works. When there is any delay in the repair work following a breakdown in the water supply, the panchayat does not intervene. At best it stages a demonstration that is reported in the local newspaper. It is all very well to raise the issue of rights, but what about duties and responsibilities?

Representing Drought

Moving away from the realities of drought and the logistical problems that it presents, let us examine the relationship of drought to the different ways in which it has been represented in folk culture. I would say that there are very few songs that deal explicitly with drought.

At best, drought is represented indirectly through songs dealing with rain, such as *barsāḷo* and *sāvan*, and more specifically, with the desire for rain. Occasionally we come across *dohās* (rhymed couplets) that deal more explicitly with the conditions of drought. For instance:

Khen, koḍh, khānsi dusi, do hāthān kirtār
Māraṇ mārag mokḷā, meh binā mat mār

TB, leprosy, cough and cold, you may give us with both hands,
We can be killed in many ways, but don't kill us without rain.

Sau sānḍiya, sau karahalā, pūt, nipūti hoe
Mehadlā to buṭhān hi bhalā, honi ho so hoe

A hundred she-camels, a hundred camels, all left childless,
What is destined to be will be, even so a few drops of rain would be a blessing.[17]

Apart from such dohās, we learn about drought through stories. My own grandmother had vivid memories of the great famine [of 1899] that afflicted Rajasthan more than a hundred years ago, which is identified as the Chhapannā (literally, 'fifty-six') famine by the Samvat Indian calendar year. This famine extended beyond the boundaries of Rajasthan to Punjab, Madhya Pradesh and other neighbouring states. In the plague that followed the famine, people had terrible experiences, which were later recalled in the form of stories and reminiscences.

One story that comes to mind concerns a Bhāmbhi, a low-caste untouchable, who stayed on in the village of Satto in Jaisalmer district, after all the other residents had fled. They left behind not only their houses and property, but also their dead relatives. Not only did this Bhāmbhi bury and cremate the Hindus and Muslims among the dead, he also looked after the property of the entire village. And he continued to do so for about a year, surviving the plague. When the plague ended, the people came back to the village to find all their possessions intact. As a reward and a token of recognition, the Bhāmbhi was given a plot of land in that village, and the fourth generation of his family is still living there today.

Another story that comes to mind involves a Rajput and his wife during a severe drought. Unable to survive where he was living, the Rajput left his home with his wife. Somewhere along the way, he came across a large *dhorā* (sand-dune). He told his wife, 'Let's stay here for the night and in the morning we will continue our journey.' The man, however, thought to himself, 'How will I survive? How can I continue this journey with my wife? Better to leave her here.' Next morning she got up to find that her husband had left her. With great difficulty she continued walking till she arrived at a village of low-caste Bhāmbhi families. She explained her situation to them. 'How will I live?' she asked. 'Don't worry,' one particular family reassured her, 'you can stay with us.' As she was a Rajput and they were Bhāmbhis, they gave her everything to eat and drink separately. They even taught her the stitching that they did for a living, and so she passed her time working with them.

A year later, the man returned to the particular dhorā, where he had left his wife. Near this place he heard news of his wife and was able to trace her whereabouts. All the Bhāmbhis treated him as their *jamāi* (son-in-law). They assured him that she had not touched their food and had lived a pure Rajput life. Later the woman left with her husband to her old home. Some time later, her father-in-law died. A message was sent to all the relations of the Rajput family, and in addition, the woman sent one to the Bhāmbhi family because she felt that she owed her life to them. When the Bhāmbhi family came to the woman's house, they were turned away as untouchables. At this point, the woman confronted her husband and said, 'You brave Rajput, who left your wife on a sand-dune to die, these are the people who saved my life. I will go with them.' And she left her home to live with the Bhāmbhis.

From this real-life story, we learn how people help each other out in the most critical circumstances of drought and plague and famine. We don't need to turn to the lives of kings and queens to learn about honour and survival. We have many stories of ordinary folk from which we can learn about their strategies of survival. These stories are now part of people's memory, which needs to be tapped in order to deepen our sense of history.

'Capturing the Clouds'—A Fable

Perhaps the strongest evidence that I have ever encountered of the predicament of drought in song was captured most accidentally on one of my research trips near Beawar, in the small town of Masuda. My purpose during this trip was to record songs sung by Bhil women. Out of the five or six women whom we were able to contact for the recording, there was one old woman, who could not sing very well because of her age. But precisely because of that, she claimed seniority and began to dictate to the other women what they should sing. I realized that there was a problem here because the younger women didn't want to sing with the old woman because she wouldn't be able to sustain the pitch. So I resorted to tact and decided that it was best to record the old woman first, and only after she had been placated would it be possible for us to record the other women without her interference.

So, with due respect, I said, 'Mother, you are the most knowledgeable person about the songs in this area. These young girls don't know as many things as you do. Would you sing something for us all by yourself?' And she said, 'Yes, I can sing alone.' Then she started to sing something like a ballad—not long enough to be an epic, but a narrative in which the characters are not specifically named, and the place and time of the events in the song are left unspecified.

The old woman's ballad began with the description of a terrifying drought. People had eaten everything that was available—all the grains, all the grasses, even all their animals: cows, goats, buffaloes, whatever. Everything was eaten, and there was nothing left. The drought became a famine. Finally, finding nothing around them, the people began to cut and eat their own limbs. But their condition got worse and worse. In desperation, they went to the court of the mother goddess and told her, 'You've tested us sufficiently. Why don't you help us?' Hearing their prayers, the mother goddess appeared before the suffering Bhils. Without commiserating with them, she took them directly to the house of a Bania.

Inside his house was a ghaṭṭi, a grindstone, on the floor. The mother goddess lifted the upper stone of the ghaṭṭi, and what did she find underneath? Hundreds of clouds. Gradually, these clouds escaped into the sky, and soon the entire sky darkened and it started to rain very heavily. Everywhere rivulets and water were flowing, and the people were happy.

Then the mother goddess seized the Bania by the hair on his head, and lifted him up and down, over and over again. Finally, the Bania cried out in pain, 'If you want to kill me then do so, but don't torture me like this.' Listening to his plea, the mother goddess said, 'All right, if you sacrifice a buffalo on my behalf, you will be spared.' But the Bania said that his caste rules prevented him from performing any kind of animal sacrifice. So the mother goddess accepted his limitation and said: 'All right, make an effigy of a *bhainsā* (he-buffalo) out of grass, then cut it with a knife. And I will accept this as a sacrifice and as an offering made to me.' So the Bania did as he was commanded to do, but as soon as he cut off the head of the grass-buffalo, the blood started oozing out of its body. And the blood flowed and flowed, mixing with the water everywhere, and gradually, the entire waters of the earth became dark with blood.

Now, this was the song sung by the woman with no accompanying instrument. It was unbelievable, I tell you. After completing the song, the old woman mentioned a temple in which the mother goddess has been envisioned as Mahishasuramardini, but instead of the buffalo, she is shown sacrificing a Bania under her foot. Though I tried to trace this temple myself, I was not able to find it. But the story of the old woman remained with me for a very long time, reminding me of the close and troubled relationship that exists in rural areas between the tribal and Bania communities.

Banias are identified as those traders in rural areas who supply all kinds of commodities—grains, clothes, utensils. To buy these items, the tribals convert their meagre resources from the forest into cash with which they obtain these commodities. More often than not they become dependent on Banias through loans, which are hard to pay back. Not only do the Banias control the cash economy in the village, they make most of their profits during periods of drought and famine. In order to deal with this exploitation, there are certain social rituals that exist in Rajasthan—for instance, while waiting for the rains, tribal groups from the Bhil community go to the houses of the Banias and plead with them not to capture the clouds. The Banias in turn offer the tribals some *guṛ* (jaggery) and say, '*Bāndhege nahi bādo ko*' (We will not capture the clouds).

This practice exists even today in some tribal areas, not unlike in the Abu region where the Garāsiās live. Here too the Garāsiās have a strong belief that the Jain Munis are capable of binding the clouds through their magical powers. And that is why we have historical references from earlier times in which Jain Munis were killed by Garāsiās, who believed that the holy men actually prevented the rain from falling in times of drought. Through such stories, we learn of drought not only in relation to its immediate physical impact on people, but in the larger mythical context of the power relations existing in rural and tribal socieities.

Perhaps there was no stronger moment in the entire process of listening to Komalda than to hear him narrate this story sung by the Bhil woman. Clouds imprisoned under the grindstone: the sheer magic of this unprecedented detail, by which the story shifts its focus from a terrifying scenario of famine-stricken people eating their own limbs to the joyous downpour of rain, made me imagine at first that this was a 'happy ending'. But the story in the song doesn't end there, and that's what makes it even richer as it proceeds to elaborate on the animal sacrifice made by the Bania—a sacrifice which eventually fills the entire earth with blood.

As always in Komalda's 'arthāv' (explanation), there is a cursory attempt to contextualize the story within the social relationships of Banias and tribal communities, but there is no 'interpretation' of the story as such, still less any metacritical reflexivity on Komalda's own caste affinities to the Bania community itself. The story of the Bhil song assumes it own autonomy as it resonates at multiple levels. There is no way of 'verifying' the text and of 'fixing' it in the process, because, like most of Komalda's oral resources, the recording of the song is lost somewhere in the numerous uncatalogued tapes of the Rupayan Sansthan. All we have is Komalda's memory of that encounter with the Bhil woman, which was fortuitously sparked during one of our very last recording sessions together, when I was picking his brains for more 'evidence' of songs dealing with drought. What emerged didn't merely jolt me (the listener) with its dramatic intensity, I believe it took Komalda by surprise as well.

4

ORAL EPICS

In this chapter, which focuses primarily on one of Rajasthan's most familiar oral epics 'Pabuji', we begin by picking up a few strands from Komalda's earlier observations on geography, vegetation, livestock and staple-food categories. In one of his passing reflections, Komalda had pointed out how much one can learn about geography from within the text of an epic itself, wherein the description of landscape and physical detail is very exact. At this point he had also acknowledged that, 'In these epics, people go on talking and talking without interpreting what they are talking about.' An ironic statement surely, because that's precisely what Komalda does: he talks and talks, without interpreting what he's talking about. Very often he seems to prioritize a significant detail—for instance, the geography contained within the text of the epic, after which he promptly moves on to making other connections. Instead of regretting these elisions, let us focus on the unexpected connections that do emerge in the course of his discourse—in this particular case, the relationship between geography and oral epics through the mediation of musical instruments.

Musical Instruments Tell Their Own Stories

It all started very innocently with my research on the musical instruments of Rajasthan. In the early stages, 'collecting information' about these instruments meant that I went to different villages, bought instruments, and wrote short descriptions of their shapes and sizes, how they are played, and how they can be categorized. Following this simple description of the instruments, it was only logical to follow up by asking: Who are the musicians? Why do they play their instruments in the first place? How did they learn to play them?

All these questions led me to think about the caste of the musicians because most of these instruments are in the hands of specific caste groups. Musical instruments have a lot to do with the heredity of particular groups and the process of learning that is passed on from one generation to another. I began to study different groups of musicians—Langas, Manganiyars, Ḍholis, Damāmis, Nagārchis, Jogis, and so on. Later in this book, I will focus in detail on the caste affiliations and social organizations of the Langas and Manganiyars (see Chapter 10). But for the moment, let me reflect more generally on the instruments themselves.

First I focused on the relationship between the musician and the instrument, but, gradually, I became more concerned with the role these instruments play in relation to singing. Only once I got to know *who* the players are and *what* they are playing and *why* the instruments are being used, did I begin to ask *for whom* are they singing and *what* are they singing. From instrument to song to epic: that was the direction of my journey.

In my collection there are about 130 instruments from Rajasthan. Sophisticated and rudimentary, different types of folk instruments. And yet, when I do fieldwork, I continue to encounter other instruments of which I was previously unaware. After my collection grew and a little documentation emerged around it, the instruments started telling their own stories. I realized that a lot of instruments perform very small functions musically—for instance, autophones or idiophones (or, as we call them in India, *ghanavādya*). These instruments, like cymbals and gongs, have a predominantly rhythmic function and are played by being struck, rubbed, or shaken. Percussive or membranophone instruments consist of different kinds of drums, like the *ḍhol*, the *ḍholak* and so on. The aerophonic instruments, like the flute, the *pungi* (gourd-pipe), and the *mashak* (bag-pipe), are wind instruments, while the chordophone instruments have strings, which can either be plucked (*jantar*) or played with a bow (*jogīā sārangi*).

The autophone/idiophone instruments are mainly played in songs and narratives dealing with folk gods and goddesses, as well as for the devotional music played specifically in numerous shrines in the rural areas. These metal and wooden instruments would include the *thāḷi* (plate), *kaṭori* (bowl), *maṭkā* (water-pot), and *chimṭā* (tongs)—instruments that are part of ordinary kitchenware. At one level, my study of these musical instruments led me to an exploration of the shrines of folk gods and goddesses, whom we will address in detail in the next chapter. But along with these shrines, my research on instruments took me on a different journey relating to oral epics. And it is this connection that I would like to elaborate on here.

In the early period of my research, I remember asking myself: What musical instrument could be common to all the thousands of villages in Rajasthan? It struck me that the one instrument that could qualify as such was the *tandurā*, a five-stringed accompanying instrument that is also called the *bīn* and *chautāro* in different parts of the state. The only role that this instrument provides is a combination of drone and rhythm, but it is absolutely fundamental to almost any singing tradition relating to the *bhakti* repertoire of songs by Nāmdev, Gorakhnath, Dharmidas, Mirabai, Kabir, Dādu, among other saints.

Another early insight related to a three-stringed *sārangi* known as *kamariā sārangi*, which is not longer than my forearm. Played in the tribal region of south Rajasthan, from Sirohi to Dungarpur, it has such a low sound that you have to place your ear to the instrument in order to listen to it. The kamariā sārangi player leads many oral epics sung by non-professional musical communities, which could include as many as fifty to sixty men and an equal number of women. While the women play the *manjirā* (cymbals), the men beat heavily on the *chāngḍi* (frame-drum). These instruments are played so loudly in accompaniment to the group singing that the kamariā sārangi is almost inaudible. So one way of understanding this situation is to see this sārangi as a ritual instrument without any specific musical function.

However, I was sceptical of this interpretation from the very beginning. During live recording sessions in the field, I noticed that whenever the sārangi player left the group to relieve himself or to drink some tea, some other person would pick up the instrument and continue to play it. Without this instrument the people would stop singing. Once, while there was a break in one of the sessions, I inspected the sārangi left behind by the player and observed how the strings had been stretched and tuned. On purpose, I tuned one of the strings higher and asked the player to adjust the other strings accordingly, after which I requested him to lead the group once again in song. I found that the singing pitch of the entire group increased, and later, when I lowered the pitch of the sārangi, I found that the pitch of the singing decreased accordingly. In this way I began to realize the function of the instrument, and the role of the musician in listening continuously to a single note that could stretch for five to ten minutes of song, or for eight to ten hours of an all-night performance. Without this little experiment with the instrument, I could never have figured out why certain instruments are essential for the singing of entire groups.

The Geography of Instruments

When we use categories like the 'instruments of Rajasthan', what exactly do we mean? The *kamāychā*, a bowed stringed instrument, for instance, is strongly associated with 'Rajasthan', but if you take it to the regions of Alwar or to Banswara, the instrument is as foreign as any other brought from Delhi. So the instruments of Rajasthan are not known all over the state. They are invariably linked to particular regions, and in this crucial sense, we can say that each instrument has its own geography. It is not geography that determines instruments, but the instruments that claim a particular geography. This is the situation.

Nowadays we don't say that the instruments belong to Rajasthan; rather, we say that they belong to this or that region. But we are not always successful in identifying any direct relationship between the instrument and the region. Suppose someone asked me to identify the geographical features where the kamāychā is played, I would associate it with the sevaṇ ghās (grass) growing areas, which I had mentioned earlier in the context of indigenous vegetation. This grass grows in areas with merely three to four inches of rainfall. It grows so high that even camels can disappear as they walk through it. This land provides the grazing grounds for non-stable-bound cows, who are free to graze anywhere. Whenever you are in this area, you are likely to hear the kamāychā.

In contrast, the *sindhi sārangi*, another stringed instrument, extends beyond the boundaries of Sind and Rajasthan to the states of Gujarat and Punjab. It is very difficult to define the geographical limits of this instrument. Throughout these regions you can encounter similar instruments, with the same musical principles and performance techniques. So it becomes impossible to identify their specific geography as such. Perhaps, it is not instruments that migrate from place to place, but people who migrate and carry these instruments with them.[1]

Take the *algojā*, a double-flute instrument but with a limited range of notes. Using three fingers on one hand and three fingers on the other, the algojā player improvises on two flutes, male and female. So rudimentary is the sound it makes that not even a tetrachord can be produced on the algojā. Once again we realize that the major role played by the algojā in singing is to provide the rhythm and the drone. Now, what geographical connections can I make for this instrument? In Rajasthan it is played where jawār is grown and in areas dominated by shepherds as also where a cattle milk economy exists. This will be true not only in Rajasthan, but also in Gujarat, Punjab, and parts of Maharashtra and Andhra Pradesh.

But there are different kinds of algojā—for example, there is one type in Rajasthan called *pāwā jodi*. This is a full aerophonic instrument; it has a separate story telling why and where it exists. A double-flute capable of playing the full octave, it produces the drone from one flute, with the melody played on the other. It is heard primarily in the cattle-breeding area. From all these examples, we learn not to move from geography into music, but rather to locate musical instruments within specific geographical regions, from which we learn how people live in these areas. Following such observations, we have tried to define where these instruments are likely to flourish and in which particular ways.

Now, once we decided to work on the oral epics of Rajasthan, their connections to geography had to be explored. As I had mentioned in an earlier chapter, when we use the word 'Rajasthan', it connotes a particular area of land determined by administrative boundaries, but culturally, this doesn't mean anything. So I started to strategize this problem of geography from the point of view of mapping oral epics. First of all, I decided that I would begin to record those oral epics in the border areas of Rajasthan alongside Madhya Pradesh, Uttar Pradesh, Punjab, Sind, and Gujarat. The oral epics sung in these border areas extend to the neighbouring states. So I thought: Let's work on the border areas, and then move inwards towards the central core of Rajasthan. I soon realized, however, that there is no such thing as a 'central core'. There are only contrasting regions.

We also discovered very soon that the oral epics correspond to specific agricultural zones, like the bājrā zone, the jawār zone, and the makkā zone, which I have already indicated. The bājrā zone, where the oral epic of *Pabuji* is located, is a cattle-breeding area rather than an agricultural one. In this zone the dominant caste group is Jat. In the jawār zone, the dominant group is Gujar, and here you find a greater focus on the Dev Narayan oral epic tradition dealing with the Bagṛāwat brothers.[2] In the makkā zone, where the dominant group is Bhil, you find epics but with no male heroes. Here women and mother-goddesses are the dominant protagonists.

In my research on folk music over the years, I have learned that the richest musical traditions invariably come from the cattle-breeding regions, and not from the agricultural zones. It is hard to say why exactly this is the case, but I have observed this phenomenon in many different regions in relation to different communities. For example, if you look at the agricultural Jāt community, which is dominant in almost eighteen districts of Rajasthan, and if you examine their musical resources and the traditions of their dependent caste musicians, you will find that their musical repertoire is not particularly rich. The same is true for many other agricultural communities like the Sirvi and Pital in the Pali area, the Kunbi and Kalbi from the Sirohi region, and other groups like the Ḍāngi and Patel in the south of Rajasthan. In distinct contrast to the rudimentary musical traditions of these agricultural communities, the Gujar community, for instance, which herds cows in the jawār zone, has a wide range of musical instruments and melodic structures, along with very strong creative inputs by Gujar women to the overall repertoire of their songs.

Again, if you ask me, why Gujars have a stronger musical tradition than the Jāts, I don't have a clear answer. However, if you asked me how exactly I assess the 'strength' or the 'richness' of any musical tradition, I would say by the number of epics sung by particular communities; by the range of musical instruments played in a particular area; and by the presence of a number of dependent communities in that area who contribute to the strength of the musical tradition, with their own creative inputs.

Moving more directly into the epics themselves, we find that each epic has its own accompanying instrument. So the Pabu story is sung to the accompaniment of the rāvanhatthā (fiddle);[3] the Bagṛāwat story is sung with the jantar (a three-stringed plucked instrument); a number of folk epics in eastern Rajasthan, in Alwar and Bharatpur, are sung to the jogiā sārangi (bowed stringed instrument), and so on. All the ancestor epics and long lays are sung on percussive instruments like the *ḍhāk* or *ḍeru*; some are sung on the *kendra*, yet another plucked stringed instrument with gourd resonator like the jantar, which bears a close resemblance to the *veena*, one of the oldest instruments in the Indian musical tradition.

Now, the problem is that when you see any rāvanhatthā player, then you find that he uses this instrument exclusively for telling the story of Pabu, and Pabu is a fourteenth century phenomenon. So what was this instrument doing before the fourteenth century? Or if you look into the jantar, it will always accompany the story of the Bagṛāwat relating to Dev Narayan, yet another fourteenth century phenomenon. So what was its function before that time? Instruments don't determine what melodies will be played on them, so then how were they selected for the singing of certain epics? Like the jantar, you have the kendra—the basic difference between these instruments is that the kendra does not have frets—and here, too, you find it as an accompaniment to stories, which do not go beyond fourteen to fifteen to twenty generations. But this instrument goes back to a much earlier time. So the question is: how do oral epics, when they start acquiring a larger presence in society, *capture* [i.e. take over] particular instruments for the telling of their stories?

As always, this kind of question comes out of Komalda's process of thinking aloud, but it is not directly confronted or answered. To trace the actual process by which an instrument is 'captured' by an oral epic requires a different historical inquiry, steeped in ethnomusicological evidence and other kinds of literary and sociological references, which are not part of Komalda's training. However, what he does bring to the complex investigation of oral epics is a sharp intuition by beginning neither with the text nor the performance of these epics, but with the musical instruments accompanying them, located within specific geographies.

Other folklorists, notably Stuart Blackburn (1989), have attempted at a more rigorous and academic level to map the geographical spread of India's numerous oral epics on the basis of distance in circular ranges: local (10–100 miles); sub-regional (100–200 miles); regional (200–300 miles), and supra-regional (400+ miles).[4] *These ranges in turn are related to three specific types of epics—martial, sacrificial, and romantic. Within the contours of this model, the epic of 'Pabuji', for example, would be classified as a 'martial' epic, one which celebrates 'external—often military or political—conflict and a warrior ethic.'*[5] *While the 'martial' type of epic can be found in all four geographical ranges, 'Pabuji' functions within 'regional' limits.*

Without undermining the utility of mapping India's oral epics in accordance with their geographical area of diffusion, what needs to be questioned are the criteria constituting the understanding of epic 'geography' in the first place. To examine the geography of oral epics in relation to statistical considerations of distance and territoriality has limited uses. For a more textured and microanalytical mapping, it would be necessary to include some of the ethno-geographical criteria that have been presented by Komalda in the earlier chapters. It is not just 'area', or 'territory', or 'direction', or 'diffusion' that determine the spread of an epic's geography, but the constituents of land, soil, water, vegetation, staple foods, and the variables of nomadic cultures. Undeniably, this knowledge, which has been presented in fragments in the earlier chapters of this book, has yet to be adequately theorized at regional or pan-Indian levels.

On different grounds, Blackburn's model has been contested by scholars like Alf Hiltebeitel (1999), who has pointed out how 'location' and 'region' within Blackburn's model function as 'sealed concepts'.[6] *Within these strictures, oral epics have no other option but to 'exhaust themselves each within their own circumscribed areas.'*[7] *And yet, as some of them (depending on their type) extend their geographical limits to 'supra-regional' levels, assuming 'pan-Indian' identities in the process, the 'deification' of the epic hero so palpable at local and occasionally regional levels (as in the case of 'Pabuji') gets systematically diffused.*[8] *There are tricky academic problems underlying such theoretical hypotheses, to which we will return but only after getting on to more basic matters.*

The Story of Pabu

For a start, we haven't even begun to describe what goes on in 'Pabuji'. Here is Komalda's very cryptic rendering of the story—I've included some variations to the story from other sources in the notes. I've also inserted necessary corrections to Komalda's narrative in square brackets within the text itself, where I have also attempted to fill in some particularly glaring gaps in his telling of the story. Following this brief description of the epic's story, we will provide more details on the context and performance of 'Pabuji', after which we will return to the vital question of 'deification', which has prematurely interrupted our narrative.

Let's begin with the bare outline of Pabu's story, and then we can start looking at it from different points of view. Before Pabu is born, his father, a king named Rao Āsthān, wanders the forest where he comes across some fairies bathing in a lake. Rao Āsthān steals one of the fairies' clothes. When the fairies come out of the lake, they return to heaven, all except the one [Kesarpari, the 'nymph saffron'][9] whose clothes are missing. Rao Āsthān approaches her and says: 'You're here on earth now, why don't you marry me?' In response, the fairy agrees to his proposal but on one condition: 'You will never enter my room without knocking at the door. The day you break this rule, I'll leave you.' So Rao Āsthān accepts this condition, and the two of them live together and Pabu is born.

Now, for about twelve months, nothing happens. But after some time the king gets curious: 'Why shouldn't I have a look at my wife without knocking at the door?' Once, he enters the room without announcing himself. Inside the room he sees a lioness suckling Pabu. Taking on the form of a fairy once more, Kesarpari says: 'Now that you've broken your promise, I have no other option but to leave.' But Pabu, who is only twelve months old at that time, entreats his mother not to go. Then, she reassures him, 'For twelve months I've held you in my lap, but when I return, you'll sit on my back.' So saying, she disappears.

Sure enough, she does come back, as a magical mare, but we will get to that later. In the meanwhile, Pabu grows up in the village of Kolu near Phalodi, which is less than two hundred kilometres from Jodhpur. Here he digs a bore-well with a lot of water, which becomes known as Gunjwā. Since there were no such wells in Kolu before Pabu's feat, it is regarded as some kind of miracle, not unlike the many miracles associated with him, as he moves from one adventure.

Pabu grazes cows for a living. One day, he thinks to himself: 'Why should I stay here all by myself for the rest of my life? Why don't I go out and claim some territory for myself? Why shouldn't I become a robber and amass wealth?' It is at this time that he joins up with his four companions—the brothers Chando and Ḍhēbo, Saljī Soḷaṅkī and Harmal Devāsi. While the first three are from Rajput groups—more specifically, the Bāghelā group of Rajputs—Harmal is a Rabāri herdsman from the Rāikā group of camel herders. With these four companions, Pabu begins his different exploits as a brigand, which include adventure, looting, and annexation of territory. While all four companions are excellent warriors, Ḍhēbo is the most valiant of the lot—he is a bit like the epic character of Bhim from the Mahabharata, a big man known for his capacity to consume vast quantities of food and opium. Among the four companions, Saljī Soḷaṅkī is an augurer who is capable of reading the future.

When Pabu and his companions get together, they face a problem: 'Without horses, how can we function as dacoits?' So they approach a woman named Deval from the Chāraṇ (bard) community, who is known for her skill in rearing and trading horses, cows, and bullocks, and request her to provide a special horse for Pabu. Deval offers them any of the horses that they can see grazing in her fields. But

Pabu insists: 'I don't want any of these horses. You have a special mare that you've kept hidden, and her name is Kesar Kalāmi [Black Saffron]. I want her.' Deval says that she does not have the mare, so how can she give her to Pabu? But on Pabu's insistence, she is compelled to admit: 'Yes, I do have Kesar Kalāmi, but I can't part with her because your brother-in-law would object.'

Now, Pabu's sister Pemā is married to Jindrāv Khīchī, and though the two families are linked through marriage, they are sworn enemies. There is a dispute connected with this enmity that I won't go into here.[10] Deval says: 'I can't afford to make Jindrāv angry. I have to graze my cattle and move around with my horses in his territory. If I give you the mare, he will create problems for me.' But Pabu pleads: 'Give the mare to me on any condition. I will accept whatever you say.' So, finally, Deval says: 'You will have to protect my herd of cows even at the cost of your life.' And Pabu agrees to that condition.

Then, he is taken into a deep underground cave, where the beautiful, jet-black Kesar Kalāmi is kept hidden. This is none other than Kesarpari, his fairy foster-mother, who had left him as child. While he rides the mare, she suddenly flies into the sky with him, leaving his companions behind. Worried by their leader's disappearance, Pabu's companions begin to threaten Deval, who advises them to play on two pot-drums (*māṭā*) to bring him back. To the rhythms of these drums, which sound like the hooves of a horse galloping, Kesar Kalāmi reappears on the earth with Pābū mounted on her, and there is a happy reunion.

Now the story shifts its location and focus. Pabu decides to go to Pushkar where he accidentally meets Gogo Chauhāṇ, a snake-god from the north-east of Rajasthan.[11] While Pabu and Gogo don't know each other personally, a small incident helps to bring them together. Gogo slips on the steps of the bathing ghat at Pushkar, and Pabu prevents him from falling. After this incident, they introduce themselves and their friendship is sealed. Pabu tells Gogo: 'I am not married, but my elder brother Būṛo has a daughter called Kelam, and I offer my niece to you.'

Pabu returns to his house and sends Chando as an emissary to inform Būṛo and his wife about their potential son-in-law Gogo. But they are not impressed: 'He's a mere snake-man, who extracts the poison of snakes and cures people of snakebites. How can we give our daughter to him?' Pabu has no other choice but to tell Gogo that his brother and sister-in-law don't accept the marriage. However, he has a plan that he reveals to Gogo: 'During the festival of Teej in the month of sāvan, Būṛo's daughter will go to the garden and play on the swing. Why don't you enter the garden as a snake, bite her, and then cure her, so that my brother and his wife will have no other option but to accept you as their son-in-law?' This is precisely what happens: Gogo transforms himself into a snake, bites Kelam while she is on the swing, and then, after all attempts to cure her have failed, she is healed after an amulet in Gogo's name is tied on her arm. Now her parents have no other choice but to accept the snake-man as their son-in-law.

When the marriage takes place, everybody offers a gift to the couple. Some people give money, others clothes and ornaments, but when it comes to Pabu's turn, he says, 'I will give you a herd of red-brown she-camels (*rātal bhuri sāṇḍiya*) from the distant land of Lanka over the seas.' No one had ever heard of such camels. So the people prevail on Pabu to change his mind: 'Why do you want to give something that we don't know and which may not even exist? Why don't you give something that is more easily available? Why bind yourself to an unrealizable promise?' Pabu listens and then says, 'When all is said and done, I will give only these camels as a gift.'

Some time later after the marriage, Kelam sends him a message from her in-laws' place: 'My sisters-in-law here are ridiculing me, for not fulfilling your promise, which you had made during my marriage. What are you doing about it?' At this point Pabu asks Harmal to find out the whereabouts of the she-camels. Belonging to the Rāikā community of camel-herders, Harmal is more likely to know about these camels than anyone else. So he disguises himself as a *jogi* (mendicant) in order to enter the she-camels' territory. I won't go into the numerous details here as to how he became a disciple of Sri Gorakhnath, who gave him many talismans by which he could protect himself on the dangerous road to Lanka.[12] So convincing is Harmal's disguise as a jogi that even his wife and mother can't recognize him. He crosses the Sind river, where he is able to trace the herd of camels, after which he comes back to Kolu, and Pabu then begins to organize the capture of the she-camels.

Once again I will avoid the specific details of the battle in Lanka, but there is a fight between Pabu and the owner of the camels, a Muslim named Sumrā. Neither of them is able to win the battle. Finally, they arrive at an agreement and exchange turbans, affirming their brotherhood. In exchange for the camels, Sumrā asks for a Chāraṇ to be appointed as a poet for his family. Pābū agrees to this request, and gives Mangu Chāraṇ of the Rathor community to Sumrā's family. Even today these particular Chāraṇs are attached to the Mehar Muslims of the Sumrā community. This is the one exceptional case where the Chāraṇ's patrons are Muslims.

While returning to Kolu with the herd of camels, Pabu stays over in Umarkot, where the king's daughter Phulande [Phulvantī] promptly falls in love with him. She asks her father to arrange her marriage to Pabu, who hesitates slightly, saying, 'Well, I can't accept your proposal myself, but I'll ask my elder brother and if he accepts, I'll come back and get married.' After sending the camels to his niece, there is a small complication in the story: Būṛo wants to marry Phulvantī himself as a second wife. [However, Pabu who is identified throughout the epic as 'the ascetic deity (*bāljaṭṭī*) of the sand-desert', makes up his mind to get married. But he lays down a condition—he will get married only after saffron is obtained in order to dye the garments of his companions forming the wedding-party. This demand for saffron leads to yet another detour in the story as a battle is waged against the owner of a saffron plot, Lakkhū Paṭhāṇ.]

Finally, Pabu and his companions are ready to leave for Umarkot, but at this point in the story Deval reappears to remind Pabu of his earlier promise to protect her animals. 'If all of you leave Kolu at the same time, this will be an ideal opportunity for Jindrāv to capture all my cows, so why don't you leave at least one of your companions so that they can protect me?' But all of Pabu's companions refuse to stay back. Finally, Pabu reassures Deval by saying that, 'If Jindrāv makes any attempt to steal your cattle, remember that I will be with you in no time, and I will see to it that you will suffer no loss.' Deval accepts his word. But all is not well, because on the way to Umarkot, Pabu encounters a number of bad omens, which the augurer Sālji

Soḷaṅkī points out. [They include a snake, vultures, partridges, jackals, and a tiger.] Pabu, however, disregards the omens and is impatient to get on his way.

In Umarkot, while the marriage ceremony is being performed—indeed, just as the couple has gone around the nuptial fire four times—the spirit of Deval appears to Pabu in the form of a bird and announces that Jindrāv has already come and stolen her cows. Immediately, Pabu cuts the bridal knot with his sword, leaves the *chānvari* (marriage pavilion) and rides away on horseback, all the way to Kolu. He is followed by his other companions, with the exception of Ḍhēbo, who has consumed so much opium during the wedding that he is sound asleep. When he gets up from his slumber, he realizes what has happened and promptly leaves for Kolu to support his companions. [It is at this point that he disembowels himself in order to placate the hunger of vultures hovering around him. Ḍhēbo feeds them with his intestines. Then, fastening his belt even tighter, he charges off on his horse in the direction of the battlefield where the war is waging against Jindrāv Khīchī. He fights wildly and is about to kill Khīchī when Pabu stops him from doing so, because he doesn't want his sister Pemā to be a widow.]

In this battle Ḍhēbo dies, but the stolen cattle are returned to Deval. Proudly, Pabu tells her to count her animals. After doing so, she points out that her one-eyed bull is missing. Initially, Pabu is angry: 'I got back everything for you and now you're saying that some animal is missing.' [At this point in the story there are some delaying tactics adopted by Deval during which time Pabu discovers the missing bull in Ḍhēbo's opium box. Deval also tells him to water her cows because they are thirsty, but the well is dry because all the water has been consumed by a genie named Susiyo Pīr. By the time Pabu has killed the genie and watered the cows, Jindrāv Khīchī has enlisted the support of his uncle Jaisingh Bhāṭī, and with their combined forces, they wage a terrible battle against Pabu, who dies in the encounter. Actually he dies only after he forces his enemy to take his sword in exchange for a whip.] As in all folk epics, where the hero is never shown dead, a *pālki* (palanquin) comes from heaven and carries Pabu away.

In the war fought with Jindrāv, Pabu's elder brother Būṛo is also killed. On learning of his death, Būṛo's wife decides to become a sati. The news of Pabu's death is also sent to Umarkot, along with his turban, and Phulvantī promptly becomes a sati. However, Būṛo's wife is pregnant, and since pregnant women cannot become satis, she orders a woman from the barber community to give her a knife with which she herself cuts open her own stomach and pulls the child out. Thereafter, Būṛo's wife takes her own life and the child (Jharda) is handed over to Deval and brought to the household of his *māmā*, Būṛo's wife's brother.

Ignorant of his heritage and the circumstances of his birth, Rūpnāth (as the child is later identified in the epic) is very mischievous. He breaks a lot of pots of the *panihāris* (water-carriers) with his catapult, apart from harassing the people in the village. One day he is challenged by a woman: 'You're up to so much nonsense with all your pranks. Do you know what happened to your own father? Why don't you take revenge on his behalf and spare us your mischief?' Thereupon, Rūpnāth, through Deval's intervention, comes to know about how Pabu and Būṛo were killed in the war and how his mother became a sati. Now, he resolves to take revenge against Jindrāv.

Remember, Pabu's sister Pemā is married to Jindrāv, so she is Rūpnāth's *buā*. It is she who instructs her nephew how to avoid all the traps and wild animals guarding Jindrāv's palace. Rūpnāth enters the palace and beheads Jindrāv. Now, Pemā had vowed that only after her brothers' deaths had been avenged, would she start churning *dahi* (curds) to make butter. As she sees Jindrāv's blood flowing through the palace, she promptly starts churning the curds, and on hearing this sound late at night, everyone in the neighbourhood comes to know that Jindrāv has been killed. Not content with killing Jindrāv, Rūpnāth starts kicking his head around like a football all the way back to his māmā's home. Finally, he kicks the ball back to Jindrāv's palace, so that his aunt can commit sati.

[In the closing section of the epic, Rūpnāth abandons all worldly activity, and takes *samādhi* in a small place near Bikaner, where he is worshipped today.] This is how the main story of Pabu ends, though one should keep in mind that no performance of Pabu would ever attempt to tell the entire story. At best it would focus on two or three episodes. What I've described for the purpose of our discussion is the action of the 'entire' story. Of course, there are many episodes and details that I have left out, but roughly, this is the story.

Clearly, this rendering of the story is not in the tradition of A.K. Ramanujan's 'Folktales from India' (1991), where the very telling of the tale conceals its own authorial signature, even while flowing with an inimitable, yet understated eloquence. Komalda's summary of the events in 'Pabuji' is by his own admission 'rough', but at the same time, it is intimate in its narrative detail. On comparing Komalda's summary with the fuller transcription of the 'entire' epic, as rendered by John Smith (1991), it becomes interesting to figure out not only what gets left out in any prose recapitulation of an epic's story, but also what gets included.

In Komalda's rendering, there are no references to the numerous skirmishes between Pabu and his adversaries like Jindrāv Khīchī's father, the Muslim cattle-raider Mirza Khan, the saffron-owner Lakkhu Paṭhān, and so on. There is no mention of Ravana, the evil king of Lanka, whom Pabu kills with his spear while fleeing Lanka with the she-camels. And yet, there are so many other details, like the references to Rao Āsthān, Pabuji's father, who is almost never elaborated on in oral performances of the epic. Likewise, Komalda dwells on seemingly minor physical details like the Gunjwā bore-well, the beats of the 'māṭā' (drums) to which Pabu returns to earth on Kesar Kalāmi's back, and, at a more symbolic level, Pabu's exchange of turbans with Surmā. Now, this last detail is particularly telling because Komalda uses it to emphasize that the Chāraṇs (bards) of the Rathor community are still attached to the Mehar Muslims. Significantly, this detail relating to an exception in the 'jajmāni' (patronage) system is given more importance in Komalda's narrative than the symbolic rapprochement of different communities in the epic—Bhil, Rajput, and Rabāri—which Komalda does not address.[13]

Despite these erasures, Komalda's cursory prose summary of 'Pabuji' can be interestingly contrasted with John Smith's (1991) elaborate translation of his own transcription of Parbu Bhopā's Rajasthani rendering of the epic, which is the only 'full' recording of 'Pabuji' to date. And yet, this textual 'fullness' is itself full of erasures, so much so that many of the details that Komalda had brought up in his twenty-minute recapitulation of the story are not to be found in Parbu's thirty-six-hour recording. Obviously, there's a lot more here than 'getting the story down from start to finish', by concentrating on a linear progression of the text through its twelve fairly sharply demarcated 'paṛvāros' (episodes). The length or brevity of the narration is not just a matter of memory, but of what constitutes memory in the first place.

In this regard, let us now examine the context *of 'Pabuji' in order to explore how different 'meanings' get generated beyond the purely structuralist logic of the story. Here the crucial connection is with the indirect, yet resonant links of 'Pabuji' with the pan-Indian Hindu epic of the 'Ramayana'.*

Context of Pabuji

There are many levels of *avatārs* (incarnations) in the Pabu story. It is believed that Pabu himself is the avatār of Lakshmana, Rama's brother from the Ramayana. Jindrāv is also represented as a ten-headed Ravana figure in the *paṛ*, or visual scroll, that accompanies the telling of the Pabuji narrative, to be described later. However, at no point in the narrative is Jindrāv specifically equated with the avatār of Ravana.[14] The same holds true for Pabu's wife Phulvantī, who is not specifically identified as the avatār of Ravana's sister, Surpanakha, even though this is how she can be described by *bhopās* (reciters) in conversation. On a minor level, Ḍhēbo is sometimes considered to be an avatār of Hanuman, though this is not fully elaborated at all. While these connections between the characters in the Pabu narrative and the Ramayana are not necessarily spelled out in the performance, all people familiar with the context of the epic are aware of the links.

Broadly, we can say that epics from the cow-breeding area, such as the Pabu epic, are always sanctified by the Rama story. In those areas where milk is the primary resource of the economy, we find stories incorporating the incarnations of Vishnu and Krishna. In contrast, wherever there is a conflict between agriculturists and cattle keepers, you will find the Bagṛāwat story sung. In such conflicts, the farmers inevitably win the battle and the sacrifices of the cow owners provide the material of the epic stories. Significantly, you will find stories on the Bagṛāwat pattern sung in the southern states of India like Andhra Pradesh, in epics like the *Kāṭamarāju Kathā* from the Telengana region.[15] The pattern never changes: large areas of land are taken over for agriculture, the grazing land shrinks, and the cattle owners lose out to the farmers. Even today in Rajasthan these tensions exist, resulting from the reduction of grazing areas and the expansion of non-stable-bound animal husbandry.

Let us focus now more closely on the Pabu epic and its links with the Ramayana. What do we find in the Ramayana itself? When Rama realizes that he can't kill Ravana, he turns for help to his brother Lakshmana, who assumes the identity of Mandodari, Ravana's wife, while mimicking the exact tone and pitch of her voice. Lakshmana (as Mandodari) enters Ravana's bedchamber and asks: 'You're fighting a great god like Rama and he's going to kill you. What is going to happen to me?' Ravana reassures his 'wife' that Rama will not be able to harm him: 'My life, my very soul, lies in the eye of one of the seven horses of the Sun. Somebody has to shoot an arrow directly into this eye, and only after the eyeball has fallen into a cauldron of burning red-hot oil, only then will I die, otherwise Rama cannot harm me.' After listening to this secret, Lakshmana leaves the room, followed by the real Mandodari who is oblivious of the situation. Getting angry with her for extracting the secret of his life, Ravana asks: 'Why did you need to know this secret?' Mandodari is surprised: 'What secret? I never asked you anything about it.' Then Ravana realizes what's happened and says: 'Tomorrow morning I am going to die.'

When Ravana is eventually killed by the secret mechanism he has divulged, Rama tells his brother Lakshmana: 'I have been able to take revenge against Ravana, but your revenge remains unrealized. You will have to take birth in the age of Kaliyuga and then only will you be able to kill Ravana in order to fulfil your vow of revenge.' This is why Lakshmana gets incarnated as Pabu in the epic, to carry out his own act of revenge against Ravana.

Regarding Surpanakha's alleged transformation into Phulvantī, there are stories that are told outside of the performance context of Pabuji. It appears that when Surpanakha is rejected by Rama after she offers to marry him, she is further insulted by Lakshmana, who cuts off her nose and ears. Before she is mutilated, however, she manages to go around Lakshmana three times, thereby ensuring at a symbolic level that she is half-married to him. In order to achieve her own salvation by being fully married, Surpanakha is compelled to return to earth in the form of Phulvantī. Here, too, her wedding is disrupted, when Deval suddenly makes her appearance in the form of a bird and Pabu abandons the ceremony. However, Pabu and Phulvantī manage to complete four rounds of the nuptial fire, so Surpanakha in her incarnated form can now claim to be fully married. She has completed the seven rounds that are necessary for any solemnization of marriage—three rounds in an earlier life with Lakshmana, four rounds in a later life with his avatār Pabu.

Despite this incarnation of Surpanakha as Phulvantī, which is not specifically narrated in the Pabu text, and the more explicit transformation of Lakshmana into Pabuji, it would be a mistake to see any direct transference of identities between the characters in the Ramayana and Pabuji's story. At best one could say that the classical epic has been grafted on to the folk story, but there is no thematic correspondence as such between the two texts. After all, Pabu does not even get to kill Jindrāv in a face-to-face encounter, quite unlike Rama who kills Ravana in the epic. It is Rūpnāth, Pabu's nephew, who kills Jindrāv, as I have described earlier. So let us not look for any literal correspondences here. What needs to be stressed is a general belief among communities like the Nāyaks, the Bhils, and the Jogis, that the Pabu story has mythic links with the epic of Rama. However, the real reason why Pabu is worshipped has nothing to do with his associations with Rama as such, but with his very direct impact on the problems of everyday life, on which I will have more to say later.

Great and Little Traditions: the dynamics surrounding the critical debates around these terms never once comes up in Komalda's discourse. To figure out his relationship to these categories, one has to turn to his one essay on oral epics (1989), and the critical interlocution it has received from scholars in the field. Alf Hiltebeitel (1999) in particular has commended Komalda's insistence on emphasizing the 'indirect' relationship between the oral and Sanskrit epics, though he is less enamoured of Komalda's vague pitch for 'Sanskritization' [i.e. 'the desire for a higher status'].[16] *For Hiltebeitel, this simply falls into the familiar theoretical trap of 'legtimization', which undermines other possible 'direct' relationships of oral epics with 'oral versions of the classical epic stories'. These folk versions of the classical epics, which emerged during the medieval period, 'supply' in Hiltebeitel's view what A.K.Ramanujan has aptly described as 'regional pools of classic epic signifiers.'*[17]

While Komalda would broadly concur with this view, he does not enter the textual, metaphoric, and framing 'signifiers' of oral epic narratives. What concerns him is the less illusory, but no less elusive realities of the 'signified'—the belief systems and group identities that provide the primary context for stories like 'Pabuji'. Certainly, at one level, it is possible to read some process of legitimization in the inclusion of classical references in the oral epic, but as Komalda makes very clear, 'Pabuji' is no mere re-telling of the 'Ramayana'. This does not mean that it has nothing to do with the 'Ramayana'—but to trace its multiple trajectories with classical origins and their folk derivatives is not Komalda's concern. What matters to him is the actual performative context and deification of Pabu in Rajasthan today through the figure of the 'bhomiyā', to which we will turn our attention now.

The Bhomiyā

The economy of the region where the story of Pabu is sung is totally dependent on the breeding of cows, sheep, goats and camels. The cows in particular are among the finest breeds in the country, which would include Tharparkaṛ, Rāṭhi, Kānkrej, and Gir (also found in Gujarat). Earlier, the tradition existed for literally thousands of cows belonging to different families in a particular village or district to be assembled at a particular place in the village. From here the cattle would be taken by a cow-herder (*gwālā*) to graze in the common land (*oran*), which I have discussed earlier in Chapter 2.

In 1962 I went to the Kolu region for the first time in connection with a BBC film on Pabuji, and I saw an extraordinary sight. We arrived at the temple of Pabuji in Kolu late in the evening. Early next morning we saw cows coming from different directions. By 6 a.m. at least a hundred cows had assembled near the Gunjwā well, where they drank from the *kheli*, or water container. Later, they all grazed together in the oran which stretches for miles around the temple. Still later, as the day got hotter, they rested under the trees, and by 4 p.m. they started walking back to their homesteads in a very orderly way. Mind you, there were so many cows, and only one cow-herder to guide them.

I bring this image up to evoke the context of the bhomiyā, which is central to understanding the Pabu story. Basically, a bhomiyā is someone who gives his life for cows, and who is worshipped after death. In the old days, it was very easy for bands of robbers or dacoits to steal cows because, as was the custom, only one cow-herder (gwālā) was appointed to take care of the cattle. Generally, the cows would return to their homes by dusk. If they did not return at the regular time, there would be cause for alarm. This would increase with the reports of people from neighbouring areas who might have seen the cows in other villages. At this point, the practice was for a war drum (*vāru ḍhol*) to be beaten in the village, whereupon all the people would gather together. Among them would be volunteers who would offer to pursue the robbers and bring back the cows. Generally, these volunteers were Rajputs, who were prepared to die in the fight.[18]

In popular stories, the actual battle with the robbers and retrieval of the cows are generally evoked in mythic terms. In most stories, the Rajput warrior is beheaded in his fight with the robbers, but he continues to fight on his horse—headless, but with swords in both hands. From his head sprouts a lotus-flower, while eyes appear on his chest. In this transfigured state, he returns home to the village on horseback, with all the stolen cows. At this point, there are a number of variations in the story. In one version, the warrior drops dead from his horse, only after women have hailed him as a headless hero. In other versions, they sprinkle a mixture of indigo and water on him, after which he falls from the horse. A shrine is built on the exact spot where his body falls. Sometimes there are as many as three shrines—one where the warrior was decapitated, another where his body fell, and the third where his horse died. These shrines can be positioned very far from each other, but in most cases, there is only one shrine for a bhomiyā in many villages in the desert region of western Rajasthan.

Keeping in mind these details, it can be said that Pabu is nothing more and nothing less than a bhomiyā, a protector and martyr to cows, who chases and engages in battle with the robbers (Jindrāv and his followers) who have stolen Deval's cows. Needless to say, he dies in the battle; if he had remained alive at the end of the epic, he wouldn't be worshipped. Pabu's story merely narrates what must have happened to many others like him, and today he is worshipped as a bhomiyā god. In the Jalor or Sirohi region, the bhomiyā is known as *māmā*, and in Gujarat, he is identified as *pāliā*.

For the cult around a bhomiyā to spread, there has to be a bhopā (shaman-priest) attached to a particular shrine, who conducts ceremonies and mediates in the everyday problems brought to the shrine by the local people. The problem could be as simple as finding a cure for ailing camels, or for protecting one's family from illness, or curing some kind of skin disease. So long as the bhopā is effective in mediating these problems, going into trance and embodying the spirit of a particular bhomiyā, then only will the shrine be considered active. However, there are many inactive shrines that continue to be given due respect by villagers, particularly during marriage ceremonies. These shrines could have been abandoned because they are no longer attached to any particular bhopā. The bhopā might have died, or his hereditary link may have been cut. In the course of time, it is possible that both the bhomiyā and the shrine attached to him may be completely forgotten. Only so long as they are perceived to have power in protecting people's lives and solving problems, will they continue to have significance. Otherwise they are likely to fade into oblivion.

It must have taken hundreds of years before Pabu's story got sanctified in the form that we know it today. I am not able to account for this process; nor am I clear of the exact relationship between the worship of Pabuji and the actual rituals of the bhopā who incarnate his spirit and then proceed to mediate in people's everyday problems. What I do know is that the figure of the bhomiyā continues to be worshipped across tribal and nomadic communities in the desert region of Rajasthan. The Rāikās, or camel herders, are particularly fervent in their worship of Pabu as a god. To hear them singing the *jhurāvā*, which is an unaccompanied song narration on the life of Pabu, is a haunting experience indeed. Through the night, you can hear their voices resonating in the darkness, serving as the sole instruments of their devotion to Pabu.

Keep in mind that there have been so many great Rajasthani warriors and kings from noble families in the past whose achievements have been commemorated in classical stories, myths, genealogies, and hagiographies. But are any of them remembered through an oral epic, as Pabu is to this day? Elsewhere I have said that these classical warriors and kings are like 'absentee' heroes—they are literally absent from folk memory and ritual.[19] But heroes like Pabu from ordinary Rajput backgrounds are worshipped as gods. How do we account for this? Once again, I would say that he is worshipped because large sections of people believe that these ordinary heroes have the power to intervene in life's manifold problems through possible solutions and blessings. So it is not so much Pabu's achievements in the epic that make him so memorable to this day, but his capacity to intervene in everyday life.

Despite Pabuji's interventionist capacity, we have no reason to assume that the cult surrounding him has emerged out of the death and subsequent deification of an actual 'bhomiyā', a real historical figure whose identity remains unknown. There are far too many unverifiable historical factors here that beg the question of history itself.[20] *Without entering the details of this heavy academic debate, it is important to stress that Komalda's views on Pabu are neither historicist nor evolutionary, despite his claim that 'Pabuji' is 'an elaborated story of a bhomiyā god'.*[21] *This is better read as a hypothesis than a thesis. In his conversations with me, Komalda repeatedly emphasized, 'I do not know how death and deification are related to the actual shaping of an epic narrative. The connections remain unclear to me.' To seek a theory in Komalda's unselfconsciously non-theoretical writing is to miss the point.*

The *Paṛ*

Moving on to more performative matters, let us now address the actual conventions by which the epic of 'Pabuji' is rendered at oral, musical, and visual levels. First, Komalda provides a brief perspective on the 'paṛ', the painted scroll against whose visual backdrop the story of 'Pabuji' is sung, generally late at night into the early hours of the morning. This will be followed by a more detailed description of three different performance traditions relating to 'Pabuji'—traditions linked to specific caste groups.

Let us address the visual dimension of the Pabu epic. The entire story is illustrated in around 172 episodes that are painted on a scroll (paṛ), which is about eighteen feet long and three and a half feet wide. Basically, there are different segments in the paṛ, which can be said to map the entire story of Pabuji. Dominating the centre of the paṛ is Pabu's court, in which a large figure of Pabu is displayed along with his four companions. On the extreme right side of the paṛ, you find Pabu's enemies—the Jindrāv and Bhāṭi courts—and in between these courts and Pabu's territory, you have smaller sections representing Deval's court, the bathing ghats in Pushkar where Pabu meet Gogo Chauhāṇ, and even a segment visualizing the Gunjwā well. On the extreme left side of the paṛ, you find Lanka, where Harmal goes to find the red-brown she-camels. This section is dominated by an elaborate figure of Ravana himself, with his ten heads and twenty hands. In between Lanka and Pabu's court, you find Umarkot where Pabu's short-lived marriage takes place with Phulvantī.

Significantly, the episodes are not painted in sequence—they are scattered all over the place, with some represented entirely on the right side of the scroll, while the events that follow immediately in the story can be found on the left side, or somewhere in the middle.[22] Because there is no sequence in the visuals, the bhopā is compelled to move from one section of the scroll to another to identify the different locations in the narrative—'Deval is here, now she goes to such-and-such place there, and here we find her again in a different place.' In short, the paṛ highlights space over time—*where* a particular event takes place is given more importance than *when* it takes place. Interestingly, the same segment or detail within a segment can be used to represent different moments in the narrative. All the bhopā has to do is to point at a particular place or figure and with his commentary he can promptly change their identities.[23]

As in almost all folk-painting traditions in Rajasthan, the faces of the characters are presented in profile, except for the demons, whose faces are presented frontally. Apart from following very specific iconographic details to represent the different figures and their gestures and action, there are clearly defined codes of colour. The paṛ uses at least five colours that are painted directly on the canvas, which is treated with wheat flour and then rubbed with a very smooth stone. The sketch of the entire painting is first made in yellow, with very faint outlines. At times, just one-fourth of the entire canvas is sketched, followed by the other parts. The tradition demands that the painting be filled in one colour at a time—first red, then green, and so on. Black is used to highlight the outlines of the figures and the boundaries between the sections. This is generally left for the very end, before the paṛ is completed.

The paṛ painters come from the Joshi community. Formerly, they all lived in one village near Bhilwara district called Shahpura in the south-east of Rajasthan. Today, at least nine families can be found living in this area in addition to the town of Bhilwara, Chittor and Udaipur. Earlier, the bhopās would go to the Joshi families and give them an advance of one rupee, whereupon a paṛ would be prepared for them. Once it was ready, the bhopās would come back to collect it and pay the remaining money. This was the traditional arrangement between the painters and the reciters of the paṛ, but today this practice no longer exists.[24]

Generally, the paṛ remains the property of a bhopā family for approximately fifty-sixty years. The vegetable and mineral dyes withstand the effects of humidity, heat, and the cold of the winter. The only exception perhaps is the green, which tends to cut into the cloth because it is made from a combination of bronze and lime juice. Today the making of the paṛ has been commercialized—each scroll costs around four to five thousand rupees. In addition, there are any number of small paintings and sketches derived from the paṛ that have entered the tourist market. Other communities have also begun to learn the art of paṛ painting, because it brings in money.

One convention hasn't changed: the paṛ painters do not teach their own daughters how to paint out of fear that, when they marry, this tradition will be passed on to other families, who would become competitors in the business. The Joshis, who come from the textile printers' caste, call themselves Nāmdevi Chhipā, because they belong to the Nāmdev sect. Other members of the Chhipā community eat non-vegetarian food and drink liquor, but the Nāmdevi Chhipā, who consider themselves Joshi, are strictly vegetarian. As a community, they have 'Vaishnavized' themselves.

Performing *Pabuji*

There are three important performance traditions around Pabu's story: *Pabuji ki paṛ*, which is generally sung by a husband-wife team, to the visual background of the paṛ; *Pabuji kā māṭā* which is sung to the accompaniment of two pot-drums (*māṭā*), with no other enactment or visualization of narrative; and yet another version of Pabuji ki paṛ, which is performed by two men, one of whom dances as a female impersonator. Now, the caste affiliations of these three performance traditions are interrelated, yet distinct. It's a complicated matter because these affiliations are in the process of changing over time.

For instance, when I first came into contact with the Pabuji ki paṛ performers (the husband-wife teams), while I was working on the BBC film in 1962, they were identified by local people as Thorī, which is an abusive name for the Nāyak caste. Today neither of these terms would be acceptable to the performers, who now insist on calling themselves Bhil. Undeniably, they seek a higher social status and would like to draw on the benefits and reservations for jobs granted by the Indian government to official scheduled caste and tribal groups like the Bhil.

I have to interrupt the narrative at this point with a story which illuminates the complexities of identifying the caste affiliations of traditional musicians and performers. During the early days of my research, I was sitting with Komalda early in the morning, quizzing him about certain facts brought up by John Smith in his authoritative study of 'The Epic of Pabuji', which I greatly admire. Lo and behold, who should walk into our conversation but Parbu Bhopā himself, the performer whose thirty-six-hour recording of the 'Pabuji' epic serves as the base for Smith's transcription and translation. After accepting my compliments on his considerable feat, Parbu mentioned with casual dignity that he himself owned a copy of John's book, on which he is featured prominently on the front cover. Suddenly, he changed the subject, and with some agitation asked Komalda directly: 'Why does he refer to me as a Nāyak in this book? This is creating problems for me and my family.'[25] *With his eminent capacity for mediation in such matters, Komalda reminded Parbu that his caste and community had indeed been identified by different names over the years, by different communities, in different contexts. Parbu accepted Komalda's comments, but his dissatisfaction with being named a Nāyak clearly rankled. 'How do you see yourself?' I asked. 'Bhil,' he emphasized.*

The problem is that the category of Bhil itself is very diffused. At one time in Rajasthan it was used to describe tribal communities who lived by the rules of their own social organizations and who were totally dependent on the resources of the forest in the Aravalli hills. Over the years, however, we have seen migrations of Bhil tribals from the hill areas into the desert zone, in Jalor, Jaisalmer, Barmer, and Sind. Inevitably, the way of life of these people has changed, and it can no longer be identified with that of the tribals living in hill settlements. So today, all kinds of groups are calling themselves Bhil—these would include the Van Bagari or Sikaria group, the Nāyak, as well as the Thorī. The earlier equation of Bhil with tribal communities in the hill region is no longer applicable.

'Bhil', I would suggest, has a wider reference, indeed a more respectable reference, which is why the Pabuji ki paṛ performers—both the husband-wife teams and the all-male teams—choose to identify themselves as Bhil today. The Pabuji kā māṭā performers, however, from the Barmer region continue to identify themselves as Nāyak. Interestingly, the all-male performers of the Pabuji ki paṛ also come from this region, but they choose to identify themselves not merely as Bhil, but as Manjhirana Bhil, which is a more respectable term. Apart from the obvious need for a higher social status, the different discriminations in caste identity are also there to control marriages across communities. So, even though there may be different

Bhil groups doing Pabuji ki paṛ in different parts of Rajasthan, they do not intermarry.

Now let us focus more directly on the performance tradition itself. In the husband-wife rendition of Pabuji ki paṛ, the man sings the first lines of each verse in the narrative, playing the rāvanhatthā, while his wife sings the rest of the verse. Each verse in the singing part of the narrative (*gāv*) is followed by an explanation (*arthāv*) given by the man in a declamatory mode. This section is invariably punctuated by cries from a selected member in the audience, the *hunkārio*, who echoes the last words of each line and occasionally engages in jocular interpolations with the bhopā, who can deliberately play with the text through rhythmic distortions. During the all-night performance there will be time for singing merely one or two episodes—for example, the episodes covering the meeting of Pabu with Goga in Pushkar leading to Goga's marriage to Pabu's niece. If the entire story had to be told, it would take three to four nights.

What is important to keep in mind is that the husband-wife rendition of the Pabu story is an hereditary function, even though it is only the men in this community who are formally initiated into the singing tradition when they are boys. Women, on the other hand, are allowed to sing in public only after they begin to live with their husbands—they may be married at a very young age, but they only leave their parents' home after puberty. How a young woman of seventeen or eighteen learns all the lines of the Pabuji epic, through informal instructions given to her by her husband and in-laws, remains a mystery. However, one should keep in mind that she has been listening to this epic since her childhood. Not only does she learn the lines of the epic to sustain the livelihood of the family, she even sings close to seventy to eighty per cent of the text in actual performance. The man playing the rāvanhatthā merely begins each line, but it is the woman who completes it. This fact is not always acknowledged.

To insert a brief critical intervention here, I should point out that John Smith is more cautious about attributing the largest number of lines sung in 'Pabuji ki paṛ' to the wife of the bhopā: 'A bhopo with an inexperienced wife will leave only the last word or two of each section to her, whilst an experienced woman will in fact sing considerably more than her husband does'.[26] *Both Komalda and John Smith, however, fail to deal with the veiled presence of the bhopā's wife in actual performance. Indeed, she does not even face the spectators but stands sideways, facing her husband, feeding* his *performance. This is not the place for an extended analysis of feminist semiotics, but future research on 'Pabuji' could well shift the focus of the research to the women performers, who are, as yet, not fully acknowledged, or even named. It is worth emphasizing in this matter that the authoritative text provided of 'Pabuji' by John Smith is based entirely on Parbu Bhopā's 'arthāv' (explanation) of the text rather than the 'gāv' (song), which is shared with his wife.*

Pabuji kā māṭā is a more economical and tightly structured performance, because here there is no use of the paṛ. In this performance, the narrative is sung by Nāyak reciters/drummers, who are not hereditary caste musicians, but professionals who have chosen to sing the story of Pabu out of devotion. The most vital aspect of this performance is the use of the māṭā, a large parchment covered pot-drum, on which very intricate rhythms are beaten out. In fact, the māṭā style of singing is more complex musically than the paṛ style because it has more variations within strict rules of rhythm and melody. It should also be kept in mind that the māṭā is mentioned in the epic of Pabu itself. Remember, how when Pabu flew into the sky seated on the magical mare Kesar Kalāmi, that Deval had instructed his companions to play on the drum to bring him back. Well, the drum mentioned by Deval is the māṭā, which still continues to be played in commemorating Pabu's story, particularly during ceremonies performed in shrines.

In the all-male rendition of Pabuji ki paṛ, the musician/reciter plays on a *gujari* or *nareli*, a stringed instrument with a semi-circular bow attached to *ghungroos* (bells). To this combination of song and music, the female impersonator, fully veiled, dances with vigorous movements, balancing *thāḷis* (brass plates) in his hand, which are manipulated in many virtuoso ways. Unlike the rāvanhatthā rendition of Pabuji where both the man and the woman share the narrative, here the male lead singer sings the entire narrative, interspersed with dances provided by the impersonator. These performers have no hereditary links with the performance of the Pabu story. Rather, like the Pabuji kā māṭā performers, they are professionals who have become devotees of Pabu. Unlike the itinerant husband-wife team, who travel along the pastoral migratory route of the Rāikās, these performers tend to base themselves in particular villages, where they are approached by interested parties to do a show in their respective village. The basic difference in their performance style is that their story-line is stronger, and the lives of local communities are more strongly incorporated into their performances, primarily through the insertion of wedding songs. These songs enable the bhopā to draw on deeply localized cultural references.

Finally, while studying the story of Pabu, there are at least two points of reference. On the one hand, we can try to reconstruct the physical and historical facts surrounding the actual period in which Pabu lived, for which we would need to turn to all kinds of obscure historical records for verification. Frankly, I am not in a position to explain these historical matters—for example, anachronisms by which an allegedly eleventh century phenomenon like the snake-god Gogo is found in a fourteenth century narrative like Pabuji. I cannot explain such discrepancies. But let us not forget that there is another point of reference for studying Pabuji, and that is *our own time*, in which Pabu's story continues to be told by many different performers from different caste groups, who interpret and tell the story in many different ways. In this present context, there are many concrete issues that need to be addressed: how the performers will be paid; why a particular episode from the story is told for the entire night; what responsibilities are assumed by the sponsors of the performance, and so on.

As in other folk rituals, we find that the Pabu performance is invariably staged to mediate a particular problem faced by a family or community. It is also performed as an offering—for instance, if a man's cows have fallen ill, or if he has no children, or if he is facing a legal problem, or if his family wishes to ward off an evil spirit. In such situations, Pabu's story can be rendered to appease the gods. What needs to be kept in mind is the faith of people at large in the power of Pabu as a deity, and not just the skill of the performance itself, which is of secondary importance. Apart from solving problems, a performance of Pabuji can also be commissioned for the installation of a new shrine or icon, or as part of an all-night session of devotional songs (jāgraṇ). This ceremony in turn could be held for any number of events in the community—the building of a new well or house, or the purchase of agricultural land.

Depending on their economic means, different communities support the Pabu performances in different ways. While the Rāikā or camel-herder and shepherd communities may not be able to afford more than the payment for the performance itself, some more wealthy members have been known to pay for the making of a new paṛ. There is also the custom of making donations during the performance itself, particularly during the sequences dealing with the marriage ceremonies of Pabu and Goga. Those spectators in the audience who can afford to make a donation can, like honorary wedding guests, have the honour of hearing their names announced by the bhopā to the auspicious blowing of a conch shell.

Basically, what we are talking about here is the performance of an epic that is meant for the entire community, which gathers together through the night near the village shrine or in an open field to hear Pabu's story one more time. This is a community celebration, even though one particular family inevitably sponsors the performance, providing the spectators rounds of tea and an early-morning snack of *lāpsi*, a sweet preparation made out of wheat. Pabu, it should be emphasized, is worshipped not because he is a great hero, but because he is an ordinary Rajput, whose spirit, once invoked in whatever form, can help in mediating and solving human problems.

The self-affirmation of the community is obviously being emphasized here at very local and material levels, but the question of deification to which it seems linked has not been fully resolved. Perhaps, instead of contextualizing this widespread Rajasthani phenomenon within the contours of a specific text ('Pabuji'), it would be more useful to explore its multiple manifestations through the narratives and ritual practices surrounding other folk deities. With Komalda's discourse

I have noticed one thing—the more it spreads at a spatial level, incorporating all kinds of connections along the way, the more one is likely to find some insight into a particular phenomenon. Like the paṛ which has no regular sequence, but which proceeds through principles of spatial contiguity and direction rather than a temporal logic, Komalda's discourse is most resonant when it is not constrained within the point-by-point argumentation of a particular position. While this refusal to accept a linear theoretical logic can be seen as a limitation, its very deviations can also be viewed as representative of another mode of thinking. Let us turn now to a broader perspective of deification within the cultures of everyday life.

5

FOLK GODS AND GODDESSES

In this chapter, the phenomenon of deification moves beyond the figure of the bhomiyā to include a wide range of folk gods and goddesses. Later, in a more personal register, through some telling exposures of the process of deification in his own family, Komalda illuminates the diverse ways in which the spirits of the dead are commemorated and placated through household ritual practices. Let us begin by situating folk gods and goddesses within the framework of their shrines.

Identifying 'Folk' Gods and Goddesses

What is 'folk' about 'folk gods and goddesses'? What makes them 'folk'? Remember what I had said about Pabuji—he is no great god in the Hindu pantheon, but a bhomiyā god who has the power to intervene in the problems of everyday life, faced by nomadic communities like the Rabāri of Rajasthan. For example, if a cow owned by a Rabāri family is ill and is not capable of giving birth to a calf, neither Lord Krishna nor Lord Shiva is likely to be approached to deal with this problem. Likewise, if there is a family problem—more often than not related to child-bearing or some mental illness attributed to an evil spirit—it is assumed that the great gods are not likely to solve the problem. At such junctures, communities like the Rabāri turn to folk gods and goddesses, who are believed to solve everyday human problems, as we will describe later on.

For the moment, keep in mind that Krishna, Shiva, or for that matter, Buddha and Mahavir are not folk gods. When devotees turn to them for personal salvation, they have to embark on a rigorous process of different disciplines—*tapasyā*, *sādhana*, *yoga*, or whatever. But so far as folk gods and goddesses are concerned, they can be approached more directly with the faith that they will be able to intervene in the most ordinary problems of everyday life. Once I understood this principle, it became easier for me to decide who is a folk god and who isn't.

Around the same time that I was beginning to explore folk gods and goddesses in the immediate context of their innumerable shrines, I was also collecting folk tales called *vrat kathā*, which are stories (*kathā*) told by women during a ritual fast (vrat). These fasts are generally held on the basis of different calculations made by women in relation to the Indian calendar (*tithi*)—so a *vrat* could be held on a particular day every week, or on the eleventh day of every fortnight, or on nights of no moon (*amāvasya*).[1] When a group of women observe the vrat together, the stories from printed booklets are read aloud, but when women are alone, they read the stories to themselves. In these stories the gods are invariably angry, but they are capable of being placated through the telling of stories. At the end of each story you will find more or less the same refrain in different words—*Jisi tarah se devi yā devatā uspe ṭuṭe, usi tarah mujh pe ṭuṭnā* (Just as the gods and goddesses blessed him or her, so also bless me). All those gods and goddesses who become angry and start harming you, those who become *rusth* (malignant) and destroy you, are also capable of making you happy, wealthy, and full of well-being (*tusth*). Rusth becomes tusth. So the deities who are able to destroy or help you in your daily life are folk gods and goddesses, and others are not.

Shrines and their Inventions

Having clarified how folk gods and goddesses can be identified at a very rudimentary level, let us now examine the shrines where they are worshipped.[2] A folk shrine could be located in a number of places, not just in an enclosed structure, but also under a tree, or in a cave. Generally, there is a platform (*chabutrā*), which varies in its construction, though in most villages it is made out of mud and cow dung with a coating of lime. Within the shrine there is always some kind of icon (*murti*). When we look at these icons, they always fall into very definite categories—heroic deities like the bhomiyā, as represented by figures like Pabu and Tejā: sati deities like Rāni Sati and Rāni Bhaṭiyāṇi; saints like Ramdev, Gogādev and Dev Narayan.[3] All these deities are very sharply defined, with specific iconographies, narratives, and symbols.

While many of these deities are linked with very familiar and established mythologies, there are others whose identities continue to evolve. Consider, for example, the figure of the folk god Bhairon, a protective deity who guards the boundaries of a particular village. However, he has other manifestations as well—for example, Ragtiā [literally 'blood'] Bhairon, who is worshipped for the possession of tantric powers; Masaniā Bhairon, who is specifically invoked on cremation grounds; the twins Kālā Bhairon and Gorā Bhairon—one black and ferocious, the other white and compassionate. More abstractly, Bhairon can be worshipped as a seasonal god in the form of Ghās [literally, 'grass'] Bhairon, who has the power to provide a good rainfall.[4] In addition, there are new manifestations like the Kāshi kā Bhairon, which I would like to describe in more detail because it indicates how folk deities in Rajasthan get invented through specific interventions.

At a popular level, the phenomenon of Kāshi kā Bhairon can be traced back to a sugar mill in Karera near Udaipur, where it appears that a labourer died shortly after Independence. After his death, he started manifesting himself as a spirit and creating a lot of trouble for the factory. So the factory owner wanted to find a way by which the labourer's soul could be put to rest. To do this he sent a person belonging to the chamār community all the way to Kāshi (Benares) in order to bring back the Bhairon from this holy city. The chamār went there and brought back the *jyot* (the holy flame) of the Bhairon. An icon of this deity was set up in a shrine in Karera itself, the location of the sugar-mill. This shrine was supervised by the chamār, who gradually assumed the role of a bhopā by coming into trance. In the course of his mediation, the labourer's troubled soul was appeased.

Now the story gets complicated. At that time Maharāṇā Bhupāl Singh was ruling over Mewar. Of his own accord, the chamār decided that the shrine should also contain a printed picture of Maharāṇā Bhupāl Singh. In addition, the factory owner, who was an Oswāl Jain, believed in Nakodā Bhairon, a deity whose shrine is located about 100 kilometres from Jodhpur on the way to Barmer. He in turn decided that a picture of the icon of Nakodā Bhairon should also be seen in the shrine. Today the shrine of Kāshi kā Bhairon has started proliferating all over the Mewar region and we have more than 500–600 shrines. If the pictures of the Maharāṇā Bhupāl Singh and Nakodā Bhairon are not seen in the shrine, then it is not regarded as Kāshi kā Bhairon. So in this way we begin to see how shrines get invented, and how they multiply.

Structures of Shrines

While collecting material from about 140 shrines, we began to identify different kinds of shrines. Open-air shrines located in fields or under trees are called *thān*. During those periods of time when the thān is associated with some kind of miracle or supernatural event, the shrine is called *dhām*. Shrines located within the interiors of rooms and huts are called *deoṛa*. Platforms of worship constructed within the homes of tribal communities are called *thada*, which are taken care of by individual families. No public worship is held in the thada, quite unlike the more widespread thān and dhām, which attract larger numbers of *yātrīs*/*jātrīs* (pilgrims) from all sections of society in Rajasthan.[5] On those days when the shrine becomes *active*—in other words, on the days when a trance ceremony takes place within its precincts—the thān or dhām is identified as *chauki*.

Apart from the fixed platforms representing the shrines, there are other kinds of itinerant shrines, such as the paṛ, which we have described in the last chapter in relation to the performances of Pabuji ki paṛ. Another form of itinerant shrine is the *kāvaḍ*, or small cupboard, which is used for recitations invoking the lives of saints and the spirits of dead people. (See Chapter 9 for a detailed description of this phenomenon.) Both the paṛ and the kāvaḍ can be regarded as performative shrines. Of course, there are even more 'human' shrines embodied by mendicants and travelling performers like the *bahurupia*, who take on the physical identities of specific deities like Hanuman, Krishna, and Shiva with elaborate costumes and make-up (*vesh*).[6] Through all these examples, it becomes obvious that the shrine is a dynamic phenomenon—it can take on many different forms and shapes, defying the architectural protocol and formality of the temple (*mandir*). In the very informality and ordinariness of its improvised structures, the shrine offers itself as an intimate space of worship.

The *Bhopā*

Central to any public shrine is the bhopā or priest, who is also called ghoṛala in the south of Rajasthan—literally, the 'horse' of this or that god or goddess. The critical difference is that while the bhopā actually gets possessed by the deity—he 'becomes' the deity—the ghoṛala is merely the vehicle of the deity. In both cases, however, what matters is how this figure, who serves as an oracle, is answerable to the gods on the one hand and to people on the other. How one becomes a bhopā is not very clear, though it is generally believed that a spirit or deity takes possession of a person without his knowledge or volition. This person is literally 'caught' by the spirit, as the expression bhopā pakaṛnā suggests.

While mediating the everyday problems of local people in a state of trance, the bhopā also plays a very important social role in rural society. After all, even though he has the capacity to go into trance, he also lives in the village. People believe in him, whether or not his trances are genuine. Without a bhopā, no shrine can be considered active. So, inevitably, when one particular bhopā dies or leaves the village for any particular reason, a jāgraṇ, or all-night singing session of bhajans (devotional songs), is held in the vicinity of the shrine. At some point during the ceremony another person from the community is 'caught' by the spirit or deity and assumes the role of the new bhopā.

The assistants to the bhopā are identified as *koṭwāl* and *hazuriā*. Interestingly, both these terms are familiar names for policemen or constables. And it is not entirely surprising that the pilgrims come to the shrine to 'seek justice' (*nyāy māngno*). These details reveal that the trance situation and the possible resolution of problems that emerges in the course of it demands some kind of supervision of the pilgrims' behaviour. After all, there is a public airing of family feuds, property disputes, marital and mental problems, infertility, possession by spirits, among other difficulties faced by people in their everyday lives. All these problems are invariably expressed after the bhopā goes into a state of trance, during which time whatever he says is interpreted to the pilgrims by the koṭwāl or hazuriā. More often than not, the bhopā does not speak directly to the pilgrims. Likewise he is never paid directly by the pilgrim. It is the koṭwāl/hazuriā's responsibility to collect the offerings made by the pilgrims for the larger maintenance of the shrine.

Elements of the Shrine

In considering the practice of worship at the shrines, there are many elements to be taken into account. There is, for instance, the use of the *jyot* (the holy flame). Different shrines use different kinds of jyot, which in turn use ghee or oil—indeed, different kinds of oil. The shape of the *dīpak* (lamp) will also vary from shrine to shrine, being defined by its allegiance to a particular class of god. Then there is the *prasād* or offering of food. Some gods and goddesses, like the Kāshi kā Bhairon, are strictly vegetarian. They can only be offered fruits and *miṭhāi* (sweets), but there are others for whom animal sacrifices are made. Non-vegetarian foods are offered to them, along with liquor. Yet another element in the worship of folk deities is incense. Different incenses are used for different gods and goddesses. Today *agarbatti* (manufactured incense sticks) have almost eliminated more traditional forms of incense used in Jain, Buddhist and Sufi shrines. In the shrines of folk gods and goddesses, the relationship of incense to *gandh* (smell, aroma) is very strong.[7]

Yātrīs

Finally, we need to address the yātrī who come for mediation to the shrines. Who are these pilgrims? What have they come for? Why do they behave the way they do? Whether people are suffering from unidentified psychological problems or physical ones like scabies, paralysis, polio, even slipped disc or whooping cough, they know exactly which shrine is appropriate for the possible cure of their ailments. It is hard to explain the state of trance to which many of them submit at the shrine. But, perhaps, trance can be described as a state in which a person behaves physically in a manner that we cannot easily relate to normal circumstances. How it happens, is very difficult to say. Maybe to a certain extent it is a form of self-hypnosis. But perhaps this is merely an interpretation that we can do without.

What we can confirm is that a number of things take place *physically* during the moment of trance. A musician has to be present; he has to be singing and playing his instrument very loud and fast. The bhopā going into trance looks very strongly into the jyot. Then, when he enters the state of trance, we find many things happening—some bhopās may move only their hands or thumbs, some shake their heads, some move only their legs, others their feet. Something happens that you can see very physically, like the rolling of eyes. All this happens for barely a minute or two, and then the bhopā starts speaking in the voice of the deity.

If you go to the Gaṭodji shrine near Jaisamand Lake in Udaipur—this is the shrine of the snake-god Gogāji[8]—there are around twelve priests who simultaneously go into trance. This trance will be physicalized through the darting of the tongue, rather like a snake. The condition lasts for barely a minute, within which time the afflicted person can raise a question that will be promptly answered by one of the priests.

There are other Hindu and Sufi shrines where it is not the priest who goes into trance, but the afflicted persons. At this point, they start shivering, shuddering, trembling, sometimes rolling on the ground, even somersaulting. In all this vigorous movement, you can sometimes see something akin to dance movement—a fluid movement of the hand or the tossing of the head; sometimes you can hear the repetition of a specific word, or a snatch of a song. In this trance situation the bhopā does not directly talk to the person who comes for relief from a particular problem. Rather, he talks to his assistant, and it is the assistant who says that this god says such and such thing, or you should do the following things if you wish to be cured.

Now, all of this depends on the people's belief, which is not an easy phenomenon to comprehend. I have come across at least two shrines near Bundi where it is believed that the gods and goddesses have actually ordered that there should be no bhopā within their shrines, and that no trance should take place there. So there are different shrines with different conditions, which are created to mediate and resolve different problems.

Women come in large numbers to these shrines to deal with their problems. Some of them suffer from fits; others have no children. We often find young girls brought to the shrines because they haven't conceived. Usually in Rajasthani society, we find that if a girl is not pregnant within a year of marriage, then the other women start gossiping, and the situation becomes the talk of the village. The family members are affected. Then the husband and wife are both taken to the shrine. When they get there they are told by the bhopā that 'such-and-such person died in your family and you didn't do certain rituals, so go and do these rituals, take this *nārial* (coconut), eat it'. Or else, 'You have not gone on such-and-such pilgrimage as you had earlier promised, so do so and your problem will be resolved,' and so on.

From a broader perspective, we can say that these shrines provide a breathing space, a two to three year period, during which time a problem can be confronted, and hopefully, resolved. At a psychological level, they provide the mediation of time for wounds to heal. That's what needs to be kept in mind. The bhopā does not directly resolve disputes or problems, but he creates the possibilities of some of kind of healing process and reconciliation.

Similarly, at the snake shrines, the point is not that the rituals at the shrine can, in actuality, cure snake-bite. The point is that 90 per cent of the snakes are non-poisonous. But people bitten by snakes are *afraid* of dying. They don't realize that the snake-bite won't kill them. Now, when they get 'cured' after visiting the shrines, the credit is invariably given to specific gods. So in this kind of way shrines mediate certain problems, and in the process, larger problems in the lives of individuals and entire families and neighbourhoods can be resolved.

I have visited many Sufi shrines, all the way from Ganganagar in the north of Jodhpur to Banswara in the south of Rajasthan. When afflicted persons in these shrines go into trance, you hear identical cries in Ganganagar and Banswara. Nobody has taught these people to cry in that way, so how does this happen? I have also heard people who have never spoken Urdu or Arabic or heard anything from the Qu'rān speak perfect Urdu and Arabic and even recite from the Qu'rān. These are ordinary people, uneducated, who speak the local languages of Rajasthan. How do we account for their use of other languages? Once the trance is over they would not be able to understand any of the words that they had earlier used. At times I have seen women in the Sufi shrines rolling on the ground, but holding on to the end of their *ghāgrā*. Is this some kind of reflex action? Or is it premeditated? Is trance another kind of performance, or is it an involuntary state of self-transformation?

Once again we end with a few questions which come out of Komalda's observations of particular ritual practices. When he does not fully understand any phenomenon, like the psychic processes underlying trance, he does not try to mystify it. On listening to him address the different states of transformation experienced by pilgrims, particularly women, it becomes clear that his observations are far removed from, say, Sudhir Kakar's psychoanalytic perspective on indigenous healing practices, in which Freudian categories are at once vernacularized, transformed and subverted within indigenous Indian psychological traditions.[9] *It is obvious that Komalda is no such psychoanalyst. In fact, I'm not too sure to what extent the psychological dimensions of material and cultural history interest him in the first place.*

At another level, it could be argued that for all the intensity of his fieldwork, he resists the kind of intense empathy that characterizes a great deal of research in the anthropological participant-observation documentation of folk ritual practices.[10] *Komalda seems to me more of an observer than a participant. Over and over again I've been struck by his restraint in addressing extreme emotional experiences, which, in critical hindsight, could be described as expositions of trauma. This restraint is not a form of self-censorship, I would emphasize, but a kind of detachment with which Komalda addresses the seeming hysteria of pilgrims seeking mediation through the trance-induced articulations of the 'bhopā'.*

Perhaps, in an even more startling register, this detachment is also to be found when Komalda talks about legacies of deification in his own family. While 'the family' often comes up in his discourse, it is rarely invoked for nostalgic or purely autobiographical purposes; rather, it is presented as a point of reference, if not an active site of research. Listen now to how Komalda continues to ground the dynamics of deification within the intimate, yet curiously anonymous framework of his own family.[11]

Deification in the Family

Many a time, when I want to understand a complex phenomenon, such as the manifestation of a dead person's soul, I try to get as much information as possible from my own family members. What's going on inside the family? For me this has been a research strategy, which has invariably yielded insights into the workings of larger social and cultural phenomena, like deification. I have evidence of deification in my family history in three different cases.

Let me begin by telling you a story. As well as my father and his elder brother, my grandmother had a third son. On the day he was born, on that very night, she had a bad dream, in which she was given a sign, that when her newly-born son grew up he would be dangerous to her husband. So, my grandmother took some opium, which was in the house at that time, and fed it to the child. Next morning he was found dead, barely twelve hours after he was born.

Six or seven months later, this child returned to haunt his mother in a dream. In this dream, he told her: 'You didn't allow me to live. Too bad, I only had six or seven years to live. I would have died anyway. But since I have already been killed, worship me as part of the *puja* ceremonies in the family.' Even today this child is worshipped in the form of a gold medallion which we call *chhink bījāsā*.

Now, this particular manifestation of a male spirit after death is known as *pitar*; in Mewar they refer to it as *purvaj*, and in eastern Rajasthan, it is known as *aut* or *aut mahārāj*.[12] Tomorrow, for instance, is *Rakhi puja*; you will see the pitar worshipped during the family rituals. Likewise, he will be worshipped during Diwali, Holi, and other ceremonies with offerings of coconut, incense, and so on. Almost every Hindu family in Rajasthan has some form of pitar or family god. The Muslim communities also have the concept of *shahīd*, which is very close to pitar. All such gods have to be childless—a pitar is one who does not perpetuate the line of his family ('*jiske āge vansh nahin chalā*').

Now, the manifestation of the pitar ended in my family with my grandmother's dream. It has not recurred. However, there is another situation in my family that is somewhat different. My father married for the first time in Sanganer. His wife gave birth to several children, one of whom survived. Then she died. My father married for a second time, and this time, his wife (my own mother) gave birth to eleven children—we are eight brothers and three sisters. Now, in this kind of situation, the first wife will invariably be deified as a *pitrāṇi*, the female version of a pitar or family god. She is also known as a *sauk*, or step-wife, or *saukarli*.[13]

In almost all rituals conducted in the family, songs will be sung to her in which she is requested not to harm the family in any way. You see, the pitrāṇi is perceived to be malignant. She can get very angry for the most trivial reasons, and she is capable of doing a lot of harm. If anything is missing in a particular ritual, she can create trouble for the family. Suppose you have a marriage function and, say, something falls short, then it has to be replaced immediately. But even as it falls short, you can be sure that some member of the family will say, 'The pitrāṇi is angry with us.' Any mishap or disturbance in the family rituals is likely to be interpreted in this way, and the pitrāṇi has to be promptly placated.

The third form of deification that is part of my family history concerns a woman who is worshipped as a sati in our rituals.[14] I remember my grandmother talking about her, as well as my mother and father. But who was this sati? The truth is that we know nothing about her life, why or when she took her life, what exactly happened that compelled her to take her life. All I know is that there is a shrine to this particular sati in the village of Namli in Ratlam district of Madhya Pradesh, which is the original native place of my family. The *munḍan* or haircutting ceremony of my elder brother from my father's first marriage took place at this shrine. Later on my family moved to Jodhpur and we stopped looking after the shrine in Namli. Then one day my father got a letter from some people in Namli informing him that the sati's thān (platform) was in very bad shape and needed to be repaired. I remember father sending one of our relatives there to have a look—this must have been between 1941 and 1943—and I remember that he sent ten thousand rupees to have the shrine repaired. Today no one knows anything about this sati, but she continues to be worshipped in our family rituals.

Indeed, she continues to hold sway in our family through a peculiar taboo, which we never fail to obey. During any marriage in our family, none of the women living in the household, or marrying into the family, can wear ornaments that are embellished with a certain type of flat jingle called *chorāsi kā ghugrā*. So, whenever any marriage is in the process of being arranged, we promptly inform the in-laws' family that no such ornament can be accepted because it has been prohibited by the sati in our household. Looking at many other satis in different families, I have discovered that they are invariably worshipped only when they lay down a certain restriction. They have to *prohibit* something in order to be worshipped.

I could easily at this point intercept an extended description of 'sati', but this subject is better addressed in detail in the following chapter. For the moment it would be useful to continue broadening the perspective on the ordinariness of deification practices in Rajasthan. 'Ordinariness' might seem too euphemistic a word for the seeming triviality by which the memory of a sati is commemorated through the prohibition of a particular ornamentation in jewellery. Certainly, this kind of folk connection does not readily get contextualized within the contemporary theorization of sati, either in its marxist/feminist or communitarian contexts.[15]

Leaving this matter for further questioning in the next chapter, we move on now to Komalda's observations on the manifestation of dead spirits, who are celebrated in households and neighbourhoods outside the immediate precincts of his own family.

Deification Outside the Family

Despite the specific circumstances surrounding the manifestations of a spirit, there are recurring factors in the larger phenomenon of deification. Take, for instance, a case in the family of my friend Vijay Dan [Detha], whose father and uncles were once involved in a feud in the village of Borunda. The feud occurred on account of some land, owned by low-caste people, which some thākurs from a neighbouring village wanted to occupy. Vijay Dan's father and uncles formed a group and put up a resistance, but the thākurs were armed with lāṭhis and guns, and in the ensuing fight as many as fourteen people from Vijay Dan's family were killed.

Now, on the one hand, the law took its course through the trials and arrests and imprisonment of the wrong-doers. But on the other hand, a totally different kind of response came from a widow in Vijay Dan's family. She had not been widowed as a result of this feud, but much earlier. This woman claimed that she had a dream in which a man came riding on a white horse; he was dressed entirely in white, and his beard was also white. According to the widow, this man wanted a shrine erected for those who had died in the feud. In deference to her dream, the survivors in Vijay Dan's family built a memorial shrine for the dead men. Today this shrine is identified with the phenomenon of *jhunjhar*, a term which refers to those people who die a violent death and who later manifest themselves as restless spirits. This is an all-Rajasthan phenomenon.[16]

What I want to point out here is that whenever the dead manifest themselves in such dreams in Rajasthan, the men are invariably in white—they ride white horses, their clothes are white, their beards are white. As for women, the colour is always red—they wear red *chuṛiyān* (bangles), a red bridal dress and ghāgrā. From Ganganagar to Banswara, this phenomenon never changes. The signs by which the dead manifest themselves in people's dreams have become a kind of language. There are no other variations in the visual signs of this dream-state. Even a child, like the third brother of my father, who barely lived for twelve hours, he, too, appeared to my grandmother in white.

Whenever shrines for the dead are constructed, they house icons that correspond to very specific circumstances in which a person died, whether it involves a pitar, or purvaj, or bhomiyā, or sati. The icons are made according to iconographic details and symbolic codes known to the sculptors. Once completed, the icon is brought to the family household where an all-night jāgraṇ is held, after which the icon is sanctified in a shrine. In tribal communities as well, icons are made in accordance with the particular circumstances surrounding the death of a particular person and the qualities of his or her temperament. In the Garāsiā community, the male and female spirits are identified as *moghā* and *moghi*, respectively; in the Bhil community, they are known as *sura* and *matlok*. Each and every person who dies in these communities is given an icon.

Here again there are death rituals in which a bhopā goes into trance while addressing the mother goddess of a particular village. In this trance he will assume the exact mannerisms of the person who has died. Supposing this person used to drink a lot, or smoke in a particular way, or wear goggles, or perhaps, he was a very good hunter, all these characteristics will be played out by the bhopā in trance. He might even ask for specific objects to be brought from the dead person's home to enhance his enactment—it could be a bow and arrow, or a gun, or a set of clothes, or whatever. In the course of impersonating the dead person throughout the night, the bhopā will at some point declare that a stone icon should be made in his honour. He will also indicate where this icon should be placed—either in front of his house or in the vicinity of a temple, or near his well, or in an open field.

After this impersonation in trance, the relatives of the dead person will go to the sculptors who make these stone icons and explain the exact circumstances in which their relative died. It is possible that the person could have died of snake bite, or perhaps he fell from a hill, or was killed by an animal, or else, he might have committed suicide, or someone might has killed him. There could be any number of explanations for a specific death, on the basis of which an icon is made representing the particular circumstances. At least this used to be the case some sixty to seventy years ago; now most of the icons have become standardized in their formulaic iconography.

And yet, specific manifestations of the dead continue to influence the construction of shrines. In the Mewar region, for instance, there was a milkman who used to bring milk daily to Udaipur from a neighbouring village. He used to drive a motor-cycle. One day he met with an accident and died on the road itself. Later, he came in a dream to his mother, and told her to build a shrine on the accident site. So, a roadside shrine was built, and what was the icon? A man riding on a motor cycle with the very number of the milkman's vehicle. You can still see that motor-cycle shrine today, even though the number has been washed out.

Interestingly, this milkman continued to visit his mother in her dreams. When I met her— it must have been about four or five years after he had died—she was still being regularly visited by her son. Whenever he manifested himself, she would go into trance and a lot of people from the neighbourhood would come to her for solutions to their problems. What kinds of problems? Everyday life problems—for example, my son is applying for a job: will he get it or not? Will my father survive this operation? Will such-and-such nephew pass his examination? Will this marriage come through? And so on. When I myself was going to be operated for cancer, one of my brothers went to a particular woman who is known to go into trance. He asked her if I would return from the hospital alive. And she said, yes, he will return safely. So, all these types of reassurances are part of everyday life. Once word gets around that a particular person can mediate with the world of the dead, the message spreads to relatives and neighbours and to larger and larger communities. Thereby household gods and goddesses begin to extend their influences beyond the family, and the deification process spreads to larger areas.

The value of Komalda's somewhat freewheeling observations here is that they suggest the widespread diffusion of deification practices in Rajasthani society. So familiar are their 'reassurances', to use his precise word, that it seems almost pedantic to use the term 'deification' to describe dreams and states of possession and trance, through which the spirits of the dead continue to be commemorated in everyday life. Perhaps the central clue here in illuminating these 'reassurances' derived from deification practices concerns the very tangible and participatory ways in which death ceremonies are practised in

Rajasthan. The dead, as Komalda will elaborate in the next section, are treated as living beings through numerous rites, rituals, and ceremonies. Here then is an account of these activities, which prefigure—and ground—the phenomenon of deification even more deeply in the processes of everyday life.

Life After Death

What interests me is the continuity that exists even after this phenomenon called death. To explore this continuity I have observed what actually happens in the day-to-day household practices following a death in the family. I have direct experience of these practices from my father's death and from any number of cremation ceremonies in my community.[17] As soon as a person dies in a Hindu household, the body is placed on the earth. If *gobar* (cow dung) or *gangā jal* (holy water) or *go mutra* (cow's urine) are available, these will be smeared on the ground before the body is placed on it. Depending on the time when a person dies, there are specific rituals to be followed. If a person dies at night, you wait for morning to break before sending messages to other members of the family.

A very important ritual concerns the bathing of the body. Here one has to follow rules concerning who has the right to bathe the body; if it's a male body, then men bathe it, and if it's a female body, women do so. I've noticed that many old people have actually prepared the clothes in which they wish to be laid out long before they die. For many years, my own mother would go on and on about the clothes that she would wear when she died. My father never said anything in this regard about his own death, but we all knew in the family that he had kept certain clothes aside for that occasion. He never directly pointed this out to us, but we all knew what he wanted us to do. Of course, there are a lot of variations from family to family as to what is wrapped around the dead body—in certain cases, the body is even left naked. Depending on the estimated time for disposing of the body, certain perfumes are used to keep it as fresh as possible.

The purchasing of the cloth for the *kafan* (shroud) and the clothes worn by the dead person involve a number of rituals. The shawl, for instance, generally has to come from the in-laws' side of the family—if, for any reason, it doesn't arrive on time, then you can purchase this cloth yourself on behalf of the in-laws, but they will have to reimburse you for it. The problem is that the circumstances of death can be so unexpected that sometimes you find yourself in a situation where you don't know what to do. So, for example, when my brother-in-law expired—he was from a family in Udaipur, but he lived in Jodhpur and died in Jaipur—it was my responsibility to go to Jaipur and buy the cloth for the death rituals. I asked my sister: 'Do you have any special knowledge about what needs to be done in his case?' And she said that in her husband's family it was the custom that the *chaḍḍi* (underwear) should be red and that there should be a thin cotton mattress placed on the *arthi* (bier).

So I went to one particular place in Jaipur, Badi Chopad, where there are some shops that deal with materials relating to death rituals. I arrived there around 4.30 in the morning, and immediately, even before I could elaborate on what I needed, the shopkeeper himself inquired about the dead person. I told him that my brother-in-law was a Mehta Oswāl from Udaipur. That was enough. 'Oh then,' said the shop-keeper, instructing one of his assistants, 'Go take this red cloth and give it to the *darzi* (tailor) to make the chaḍḍi, and take this cloth for the mattress. If he is from that family and that caste, then this is what needs to be done.'

Once you get the necessary clothes for the dead person, which have to be made in a particular way, you have to then concentrate on how the body should be carried. There are specific rules that have to be obeyed in this matter. Once the body is lifted on your shoulders, you have to utter a cry that signifies, 'We're taking you with us'. Which end the head is placed, which end the feet, all these details matter. Before arriving at the cremation ground, there is a platform on which you place the body and reverse its position. In certain rituals, there are sweets that are distributed to dogs at this time. Finally, the body is taken to the cremation ground. Here there is a particular system of preparing the fire and arranging the wood on the pyre. The body is placed on it in a certain way. The fire is lit. Who sets fire to the pyre is a very critical matter—in family disputes, this can result in a great deal of tension.

After the cremation, the rituals are not over. On the third day, you have to collect the ashes and the bones of the dead, which are gathered in a red *theli* (bundle) for women, and a white one for men, but you can't take it inside your house. It has to remain outside or you have to keep it in the temple near the cremation ground. When you go to Hardwar to immerse the remains of the body (literally called '*phul*', or flowers), there are other rituals that need to be followed. If four people, for instance, are going to Hardwar for the final rites of a dead person, they will buy five tickets. After all, one of their relatives is travelling with them. If they order tea or food, they will always order for five persons—they may give away the fifth share to someone, but they will always order for five. However, when they return home, they only buy four tickets. By this time they will have requested the Bhairava of Ganga, Lord Shiva's attendant, to accompany them so that the person whose phul have been immersed in Hardwar will not return home with them.

There are so many details that can be observed in the death rituals, from the moment a person dies in a particular place to the immersion of his or her ashes. I have personally counted almost 170 such details to be dealt with in the minute rituals that have to be followed at home, including all the arrangements of food that has to be specially prepared and sent from the in-laws' house—the bitter food (*kaḍuva kāvā*) as it is called. Even many days after the cremation is over, the rites continue in Hardwar, as one negotiates with *panḍās* over the payment for performing specific ceremonies, and so on. There are rules involved at every step of the way, which makes death a very vital phenomenon in the lives of people in India.

In contrast, I remember talking to a very dear friend of mine from France, whose father had died. I asked her: How did it happen? Can you explain it to me? What kinds of ceremonies did you observe? She told me that her father had died in hospital. When he died, she had informed all her brothers and sisters and they met together and contacted a particular cemetery at a neighbouring church for the funeral. But the church authorities couldn't give a date for the funeral until eleven days after the man's death. Only on the eleventh day was it possible for him to be buried. I asked my friend: 'What happened during the eleven days? What did you do together? What kinds of ceremonies did you participate in? She said: 'Well, the body was put in the morgue, we all went back to our respective homes, and on the eleventh day we got together again, and buried our father. That's all.'

Now this is very different from the Indian situation. As I look back on all the rites and rituals of death that I have experienced, I realize that in all the hundreds of little things that happen after a person dies, you continue to treat the dead person as a living being. That is the basic point. Now, to my mind, if you are capable of treating a dead person as a living being immediately after his or her death, then he or she can live for eternity. The dead can be with you forever.

Even as this sounds like a very beautiful sentiment, I can hear Komalda saying: It's not just a sentiment but a set of practices *by which the dead are treated as living beings. These practices enlarge in perspective and take on other-worldly dimensions when the dead person in question appears in someone's dream or takes possession of a family member, or gets invoked through a shamanic rite. Through such mediations, the process of deification begins and grows. It is true that not everyone who dies is necessarily deified, but the possibilities of sustaining a 'life after death' cannot be ruled out for anyone.*

As always, there is a realistic undercurrent to Komalda's conjectures, as he acknowledges the limits of remembering. Even the deified can be forgotten. Once again, he returns to the sati from his own family history, and speculates on her status. 'Our sati,' he says, 'is in Namli, and here we are living in Jodhpur. There are no family members left in Namli any longer. Today a "pujari" (priest) from that area has taken over the shrine, which is now being worshipped by the entire village. Who exactly is being worshipped here I cannot say, but we continue to think of the shrine as a family responsibility. And in that sense the sati is still alive for us.' With this thought let us now focus on the phenomenon of sati in broader regional and folk contexts.

6

SATI

Listening can be very demanding, particularly if the subject in question is as difficult and painful as sati.[1] *I cannot deny that this session didn't quite 'work' for me—there were any number of gaps and breakdowns in the recording, and it was obvious that Komalda was not entirely in grasp of the facts surrounding the history and resurgence of sati in contemporary India.*[2] *Perhaps, the easiest thing for me would have been to omit this session altogether. But I also realize that this would have been something of an evasion, if not a cop-out, because it would have glossed over the inconsistencies not only in recording, but in listening to a problematic description of sati in a folk register.*

Instead of covering up these gaps and inconsistencies in Komalda's recording (and my process of listening), I have attempted to highlight them through my transcription. My strategy here has been to edit (and collate) the fragments from the recording, interspersing them with my comments, which are more interventionist than in the earlier sections. As will become clear, the focus in Komalda's narrative is on fragments of stories, rather than on any analysis of the larger social phenomenon of sati itself. To provide a fuller context of the politics of sati, which I think is unavoidable within the highly contentious and voluminous literature on the subject,[3] *I have added critical notes to supplement—and question—Komalda's perspective.*

How do we begin to understand the phenomenon called sati? As I told you earlier, in my own family there is a sati and she is strongly associated with the prohibition of one particular custom, which is what compels her to be worshipped in my family to this day. Now, of course, for other people, from outside of the family, she has no significance at all. The point is that some satis can be understood only within the context of individual families. They have no larger public significance.

Take the case of my late friend Narayan Singh Sandu. In his family, about three or four generations ago, a woman from the Chāraṇ community became a sati. It is said that even earlier in the family history there had been another sati, but this first sati is not worshipped in the Sandu family because she did not lay down any law or order that had to be followed in the family. But the second woman who became a sati laid down the particular law that no one in the Sandu family should ever construct a first storey to their house. To this day, this particular *okh* (taboo) is strictly observed. One of Sandu's relatives did try to build an additional storey to his house, not in the village he came from but in the urban area to which he had migrated. And he found that this created a lot of problems for his family—illness, death, all kinds of tensions. Finally, he had to remove this additional storey in order to get peace of mind.

Now, while all satis are linked to specific families, only a few of them get deified. Among those who get deified, some of them begin to be worshipped outside of the boundaries of their community, as other social groups begin to claim them, on their own grounds. I shall tell some stories of such satis later on, but for the moment, let me focus on those satis who are very strongly linked to particular communities.

Sati Stories

a. Jhumā Sati is worshipped in a large part of the Thar desert in the Barmer district. Her origins are linked to a village called Mithrau, at present located in Pakistan. It seems that in earlier times there were many raids on this village by the Baloochi people. Finally, the villagers of Mithrau decided that someone from their village should become a sati—perhaps, out of fear of this sati, the Baloochi's atrocities would stop. The problem was to decide who should become the sati for the entire village. Finally, the villagers recalled that a number of women from the neighbouring village of Harwa had become satis. So they decided to bring some sand from that village and scatter it on the ground in their own village, so that the women of Mithrau could walk on it—and who knows? Maybe one of them would find the power to become a sati.

It was at this point that a woman from Mithrau claimed that, as a resident of Harwa in her unmarried years, she had walked on that sand. So she offered herself as a sati for the village. Mind you, her husband was alive, she had two children, and yet she decided to become a sati. When all the preparations for the sati were going on, her eldest son began to have doubts about her sincerity. He thought that perhaps his mother was under some emotional pressure on account of the larger predicament of Harwa, and therefore she had offered to become a sati under duress. He believed that when the fire began to burn her body, she would try to run away from the *chitā* (pyre). To prevent this possibility, he built a barricade of thorns around the pyre so that she would not be able to escape. By this time the woman realized what was on her son's mind, and she cursed him. She said that in every generation born into his family there would only be one son, and he would go mad by the time he was sixteen years old.

Over the years, members of this family have migrated to India from Pakistan, along with many other Hindu refugees during the Partition and the Indo-Pakistani war—they have settled in a particular area around twenty kilometres from Barmer, and the mother's curse has come true. In each successive generation of this family there has been just one son, who invariably goes mad in the prime of his youth.

Another prophecy that Jhumā Sati made before dying has also come true. Mithrau had been a predominantly Muslim village in her time, with a few Hindu families living in their midst, such as her own. Just before dying, Jhumā Sati had declared that no mullah would be able to do the *āzān* (the call of prayer) from the *masjid* (mosque) in Mithrau: '*Āzān nahi lagā sakte*' (No call of prayer can be made). To this day, a peculiar feature of this village, or so I have heard from those Hindu families from Mithrau (now in Pakistan) who have settled in Barmer, Rajasthan, is that there is '*namāz* without *āzān*'. The descendants of Mithrau continue to regard Jhumā Sati as their patron deity.

b. Yet another sati with an unusual history is Gomā Sati. Her story involves a band of robbers who steal cows from a particular village. As they are fleeing with the cows, they meet Gomā, a Chāraṇ woman, on the way. She recognizes the cows and demands to know where they are being taken. When the robbers brazenly affirm their theft, she protests and threatens to kill herself by cutting off her own limbs. The robbers are not taken in by what they assume to be a wild threat, and Gomā takes her own life. Today she is worshipped as a sati in the region around Beesoo, Sheo, Barmer and Jaisalmer not only by Hindus, but by Muslims as well.

Gomā Sati has the particular power to prevent fire. Most of the huts in the desert region are made of different kinds of grass and mud; dry thorny plants and creepers are used for the hedges, which surround each hut. A simple fire could set a village ablaze. Gomā Sati is capable of providing protection against such fires. Interestingly, her powers are assumed to travel beyond her place of worship. When Shafi, a young Manganiyar musician, died during a foreign tour in Belgium—a leak in a gas stove resulted in an explosion, that burnt his entire body—his death was, at one level, attributed to Gomā Sati. (See Chapter 11 for more details on this tragic event.) Some of the musicians in his touring party believed that they had not adequately worshipped Gomā Sati before leaving their native place. Perhaps, if they had followed the rituals, such an accident could have been averted. This is one instance of the intensity of faith in Gomā Sati, who is worshipped as a goddess.

c. Another unusually powerful sati is Bāḷā Sati, who died just a few years ago. What was her situation? When her husband died, she wanted to become a sati, but the people in her community prevailed on her not to take her own life because the legal repercussions could affect all of them. They suggested that since her husband's elder brother had a son, and she had no sons of her own, she should adopt this boy and live with his support. Reluctantly, she agreed to this proposal.

After a few years, however, this son died as well. Now Bāḷā was determined to become a sati with her adopted son. Again the people of her community tried to reason with her, but this time she was very adamant. So they locked her up in a room and provided her with food and water from the ventilator. In this way, she lived for almost two months. Finally, when they opened the door, they found that she had not eaten or drunk anything in all that time. In this condition, she continued to live for many years, refusing to touch any food.

When she used to come to Borunda to attend all-night jāgraṇs, I had an opportunity to meet her. She was a very simple woman—all her life she would insist that nothing should be done to deify her. Indeed, she never seemed to take her condition very seriously; but after her death, she was deified against her wishes. Today Bāḷā Sati is a big phenomenon in this region—every third person from Jodhpur would know about her and believe in her miraculous powers. It's important to keep in mind that 'Bāḷā' refers to the village of this sati; her own name is never invoked. She is identified with the village itself.

From these stories, it becomes clear that there are diverse practices of and motivations for sati. While Komalda categorizes all three of the satis described above within the context of 'community', there are different understandings and affirmations of community at work here. Jhumā Sati, for instance, is prepared to take her life in order to protect the village, but not before cursing her own son for disbelieving her integrity, and not before laying down a law that the Muslims in 'the community' will no longer be able to hear the 'āzān'. Gomā Sati has fewer qualifications in her visceral response to the theft of cattle as she cuts her own limbs rather like a bhomiyā, a martyr for the protection of cows. Bāḷā Sati, who is the only sati whom Komalda acknowledges meeting, is far more difficult to 'read', because she consciously allows her life to waste away, after the two men in her life fail to protect her—her husband and adopted son.

At one level, Bāḷā Sati's 'choice' to reject nourishment through food and water calls to mind a ritualistic practice among Jains called 'santhara'. This practice is generally undertaken when a person is dying and has reached a terminal stage; from this point on, he or she will not eat or drink anything till the moment of death. It is believed that when a person takes the vow ('pāchak') of 'santhara', his or her status is transformed from a worldly ('laukik') to an otherworldly ('alaukik') one. At another level, however, Bāḷā Sati's choice to slowly terminate her life cannot be separated to my mind from a very deep, yet inscrutable dimension of subjectivity that defies ready analysis.

In a more critical register, it could be argued that the very enigmas presented by these stories are precisely what enable them to feed patriarchal endorsements of sati at mythological levels. The women described in these stories may not be 'pativratās' (faithful wives) in a conventional sense, but they represent exemplary models of courage and endurance in their seemingly innate capacity to sacrifice themselves 'voluntarily'. And yet, can I deny the difficulties in assessing this much-mythologized 'voluntarism'? For the first time in listening to Komalda, I sense a schism between the 'folk' and the 'contemporary' through his inability to link these stories around sati with the actual practice of 'widow-immolation' in contemporary times.[4] *Keeping in mind highly politicized figures like Roop Kanwar, I cannot deny that it is hard to listen to 'stories' that don't seem to address the dimension of violence, either against women in general, or against satis in particular.*

At the same time, it is also possible to read in Komalda's sati stories a value-system that is not easily accommodated within the framework of modernity. Without valorizing this non-modern belief system as providing the foundations for an 'authentic' Indian [Hindu] identity, against 'modernity, westernization and materialism',[5] *it would be useful to listen to more of these stories if only to complicate the historical evidence surrounding sati today. In the story that follows, Komalda provides a very different instance of a sati, whose story has been claimed by a traditional musician community for its own sustenance.*

Rāni Bhaṭiyāṇi and the Manganiyars

Let me tell you a story in this regard around the legendary figure of Rāni Bhaṭiyāṇi. She was married to Kalyan Singh, but it was rumoured that she was close to her younger brother-in-law, Sawai Singh. Both the brothers went off to fight a battle, and in the fight Sawai Singh was killed. However, Kalyan Singh sent a message home to his wife stating that *he* had been killed, whereupon Rāni Bhaṭiyāṇi decided to become a sati. Finally, when Sawai Singh's turban was brought home, it became clear to everyone that he had died, and that Kalyan Singh was very much alive. At this point Rāni Bhaṭiyāṇi became a sati but with the younger brother of her husband.

Today she is worshipped in Jasol as Rāni Bhaṭiyāṇi, since she was from the Bhāṭi community, but she is also known by other names. In Jaisalmer, for instance, she is worshipped as Bhuāsā—'*bhuā*' being the name for father's sister. Originally, Rāni Bhaṭiyāṇi came from Jaisalmer, and therefore she is regarded as a daughter of that city. There are hundreds of Rāni Bhaṭiyāṇi shrines all over western Rajasthan and Gujarat—practically every third village will have one such shrine, around which you are bound to find a bhopā coming into trance, with a large number of worshippers from the musician caste groups. In Jaisalmer, the Manganiyars attend the shrine of Rāni Bhaṭiyāṇi; in Jasol, the Ḍholis, another musician caste, attend the shrine, and indeed, in many other parts of Rajasthan, Rāni Bhaṭiyāṇi is *alive*. Her shrines are very active, with musicians from different caste groups singing devotional songs (*oḷakh*) in her name. Hundreds of pilgrims seek out Rāni Bhaṭiyāṇi's mediation to resolve their problems, particularly in relation to physical disabilities of various kinds.

There is an interesting story to this legend that attempts to explain how the Manganiyars owe their allegiance to Rāni Bhaṭiyāṇi. It appears that after she became a sati, one Manganiyar came to her in-laws's place in Jasol to seek his *bhati*, which is a traditional payment that is made to Manganiyars from the families into which their patron's daughters get married. The details of the story are unclear, but it seems that this Manganiyar was sent off by Rāni Bhaṭiyāṇi's in-laws to search for her on a palace up the hill.[6] On the way, the Manganiyar encountered an apparition of Rāni Bhaṭiyāṇi who gave him her jewellery, while instructing him specifically not to return to her in-law's household. The Manganiyar, however, broke his promise thinking that he would be able to get even more money from the family. Predictably, they drove him away after taking away all the jewellery. Once again, on his way back home, the Manganiyar encountered the spirit of Rāni Bhaṭiyāṇi, who accused him of breaking his word: 'Why did you go to their place? I would have done everything for your community.' However, she also added: 'Never mind, you lost what I had gifted you, but now the Manganiyars can earn their living by singing songs (oḷakh) at my shrine, and through this service, I will support them.' This tradition continues to this day, as a large number of Manganiyars continue to earn their livelihood by singing songs in Rāni Bhaṭiyāṇi's honour.

There are a few facts that we can draw from this story. One, the status of Rāni Bhaṭiyāṇi as a sati has been linked with her patronage of the Manganiyars, who regard her as one of their chief patrons. But it should also be remembered that Rāni Bhaṭiyāṇi is not just a sati, she is also a pitrāṇi, the first wife of a man who marries again, and whose malignant spirit has to be appeased. It appears that after Rāni Bhaṭiyāṇi died, her husband Kalyan Singh married for the second time. When Rāni Bhaṭiyāṇi began to trouble her in-law's family as a malignant spirit (pitrāṇi), the situation became so intolerable that the entire family had to leave Jasol and settle in Balotara. Eventually, they were able to return to Jasol but only after a temple had been built in her honour, following which her spirit was appeased.

Once again, through the multiple levels of this story, one can see how traditional communities can claim particular shrines in order to perform ritual services, on the basis of which they can earn a living. This right to worship is viewed as a gift, which becomes all the more striking when one considers that the Manganiyars are Muslims serving at a Hindu shrine—a sign of a syncretic form of worship which exists in other parts of Rajasthan as well.

With the story of Rāni Bhaṭiyāṇi, we move from the psychological dimensions of sati as a form of self-sacrifice to more material considerations in which sati seems almost like a pretext for other kinds of economic and social transaction. In this particular case, the transaction involves a community of traditional musicians, the

Manganiyars. How exactly the legend of the Manganiyar meeting Rāni Bhaṭiyāṇi got 'invented' and disseminated is not clear. But even as the legend intensifies through multiple and often conflicting versions, the history surrounding Rāni Bhaṭiyāṇi's death become increasingly more obscure. This, as some critics of sati would argue, is one of the central tropes around which the larger narrative of sati is built. Its 'reality' is both generated and consolidated through fiction—not merely heroic but romantic tales. Let us examine two such fragments of romance.

The Romance of Sati

Another sati widely worshipped in Rajasthan today who comes to mind is Ḍhoḷan Sati. What is her story? It appears that a Ḍholi woman was once passing through a forest in the Aravalli hills with her husband. Three or four men waylaid the couple and attempted to molest this beautiful woman. Her husband fled in terror leaving her with no protection whatsoever. Meanwhile, another man, a Rajput, arrived on the scene riding on a horse, and seeing the woman being molested, began to fight the assailants. In the struggle, he died, and the Ḍholi woman decided to become a sati with this man. Today she is worshipped every year in a massive *mela* (religious fair) that is held in her honour near Raipur in Pali district. There is also a Sādh Sati in Ṛās-baḅra, whose story is somewhat similar. She too did not cremate herself on her husband's pyre, but died for another man.

Yet another story, this time of an entire community tracing its origins to a sati, can be linked to the Surānā, a sub-caste group of my own community, the Oswāl Jains. The story of this group revolves around a beautiful girl from Nagaur, who attracted the attention of a Mughal *subedar*, or military official. Even though she was betrothed to someone else, he tried to put pressure on her to marry him. So she challenged him, promising that she would attach herself to him if he could catch her. In the climactic event of the story, it appears that as the subedar was hunting her down, just at the critical moment when he was about to catch her, the woman from Nagaur mysteriously disappeared into a tree, where she became a sati. Even today the Surānā regard this tree as a shrine commemorating their origins.

In both these stories there is 'another man' involved. In the first case, Ḍhoḷan Sati dies for a man, significantly upper-caste (Rajput), who attempts to protect her honour when her husband abandons her. In the second case, the 'other man' (ostensibly from another religious community) is the abductor himself, who ultimately fails to catch the woman as she disappears into a tree. While the 'voluntarism' of Ḍhoḷan Sati in taking her life would seem to be self-directed, the second example is clearly marked by supernatural mediation. Finally, while Ḍhoḷan Sati is married, the other sati remains single.

How does one read the 'idealization' of honour and love in such stories? The feminist theorists Sudesh Vaid and Kumkum Sangari (1991) do not quite answer this question as they encounter one such romance during their rigorous fact-finding investigation following the 'immolation' of Om Kunwar in Jharli village of Sikar district in 1980. The villagers of Jharli tell Sangari and Vaid that only one other case of 'widow immolation' had taken place in their village 'about 200 years ago.' And this incident is commemorated in a small memorial which tells a story of 'adolescent love', involving 'an unmarried *girl of the Gujar caste [who] is supposed to have immolated herself for an Ahir youth.'*[7] *While brushing aside the 'idealization' of such romantic tales, Sangari and Vaid have little to say about the structures of belief, ideology, and consent contained in the folklore surrounding such tales, even as they prioritize the 'hard facts' relating to caste, economy, and patriarchy in their exacting social scientist analysis. Perhaps the subtle hegemony of folk romance could be one of the most tenacious components in consolidating the 'belief' in sati itself, precisely because it does not appear to be ideological.*[8]

Conditions of Sati

There are satis who are worshipped neither in the family in which they are born, nor in the family into which they have been married. Some satis are not worshipped at all. Significantly, there is no report whatsoever of the satis from royal and jāgirdār families ever being worshipped. I should make it clear at this point that I am referring specifically to the effects of the primogeniture inheritance laws in these families, which ensure the unconditional right of the eldest son in the family to inherit everything. Of course, he is free to share this inheritance with his brothers and other relatives, if he so desires.

When a king died in one of these royal families, or more critically, when he was defeated in battle, it is well known that any number of women would throw themselves on his funeral pyre in a collective form of sati known as *jauhar*. Not all of them were *rānis* (queens)—they were *pardāyats*, *badarans*, *bhagtans*, among other female consorts, entertainers, musicians and companions of the king. When they would cremate themselves along with the body of the king, who would have the responsibility of worshipping them? The king's family? No, they were from other caste groups. Their own families? No, they had broken ties with their own kin and entered into non-marital relationships. The fact is that there was no public worship for these satis, because they were not deified. They never entered what I would call 'the worship mode'. This would apply to the most legendary of all satis from the royal family, Rāni Padmini herself, around whom many stories have proliferated, but is she worshipped? The answer is no.

Why do some satis enter the 'worship mode' while others do not? Take the case of Sugan Kanwar from Jodhpur, who could be described as a post-Independence sati. An educated woman, she was the wife of a brigadier, Jabar Singh. When he died, she became a sati, after which she continued to manifest herself to different people in and around Jodhpur. It is said that it was through her intervention alone that the city was protected during the first Indo-Pakistani War in 1965, when many bombs were dropped in the Jodhpur area. Only Jodhpur prison was damaged during the bombing and a few people died, but the rest of the city was left untouched, all because Sugan Kanwar allegedly would catch the bombs in her hand before they dropped, and throw them outside the populated areas of the city. This was the kind of myth that spread during the war. I remember how often this story would be repeated, whenever we would hear the Pakistani planes flying in our air space.

Sugan Kanwar would be a good example of the public worship of sati, as opposed to the family worship of sati, which I spoke about earlier. In both cases a process of deification takes place, even though in the first place the dissemination is much wider, and in the second case it is restricted to a particular family. The worship of a particular sati will depend to a large extent on what provokes her to take her life in the first place. As we have already described the situations represented by Jhumā Sati, Gomā Sati, and Bāḷā Sati, a woman may decide to become a sati for reasons that are related not to her individual family, but to the larger community. But whether the essential relationship of the sati is to family or to community, the point is that she has to manifest herself in the lives of people after her death either through dreams or miracles attributed to her.[9] Without these signs, there can be no sati in worship.

Actually there are signs that prefigure the actual event of sati, notably the manifestation of *sat*. This *sat* ['essence of purity'] refers to a very specific type of feeling that seizes a woman before she commits sati.[10] *Sat ānā, sat uṭhnā*—these expressions indicate that the *sat* 'comes' (*ānā*) to a woman, or it 'rises' (*uṭhnā*) within a woman. In fact, the community surrounding the woman does not immediately accept the authenticity of the woman's feeling when it first manifests itself. Rather, she is tested through certain kinds of rituals. One common practice is to melt indigo-dye (nīl) into some water and throw it on the woman; if she is dissembling, then the so-called *sat* within her will subside. Only when the people are convinced that hers is a genuine *sat* will they proceed with the preparations for the sati event. Then she will be made to wear her bridal clothes, adorned with ornaments and jewellery, and taken in a procession with drums following the bier (*arthi*) on which her husband's body is placed. In the funeral pyre (*chitā*) she is generally shown seated with her husband's head resting on her lap, and when the pyre is lit it has to be witnessed by at least one Chāraṇ. At least this was the case in older days, as I learned from my friend Narayan Singh Sandu, whom I have earlier mentioned—he told me that as a child he had been made to witness one such sati. The evidence provided by a Chāraṇ is traditionally considered necessary for assessing the authenticity of sati.

What Komalda is presenting here, it could be argued, is a very normative and essentialized reading of the 'sati' event, which totally contradicts his earlier stories, in which there would appear to be many different kinds of sati. Here the sati is once again reduced to the heroic figure of the widow burning on her husband's funeral pyre. Needless to say, every single detail of the 'evidence' surrounding the manifestation of 'sat' leading to the burning of the pyre can be read within the context of coercion, if not deliberate mystification. In this regard, the actual struggle and desperate resistance of 'satis' like Roop Kanwar of Deorala, for instance, are now well established, even as their murder is apotheosized with all the devotional fervour attesting a miraculous event.[11]

Likewise, on the mechanics of deification in contemporary India, there can be little doubt about the intricate collusions of family, local priests, religious institutions, fundamentalist organizations, temple bureaucracies, and big business houses primarily from the Marwari community, in contributing to the lucrative industry around sati. On these matters, Komalda is keenly aware—the Jai Santoshi Ma phenomenon, after all, is centered in Jodhpur.[12] *But tellingly, he does not address it at all, as much as I try to integrate it in our discussion. Neither is the massive phenomenon surrounding Rāni Sati pursued, even though Komalda acknowledges in passing its links with the Agarwal community and its diverse capitalist affiliations on an all-India basis.*[13]

Instead of pushing the obvious theoretical issues relating to the commodification of religion, promoted by new technologies and the vested interests of upper-caste communities, with growing communal agendas, I realize that it is best to address Komalda more directly on these matters. So, finally, in our last discussion on the subject, I asked him: 'How do you see the manifestations of sati today, *as represented by figures like Roop Kanwar?' He responded with these exact words: 'It's a hysteric situation created by society.' 'Who or what is creating the hysteria?' I asked. And promptly, he said: 'The Hindu social value system.' At this point, I dared to insert a key word, 'Patriarchal?' 'Definitely patriarchal,' Komalda emphasized. But at the same time it is clear that Komalda does not see sati as an exclusively patriarchal phenomenon, as the following statement testifies.*

Enigmas of Sati

For me the individual circumstances that compel a woman to become a sati are very important. Only on the basis of these circumstances can we come to some conclusion regarding the event. Even if we accept that there is tremendous pressure being put on women in general by patriarchal society, what is it that makes that *one* woman out of thousands become a sati? Yes, we can turn to disputes relating to property and dowry—these can provide a certain kind of evidence. But there are other cases that are much harder to comprehend. I know of at least one such case in recent times where a sati—I would not like to mention her name, because this could create problems—was all her life totally unfaithful to her husband and everyone knew it. Even he knew about her numerous affairs and would acknowledge them to his close friends. And yet, on his death, she became a sati. What do we make of this?

To my mind we need to look into all aspects of different kinds of sati in order to arrive at a clearer perspective on the overall phenomenon. Rāni Bhaṭiyāṇi, Ḍhoḷan Sati, Gomā Sati, Bāḷā Sati provide us with individual histories that are not addressed in the more abstracted perspective on sati which we encounter in sati songs sung only by women in all-night *rātijāgā* sessions, following birth, marriage, and death.[14] Here the satis invoked in the song are linked to larger rituals, symbols, and ceremonial details. They tend to focus on an iconographic description of different parts of the sati's apperarance, costume, accoutrements, as well as on her adventures. Against the generalized rhetoric of these songs, we need to acknowledge that each sati story carries its own nuances. There is a Rajasthani proverb that is well worth recalling in this regard —*Sati Mātā, thāne kai dīse*? (Mother Sati, what do you see?). Basically, she acknowledges three things: *Mhāro pati mar gyo, mhe bālu, mhāra ṭābria ruḷtā dīse* (My husband is dead, I'm burning, and I can see my children crying). The situation described in this proverb applies to many satis, but their individual contexts are remembered in different ways.

On a more personal note, I think of my own wife Indira, who has an enormous respect for sati and is all praise for it. If I ask her in jest, '*Mere marne per sati hone ko taiyār ho*? (After I die, will you become a sati?), it is very interesting that she won't say 'no' outright. On the contrary, her response is more likely to be, '*Hamāre aise bhāgya kahān hai*?' (Are we that fortunate?)

At this point, Komalda cracks up and laughs. I think he realizes the total absurdity of the situation. That something so unquestionably oppressive as sati can be addressed not through outright denial or opposition, but through a kind of wish-fulfilment, is what makes Indiraji's comment so unconsciously ironic in its caustic matter-of-factness. However, her comment is also telling in so far as it testifies that sati is not necessarily within the orbit of every woman's choice. For her, it would seem to be a matter of destiny, if not divine privilege. But clearly this is not the only response to the subject, as is evident from the subaltern responses of a wide range of low-caste rural women in Rajasthan, who have no illusions that pro-sati attitudes are also 'anti-woman.'[15]

Woman as Witch

This brief session which followed immediately after Komalda's somewhat scattered comments on sati takes the subject of women's oppression into a different direction—one of Komalda's many strange, yet oddly cogent connections that makes the act of listening to him so riveting. As always, the history underlying this connection is not substantiated, but it poses a significant provocation. Following the official ban on sati by the British in 1829, intensified by all kinds of social reforms on an all-India basis, Komalda claims that there was increasing pressure on the princely states and jāgirdārs in Rajasthan to control the occurrence of sati. In reality, acts of sati intensified as a consequence of the colonial legislation, which for some critics is linked to the epistemic violence inherent in the imposition of an 'enlightened' western law.

A more provocative conjecture put forward by Komalda is that the campaign against sati coincided with the opposition to local practices of witchcraft. A woman branded as a witch represented the reverse side of the apotheosis of woman as sati.

By the late nineteenth century, even while women were burning themselves on their husbands' funeral pyres, witches were being killed and lynched practically all over India in large numbers. Almost every village had a story to tell about a woman who had been lynched mercilessly. It was believed that a witch could not be shot or killed by a sword; she had to be axed, or else, she had to be hung on a tree upside down and burned to death with a fire containing chilli. Such myths circulating around the witch were rampant, and they continue to this day.

But before proceeding, let us be a little precise here about our use of words. Instead of using the word 'witch', which connotes many things, it would perhaps be better for us to stick to the Hindi word '*ḍāyan*', or the more popular usage in Rajasthani, '*ḍākan*'. This is how a woman suspected of witchcraft, or of black magic, would be identified by villagers in common parlance. A ḍākan is always a living woman, quite unlike a *chuṛēl*, a dead woman who manifests herself as an evil force. It is believed that a ḍākan has the capacity to harm others by the evil eye, the evil word, or sometimes by simply praising anything. Take, for instance, this microphone into which I'm speaking. A ḍākan could say, 'Oh, what a beautiful microphone', and it would be in pieces the very next moment. Another belief surrounding the ḍākan is that she consumes children's livers (*kalejā*). If many children happen to die in a village, it is assumed that a ḍākan may be operating there, and this assumption very often leads to a general consensus in the village community that such-and-such woman is a ḍākan and should be killed.

In our own times, whenever we read in the newspaper that a woman has been killed with an axe, we can be sure that she had been marked as a ḍākan. This is the case not only in Rajasthan, but in Gujarat, Maharashtra, and in other states of India as well. Since the public lynching and killing of ḍākans are no longer possible without legal consequences, they tend to take place very secretly in the interior of remote villages. Most of these killings are not even reported. But if you go the villages and win the confidence of the people living there, you can ask them, '*Yahān koi ḍākan hai*? (Are there any ḍākans here?), and you can be sure that some will be identified. Of course, none of these women would identify themselves as ḍākans, which raises the difficult question: how can we be sure about their role?

When I was studying this phenomenon, I would ask the villagers: When these women come in your presence, what do you do? And I found out that even if the woman asked for a very simple thing, like water, for example, all the people around her would start running to get her water, just to keep her happy. If she happened to pass by someone's house and saw the woman of the house, say, cleaning the rice, or stitching something, she would only have to make a casual remark about these activities and she would be presented with rice or a new piece of cloth. The basic response of the villagers, I realized, was to placate her and keep her happy at all costs, and not to allow their children to be anywhere near her.

How does a woman become a ḍākan? Most people in the village acknowledge that they don't know. However, I have come across some involuntary practices by which women get initiated as ḍākans. An existing ḍākan, for instance, could ask a woman in the village to listen to one of her stories, while providing the *hunkāra*—the response to a story through onomatopoeic sounds ('hu', 'ha', 'hmm', and so on). On finishing the story, the ḍākan will tell the *hunkārio* (respondent), '*Jaisi main hun, vesi tu ho jā*' (Just as I am, so you become). At this point, the woman feels compelled to take on the role of the ḍākan and proceed with her life accordingly.

Another source of initiation arises when any woman wears the discarded clothes of a ḍākan after her death. These are involuntary practices in so far as the initiated do not actually choose to become ḍākans; they are accidentally initiated into believing that they have become so. Of course, there are other folk Tantric practices in which ḍākans play on fears, by throwing grains, or seed, or chilli on people's bodies, or by making an effigy of a person's body out of flour and sticking pins into it, or by chanting mantras, and so on.

It's important, I think, to differentiate these very local practices and beliefs from the more ritualized forms of initiation into cults. There are, for instance, some particularly secret rites that revolve around the figure of Hanuman. Here I am not referring to the familiar monkey-god deity, Dās Hanuman from the Ramayana, the great bhakta of Rama who serves him unconditionally. I am referring to the totally different figure of Vīr Hanuman or Mahavīr Hanuman. 'Vīr' here does not mean 'brave', it does not connote a warrior. Rather it refers to the well-known saying *bāvān vīr chosaṭh joganiā*. This literally refers to fifty-two male malignant spirits (*vīr*) and sixty-four female malignant spirits (*joganiā*). And who is the owner and master of all these spirits? Hanuman himself. The spirits are malignant and can harm people when they possess individuals dabbling in black arts and magic, but ultimately the practitioners have to humble themselves before Hanuman and seek his blessings.

How do these practitioners assume the power of these spirits? The rituals are at once secretive and well established. It appears that people who aspire to empower themselves through these vīrs and joganiās have to go nine or eleven times to a Hanuman shrine on Tuesday night after midnight. The shrine is generally situated outside of the precincts of any village, and it is mandatory that the worshippers should go to this shrine alone and return alone. After these nocturnal visits, week after week, the worshipper has to strip himself of all his clothes, and in this naked state, embrace the figure of Hanuman, after adorning it with garlands and *sindur* (vermilion). When he completes this ritual practice, it is assumed that the worshipper acquires one vīr, which he is in a position to use for any malignant purpose of his choice. If he wishes to acquire yet another vīr, he has to re-embark on the same ritual process again.

Now what is significant about this process, as opposed to the initiation of a ḍākan, is that it is voluntary, even if the practices involved are secretive. A ḍākan, however, has the possibility of evolving from someone who has been initiated against her will, into a different kind of being. From being maligned as a woman capable of doing only bad things to the people around her, she can become respected for her knowledge of the past. It is believed that if a ḍākan does not harm anyone and keeps her power intact, she is capable of becoming a *siyāri*. In this state, she has the capacity to look into at least six months of a person's past life.

Despite this concession, I would say that in the final analysis all these manifestations of women—ḍākan, sati, pitrāṇi—are linked to some notion of an essentially impure, if not malignant, power that is specifically attached to women. In its extreme manifestations, possession of this power only serves to denigrate women. Let us be very clear that, in the case of the ḍākan, it is not the woman who identifies herself as such; others in the community mark her as a ḍākan. Of course, there have been cases where women who have been suppressed within their families have *pretended* to be ḍākans, and mind you, they can wield an enormous power in this state.[16] So falsehood can be used as a technique of empowerment, and it can be effective for some women at least.

For the most part, however, I would have to say that that the branding of women as ḍākans only serves to demean them. It is not insignificant in this regard that when you ask villagers to actually name the ḍākans in their village, invariably you will find that they will name the ḍākans by caste, and they are usually from the lowest of castes including the most downtrodden sections of society. Upper-caste women are rarely marked as ḍākans, but it is the poorest of the poor who get branded in this way, as women with malignant powers.

This succinct section reveals to me that Komalda is at his best when he reports or generalizes on certain phenomena on the basis of intensive fieldwork. Despite its skeletal framework, the comments here on the 'ḍākan' reveal some concrete aspects of her process of initiation, branding, and caste-ing. Here, unlike in the sati section, Komalda tells no stories about 'ḍākans' as such, even though the loosely assembled facts resemble the raw material for an ethnographic fiction. The focus is on the context of superstitions in Rajasthani rural cultures in which the 'ḍākan' is perceived, and indeed, 'constructed'. Unlike in the sati section, where the tricky issue of 'voluntarism' was not fully confronted, it is clear that the 'ḍākan' is not self-identified, but named and marked by others.

7
WOMEN'S SONGS

It is one thing to listen to songs, it is quite another matter to transcribe them into words on a printed page. Towards the end of this chapter, we will provide the texts of four songs, which will reveal different modes and strategies of transcription. Instead of agonizing about the inevitable failure to translate the musicality of songs into words, it would be more useful to focus on what can be said about them by way of content, social context, vocabulary, and textual improvisation.[1] *Komalda's comments in relation to these areas of inquiry are particularly precise. Without any jargon derived from ethnomusicology, still less any postmodern 'thick description' on 'the grain of the voice', he spells out some recurring characteristics that he has encountered in his own listening of women's songs over the years. While the observations are made in a matter-of-fact way, their precision is illuminating.*

After Independence

When we talk about women's songs, we are not just addressing the songs sung by women at different social gatherings related to childbirth, marriage, birthdays, or singing sessions organized by 'ladies *sangeet*' (as they are called), we are calling attention to those songs that have been composed by women themselves. For centuries women have been expressing themselves through language and music in these songs—songs from which we can learn about how they see the world, both the outer world and their own inner worlds. These songs reveal that women are not just 'preservers of tradition', as they have been made out to be, most frequently by men. Rather, they are composers in their own right.

Historically, however, this is not readily recognized. And the reason for this is that since Independence, we have actually seen a mass withdrawal of women from participating in professional women's groups, at least in the rural sectors. This is certainly true of the Damāmi group, which, at one time, used to be dominated by women singers. The men were merely their accompanists. Today they are rarely heard in public, though some of the women from this group are beginning to work as music teachers in schools. The Ḍholi women have also been affected because their men have prevented them from singing in public. Today there is just one Ḍholi group from the town of Nagar near Barmer where the women have started singing on a regular basis. It is the same story with the Manganiyars, whose women used to play an active role in the singing of ceremonial songs in the homes of their jajmāns (patrons), particularly during weddings.[2] Today there are only three professional Manganiyar women singers, notably the disabled Rukmabai, who has managed to resist the male domination of the field by singing in public both at home and abroad. But she is an exception.

It could be asked why we are seeing this decline in the participation of professional women's singing groups. One reason could be that the men in these communities have come to regard singing in public as a low-caste activity that unavoidably demeans the social status of the community itself. It is assumed that the prospect of women travelling to other places and performing for other men can only increase the possibilities of scandal for the family and a subsequent decrease in social prestige for the family itself. And yet, it is interesting to point out that even as we are seeing a mass withdrawal of women folk singers from the Damāmi, Ḍholi, Manganiyar, and Nagārchi groups, we are seeing a simultaneous rise in the participation of women from middle-class and upper-caste groups. These women sing their own versions of 'folk' songs in public concerts and recitals on radio programmes. So there are two contrary movements at work in the post-Independence period, where, on the one hand, there is an absence of prestige attached to public singing among low-caste women's groups. On the other hand, we are seeing an increase in prestige and heightening of family status for women singers from upper-caste society.

Recurring Features in Women's Songs

I would now like to make some general points on women's songs in Rajasthan, sung both by the professional groups mentioned above and nomadic communities like the Kālbeliā, as well as by non-professional singers like housewives who sing for different kinds of ritual and family occasions. While there are obvious differences in the contexts of these different singing traditions, they do share some common affinities, cutting across caste, class and community.

First of all, it needs to be kept in mind that most women's songs have no fixed beginnings, middles or ends. If, for instance, you record a woman singing a particular song, and you then re-record the same song a couple of hours later, you will find that the sequence of the song is no longer the same. The seventh line could become the third line, the third line could become the thirtieth line, or something like that. So this is one factor that we always have to keep in mind—the sequence of women's songs varies considerably from rendition to rendition.

Secondly, women's songs are rarely, almost never learned by rote, and yet, a woman who may never have heard a particular song earlier can join in after listening to it for a few moments. There are obviously some formulaic images and words within the songs themselves, certain associations and melodic patterns, that facilitate this kind of 'memory'. I will have more to say on this later.

Third, while these songs are never sung solo but are always group compositions, it's important to realize that women rarely have an audience for their songs. They could be singing somewhere in the house, or in the courtyard, but you won't find people listening to them. Now, this raises an interesting question—if the women are not singing for anybody, then for whom are they singing? Themselves? Clearly, they don't wish to 'influence' others through their singing.

This brings us to the fourth point—namely, that in women's songs, the question of creative or musical or textual 'excellence' does not arise. Indeed, if any woman considers herself 'excellent' and tries to sing more brilliantly than the others, then she is not likely to be accepted by the larger group. Individual 'excellence' as opposed to collective expression will not be tolerated.

The cues for group singing are built into the very structure of the songs themselves. Most of the lines are repeated at least twice—so maybe the first time round, only three women will sing a line, but when it is repeated, the whole group of five or ten women could join in. Then also, we need to keep in mind the importance of the refrain in women's songs. Very often these refrains run into entire stanzas, which are repeated over and over again, with perhaps only one word or line changed. This makes it easier for women to follow the song and sing it together.

In this regard, I remember my own wife when she married me at the age of fourteen. She had come to my home-town, Jodhpur, from Shahpura in Mewar state—and I remember how during the ceremonies, when wedding songs from Marwar were sung, she would initially be hesitant to sing because she hadn't heard those songs before. But then, after hearing one or two lines of a song, she would join in as if she had sung that song all her life. And this is not an individual case, but representative of a large body of women's songs and the women singing them.

At a musical level, it has to be noted that whenever there is a group of women singing there will be one woman in the group who leads the song. In Rajasthan she is known as *ugarne wāli*, literally 'the one who leads the song'. Now, how will she be selected? She is certainly not a woman who knows the song better than the others. She is more like a musical instrument, or a pitch-fixer, the one who fixes the basic pitch for the entire group. So, in a particular group of four women aged between seventeen and fifty, say, it is not likely that the seventeen-year-old would be regarded as an ugarne wāli because her pitch would be too high for the older women to sustain. The woman selected will be one whose pitch can accommodate, and in the process, control the pitch of the other women. This selection process is generally worked out among the women themselves; it has nothing to do with seniority as such.

At a more technical level, women's songs are generally structured within a range of four notes. There are of course a few songs that have more complex melodic patterns using more notes, but for the most part, the songs are confined to four notes. When we look into the notation of these songs, however, we find that one of the notes is invariably from a lower octave. So, in essence, the four notes in the songs span two octaves, which accounts for the melodic richness of these songs despite their minimal notational structure.

Thematic Content

Now, if we turn to the thematic content of the songs, we should keep in mind that the women's capacity to memorize songs is activated not only by verbal and musical associations, but through a very intimate knowledge of all the things that constitute the content of these songs. The relationship of women to their inner selves, to each other, as well as the patterns of behaviour in society, the activities of everyday life, nature and environment, animals, trees, the moon and sun—all these aspects of life are part of the subject matter of women's songs. So it is not difficult to conduct research through songs, as many women's organizations are doing, on women and health, women and childcare, women and their rights, and so on.

Sexuality, for instance, is an important part of folk songs, though the content and treatment vary according to different caste groups. Obscenity figures in songs celebrating Holi and in *gāḷi* (literally 'abuse') songs, which are sung during marriage ceremonies, generally to tease the bridegroom's family. Here one can find bold expositions of male-female intimacies and diverse forms of sexual behaviour. The sexual content of songs from low-caste groups is more closely related to everyday life. Here it is not just specific sexual encounters that matter, but the very connection of sexuality with the bodies of women as expressed in their clothing, gestures, and social customs. Take the practice of breast-feeding a child, for instance. In upper-caste society, women do not feed their children openly; their bodies have to be concealed. But in low-caste and tribal contexts, it is perfectly normal for a woman to feed her child by exposing her breast in a public space. There is no shame attached to this whatsoever, as indeed there is no condemnation of what could be branded as promiscuity and polygamy in middle-class Hindu society.[3]

Many women's songs deal indirectly with issues relating to health care. I say 'indirectly' because any song as such merely presents a description of a particular situation, using figurative language. Our task is to unearth the real meanings underlying the poetry, so that the songs can function as a window to society at large. For example, there are a number of songs dealing with pregnancy, during which time women yearn to eat certain foods. A woman may want to eat *imli* (tamarind) or *keri* (raw mango) in the song, but in real life, it is very likely that she could crave for much baser substances like *miṭṭi* (clay) or *koylā* (coal). There are any number of cravings and rejections that need to be taken into account when interpreting, say, a song dealing with a woman's pregnancy. Once again, we have to make the necessary correspondences by relating the song back to what is actually happening in the everyday lives of women. There can be no literal reading of a song as such.

Very popular among women's songs are a large number dealing with spices such as *sūnṭh* (dry ginger), *dhaniā* (coriander), *jīrā* (cumin) and *ajmā* (ajwain). In fact, there must be at least thirty to forty songs dealing specifically with ajmā, the spice given to women during pregnancy and post-natal health care. There's a whole culture that is evoked in the ajmā songs, which describes how it is bought from particular shops, how it is cleaned, pounded, mixed with ghee, cooked, and eventually served to women. Note that, though a song could focus on a mother, it is not the mother who sings the song but the women around her, who celebrate the joys and trials of motherhood. In some of the songs, the situation becomes more explicit as the pregnant woman attempts to conceal her birth-pangs. She does not want other women in the neighbourhood to hear her cries and be troubled, or else she doesn't want to be obliged to them. In such cases, the woman turns to her husband to buy ajmā from the market to alleviate her pains.

In other songs relating to childbirth, a woman starts complaining that she has a pain, but she doesn't want to acknowledge its link with childbirth. So others are compelled to question her: Are your eyes giving you trouble? Do you have a toothache? Do you have cramps in your legs? Finally, she reveals to her husband, '*Mhāro pēṭ ghas mas dukhe.*' Now this is a very specific expression, quite different from other expressions like '*pēṭ dukhnā*' (stomach pain), '*pēṭ me maroḍā āve*' (literally, 'there are worms in my stomach', referring to spasms), or '*pēṭ me ghad ghad hove*' (rumbling in the stomach). When the woman says '*ghas mas pēṭ dukhno*', you can be sure that it refers to the birth of a child.

Now, terms like these are known at very local levels; they get interwoven with other formulaic things, which have a logic of their own, and together they constitute the meaning of the song. Very often there are chains of associations through elaborations on a particular category—for instance, in dealing with kinship ties included in welcome songs (*badhāwo*), the song can include everyone in the family, but in order of seniority. In one particular example of this genre, a woman welcomes all members of the family during a wedding ceremony, beginning with her father (*bāp*). She then moves on to acknowledge her mother (*buji*), elder brother-in-law (*jeṭhji*), elder brother's wife (*bhābhi*), younger brother-in-law (*lālji*), all the way down to the younger sister-in-law (*dhīv*), her husband (*jawāi*), and finally, to the father's second wife (*sauk*), who is there illegally alongside the lawfully wedded wife.

Not only are these categories placed hierarchically in descending order of importance, the similes that are used to describe them also change in poetic content. So, if the more respected members of the family are compared to the 'full moon of the rains', 'cluster of stars', a 'flash of lightning amidst the clouds', the 'glow of the lamp' and so on, the second wife is 'like the shoe of the left foot' (*dāwā pagri mojaṛi*). It should be noted that in actual wedding situations the order of invocations in the song can be re-adjusted depending on the arrival or the presence of a particular person in the family. So, for instance, the singer of the badhāwo (welcoming song) could be singing about the lālji (younger brother-in-law), but if the jawāi (husband of younger sister-in-law) lands up at that time, then the singer could promptly shift from the verse he is singing to the verse celebrating the jawāi's virtues. The references and similes in the song would remain exactly the same, but the placement of the person being referred to would change.[4]

In such songs, where there are lists of relatives, a lot depends on who is included and who is left out. Accordingly, the song either decreases or increases in length. Likewise, there are numerous songs dealing with ornaments, and here there are very specific norms and taboos as to what a child, an unmarried woman, a married woman, and a widow can either wear or cannot wear. All these ornaments reveal the social status of women; they have specific social functions; and more intimately they are all related to particular parts of the human body. For instance, there is this one ornament, the *okhari*, that is worn on the middle part of the ear. The belief is that, when a woman miscarries a number of times, she can free herself of this problem if she wears this particular earring. Now, such minute details enter the text of songs in connection with particular ornaments, and it is very revealing what they suggest about a woman's social status and condition.

For example, in wedding songs where particular ornaments are listed and described in detail, there are specific associations between particular ornaments and the kinship ties of those relatives who make these gifts. So, the *nath* or nose-ring would be associated with the maternal uncle, the *kadā* or thick anklet with the in-law's family, the necklace (*hār*) and bangles (*chuṛiyān*) with the father's side. Who gives what is an important dimension of these songs, which are part of the memory house of women. The ornaments are intricately related to the contexts and social relationships of a given cultural situation, and as such, they have their own inner logic and sequence.

Now, all these songs describing family members or ornaments or spices are structured from stanza to stanza, with each stanza more or less independent. Consequently, there is some kind of jump between the stanzas as the song proceeds. However, in narrative songs, where a particular story unfolds, there is less of a jump because the women have to remember how one stanza is linked to the next in order for the narrative content in the song to develop into a story.

Narrative Songs

Now I would like to describe one song drawing on childbirth customs, but set within the framework of a story. The song I have in mind is entitled *Gūgri*, which refers to a particular kind of Rajasthani food preparation made out of pounded cereal. The custom is that, whenever a male child is born in any Rajasthani family, some gūgri is prepared and a very small quantity is distributed to each of the houses in the neighbourhood and to close relatives in the kin group. This custom is merely a way of saying that 'there's a birth in the family'—an auspicious sign. In this song, a child is born to a woman, the gūgri is prepared, but the woman tells her husband not to give any to her *nanad* (husband's sister). So the husband agrees, but, after distributing the gūgri to all the relations, he feels bad about ignoring his own sister. Finally, he gives into his feelings and presents his sister with some gūgri and returns home. On being questioned by his wife, he is compelled to admit that, 'Yes, I did give gūgri to everyone and I couldn't resist giving some to my sister as well.' His wife becomes enraged and demands that he bring the gūgri back, or else she threatens not to feed the child. The husband has no other choice but to return to his sister and ask for the gūgri back. 'My wife,' as he tries to explain, 'is from another family, and she doesn't understand the relationship between brother and sister.'

At this point, the song presents an interesting problem. Since only a handful of gūgri is normally given to relatives, there is none left in the sister's home. 'My children have eaten it all up,' as she informs her brother. 'But wait,' she says, 'I have a substitute.' She goes to the goldsmith's shop and gets some rice made out of gold and gives it to her brother. 'Here,' she says, 'give this to your wife. Since the gūgri you gave me is already eaten, I can't return it, but take this gold instead.' The husband returns to his wife and presents her with the gold rice, and the song ends there.

Now this is one kind of narrative that one finds in women's songs. It does not mention any particular place, the characters are not named, it's a general type of family situation where the woman leading the song, the ugarne wāli, is free to use her imagination and enlarge the narrative space. What interests me here is to understand why a sister should be debarred from receiving a gift that comes from her own brother. As I see it, this song tells us something very deep about a social custom that we have in Rajasthan—*hānti aur pānti*. Hānti means anything that is given by your own 'hand' to anybody, while pānti refers to succession rights in property. The rule is that a daughter in any Rajasthani household has the right of hānti, but not pānti. So, for instance, every time there is a pūja in my own house, the prasād will be eaten by my daughters. My sons, my sons' wives cannot share it because they have a right in the property, which is debarred to my daughters. Now this kind of context relating to hānti aur pānti comes up in any number of social ceremonies and rituals. So the song that I described earlier tells us that sisters (and sisters-in-law) have rights over certain things, and no rights over others.

Of course, there are different interpretations of the gūgri song—it can be sung in twenty lines, or as many as one hundred lines. It all depends on the women improvizing it, who use their own imagination and musicality to extend the life of the song from one rendition to another. Truly, women do not merely preserve tradition; as I said earlier, they are composers in their own right. There is no better way to pay tribute to their compositions than to listen to some of the songs that follow.

* * *

'Listening to the songs' is perhaps an overstated function of what we are prepared to share with the reader here—a transcription of four songs, two of them with a detailed transliteration of the 'original' Rajasthani vocalization of the song. Note that I use the word 'vocalization' as opposed to 'dictation'—these discriminations will become clear as we proceed with the songs themselves.

The text of the first song 'Rekhaṇ' (Locust), sung by the women from the nomadic Kālbeliā community, has been drawn directly from a tape-recording of the song. On being requested by Komalda to contribute to his 'pashu-pakshi' (animal-bird) song collection, the Kābeliā women spontaneously came up with the selection of 'Rekhaṇ' themselves. Komalda had not heard it before and was struck by its dramatic intensity: a solitary locust, abandoned by her community, is confronted with the task of protecting herself and her children. The transliteration of the song from Rajasthani into English is a verbatim transcription of all the words, expressions, lines, repetitions and refrains in the song, as it was actually sung during that one recording. Needless to say, if the same women had to sing the song again, the lines in the text would be shifted around. But here we have a fairly accurate—and to my mind, tonally and rhythmically sensitive—rendition of the song in words.

Rekhaṇ

Locust

Aṭhe rī uḍiyori rekhaṇ Rohet dhāḍo diyo
From here flew the swarm of locusts and landed at Rohet
Aṭhe ri uḍiyori rekhaṇ Rohet dhāḍo diyo
From here flew the swarm of locusts and landed at Rohet
Thānrā bachhadā ruḷ jāyi rekhaṇ
Your children will be lost and scattered, oh locust
Pari uḍe ni e
Why don't you fly away now?
Thane mārwā ne āyā rekhaṇ
They are coming to kill you, oh locust
Pari uḍe ni e
Why don't you fly away now?
Thane mārwā ne āyā rekhaṇ
They are coming to kill you, oh locust
Pari uḍe ni e
Why don't you fly away now?

Kāndā re khāyegi mūlān re khāyegi
The onions are all eaten, the radishes are all eaten
Khayegi sabki bāḍi
Everybody's vegetable gardens eaten bare
Kāndā re khāyegi mūlān re khāyegi
The onions are all eaten, the radishes are all eaten
Khayegi sabki bāḍi
Everybody's vegetable gardens eaten bare
Mhārā pātalīye pagā ri rekhaṇ
My locust of slender feet
Pari uḍe ni e
Why don't you fly away now?
Mhārā pātalīye pagā ri rekhaṇ
My locust of slender feet
Pari uḍe ni e
Why don't you fly away now?
Thane mārwā ne āyā rekhaṇ
They are coming to kill you, oh locust

Pari uḍe ni e
Why don't you fly away now?
Thānrā bachhaḍā ruḷ jāyi rekhaṇ
Your children will be lost and scattered, oh locust
Pari uḍe ni e
Why don't you fly away now?

Aṭhe ri uḍiyori rekhaṇ Rohet ḍhaḍo diyo
From here flew the swarm of locusts and landed at Rohet
Aṭhe ri uḍiyori rekhaṇ Rohet ḍhaḍo diyo
From here flew the swarm of locusts and landed at Rohet
Mhārā pātalīye pagā ri rekhaṇ
My locust of slender feet
Pari uḍe ni e
Why don't you fly away now?
Mhārā pātalīyā pagā ri rekhaṇ
My locust of slender feet
Pari uḍe ni e
Why don't you fly away now?
Thāre dābariyā naināṇ ri rekhaṇ
For your large eyes, oh locust
Pari uḍe ni e
Why don't you fly away now?
Thāre dābariyā naināṇ ri rekhaṇ
For your large eyes, oh locust
Pari uḍe ni e
Why don't you fly away now?

Kāndā re khāyegi mūlān re khāyegi
The onions are all eaten, the radishes are all eaten
Khāyegi sabki bāḍi
Everybody's vegetable gardens eaten bare
Kāndā re khāyegi mūlān re khāyegi
The onions are all eaten, the radishes are all eaten
Khāyegi sabki bāḍi
Everybody's vegetable gardens eaten bare
Mhārā pātalīyā punchhā ri rekhaṇ
My locust of slender wrists
Pari uḍe ni e

Why don't you fly away now?
Mhāre gulguliye gālān ri rekhaṇ
My locust with round cheeks
Pari uḍe ni e
Why don't you fly away now?
Thānre dābariyā nainān ri rekhaṇ
For your large eyes, oh locust
Pari uḍe ni e
Why don't you fly away now?
Thānrā bachhadā ruḷ jāyi rekhaṇ
Your children will be lost and scattered, oh locust
Pari uḍe ni e
Why don't you fly away now?

Kāndā re khāyegi mūlān re khāyegi
The onions are all eaten, the radishes are all eaten
Khāyegi sabki bāḍi
Everybody's vegetable gardens eaten bare
Kāndā re khāyegi mūlān re khāyegi
The onions are all eaten, the radishes are all eaten
Khāyegi sabki bāḍi
Everybody's vegetable gardens eaten bare
Thānre pātalīye punchhā ri rekhaṇ
For the sake of your slender wrists, locust
Pari uḍe ni e
Why don't you fly away now?
Thānre gulguliye gālan ri rekhaṇ
For the sake of your round cheeks, locust
Pari uḍe ni e
Why don't you fly away now?
Thāne mārwā ne āyā rekhaṇ
They are coming to kill you, oh locust
Pari uḍe ni e
Why don't you fly away now?
Thāne mārwā ne āyā rekhaṇ
They are coming to kill you, oh locust
Pari uḍe ni e
Why don't you fly away now?

Thānrā bachhadā ruḷ jāyi rekhaṇ
Your children will be lost and scattered, oh locust
Pari uḍe ni e
Why don't you fly away now?

The implicit contrast here is between a solitary, abandoned locust, and a swarm of locusts ('fākā'), which is not specifically named or described. The marauders who are out to kill the locust and her children also remain anonymous. However, it's obvious from the feminization of the locust (which is grammatically vivid—'pari *uḍe ni e') that she is being targeted by men. As Komalda puts it, 'She runs the risk of being devoured by men.'*

It is a known fact that Kālbeliās and other nomadic tribal communities eat locusts, which they collect by the sackloads and later fry and eat as snacks. So menacing is the attack of locusts—'itnā jabardast,' as Komalda adds—that the entire sky is darkened, and, within minutes, all the vegetation of a surrounding area can be destroyed. This menace of the 'fākā', therefore, is a given reality within the social context of the song. And yet, the 'rekhaṇ' in question is beautiful—she has 'slender feet' and 'delicate wrists'. As for her 'round' cheeks, we don't have an appropriate English word for 'gulguliyā', but it connotes many things including the shine and glow on chubby cheeks, soft as sponge, which are almost edible, not unlike sweet 'pakoras' made of wheat flour and jaggery called 'gulgulā'.[5]

* * *

Gāḷi

We turn now to a song which falls under the category of 'Gāḷi', which literally means 'abuse', but which applies more generically to a type of teasing and jesting song, which is generally sung during wedding ceremonies, in which, more often than not, the bridegroom's party is subjected to ridicule. Call it the prerogative of the bride's party, but the raillery in question can border on the obscene, including sexual innuendoes and references to male and female genitalia. While the particularly risqué songs are not sung in formal gatherings, there is another kind of 'Gāḷi' song represented here that is more respectably jocular, though the sexual innuendo is not entirely absent.

In this particular song, the butt of ridicule is an ostensibly unmarried male relative ('sagoji') from the in-law's side, whom we refer to as 'in-law' in the translation rather than as 'relative' or 'cousin'. Helter-skelter, he goes around from one shop to another acquiring different things for the wedding ceremony. But all he brings back each time is a 'woman'—more specifically, a doll ('thābak-thaiyān') made of clay, wood, cloth, and gold, respectively. In each case, he is 'left behind', the still unmarried male. Here again the song is translated alongside Rajasthani transliteration into English, including all the repetitions and refrains.

Dauḍiyā sagoji kumhāriyā re giyā thā
Running went the in-law to the potter
Dauḍiyā sagoji kumhāriyā re giyā thā
Running went the in-law to the potter
Miṭṭi re ghaḍ lāi rayā 'thābak-thaiyān' sago yun rahyā
A doll made of clay, he brought back,
Oh in-law! Left where he was!
Miṭṭi re ghaḍ lāi rayā 'thābak-thaiyān' sago yun rahyā
A doll made of clay, he brought back,
Oh in-law! Left where he was!

I miṭṭi re kāin bharoso
How can this clay be trusted?
I miṭṭi re kāin bharoso
How can this clay be trusted?
E chhānṭ paṛe gaḷ jāye rayā, 'thābak-thaiyān' sago yun rahyā
A few drops of water will melt it away, this doll
Oh in-law! Left where he was!
Are, chhānṭ paṛe gaḷ jāye rayā, 'thābak-thaiyān' sago yun rahyā
A few drops of water will melt it away, this doll
Oh in-law! Left where he was!

Dauḍiyā sagoji suthāriyā re giyā thā
Running went the in-law to the carpenter

Dauḍiyā sagoji suthāriyā re giyā thā
Running went the in-law to the carpenter
Lakṛi re ghaḍ laī rayā 'thābak-thaiyān' sago yun rahyā
A doll made of wood, he brought back,
Oh in law! Left where he was!
Are lakṛi re ghaḍ lāī rayā 'thābak-thaiyān' sago yun rahyā
A doll made of wood, he brought back,
Oh in-law! Left where he was!

Iyen lakṛi re kāin bharoso
How can this wood be trusted?
Iyen lakṛi re kāin bharoso
How can this wood be trusted?
E to suḷo paṛe suḷ jāye rayā, 'thābak-thaiyān' sago yun rahyā
It will get infested and rot, this doll
Oh in-law! Left where he was!
E to suḷo paṛe suḷ jāye rayā, 'thābak-thaiyān' sago yun rahyā
It will get infested and rot, this doll
Oh in-law! Left where he was!

Dauḍiyā sagoji abe sonāriyā re giyā thā
Running went the in-law now to the goldsmith
Sonāri ghaḍ lāi rayā 'thābak-thaiyān' sago yun rahyā
A doll made of gold, he brought back,
Oh in-law! Left where he was!
Are, sonāri ri fare ghaḍ lāi rayā 'thābak-thaiyān' sago yun rahyā
A doll made of gold, he brought back again,
Oh in-law! Left where he was!

Are iyen sonā re kāin bharoso
How can this gold be trusted?
Are iyen sonā re kāin bharoso
How can this gold be trusted
Are, chor paṛe lāi jāye rayā, 'thābak-thaiyān' sago yun rahyā
A thief will steal it away, this doll
Oh in-law! Left where he was!
Are, chor paṛe lāi jāye rayā, 'thābak-thaiyān' sago yun rahyā
A thief will steal it away, this doll
Oh in-law! Left where he was!

This is a considerably more tricky song to translate than 'Rekhaṇ'. First of all, there is the problem of figurative vocabulary—what, for example, is the 'thābak-thaiyān' which the man keeps bringing back from the potter, the carpenter, the tailor, and the goldsmith? The expression itself—'thābak-thaiyān'—is onomatopoeic, a nonsense word, suggesting a flighty, flirtatious coquette of sorts. 'Thābak-thaiyān' also connotes movement, and brings to mind earthen dolls whose head and hands and limbs are pivoted in such a way that they can move in different directions, simultaneously. Whatever the connotation of 'thābak-thaiyān', the point is that the lone relative ('sago') from the in-law's side is left without a real woman. All he succeeds in collecting are counterfeit women. And therefore, the somewhat sexist equation of 'woman' with 'doll' is tempered by the fact that the butt of ridicule in this song is the man himself. The ridicule deepens when one considers that this man would inevitably be compared to an actual male relative, in all probability from the bridegroom's party.

Rātijāgā Songs

We now present two songs that are sung during a ceremony called 'rātijāgā'—an all-night singing session that needs to be differentiated from the jāgraṇ, which has come up earlier in the book. The content of the songs in any jāgraṇ, whether it is held for the sanctification of a new house or well or in thanksgiving for an auspicious occasion, is primarily devotional. In such singing sessions the majority of the songs would be 'bhajans' (hymns) composed by Bhakti saints like Kabir and Mirabai and the singers would be men.

In contrast, the rātijāgā ceremony involving women is generally held for three specific occasions—birth, marriage, and death. What is interesting about the rātijāgā songs is that they exist in two independent clusters—one deals with ritualistic figures like the pitar, pitrāṇi, sati, and bhomiyā, whom we have addressed in earlier chapters. However, at some point during the night—and this is particularly true for marriage ceremonies—there is a shift from the ritualistic context of the songs to what could be described as singāru gīt, songs with an erotic theme and idiom.

These erotic songs in the rātijāgā are invariably sung on the first night when the bride and groom are together. Before the bride is brought to the groom's place, a pūja is conducted in honour of the god Ganesh, following which someone in the family sketches a painting on a wall called māyā. This is generally a very rough sketch in turmeric made up of triangles and lines and other icons, which depict the elemental figures of a man and woman symbolically tied together. In earlier days, the bride would be made to sleep all by herself in this room containing the māyā sketch. Today this is not the case, but the rātijāgā ceremony takes place here.

Both the songs represented here—'Moriyo' (Peacock) and 'Jetal De' (the name of the woman around whom the events in the song revolve)—are tales of adultery and violence. Both of them tell stories that challenge orthodox social norms and behaviour in a highly transgressive way. This breaking of rules makes one question whether the songs serve some kind of psychological release for the women singing them. However, it should also be pointed out that these songs are not always sung in their entirety, and their content is often glossed over in the desultory singing that characterizes the actual performance of rātijāgās today. So, the 'transgression' that I am pointing out is perhaps more vivid in reading these songs, than in actually listening to them in their performative context.[6]

Since these are narrative poems, I won't attempt to summarize their stories, but will leave you to read how their stories unfold in a balladic form. What is presented here is simply the English translation of both poems, and not their transliterations. Not only are the songs rather long, the translations presented here are based on literary transliterations (in Hindi and Rajasthani) of the songs, rather than any attempt to capture their musical sense. In this sense, they are different in their presentation from the transcriptions of 'Rekhaṇ' and 'Gāḷi' represented earlier.

Moriyo (Peacock)

The Rajasthani text of 'Moriyo' was transliterated by Komalda's colleague Vijay Dan Detha into Devanāgari script and rendered into Hindi on the basis of a dictation *of the song that was made to him by his relative Chiman Dan Detha's wife, Sayar Kanwar.*[7] *It appears that she had learned this song in her native place in Rojas, before she left for the village of Borunda to get married at the age of nine. While Vijay Dan is meticulous in capturing the narrative, his version in Hindi is essentially a 'poetic' rendering of the song, and not, as Komalda emphasizes, a rendering of the actual 'chhand' of the song. To capture the 'chhand' one needs not just the metrical and stanzaic arrangement of the song, but its actual breathing pattern, repetitions, refrains, and expressions made during the act of singing. Whenever transcripts of songs are made on the basis of a dictation, rather than on a recorded version of the song, this is the inevitable outcome. Having made these qualifications, here is a fairly literal English translation of 'Moriyo' (Peacock). Note that the two sisters-in-law mentioned in the first lines of the poem are the nanad (husband's sister) and the bhojāi (brother's wife).*

Moon, O moonlit night
Two sisters-in-law set out to fetch water.
They go, go to the big pond
Keep the pitchers on the bank
Hang the pitcher rings on tender jasmine boughs
Wander here and there through the meadow
Pluck tender stems to brush their teeth.
Rub and wash their feet
Rub, shining bright, the ivory armlets,
Rub and wash their hands
Brush their thirty-two beautiful pearl-like teeth.
A radiant peacock sits at the edge of the pond
Opening its wings, it canopies the pond.

'O Indra's peacock, move aside a little,
Let me wash and fill the pitcher.'
'O lovely maiden, unveil your beautiful face first,
Then wash and fill your pitcher.'
'No, dear peacock, the veil shall not open,
It unveils only in the pleasure palace
It unveils only in the cloud palace.'

'Look, oh husband's sister, behold the beauty of the peacock.
He is twice as handsome as your brother.'

'Go, O sister-in-law, follow the peacock,
I shall marry my brother to the beautiful young lass from the fortress.'
'Take, O sister-in-law, my colourful sash,
But do not go and tell your brother.'
'Burn and set fire to your colourful sash
But I shall certainly go and tell my brother.'
'O sister-in-law, take my jewelled necklace
But do not tell your brother.'
'Burn and set fire to your jewelled necklace
But I shall certainly tell my brother.'

In front strutted the peacock
Closely followed by the princess of the fortress.
Step by step strutted the peacock to the forest
Followed by the princess of the fortress.

'O my unfortunate brother,
Spread the carpet and sit on it
For your lady has crossed the mountains
To live with the peacock.'
'Liar, O sister, do not lie,
My wife is in the pleasure palace
My wife is in the cloud palace.'
'Go brother, go and look in the pleasure palace
Go, O brother, and search the cloud palace,
There fly the crows and swoop the eaglets.'
The brother went to the palaces only to find crows and eaglets.

One hundred and fifty horses and riders
One hundred and fifty set out on foot.
Step by step with the peacock
To the forest trailed the princess of the fortress.
All of them entered the garden.
The radiant peacock sitting on a bough,
The princess resting against a tree trunk.
Stretching the arrow on the bow, the prince killed the peacock.
The prince hid the peacock.

'O fair woman, clean, roast, and sizzle this meat
Together we shall sit and eat.

Serve, serve it in a jewelled bowl.'
The prince and his fair princess sat down to eat.
'O queen, you followed the peacock,
Now why are you eating its sweet meat?'

Mad, mad, the princess went mad with anger.
She threw the jewelled bowl into the yard.
'Go, O maid, go to the printer's market,
Get printed on my veil, the radiant peacock.
Go, O maid, go to the goldsmith's shop
Get carved on my head-ornament the radiant peacock.
Go, O maid, go to the engraver's shop
And get tattooed on my eyes the radiant peacock.'

The central motif of the poem involves eating the meat of one's beloved—an archetypal motif found in ballads worldwide. What is particularly strong about the treatment of this motif is not despair, but the rage that gets unleashed as the princess throws the bowl from which she has eaten the peacock meat, and defiantly sets out to 'imprint' her dead lover on her body. Almost flaunting her infidelity, she reaffirms her passion for the peacock. And significantly, the song ends on this note of passion rather than on retribution or reconciliation.

Jetal De

In the next song, there is a more complicated story around adultery involving not just the woman's husband, but her father as well. Unlike 'Moriyo', *where the princess herself is involved in adultery, here we confront the figure of the 'other woman' in the form of a beautiful maid-servant.* 'Jetal De' *is not exactly a dictation, like the text of* 'Moriyo', *but neither is it a transcription based on an actual recording. It is an intimate rendering of the song in prose, transcribed by Shrimati Mohini Devi, who belongs to the Shrimali Brahman community, from whom this version of the song is derived.*[8] *Once again, it should be noted that there are no stanzaic divisions in the original transcription, but these have been inserted in the English translation of the song to facilitate the identification of the numerous characters involved in the narrative.*

'Father, O my father, get me married,
My girlfriend is going to her in-law's home.'
'I've wandered, wandered, O child, in many places
There's no one to match you in the clan.'
'O father, at the far end of the sea,
Jagpati is worthy of being my husband.'
'Jagpati, O child, is a big lord,
And big people ask for a lot of dowry.'
'You, you, O father, are also a big lord,
Father, give the dowry to the lord across the sea.'

The rice is being sieved, the pulses are being ground,
The daughter Jetal De's wedding is taking place.
The wedding band is playing, the festive drums beating,
Jagpati has arrived to wed her.

The first time round, the big lord [Jagpati] and the daughter [Jetal De],
And Jeto asked for dowry.
'I'll give, give, O daughter, I shall give gold,
O daughter, I'll give sparkling silver.'
The second time round, the big lord and the daughter,
And Jeto asked for dowry.
'I'll give, give, O daughter, I shall give a herd of elephants,
O daughter, I'll give racehorses.'
'I won't take, won't take, O father, the herd of elephants,
I won't take, O father, the racehorses.'
The next time round, the big lord and the daughter,
And Jeto asked for dowry.
'I'll give, give, O daughter, a pearl necklace,
O daughter, I'll give knotted armlets.'
'I won't take, O father, the pearl necklace,
I won't take, O father, the knotted armlets.'
The fourth time round, the big lord and the daughter,
And Jeto asked for dowry.
'I'll give, give, O daughter, a storehouse of provisions,
I'll give, O daughter, the keys to a treasure trove.'
'I won't take, won't take, O father, the storehouse of provisions,
I won't take the keys to the treasure trove.

But take, I shall, I shall, O father, the beautiful maid-servant,
Who would add lustre to my home.'
'I'll give, give, O daughter, I'll give the beautiful maid-servant,
But having taken her, don't repent later on, O daughter.'

On a day before the full moon, the night of the gods,
Elder brother-in-law Dilip will have a *rātijāgā* sung through the night.
'O younger brother's wife, Jetal De, come soon
Without you there can be no midnight prayers.'
'O brother-in-law, my left eye is paining,
There's no one to look after the house.'
'O brother's wife, tie a bandage on your eye,
And ask the maid, the beautiful one, to look after the house.'

'Maid, O beautiful one, listen to what I'm saying,
Don't light the lamp for my big lord [Jagpati].
Maid, O beautiful one, listen to what I'm saying,
Don't make the bed for my big lord.'
As soon as the wife Jetal De left,
The maid's heart leapt with joy.
She opened the vanity box, adorned herself,
And lit the lamp, the beautiful maid.
As soon as the wife Jetal De left,
The maid's hands pressed the feet of the big lord.
Pressed the feet softly, and the big lord awoke.
The maid and the lord got lost in love play.

A message reached the wife Jetal De.
'Your house and husband have been ensnared by the maid, the beautiful one.'
The wife Jetal De got furious
And ran in anger.
'O beautiful maid, come out,
I'll stuff your body with salt.
Beautiful maid, why are you so scared,
Everything taken, your right hand acts as a backrest.'[9]

She called, called for a messenger,
And sent a letter for her father to read.

'Father, O Gokulchand, come fast,
The beautiful maid has held my house and husband.'
Came the father and asked what was in her heart,
'O daughter, how comfortable is your in-law's home.'
'Wheat chapatis, with cow-milk butter,
Your daughter has a two-year old son.
Quickly, quickly, ask the lord what is in his heart,
For whom has he turned his back on Jetal De.'
For qualities, no one like Gokulchand's daughter,
For looks, no one like the beautiful maid.
'If I get angry, the clan will be put to shame,
O daughter, the lord cannot be killed, just bear it.'

She called, called for a messenger,
And sent a letter for her brother to read.
'Brother, O Udaichand, come quickly,
The beautiful maid has taken my house and husband.'
Came the brother and asked what was in her heart,
'How comfortable is your in-laws' home.'
'Wheat chapatis, with cow-milk butter,
Your sister has a two-year-old son.
Call, O call, Jagpati, and ask what is in his heart,
For what reason has Jeto been set aside?'
For qualities, no one like Udaichand's sister,
For looks, no one like the beautiful maid.

Pulling out his dagger, with heart full of anger,
The brother ended his sister's pain.
'Listen, O my brothers-in-law,
Don't ever take any maid for dowry.
Long live, my true brother,
The one who released his sister from sorrow.'

Once again it is necessary to spell out some facts of the possible 'performative' context of this song. If it were sung during a 'rātijāgā', it is likely that the entire song would not be rendered. But the women singing the song would know the story, in all probability, in somewhat different versions. While in this particular version of 'Jetal De', the brother stabs the maid with a dagger, in other versions (according to Komalda), she is incarcerated in a wall. The point is that she is punished for sleeping with the lord. And yet, if one didn't have this context, and if one relied on the text of the song alone, then it's not entirely clear who is being killed. When I first read the text, it seemed possible that Jetal De herself was killed. As I have come to learn, this is not the case. Regardless of the variations in the song, there are certain core elements within the story of 'Jetal De' that survive in different renditions—and one such element is the death of the maid-servant.

And yet, despite these fixed elements, what remains unsaid *in these songs is perhaps more potent than what is said. Komalda points out at least one critical fact—that the beautiful maid (identified as 'marhatti nār') is from Jetal De's own home, and she is obviously the most precious gift made by Jetal De's father. He parts with her only after his daughter has rejected all the other riches promised to her as part of her dowry. It is Jetal De who 'takes' the beautiful maid, and in the process, as Komalda interprets, spares her mother further humiliation and pain, because the maid is sexually involved with the father. Significantly, the father warns his daughter to watch out for the maid, and sure enough, Jetal De's husband (Jagpati) is seduced by her. While being duly punished, the maid is also acknowledged for her 'looks' ('rūp'), while Jetal De is honoured for her 'qualities' ('gun'). Beauty and virtue are clearly juxtaposed, and though virtue seems to win out at the very end, the power of beauty is duly acknowledged.*

One last note is worth indicating here: the night of adultery when Jagpati is ensnared by the maid, is also the night where a 'rātijāgā' is being held in the house of Jetal De's elder brother-in-law. Whether or not this detail is recognized in the act of singing the song during an actual 'rātijāgā', the point is that the text contains its own self-referentiality to the context of its utterance, testifying to the larger reflexive dimensions of 'meta-folklore'.[10]

8

TERĀTĀLI

Following the session on women's songs, I thought it would be useful to explore dance and movement-related performance traditions by women. I was particularly drawn to Terātāli, a highly ritualized dance form, which has now been secularized in its virtuoso renditions in numerous Rajasthani cultural programmes, both in India and in festivals abroad. I should have known that what would concern Komalda is not the mere technicalities of this dance form, but its context in a particularly fervent and widespread mode of worshipping a folk deity called Baba Ramdev. At least this is how Komalda began by identifying the deity, but as we shall see in the course of this narrative, he is also recognized as Ramdev Pīr or Rāmshāh Pīr.

How a Hindu deity identified as an avatar of Vishnu-Krishna is also, simultaneously, regarded as a pīr, or Islamic saint, is what this narrative unfolds in the process of numerous turns and twists. Instead of anticipating these transitions, however, it would be more appropriate to discover them as they get articulated. This section begins with a rather sedate description of Terātāli, marked by its emphasis on functionality rather than performativity. However, there are surprises ahead.

The Performance Tradition

Terātāli is a dance form performed by the women from a caste group called Kāmaḍ.[1] Singing and dancing in a seated position, the women use *manjirā* (cymbals) with elaborate gestures and movements, at times rotating and swaying their bodies, at times lying on the floor. The women are accompanied by men playing the tandurā, a drone-like, five-stringed instrument, punctuated by the rhythms of the ḍholak (drum), the *tāl* (a heavy cymbal), and occasionally, the khaṛtāl (wooden clappers). Drawing on a repertoire of devotional songs, Terātāli celebrates the life of Baba Ramdev, who is said to have lived between the late fourteenth and early fifteenth centuries. He is worshipped as a god, primarily by large sections of the scheduled castes, not only in Rajasthan, but in Punjab, Gujarat, and parts of Madhya Pradesh, and Uttar Pradesh as well.

In my view, Ramdev's sanctification needs to be situated alongside many other religious philosophies and practices like Sikhism, Sufism, and bhakti-related practices involving the teachings of Vallabhacharya, Namdev, Kabir, Mirabai and so on. The point I would emphasize is that if these conversions succeeded in the medieval period primarily among occupational and low-caste caste groups, it is because they offered the possibility of salvation to every human being. Without an advocacy of equality, these conversions could not have succeeded.

In the early half of the last century, a large number of groups practised Terātāli, including women who were patronized by the low-caste Meghwāl community in the Nagaur district, associated with leather work and weaving. Some Terātāli groups were also sponsored by the Nāth community in the Udaipur-Pali district. Following a sudden decision on the part of the community in Nagaur to stop their women from dancing in public, there were almost no Terātāli groups active in this area in the post-Independence period.[2] Only in recent years are we beginning to see some groups returning to the dance in the Nagaur and Ajmer districts, but their patrons are more likely to be based outside of Rajasthan in metropolitan cities like Chennai and Kolkata. In the Udaipur-Pali district as well, there are about 100 Terātāli groups that continue to be sponsored by the Nāth community, but, by and large, these groups earn their living by singing devotional songs in all-night singing sessions (jāgraṇ) of different communities. They have also started to participate in radio and television programmes, as well as in cultural festivals in India and abroad.

Central to the movements of the dancers is the virtuoso use of manjirā. Indeed, at one time we used to think that the name Terātāli referred to 'thirteen cymbals'. But this is not the case, because there are more than thirteen cymbals on the body of each dancer. Apart from a pair of cymbals held in each hand, there are about nine cymbals tied to each leg, and additional cymbals tied to the upper arm and shoulder on either side. So there are many cymbals, the exact number is not the issue.

Basically, there are three ways in which the manjirā are struck to produce different intensities of sounds, accompanied by different rotational gestures of the hands or flicks of the wrist. The cymbals can be clashed against each other using both hands, or else they can be played against each other in each hand. Some of these gestural rhythmic patterns evoke a chain, which is called *sākaliā*. Other movements involve the use of a cord which is struck from a distance, say from the cymbal tied to the upper arm to one on the legs—this throwing or flinging movement of the cord from cymbal to cymbal is called *chhuṭ manjirā*.

Obviously, these movements necessitate skill for which some basic training is required. Informal practice sessions take place during any spare time to be found in household routines, when different members of the family are sitting together. Each movement will be practised over and over again for a couple of months, till the skill becomes virtuosic. Most Terātāli groups are made up of extended families, including not just the husband, wife, and their children, but their relatives as well. Since it is the women who play the cymbals, they play a crucial role in the rhythmic rendering of the songs. Interestingly, there are a lot of gestures that come directly from women's household activities, like pounding the grain, separating the wheat from the chaff, spinning the *charkhā*, churning yogurt. Within these seven or eight gestural patterns, there is the potentiality for creating all kinds of movements that can highlight a particular text.

As a general principle, folk dances rarely enact or illustrate the situation described in a song, focusing instead on rhythmic movements that are entirely physical, and not expressive (in the sense of the *abhinaya* used in classical dance traditions). But today one can see, in folk dance traditions like Ghumar, the actual representation of particular actions described in a song—it could be eating a *laḍḍū*, or applying *kājal* to the eye, or some such small action. Earlier, such translations of the text into body movement were rare in rural performances. If at all gestural movements were used, they would be quite different from what the text was saying.

However, there are a few songs in the Terātāli repertoire in which the text is enacted with very suggestive expressions. A Mira bhajan comes to mind in which she is addressing her lover, who is totally silent. She entreats him: 'You see my pain as I express my love for you, why don't you speak a few words? We have a lot of fights—is that why you're not responding to me?' This is a love-quarrel situation (*jhagṛā-ṭanṭā*), in which the Terātāli dancers, while singing the song, almost involuntarily use their hands and other parts of their bodies to express the text. By and large, however, there will not be any perceptible *effort* on the part of the dancers to render these emotions. Their gestures are at best undertones, *chhoṭā rūp*, small expressions of the larger situation.

As for props like the *loṭā* (metal pot) and the *talwār* (sword), used by the Terātāli dancers while they dance in a seated posture, these are obstructions that further complicate, and thereby enhance, the intricacy of their rhythmic and gestural patterns.[3] It is very simple: If you are dancing with your hands free, then one kind of movement will emerge. But suppose you hold a glass in your hand, then the movement will change. Likewise, if you hold a long stick in your hand, it will change yet again. In Terātāli, the cymbals and the cord used to strike the cymbals can be regarded as extensions of the hand. The sword as such has no specific symbolic significance. It is no more than a ritual object that one encounters in many locations, situations and performative contexts. For instance, when bhopās go into trance at the shrines of folk gods and goddesses, they often hit themselves with the edge of a sword. Or else they rub their bodies with it. Swords do not merely exist for attack and defence. They are also worn by bridegrooms in marriage ceremonies, or presented as gifts in royal families; they can be highly decorative artefacts made in gold and studded with diamonds. I would not read any iconographic significance into the fact that the sword is placed horizontally in the mouths of the Terātāli performers. This object merely presents a certain obstruction that demands a negotiation of space on the part of the dancers, as they manoeuver their cymbals in different patterns and directions, while lying on the ground or swaying from one side to another. Likewise, the balancing of the loṭās on the head contributes to the virtuosity of the performance.

With such performative inputs, it is not surprising that Terātāli has made a transition from its ritualistic context to all kinds of secular entertainment. Unlike those women's songs for which there is no audience as such, the Terātāli singers have always had audiences for the jāgraṇs in which they have participated. Whenever there is a gathering of people, there is a tendency on the part of performers to improvise, and to create certain effects by which the attention of the listener or the viewer can be held. So I would say that the instinct among Terātāli performers to dance and to sing *for others* has always been there. And, therefore, it has not been difficult for them to appear on the contemporary stage as performers.

However, when they perform for specific ritual or religious ceremonies, the performance can last for anything between eight to twelve hours. Urban performances on proscenium stages are an entirely different matter. Here the Terātāli performers have no other option but to cut down on the number of gestures and movements, which are generally compressed into short items of twenty to thirty minutes duration. The dramatic shifts of energy in these items are necessary in order to sustain the interest of urban audiences, who are not likely to sit through twelve hours of any ritual performance, which requires a very different concentration and sustenance of energy.

The Ritual Context

Before Independence, there were very few temples of Baba Ramdev, but today it is almost impossible to find a single village without a Baba Ramdev shrine. Significantly, the Kāmaḍ, who were earlier active in Terātāli in the Nagaur district in particular, have now become the official priests of Baba Ramdev.[4] So basically, what we have to keep in mind is that Terātāli is strongly attached to the devotional and ritualistic practice of worshipping Ramdev in the bhakti mode. In the all-night performances that are held in the villages, long stories on Baba Ramdev are sung, along with the bhajans of Kabir, Mira, Dharmidas, and Harji Bhaṭṭi, one of Ramdev's disciples who composed many bhajans commemorating the miracles of his guru.[5]

Interestingly, these all-night ceremonies, which include the ritual of *ārtī* and the chanting of *stutis* (panegyric verses) in honour of Ramdev, are called *jamā*, not jāgraṇ. [The word *jamā* is derived from the Arabic *jamāt*, which means 'congregation of the faithful'.][6] While there are some jamās where only bhajans are sung, without any performance of Terātāli, it is the musical and textual content of these devotional songs that matters more than the technical virtuosity of the performance. I have noticed at some of the jamās that I have attended how the music slowly changes in the course of the night. From the singing of Guru Mahima, bhajans sung in praise of the guru, the songs change in content, relating to more worldly matters, temptations, and conflicts which obstruct the following of the right path. Later in the course of the night, the songs become more abstract and philosophically complex with a strong metaphoric idiom. As the dawn breaks, the rāgas change and there is a return to purely devotional music, celebrating the *līla* (divine play) of *devi-devatā* (goddesses and gods). These shifts in rāga and devotional content correspond to the passage of time in the course of a single night. While not everyone among the listeners is likely to identify these shifts, there are a few initiated listeners who would be aware of the larger religious and ritualistic associations of the music.

So far I have been using the word jamā as a special kind of jāgraṇ, or all-night musical rite, in which the spirit of Baba Ramdev is invoked. But the word has other associations to which I would like to turn now. Jamā is an elusive category. In one particularly important song-narrative entitled *Rupānde ri bel*, we get the impression that the jamā is a kind of secret night ceremony. A *bel* is a poetic composition that is longer than a ballad, but shorter than an epic. While an epic covers at least three generations, a bel focuses on one generation, and generally on one character or figure with all the accompanying episodic material. Now what is interesting is that Rupānde ri bel narrates the happenings at one particular jamā, and it is also sung in jamās celebrating Baba Ramdev today. However, the jamā described in this bel is unlike anything that I have seen. When I ask people whether such a jamā exists or not, they say, 'Yes.' But when I ask, 'Have you participated in one?', they say, 'No.' When you listen to Rupānde ri bel, you realize that the jamā is not just about devotional music that brings together a group of people in the course of a night, it is an altogether different phenomenon.

In the story of Rupānde ri bel, we learn that Rupānde, the second wife of King Mallināth, sneaks away every night to attend the jamā of Dhāru, a guru from the Meghwāl or chamār (leather-worker) community.[7] Jealous of Rupānde's influence on the king, the first wife reveals to the king how Rupānde disappears every night to some unknown place. At first the king doesn't believe her, but one night he decides to check up on Rupānde for himself. In her bed, he discovers a *nāgini* (snake) and an anklet—forms that resemble the sleeping body of Rupānde, but she is not there.

So where is she? Listening to the distant drone of a tandurā, the king follows this sound all the way to Dharu's jamā. It is in full swing, with a lot of people gathered together, both men and women, some of whom are being served meat by his wife. Secretly, he watches the entire scene and plans to expose his wife in the fort. In the confrontation between husband and wife, Rupānde holds a *thāḷi* (brass plate) containing the prasād from the jamā, which is covered with a cloth. The king challenges her: 'Where were you? And why?' She refuses to answer. Finally, he orders her to reveal what is hidden in the thāḷi. She says, 'Flowers.' He disbelieves her and claims that it must contain meat, the prasād from the jamā. As Mallināth whisks the cloth away with his sword, he sees flowers.

With this miracle, the king is convinced of his wife's powers, and he volunteers to become the disciple of her guru. His wife responds by saying that it will be difficult for him to join her *panth* (sect). She lays down certain conditions: the king will have to behead his only son and kill his favourite horse. By complying with these conditions, the king proves that he too can become a true *shishya*, like his wife. With the guru's blessings, his son and horse are returned to life.

Roughly, this is the story of Rupānde ri bel. It is often sung in jamās, compelling us to think of the multiple meanings that can be attached to this all-night ceremony. What kind of religious experience does it represent? I am not clear. There have been some attempts to link the practice of the jamā to medieval Ismaili connections, but I have never come across any reference to the Ismaili faith in my interaction with Meghwāl and other low-caste communities who worship Ramdev as a god. However, Ramdev is also known as Rāmshah Pīr, and it would be interesting to question what are those qualities or actions by which Ramdev is identified as an avatar of Vishnu-Krishna and as a pīr. How do these two contexts interrelate? At what points do they synchronize? I don't have answers to these questions, but there are two stories that could help us to trace some of the hidden connections.

Before we get on to narrating these stories, which in turn will open up new stories, it is necessary to provide some much-needed context on the seminal role of the Ismaili sect in the growth of the Ramdev cult. Here one has to draw on the rigorous, yet highly inflected research of Dominique-Sila Khan (1996, 1997), in which we learn of an intricate series of religious conversions that took place in Rajasthan between the thirteenth and fourteenth centuries, in which low-caste communities and sects ('panths') came under the influence of Ismailism.[8] *Based in Multan and Ucch, the Ismaili branch of the Shia faith, originating in the eighth century* AD, *had resisted the Shari'ā (orthodox Muslim law) and propagated its faith through a series of missionary activities called 'dawā'. Known for their subtle capacity to spread their faith through acculturation rather than coercion, concealment of identity ('taqiyyā') rather than overt propaganda, Ismaili missionaries ('dai') interacted with existing sects and religious groups in Rajasthan. Notable among the missionaries was Shams Pīr or Samas Rishi, who is said to have converted Ramdev's grandfather Raṇsi Tanwar, on whom we will have more to say later.*

For the moment, it is important to note that the faith associated with Ramdev combining Ismaili and indigenous religious and ritual practices in Rajasthan has been identified by many names: the Alakh Panth (or the worship of the 'formless' god); the Kāmaḍiya Panth (the sect of the Kāmaḍ to which the Terātāli perfomers belong); the Maha Panth (the 'great sect'); and the Nizār Panth or Nizāri Dharm, which is considered to be the most sacred and secret of its numerous names.[9]

Significantly, Ramdev himself is not credited with creating a new sect as such, in so far as he did not lay down any scripture or ritualistic code of worship for his followers. Rather, he can more accurately be perceived as spreading a religious movement that already existed, extending it to newly-found converts in the most downtrodden sections of low-caste Hindus, notably the Meghwāls, who are also derogatorily referred to as Dheṛh because of their association with the removal of dead cattle. Significantly, Ramdev was for a long time identified as the 'god of the pariahs' ('dheṛhon ka dev').[10] *While this is no longer the case as he is claimed by many other middle and upper-caste groups, the stigma of untouchability is still attached to his name, compelling the scheduled castes of the Meghwāl and Kāmaḍ to reassess their claims on Ramdev as his erstwhile primary devotees and priests, respectively.*

With this historical context, we can now begin to situate the stories that follow in a more reflexive way. As always, Komalda tells his stories without interpreting them. While this is an effective—and in some cases, the only—appropriate way of sharing folklore, the point is that there are many different versions of the stories. And these different versions say significantly different things about the Ramdev phenomenon. I have no other choice, therefore, but to intervene in the narrative, by pointing out its ambivalences through conflicting material.

Folklore around Ramdev

One very popular story circulating around Ramdev is that he was visited during his lifetime by Panch Pīr, or five holy men from Mecca, who asked to be fed with beef. Since Ramdev was a Rajput it was not possible for him to comply with their request. But he realized that he was being put on trial, and that these pīrs were celestial representatives. So, in deference to their wishes, Ramdev killed a *bachhaḍā* (calf) and served its meat to the pīrs. But this was not enough for them. They wanted to eat this meat in their own vessels and plates, which they claimed to have left behind in Mecca, and without which they refused to eat. So, using his miraculous powers, Ramdev managed to transport those very vessels for them to eat in. After they had finished eating, he requested them to leave all the bones of the meat on the *dastarkhān*, the cloth on which the food is served, and not in any other place. Thereafter, Ramdev placed his hands over the bones and said, '*Jeevto vejā*', and the calf came to life again. For these miracles that he was able to perform before the Panch Pīr, Ramdev himself began to be regarded as a pīr.

There are at least two ways of reading this story. On the one hand, it can reveal Ramdev's deference to the Panch Pīr and his process of conversion to Ismailism, but on the other hand, it can be read as a form of one-upmanship by which Ramdev reveals that his miraculous powers are superior to those assumed by the Pīr. The point is that Ramdev manages to outwit the Pīr, and for this reason, this story is more likely to be endorsed by those Hindu followers of Ramdev who no longer need any Ismaili credentials to prove the innate superiority of their indigenous and increasingly Hinduized faith.

Now, this is one story, which is sung in many different songs, along with other miracles as well. There's another story, which is a bit confused in my mind, that was told to me by a Manganiyar musician, Murad. It concerns another holy man called Samsu Pīr with great miraculous powers, who was a close friend of a particular Bania. Now it appears that while this Pīr had gone away somewhere, his friend died. On returning, the Pīr was stricken with grief and used his power to revive his dead friend. However, when the Bania came alive again, the people protested and told the pīr that he had no right to do anything that only God could do. And for transgressing this law, they decided to punish the pīr by removing the outer layer of his skin. Thereafter, whenever Samsu Pīr would move around in raw flesh, people would flee from him in terror. Many days passed like this as he wandered the streets, unable to eat anything or receive alms as a fakir.

One day, he came across a woman on the roadside cooking a meal in a pot, who ran away in fear when she saw him. Then Samsu Pīr requested the sun to come nearer to the earth so that the food in the pot could be cooked. Responding to his prayer, the sun drew closer to the earth, and all the people became restless and agitated as the heat intensified. In panic the people entreated Samsu Pīr to send the sun back so that they could all live in peace. The holy man interceded on their behalf, and the sun retreated. In gratitude, the people suggested that he should go to the Ganga and take a dip in its waters. So he went to the holy river, took a dip, and miraculously, his skin came alive.

Here the story gets a bit unclear in my mind—I'm not sure if Samsu Pīr manifested himself as Ramdev, after settling down near the Ganga. In another version of the story, it appears that Ajmal, the father of Ramdev, who was childless, approached Samsu Pīr to give him a child, and it is through the Pīr's intervention that Ramdev was born.

Now at one level, this story has some parallels with Ismaili sources that I have later come to know of. But Murad who told me the story didn't know anything about the Ismaili religion or its conversion practices in earlier times. I myself have not encountered it in any direct way, and I don't know how traces of Ismaili rituals still continue in the practice of jamās or the worship of Ramdev. But I do know that he has assumed a god-like significance for large cross-sections of the population, primarily from low-caste groups, including Muslims, and that he is worshipped across religious communities primarily for his miraculous powers.

I would take Komalda's qualifications very seriously when he acknowledges the confusions in 'the story', as he remembers it being told to him by the Manganiyar musician Murad. For a start, 'the story' itself would seem to be a combination of at least two stories, which themselves have different versions. Secondly, even as 'the story' is being narrated by Komalda's own admission without any reference to Ismaili sources, the point is that they are inscribed within the Ismaili literature surrounding Ramdev.

To begin with the simpler (or, at least more cryptic of the stories), relating to Ramdev's birth: In one version, he is born as the avatar of Vishnu-Krishna after his childless father Ajmal receives a boon from Lord Krishna himself at the holy 'tīrtha' (pilgrimage site) of Dwarka.[11] *But in an earlier version of the story, Ajmal does not go to Dwarka but to Multan, the ecclesiastical centre of the Nizār Panth, where he meets Shams Pīr (either alive or as a manifestation), who declares that Ramdev will be born as* his *incarnation.*

Now, in Komalda's version of 'the story', the character whom he describes as 'Samsu Pīr' is linked to Ramdev's birth, though the facts are unclear. It is more than likely that this 'Samsu Pīr' is another colloquial rendering of the great Ismaili missionary Shams Pīr, who converted Ramdev's grandfather (and Ajmal's father), Raṇsi Tanwar. In this conversion story, which has a canonical status in Ramdev folklore, there are ironic echoes—and reversals—of Komalda's story.

The clue to my mind concerns Shams Pīr's skin disease. According to Komalda, the top layer of the pīr's skin is removed by irate Hindu devotees, who protest his miraculous action in bringing his Bania friend alive. Strangely, this story does not figure prominently in Ramdev folklore. Instead, the canonical story revolves around Shams Pīr's curse of Raṇsi Tanwar (Ramdev's grandfather), who is inflicted with leprosy, after he dares to attack the caravan of the pīr who is travelling through Rajasthan, disguised as a Hindu mendicant. Not unlike Komalda's Samsu Pīr, Raṇsi Tanwar goes from house to house begging for alms as a leper, until he meets a poor untouchable weaver named Khiwaṇ, whose guru is none other than Shams Pīr himself. On Khiwaṇ's insistence, Raṇsi Tanwar presents himself before the pīr, who cures him without realizing his true identity. Once he recognizes Raṇsi Tanwar as the brigand who attacked his caravan, Shams Pīr is angry and promptly curses not only Raṇsi Tanwar but Khiwaṇ as well. Finally, he relents not by removing the curse entirely, but by acknowledging that both these men will die heroic deaths. This is precisely what materializes as Raṇsi Tanwar and Khiwaṇ are killed in the court of the Sunni ruler of Delhi. Miraculously, however, instead of blood, milk and flowers pour out of their bodies, and these get magically transported to the holy sites of Naraina (for Raṇsi) and Dudu (for Khiwaṇ).[12]

Now, this is one of the primary myths memorializing the different sites of worship in the Ramdev cult. If we look back to Komalda's story, the primary difference is that 'Samsu Pīr' is afflicted by skin-

disease, and then cured through the divine mediation of the Ganga. Once again, it is not difficult to read here a very different religious intervention by which the [Muslim] Pīr is tamed and rejuvenated by a specifically Hindu blessing through the sanctification of the holy river.

Secret Rites and Rituals

Let us turn now to yet another problematic aspect of the Ramdev cult, which has come up earlier—the 'jamā'. Here Komalda does not dwell on the material aspects of this sacred ceremony, which is known to initiated believers through specific signs, or of what remains of these signs through traces and remnants in obscure rituals. Among these signs are the 'paṭh' or wooden seat of the invisible God, Alakh; a pair of footprints ('pagliyā'); an earthen jar filled with water ('kalash'); the 'jyot' or sacred light, among other icons and ritual objects.[13] *Without attempting to describe what he has not seen himself, Komalda uses the 'jamā' as a link to speculate on the existence of other secret rituals and sectarian rites in rural Rajasthan.*

To get back to the jamā, I know that it's not exactly a jāgraṇ. There are many rituals involved in jamās, whose Ismaili or, for that matter, Islamic connections may not be clear at all. Certainly, I have no direct evidence of anything approximating the kind of jamā described in Rupānde ri bel. Even if the jamā described in this poem may no longer exist, the point is that it opens up questions relating to the prevalence of secret rites and rituals in rural Rajasthan. It is to these rites and rituals, and the sects constituting them, that I would like to turn my attention now.

A secret sect is one that a person can join, but his or her participation remains unknown even to the immediate family. A son, a mother, or a father could all be members of the same sect incognito. One such society is the Mailā Panth, literally 'dirty sect', which I first came to know about through a sweeper who was working for my folk research institution in the village of Borunda. This man wanted to leave his job, and he wanted his son appointed in his place. Since he was not a very good worker, I was not willing to comply with his request. However, I was curious to know why he wanted to leave. Then the sweeper said that his father had recently died, and that he would have to substitute for him in the Mailā Panth. At this point, I was curious and asked him what this panth was all about. Then he said that both his father and mother had been members of the sect, but neither knew about the other's participation. Before his mother had died, she had disclosed her involvement in the sect, whereupon one of the sweeper's brothers had been initiated into the Mailā Panth. This was its process of recruitment: at the death of any member of a family, another relative had to join the sect.

Now that the sweeper's father had died, after disclosing his own participation in the Mailā Panth, there was no other alternative but for the sweeper himself to follow his father's panth. There was also an economic benefit involved, since the sweeper's brothers were prepared to forgo some *bighās* of land in exchange for the sweeper's acceptance of the panth. So it was to his advantage to leave his job in Borunda to join the panth.

Obviously, there were a lot of inconsistencies in what I was hearing. If the sweeper's brother had earlier joined the panth, then surely it was no longer a family secret. And nor was it a secret for the sweeper himself to join it since he had clearly discussed the matter with his family who were prepared to part with some of their land. Nonetheless, I was curious to know more, so I made a deal with the sweeper. If he could tell me more about the Mailā Panth, I would be prepared to give his son the job. He agreed so long as I would keep the information to myself and not talk about it to anyone. I accepted.

Then he told me that when his father had died, he had been buried, not cremated. One guru of the Mailā Panth from the small town of Pipar had taken the sweeper to the burial place, but only after tying his eyes with cloth so that he would not recognize the way. It was at this burial place that the sweeper was initiated into the panth, after accepting the guru.[14] The sweeper also told me that he and his associates would go for jamās, and that they would sing devotional songs. Here they would interact with members of the panth from the upper-castes as well. Without disclosing names, he claimed that Rajputs, Malis, and Jains, both male and female, would come for the

Mailā Panth sessions. He also spoke of a particular jyot (light, sacred flame), called *hingḷāz ki jyot*, where the wick is made out of a cotton fibre called *kokdi*. He said that outsiders to the panth could not see this flame. If they did, then they would have to become members of the panth. While he was not prepared to reveal what they ate at their secret meetings, he did acknowledge that after eating, all the left-overs had to be buried. Even animals, like the dog, the cow, or the bull, would be treated as members of the panth if they ate that food.

After hearing all these details, I was still very unclear. 'What is there to hide about it?' I asked the sweeper. 'Why did your parents not tell you that they were going to the panth? Why this secrecy?' Then he told me, 'Don't ask me any more questions. I am bound by my word and by the rules of the panth. I can't tell you any more.' 'Anyway,' I said, 'do me a favour. Just tell me the places where you hold your all-night ceremonies, whether it is in this or that village or someone's house, or wherever. Where do you meet?' He didn't realize why I was asking him the question, so he told me all their meeting places. Later, when I tried to find out from those very villages and neighbourhoods whether any all-night bhajan sessions had been reported in that area, I was told that none had taken place. So either the sweeper was giving me wrong information, or else their meetings had nothing to do with singing and were held in total secrecy. I couldn't get any more information.

From what I have learned from other sources, Mailā Panth appears to be a ritualistic sect for those low-caste communities who cannot afford to go to Hardwar to perform the rituals for the dead. Instead, they turn to the burial practices of the Mailā Panth. More critical views of the Mailā Panth, offered by counter-sects like the Kabir Panth and the Ram Snehi, tend to view this panth as an orgiastic society. There are all kinds of stories associated not just with the Mailā Panth but with the Kānchli Panth and Kuṇḍa Panth—stories associated with free sex, indiscriminately of any filial relation. A woman's bodice (*kānchli*), for instance, can be placed in a clay pot (*kuṇḍa*), and any man picking it up can have her for the night, whether it happens to be his mother or sister or whoever.

It should be kept in mind, however, that such stories have been confirmed primarily by erstwhile followers of the Mailā Panth who have been 'rescued' by counter-organizations like the Ram Snehi, in small places like Khedapa and Gotan. The question could also be raised: why are these groups objecting to the Mailā Panth if they themselves have not been involved with it at some point in time? There would seem to be some kind of secrecy in the very relationships between these panths.

In the very absence of verification and authentication of basic facts, Komalda's comments on secret societies with ostensibly orgiastic agendas can be regarded as provocative. Once again we need to turn to the scholarship on the subject, notably to Dominique-Sila Khan's (1997, 1998) carefully honed analysis, to derive a clearer idea of the 'kuṇḍa panth', ' kānchli panth', and so on.[15]

Clearly linked to 'left-handed' Tantric ritual practices, the 'kuṇḍa panth' has two forms—the 'bīsā panth' (literally, sect 'twenty'), which is more 'secretive' than the 'dasā panth' (literally, sect 'ten'), and which does not seem to have the approval of all members of the Nizār Panth. In the 'bīsā panth', all the Tantric 'pānch makārs' (five substances)—meat, fish, wine, grain, and sex—play a vital part in the rituals. What Komalda describes as 'kānchli panth' could be regarded as an intensified exploration of one particular 'makār'—notably, 'mithun' (sexual intercourse). From Khan's commentary, we learn that, 'After the ritual copulation each woman must collect in the palm of her hand the semen virile of her partner, which she deposits into a round flat earthen vessel called "kuṇḍa". At the end of the ceremony all the sperm is mixed with "churmā" (a traditional food offering made of millet, ghee and sugar) and partaken as "prasād" [sacred food] by all the members of the sect. It is named "pāyal".'[16]

There is much more elaboration that could be made of these sexual rites and rituals, but the primary fact that needs to be highlighted here concerns the crucial area of secrecy. This exposure of secrecy raises a number of questions. At an ethical level, one has to contend with the issue of voyeurism from which academia is not free. To what extent a secret remains a secret once it is articulated in any form of discourse—scholarly or anecdotal—is also a complex question. Indeed, is the Nizār Panth any longer a secret society, as its 'unclean' rites get sanitized and neutered through the process of 're-Hinduization'? Indeed, is 're-Hinduization' the right word for a mass phenomenon in which Ramdev is being worshipped in the mega-temple complex of Ramdeoṛa like any other upwardly mobile Hindu god? Are his Ismaili origins discernible to any other than his most exacting scholars and die-hard disciples?[17]

Today the worship of Ramdev in Ruṇichā-Ramdeora is assuming a massive all-India pan-Hindu phenomenon, inevitably controlled by the upper castes, in which the Ismaili traces of the Ramdev cult can barely be detected. This Hinduization of Ramdev is in the process of displacing a more 'syncretic' form of worship from an earlier time. But this is not the entire story, as we have attempted to trace in the course of this chapter, because the residues of Ismailism have not yet been erased. Komalda is aware of this, but not without complaining, 'Inme bahut jhamela hai' (This is a messy area). 'At some point,' as he puts it perceptively, 'we need to leave the secrets alone.'

9

PUPPETRY

This session on puppetry was sustained with such a steady flow of thoughts and facts that it was not necessary to interrupt Komalda by asking too many questions. Unlike in the earlier sessions on sati and the linkages of Ramdev with Terātāli, where the basic facts were blurred in Komalda's mind—indeed, his memory was playing tricks all the time—these comments on puppetry are a lot more concrete. Grounded in a nuts-and-bolts approach to the techniques and performance tradition of Rajasthani puppetry, there is no attempt on Komalda's part to link this tradition more philosophically or symbolically with other puppet traditions. The focus here is very much on secular entertainment, even though this is not theorized vis-à-vis the instrumentalist and ritualistic functions of other puppet traditions in India.

What prevents this session on puppetry from becoming banal in its rudimentary facticity is a very intuitive and telling shift that takes place somewhere in the middle of the narrative. Once again I am surprised by this capacity in Komalda's discourse to shift gears into a more elusive area of investigation—in this particular case, the dual identities of traditional performers and ritual practitioners. I shall leave you to discover this shift when it appears, but for the moment let us begin with the nitty-gritty of puppetry itself.

'Origins'

In Rajasthan, there is only one tradition of puppetry—the marionette tradition—in which the puppets are manipulated by strings. We have no examples of shadow or glove puppetry. It is possible that this string puppet tradition could have migrated all the way from Rajasthan to Maharashtra, Karnataka, and West Bengal, but we can't be sure. In fact, there is no clear evidence about the origins of puppetry in Rajasthan itself. All that we have are some legendary stories that pass off as history.

Invariably, if you talk to the puppeteers themselves, they will invoke the name of some emperor—it could be Akbar or Shah Jahan or Aurangzeb—to validate the origins of their art. More often than not, the story they tell—and there are many versions— revolves around a dispute of performing rights between the Rajasthani puppeteers and the so-called Persian puppeteers who practised their art at the court of the emperor.[1] According to the legend, these court puppeteers claimed that their puppets had life and could not die. The Rajasthani puppeteers took up the challenge and told the emperor: 'Let the puppets from each of our groups be immersed in a well. The group whose puppets survive will have the right to do puppetry, while the other will not.' Now, what does seem clear from the story is that the court puppets were made out of *papier-mâché* (*kāgaz-miṭṭi*), whereas the Rajasthani puppets were made from wood. So, inevitably, when the puppets were sunk in water, the kāgaz-miṭṭi puppet disintegrated, whereas the wooden puppet came out glowingly alive. Today Rajasthani puppetry is identified by one name only—*kaṭhputli* (literally, *kaṭh*, or 'wood'; *putli* or 'doll', 'figure').

However, even as the Rajasthani puppeteers won their particular right to practise puppetry, their skills in this art were still rudimentary. So they turned to the court puppeteers for instruction and regarded them as their *ustads* or teachers. In fact, at the time when I first entered this field in the early sixties, the older puppeteers claimed that they would pay an annual tribute to a Muslim *khalifā* (master) living in Delhi. A percentage of whatever the puppeteers earned in the course of the year would be passed on to the family of the khalifā as a tribute to what they had learned from its tradition. Of course, all this remains more in the area of legend rather than history, but this is how the puppeteers themselves explain the origins of their craft.

Materials and Construction

In earlier times, the wood used for the puppets was taken from the *ākṛā* plant, which grows profusely in the desert. This wood is known to be light and insect-resistant. The wood of the *boraḍi* tree was also used—the tree which produces the fruit *ber*, which is available in many parts of India. Boraḍi wood was also used to make the handles of different implements relating to agriculture and carpentry, because there's a spring in this wood that comes in very useful for such implements. Nowadays, puppeteers in Rajasthan tend to use the wood of the *aradu* tree for their puppets; this wood, which is very light, is generally cut when it is still a bit tender, so it's easier to mould and sculpt. The only implements used by the puppeteers are a small axe and a razor (*ustra*).

Earlier, the puppeteers would not make the puppets themselves. Rather they would seek out the services of a particular sub-caste of the puppeteers called Parpar. Other craftsmen, who were known for their handicrafts, including wooden toys, horses, elephants, and also the kāvaḍ (miniature cupboard serving as mobile temple), lived at a place called Bassi near Chittor. About sixty years ago, they used to make puppets as well. Today, of course, other caste groups have taken to making puppets for tourist and commercial purposes. The puppeteers themselves, however, still come from one caste group called Bhāṭ from the Nagaur district of Rajasthan, on which I will have more to say later.

Stylistically, the male and female figures of the kaṭhputli tradition bear some resemblance to Rajput miniature painting. At no point is there any attempt to make these figures realistic. From the shape of the beard or the moustache to the elongation of an eye, there are mere suggestions for the identification of each character. The male figures are generally divided into two categories—Hindu rajas and Mughal nawabs. Then there are women characters, notably dancers, and any number of animals like the elephant, the horse, the crocodile, the camel, and the snake. All these figures are constructed in such a way as to facilitate specific movements. The structure of the puppet is directly related to how the puppeteers want them to move, so the puppets are linked to very distinct manipulative techniques.

While some puppets are carved in wood all the way to the torso of the body, the heads of others are carved without necks, while some puppets have rather long necks attached to their heads. The rest of the body is made from cloth attached to the wood. In other words, there are no leg controls in Rajasthani puppetry—all movement in the lower part of the body is suggested through the flow of the garment, like the ghāgrā worn by the women characters, and the *jhaggā* worn by the male characters.

Once the puppets are carved out of wood, they are coloured. Earlier, indigenous colours were used, mixed with vegetable dyes—they had a matt finish, very different from the kind of shiny, bright colours used today. There is no symbolism as such in the use of the colours, as in classical performance traditions. The primary source of differentiation between the characters is to be found in their costumes and facial appearance. The Hindu and Muslim male characters, for instance, have differently shaped beards—a beard parted in the centre would connote a Hindu character, whereas a full beard suggests a Muslim character. Despite this differentiation between 'Hindu' and 'Muslim', one should stress that this has nothing to do with religious discrimination—it is simply a form of physical identification. Indeed, at no point in the history of puppetry in Rajasthan has religion been a factor to contend with. Of course, the puppeteers have other ritualistic functions, but we will get to that later.

In the making of all these puppets, the 'line' of their construction is very important. This line is calculated in relation to the size of the puppet being made. It's interesting to see the puppeteers make a four-legged animal like a cow or horse or elephant, by adding four sticks for the legs. However, it's only when they add the fifth stick, for the spine of the animal, that they can say this animal has *jīv*. In other words, 'life'. The anatomy of all the puppets is reduced to a basic minimum, but their dynamics matter. The bigger the puppets, the fewer the possibilities of animation and manipulation. It's the smaller puppets that are more mobile and dynamic.

Techniques of Manipulation

Let us continue to describe some of the mechanisms of the puppets relating to their movement. If the puppet is manipulated by only one string, then this is attached to a nail in the front of its head. Now obviously, with one string alone, the movements of the puppet are limited to standing up, facing the audience and walking with a bobbing motion. The second form of puppet manipulation is made possible by a loop attached both to the upper forehead in front and the nape of the puppet's neck behind—with this loop, the puppet can bow and do many other things. With three strings, one or both of the puppet's hands can be manipulated, depending on the skills of the puppeteer. The largest number of strings, around six, will be used for particularly virtuoso puppets like the dancer Anarkali, who in recent performances has been transformed into Hindi film actresses like Hema Malini.

One other important fact needs to be kept in mind: Rajasthani string puppets are perhaps the only example of their kind in the world where a control or cross is not used for manipulation. In other words, all the strings are attached to the puppeteers' fingers directly, which demands a great deal of virtuosity. In the hands of a master puppeteer, the puppets can be very graceful and move with no jerks whatsoever. The smallest of movements can be meaningful. It's interesting to examine the position of the puppeteer's hands, one palm facing outwards, the other downwards; when there is a change in movement or direction, these palms are reversed. So there is always some kind of an oppositional energy at work in the hand movement. Another important factor is that the elbows of the puppeteers cannot rest on anything. They have to be free. This means that the puppet should have very little weight in order to be moved nimbly.

Repertoire

Now let us talk about the specific items included in kaṭhputli. If you talk to any of the puppeteers, it becomes very clear that they prioritize the story of Amar Singh Rathor. This headstrong and proud Rajput chieftain belonged to the royal family of Jodhpur during the reign of Aurangzeb.[2] Though he was the elder of two brothers, and therefore had the right to rule Jodhpur or Marwar State, his father disinherited him in favour of the younger son, Jaswant Singh, who was made king. Despite being disinherited, Amar Singh Rathor, was made the subedar of Nagaur district, which was directly controlled by the Mughal emperor in Delhi. The story of his death basically centres around a conspiracy in the court, spearheaded by the emperor's brother-in-law, Salābat Khan. When Amar Singh Rathor goes to his village to get married, he overstays his leave from the court, and when he returns Salābat Khan takes advantage of this lapse by provoking him through the imposition of a fine that Amar Singh refuses to pay. A fight follows in which Salābat Khan is killed and Amar Singh Rathor flees. However, his nephew Arjun Gaur is drawn into the conspiracy and, after falsely winning over the confidence of Amar Singh, betrays him by killing him in the court itself. Later, in retaliation, a youth named Ram Singh challenges Arjun Gaur to a fair fight, and in this confrontation Arjun Gaur is killed. Finally, the body of Amar Singh is taken back to Nagaur where he is hailed as a hero.

Now this is a very rough outline of the story. It is important to keep in mind that this story of Amar Singh Rathor is popular in any number of folk drama forms in Rajasthan, eastern Uttar Pradesh, and Madhya Pradesh; you can find different renditions of the story in the secular performance traditions of *khayāl*, *nauṭanki*, and *māch*. Within the kaṭhputli tradition itself, the entire story of Amar Singh Rathor as I have described it is not enacted. At best, it provides a framework within which a few elements of the story are rendered in a very rudimentary way, following a series of skits and tricks, which constitute the main part of any kaṭhputli performance.

Generally, the play begins on an empty stage. The first characters who appear are workmen—a *beldār*, who digs and flattens the mud, a sweeper (*bhangi*) and a water-carrier (*bhisti*), who sprinkles water around the stage. Then, at the announcement of a court usher, a number of Muslim nawabs and Hindu rajas are welcomed and positioned in the court according to their status. Eventually, the emperor makes his appearance and demands entertainment. A number of items follow, though there are many that are no longer included in the contemporary repertoire.

Over the years I have seen many memorable figures, such as

Gangaram Māli, a juggler who tosses balls around the stage and even suspends them in the air; a Kālbeliā snake-charmer who is bitten to death by a dancing snake, which then sucks the poison out of the charmer. There are other items like Paṭṭebaj, involving two sword fighters engaged in combat, as well as the mimic Shaukeen Khan, who imitates a rooster crowing, among other animal and bird sounds, which are produced by the puppeteer through a *boli* (squeaker) held between his teeth. Most popular of all is a skit around the *dhobi* or washerman who is eaten by a crocodile, while his lusty and unfaithful wife seeks out another partner.

Yet another interesting item concerns Sakuri Julāhi, a female carpet-weaver from the Julāhi community. She is given some ten kilos of wool to weave a carpet for the emperor, but when she completes the task, the carpet weighs only five kilos. Subsequently, she is cross-examined by the emperor, who asks her what happened to the remaining wool. Then she reveals that such-and-such officer confiscated so much wool from her, yet another took some more, thereby indicating the state of bribery in the kingdom. Needless to say, this is a social comment on the widespread corruption in India today. Finally, when the emperor demands that the wool be returned, a member of the audience is generally requested to come on stage and draw the wool out of the weaver's body. And then follows the trick, as long threads are drawn from the puppet's belly, which are actually concealed in the hollow of the puppet's neck.

There is yet another puppet item that is no longer in the repertoire. This revolves around the very important Sufi *fakir* (saint) called Naugajā Pīr, who is believed to have performed many miracles during the medieval period in the Nagaur and Ajmer districts of Rajasthan. What is important about this puppet is its manipulation by a rod attached to the neck, which could be stretched to different heights. In all probability, this mechanism was a response to the widely held belief that Naugajā Pīr could manifest himself in different ways to his devotees, some of whom actually saw him with an elongated neck. Sadly, he is no longer remembered in the kaṭhputli tradition today, and this is a loss because Naugajā Pīr was the only rod-puppet in kaṭhputli. Today only a few old puppeteers remember this particular figure, and how he used to enter the stage with striking effect.

Yet another mysterious figure who can still be seen in the kaṭhputli repertoire, is Bangāli Jādugar, a magician from Bengal. He continues to entertain audiences by separating his head from the rest of the body, not only with one hand or both hands, but with his legs as well. A lot of dexterity is involved on the part of the puppeteer to control the movement of Jādugar as he dances around the stage, headless. It needs to be kept in mind that there is a lot more animation in manipulating these seemingly trivial puppet figures than the characters represented in Amar Singh Rathor's skit.

Performance

There are some important conventions relating to the performance of kaṭhputli. One very important point about the narration of the play is that it is rendered in the third person. So the dialogue will always proceed through prefatory statements such as, '*Amar Singh ne ye kaha*' ('This is what Amar Singh said'), and '*Salābat Khan ne ye jawāb diyā*' ('This is how Salābat Khan responded'), never in the first person. Even the modes of address are stylized and distanced—so Amar Singh is never directly referred to as Amar Singh, but rather, as 'Amar Singh *ki tasvir*' (literally, the 'picture' of Amar Singh). The moment it is accepted that the characters are merely 'pictures', then they can afford to cross all boundaries of space and time.

In this regard, what we find in a number of contemporary performances is the juxtaposition of historical figures from different ages, like the emperor Ashoka, the legendary Vikramaditya, Rana Pratap, and even Shivaji. At one level, this is anachronistic, but these figures add colour and vibrancy to the court scenes. And personally, I don't think there is anything incongruous about such juxtapositions—after all, even in my room, I could have a picture of Mohenjo-daro alongside Mahatma Gandhi, and both of them exist for me and share the same space, even though they cross the boundaries of time.

The convention that the puppets are not 'real' is further enhanced by the fact that they never speak to each other. Dialogue exists only with the drummer sitting alongside the makeshift stage in full view of the audience, who interprets what the puppeteers themselves recite in a very shrill and disguised voice through a squeaker (boli).

So, at every level in the performance, there is an attempt to stylize not only the portrayal and movement of the characters, but their voices as well. Sometimes there is live audience participation, as in the skit about a fictitious British army officer called Pilpili Sahib. He has an army of either six or nine or twelve soldiers, who march past in a parade—these figures are tied together three by three on sticks, so that they seem to move in unison.

The skit begins with Pilpili Sahib asking the audience if anyone wants a job. Generally, a young boy volunteers to be the recruit for the performance, and what follows is a hilarious exchange between the puppeteer (his voice disguised through the squeaker), and the boy. Here is one exchange of questions and answers that I recall from performances in the past:[3]

Sahib : Are you tough or soft?
Boy : Very tough.
Sahib : Male or female?
Boy : Male.
Sahib : Men have moustaches. Where are yours?
Boy : (Mimes twisting a moustache and coughs gruffly).
Sahib : Will you serve me?
Boy : Yes.
Sahib : How much salary do you want?
Boy : Twenty thousand rupees.
Sahib : What will you do with the money?
Boy : Find a good girl and marry her.
Sahib : One or two girls?
Boy : One.
Sahib : Dark complexioned or fair?
Boy : Fair.
Sahib : Married or a virgin?
Boy : I'd prefer a virgin.

Following this repartee, Pilpili Sahib proceeds to perform a series of funny movements, actions, and gestures that he requires the boy to imitate—for instance, he runs from one end of the stage to another, he rolls over, and so on. This results in a free-for-all improvization. At one point, the puppet turns upside down, with his legs suspended in the air. The boy, in a frenzy of 'play-acting', attempts to copy him, but obviously fails to do so. And the skit draws to an end, with the puppeteer ridiculing the boy's physical abilities, extending it by innuendo to his assumptions of sexual virility. The audience is highly entertained by all this fun.

In all these items, there is no attempt to tell any one continuous story. They are simply skits separated by announcements and commentary, involving very specific skills around particular tricks—the juggling of balls, or the removal of wool from a puppet's interior, or whatever. When the episodes from the Amar Singh Rathor narrative are performed, they too retain this quality of the skit. There is no attempt to tell the entire story from beginning till the end. Only after these skits have been performed will the story of Amar Singh Rathor be rendered, but in very brief scenes, generally involving fights and battles—for example, Amar Singh beheading Salābat Khan. What is important is that at the end of the performance the stage is covered with dead bodies, as the puppets are piled one on top of the other. Then they are all removed and the stage is empty once more, just as it was at the start of the performance.

Why the episode of Amar Singh Rathor is treated as a skit, why its story is never told from beginning till the end, why it continues to be a central part of the 'kaṭhputli' repertoire, even though it is not treated any differently from the rest of the skits: these questions are not answered by Komalda. And perhaps, there are no clear answers available from even the 'kaṭhputli' performers themselves. This is how their performance has evolved over the years and assumed the logic of a particular set of conventions. Perhaps, one reason why the Amar Singh Rathor narrative has been included in the 'kaṭhputli' repertoire is to inscribe the low-caste puppeteer's fictitious allegiance with the martial Rajput lineage. However, this 'Rajputization' is not represented with any particular reverence. Amar Singh Rathor is just another puppet, whose death provides the occasion for virtuoso fighting techniques in the 'dhishum-dhishum' tradition of 'action' in Hindi cinema.

Instead of answering questions relating to the hermeneutics of folk puppetry, still less to their 'subaltern' qualities, Komalda moves out of formal considerations of puppetry into a broader and more complex reflection on the social identity of the puppeteers themselves.[4] *Significantly, he does not attempt to link this identity to the actual performance of the puppeteers; rather, he broadens the context to dwell on the duality of identity formations upheld by other Rajasthani performers, from both the entertainment and ritual service sectors. Once again, as in the earlier sections of this chapter, I would emphasize that there is a sequence in Komalda's process of thinking about 'dual identities', which I have simply reproduced in transcription with minimal editing.*

Dual Identities

Now let us turn our attention to the puppeteers themselves, who belong to the Bhāṭ community. And Bhāṭs, as I have mentioned earlier in the book, are primarily genealogists, whose patrons come from the low-caste Meghwāl community. The kaṭhputli Bhāṭs are from the Nagaur district and neighbouring areas like Sikar, Kishangarh, Ajmer, and Churu. Now the funny thing is that if you go to Nagaur and ask people there, 'Where do the kaṭhputliwallas live?', you won't get an answer. Even the Meghwāls in the area will not be able to identify the puppeteers. The reason for this is that, till quite recently, the puppeteers were primarily identified as Naṭs, who even today are identified with acrobatics rather than puppetry.

I still remember how in the early period when we used to do fieldwork in Nagaur, the puppeteers themselves would plead with us not to tell their patrons about their work. But it so happened that, on one particular trip, a group of puppeteers were showing us some of their puppets outside their hut, and a few women from their patron's family walked past. I remember how surprised these women were to learn about the puppeteers' craft. For a long time, puppeteers simply did not perform kaṭhputli in their own district; they identified themselves primarily as acrobats and as genealogists of the Meghwāl families.

Now, this phenomenon reveals an interesting problem concerning the hidden status by which a community can live a double life. This is true not only of kaṭhputli puppeteers but of many other performing and ritual-serving communities. In other words, these communities are identified in different ways in different geographical areas of the state—the people from one area would not know what they are doing in the other, and *vice versa*. So, what emerges is two contexts of ignorance that exist side by side. In the process, there can be no fixed identification for any one community. I will give you three such examples.

a. *Kāvaḍ*

Let us take the example of the kāvaḍ tradition. What is a kāvaḍ from which the community derives its name? It is first of all an object in relation to which their performance of recitation is based. You could say that it's a cupboard, a miniature wooden temple, about one and a half feet long, and about nine to ten inches wide, with large flaps that are hinged together. Within the kāvaḍ, there is generally a deity or deities, carved out of wood and nailed to the structure. You can find figures from the Hindu pantheon like Vishnu, Lakshmi, and very often, Rama, Sita, Lakshmana, and Hanuman. Other mythical and sacred figures are generally painted on the wooden flaps of the kāvaḍ—here you come across local saints like Dhannā Bhagat, Pipā Bhagat, Sen Bhagat, along with all the stories and miracles associated with them.

But along with these deities, you also find contemporary human figures, such as husbands and wives embroiled in humorous domestic situations—the wife, for instance, could refuse to do housework, like cleaning the rice or grinding the wheat, while the husband threatens to beat her with a *jhāṛu* (broom). This kind of visual improvisation is not likely to be found in representing the more sanctified figures from Hindu mythology. In other sections of the kāvaḍ, there could be symbolic images relating to life after death, suggested through odd contemporary images like a passenger travelling in a train, or an aeroplane flying in the air. These figures can be linked to the souls of dead ancestors journeying elsewhere.

Now, what happens is that, when the Kāvad is recited, it is not just the stories around Rama, Sita, Lakshmana, or Vishnu that are narrated. Generally, the recitation is improvised around a particular person who has died in some household. It's important to keep in mind that this recitation is not sung but chanted—therefore it is not accompanied by any musical instrument. The function of the Kāvaḍ reciter is more ritualistic than the entertainment provided by folk performers. After seeking out details of the death in a particular family, he chants a tribute to the dead person, after which the family makes an offering. Like any offering made in a regular temple, it is not paid directly into the hand of the reciter, but placed in a drawer in the bottom of the kāvaḍ. Very often, there are a few empty panels on this itinerant temple. In such cases, the Kāvaḍ reciter will promise the family to get the image of their dead person painted on one of the blank spaces.

During our research, we came to know that most of the practitioners of this tradition hail from a small village known as Govindgarh near Ajmer. We had actually heard some of these practitioners recite Kāvaḍ for us, and yet, when we went to Govindgarh, we found these very same people denying any link with the tradition. When they took us inside their own homes, however, that's when they told us, 'Please don't tell local people that we work on Kāvaḍ in other areas, otherwise our jajmāns (patrons) will create problems for us.' So, like the Bhāṭs, who were identified as Naṭs (acrobats) and genealogists in their own home base of Nagaur, while earning their living as puppeteers elsewhere, these practitioners of Kāvaḍ were also recognized as genealogists in Govindgarh. More specifically, they were identified as the panegyric poets for the Jassā Bhāṭi community, their primary patrons. Outside of Govindgarh, however, they were identified primarily as the Kāvaḍ reciters.

Once I had a strange experience with an actual performance of Kāvaḍ in Jodhpur. After recording a particular practitioner, we had an opportunity to question him about the ritual practices surrounding the recitation. And, to our surprise, he had in his possession something like thirty to forty kānchlis (bodices). He said that this was one of the major offerings made to the Kāvaḍ. Why this offering should be made we are not at all clear, except that it is very much a woman's offering. Perhaps it is made as some sort of protection for one's self, or for one's mother, of for one's own child.

When the Kāvaḍ recitation is performed for the dead in any individual family, then, in such cases, the local saints and deities become very important for the recitation. Dhannā Bhagat is invoked for the Jāt or agricultural community; Pipā Bhagat for the Chhipa community, consisting largely of cloth printers; and Sen Bhagat for the *nāis* or barber community. Now the point is that the residents of Govindgarh, which is the home base of the Kāvaḍ reciters, know nothing about these recitations being made for other communities. For the people of Govindgarh, the Kāvaḍ reciters are identified primarily as the panegyrists of the Jassā Bhāṭi community. But this is not the case, as I have tried to point out. The Kāvaḍ community ensures its means of livelihood through the sustenance of two related professions, one of which is kept hidden from the other.

b. *Ḍākot*

One other community with dual functions is the Ḍākot, who also perform brahmanical ritual functions for low-caste communities in villages all over Rajasthan, while being identified as astrologers (*jyotishis*) for upper-caste families in Gujarat and Maharashtra. Recognized in their respective villages as the chief priests of Shaṇi Maharāj, a potentially vindictive deity who has to be constantly appeased, the Ḍākot are identified as the horoscope makers of low-caste people. They themselves are involved in the rituals of low-caste groups and eat meat, drink liquor, and are generally treated as low-caste people themselves.

However, when they migrate from Rajasthan to neighbouring states like Maharashtra and Gujarat, they assume the role of Brahman astrologers and perform many rituals within upper-caste households. Here, through an assumed knowledge of *jyotish* (astrology), a few Ḍākot have been known to probe the innermost secrets of rich households—secrets that are hidden from the family members themselves. There have been cases where having probed particular secrets from an individual, it is rumoured that some Ḍākot have resorted to blackmail, extorting a great deal of money in the process.

Needless to say, one has to be a little careful about exposing such practices. However, from what I have learned from my own experience in a particular village[5]—at one time, there were some thirty to forty Ḍākot families living there—I discovered from the local post office that large amounts of money would be regularly sent to these families from their relatives in Gujarat or Maharashtra. On the one hand, one could say that these amounts were the payments received by their relatives for the performance of different *yagyas* in cities like Mumbai and Ahmedabad. However, as I got to know from one of the most prominent and educated members of the Ḍākot community in this particular village, this was only one side of the story.

From this man, I learned on the strictest confidence that he was able to enter a rich Seth's family by assuming the role of an astrologer. In this particular household, the Seth's son had recently died but the widowed daughter-in-law continued to live with the family. By performing all kinds of pujas and astrological rites within the household, and becoming very intimate with their daily routine, it became fairly obvious to the Ḍākot that the Seth was having an affair with the daughter-in-law. In due course, she became pregnant, and it was around this time that the old man opened himself to the 'astrologer' seeking a way out through an abortion. After assuring the Seth that the abortion could be successful only through the performance of several pujas, the 'astrologer' then proceeded to blackmail him. As this Ḍākot resident revealed to me—he was a very respectable member of the village by that time, living in a large house and with all his children well educated—he had made most of his money through such clandestine practices. However, he also added that he never used the incriminating information on which he based his blackmail for any other purpose apart from extracting money from his employers.

So, once again, we have an example of a double identity. Within their own place of residence, the Ḍākot don't wear a *janeu* (holy thread), but this is very prominently displayed when they work outside as astrologers, where they pose as Brahmans. As I have described, their hidden profession remains unknown to the people living in their own village.

c. *Pāviā*

In a very different context, we encounter yet another example of such a discrepancy in the lives of a musician community in the Sirohi region called Pāviā. This is also the name of their sārangi-like instrument, which is used for accompanying their songs on the lives of mythical kings such as Harishchandra and saints such as Malaygir. What is so haunting about these songs is that they are sung early in the morning, before the break of dawn, during the winter months, as the Pāviā singers go from house to house in the village. As payment for these auspicious songs, the Pāviā receive money, food, and woollen quilts.

Now, the Pāviā are a nomadic community, and what I have observed about nomads is that their camps (*ḍerā*) are constructed in very specific ways. By looking at the makeshift dwellings in these camps it is possible to identify the specific community living there—it could be the Kālbeliā or the Ghaṭṭiwāl or the Kuchbandiā. When I had visited Sirohi, I noticed that the Pāviā lived in rounded structures made out of a bamboo framework, covered with cloth and waste materials. On one occasion, I happened to be travelling in the south of Rajasthan in the tribal area of Panarva, which is located in the midst of a thick forest. Quite by chance I happened to see a nomadic camp in this area with the same dwellings that I remembered seeing in Sirohi. Entering the camp, I also found the pāviā instrument lying around. So when I asked the residents of the camp, 'You must be Pāviā?', I was taken aback when they said, 'No.' I pointed out the instrument, and promptly, someone came and took it away, while another person denied that it belonged to them. It was obvious to me, however, from the way they were talking that they didn't want to reveal their identity. So, I accepted the situation, took a few notes, and went away.

Later, I asked the tribal people in the area who these camp dwellers were. And they said that the people I had seen in the camp were bone-collectors. Their job was literally to collect the bones of animal carcasses. This explanation made it clearer to me why it was necessary for the Pāviā to separate their two professions. On the one hand, they could be open about singing mythical and devotional songs, because this was a function for which they received some recognition and respect. On the other hand, it made sense for them to keep their other profession of bone-collection hidden, because it could be one of the most menial jobs, associated with the most downtrodden and marginalized of communities. We also need to keep in mind that these two jobs are seasonal—the singing takes place in the winter months in the Sirohi region, while the bone-collecting takes place during the rest of the year, when the Pāviā re-assume their nomadic life and wander from village to village.

Back to the Puppeteers

Underlying all the examples that I have given so far to demonstrate the hidden professions of many folk performers and ritual practitioners is the very real need to safeguard patronage rights. Today the identity of Rajasthani puppeteers practising kaṭhputli is well-established, but till quite recently, they never performed in their own home district of Nagaur. Actually, the jajmāni system for the Naṭ or acrobatic community, from which the puppeteers diverged to pursue their profession of kaṭhputli, was very fragile to begin with. After all, this system operated on a village to village basis, so, as the population of the Naṭs increased and the number of villages remained more or less the same, it became inevitable that some of these acrobats needed other patrons. To acquire new patrons, they needed to pursue different jobs. Hence, puppetry began to gain a new legitimacy.

Today, the puppetry community in Rajasthan wants to be addressed as Bhāṭ, and that, technically, is the caste group to which they belong. But in actuality, they are more often than not referred to as Balāiyon ke Naṭ, literally the Naṭs of the leather-workers known as Balāi. It is for these groups that the puppeteers provide genealogical records and sing during family celebrations and rituals. Even today, if you go to the village of the puppeteers and ask for directions to their homes, you would still have to identify them as 'Baḷāiyon ke Naṭ'. However, in their interactions with other communities in Rajasthan, they would like to be identified as Bhāṭ. If they migrate to Delhi and live in settlements around Shadipur Depot, then they tend to call themselves Bhaṭṭ; they are also formally addressed as Bhaṭṭ Sahib. In these changes of name, it is obvious that a process of brahmanization has taken place.

But, more important, what needs to be kept in mind is that the puppeteers are among the most migrant of all performers in India. Today, you can find communities of puppeteers living in Delhi, Kanpur, Allahabad, Kolkata, Mumbai, Bangalore, Chennai, just about everywhere. These wandering performers have gone with their puppets to schools, to panchayats, to cultural organizations; they have managed to eke out a living through these performances. And now we find at least some of them settling in these cities and owning small apartments. Despite this migration, however, the puppeteers remain very loyal to the place they belong to, and you can be sure that, for all marriages and other household ceremonies and rituals, they will return to their village in the Nagaur district to fulfil their obligations.

Up until the seventies of the last century, it was customary for the puppeteers to set up camp on the outskirts of a particular village or town. After walking around with a few puppets in hand, invariably followed by a number of children, they would seek a nominal advance of one rupee, or a small amount of money, for a night's performance. Then they would set up their *tambuḍi* (tent), which was pitched around seven bamboo poles. To this they would add the *jhālar* or upper frill of the stage; the *dyoḍi* or backdrop curtain, behind which the puppeteers stand manipulating the puppets out in front; and the *tibārā*, or front curtain within which the puppets are framed in some kind of depth-of-field perspective. Today the arrangements of kaṭhputli performances are far less elaborate. In open spaces, the tambuḍi has been replaced by a make-shift stage with two light-weight cots placed horizontally side by side, providing a convenient back wall against which curtains are draped. For indoor performances in urban areas, however, there are no such preparations, as the performances are held in assembly halls, in schools, or in community centres or in the premises of NGOs. There are new arrangements for these contemporary performances, to which the puppeteers have adjusted, and the show goes on.

While there is a return to puppetry in the conclusion to this chapter, the significant point is that Komalda focuses on puppeteers rather than on their craft. This is a leitmotif in my process of listening to him—almost always, he will begin with a form, say, a dance form like Terātāli, and almost immediately, he will contextualize it within the lives of specific communities and almost forget about the form altogether. Here, in the section on puppetry, there is a fairly extended description of the practice of puppetry, but the narrative shifts into other identifications with ritual performers like the Kāvaḍ reciters, astrologers like the Ḍākot, and musicians like the Pāviā.

Komalda's connection of different communities through the problematic of their dual identities needs to be contrasted with the more current rhetoric in multicultural studies on 'multiple' and 'hybrid' identities. While the postmodern rejection of monolithic identity formations operates within the context of 'cultures of choice', the arguably 'non-modern' upholding of dual identities by communities like the Kāvaḍ, the Ḍākot, and the Pāviā can more readily be justified on the basis of economic necessity and social mobility. These distinctions need to be made if only to resist the slippage between 'non-modern' and 'postmodern' realities, to which communitarian theorists often succumb in their larger critique of modernity.

10

PROFESSIONAL CASTE MUSICIANS

As we move towards the final three chapters of the book, which have been structured in sequence, we focus on the primary area of research in which Komalda has distinguished himself over the years—Rajasthani folk music. He is a pioneer in this area in more ways than one. We begin with an examination of the hereditary profession and skills of two traditional musician groups—the Langas and Manganiyars—with whom Komalda has a relationship going back more than forty years. There will be more intimate insights into their relationship in the next chapter within the larger context of the globalization of Rajasthani folk music, but here we will concentrate on the systems of patronage and social organization of traditional musician communities, along with their modes of transmitting musical knowledge.

Within the social background of the Langas and the Manganiyars presented here, there is a reading of caste grounded in the materiality of specific occupations. Clearly, this funcionalist approach to caste has fallen out of favour in the more contemporary literature around the politicization of caste vis-à-vis the dalit struggle, the policy of reservations, casteism in electoral politics, and the more recent attempt to internationalize caste as race. Without addressing these immediate controversies, Komalda contextualizes caste groups within specific professional traditions with self-governing laws and customs. Without polemicizing this context against the larger theorization of the 'narrative of community' in subaltern studies,[1] *Komalda merely states some basic facts relating to the communitarian social structures of the Langas and Manganiyars, whom he specifically describes as 'professional hereditary caste musicians.'*

Modes of Patronage

At the very outset I would like to emphasize that if folk music has survived over the centuries in India, this is not because of the support it has received from kings and jāgirdārs. It has survived because of the very concrete support provided by local castes, communities, and people at large, cutting across different religious groups. Even today, after Independence, the patrons of traditional musicians come from particular families, and not from the State, which can merely recognize talent by awarding fellowships and awards. But the State can neither create nor sustain talent. For the survival of traditional musicians, we have to look elsewhere.

Now, in my view, caste operates like a polytechnic. As a technical school for indigenous skills, it provides a basic education in a particular skill to a range of workers, who are recruited within specific groups. The tailor, barber, cobbler have their own organizations, which continue to develop certain crafts which are of use to society. There can be no doubt that these are necessary services, without which society would not be able to function properly. All the technologies learned in these institutions have traditions of learning which are passed on from one generation to another.

At one level, musicians are no different from other dependent caste groups who provide specific services, like the potter, carpenter, ironsmith, and cobbler. The relationship between these artisans and craftsmen who provide concrete material or technical services and their patrons is described as *birat* or *āyat*. While birat is sustained by hereditary links between patrons and those who serve them, the relationship determined by āyat is more contractual.[2] Both relationships are based on the barter economy, whereby the craftsmen receive a share of the crop from their patrons' fields in exchange for their services. While birat and āyat focus on physical services, the jajmāni system is more specifically linked with ritual functions involving the genealogy of the patron's family and the conducting of different ceremonies, both social and religious. It is within this framework that traditional musicians from the Manganiyar and Langa communities work out their relationships to specific patrons (jajmāns).

It is true that in today's world of international performance, which we will describe in detail in the next chapter, many of these musicians are now travelling abroad and earning good money—but how many such musicians would there be? At most, two hundred, but for the thousands of other Manganiyars and Langas, the jajmāni system remains their primary source of income. Even those among them who cannot sing will have to be supported by the patrons, because it is assumed that this man's son or grandson may be able to sing in the future. The patron is obliged to sustain these hereditary ties regardless of the quality of the singer's voice or musicianship.

This obligation to patronize the musicians on hereditary grounds is quite different in effect from the performing arts situation, where it is the more proficient musicians and singers who get selected for tours or for concerts in five-star hotels and other tourist venues. This kind of selective opportunity does not exist for the jajmāns of traditional musicians. And it is for this very reason that the entire musical system of the Langas and Manganiyars has been able to survive as a caste institution, otherwise it would have broken down a long time ago. After all, if one had to go by the criterion of 'quality' alone, then all patrons would want the Manganiyar musician Sakar to play the kamāychā for their festive and ritual occasions, because he is such a fine artist. But what then would have happened to the others in the community? This is what we have to keep in mind.

Even in extreme cases when singing traditions have been proscribed, the patronage system continues. For example, there was a time when the future of the Surṇāiā Langas, who used to play aerophonic (wind) instruments for the Mehar Muslims, was called into question. This followed a period when they became very staunch *murids* (devotees) of the Pīr of Pagaro, an orthodox Islamist, who declared that there should be no more singing in the Surṇāiā Langa community. So, almost overnight, hundreds of Langas could no longer play their instruments for which they received payment from their patrons. But did that mean that their patrons left them in the lurch? The answer is 'no'. Even today they continue to be paid the exact amount that had been agreed upon earlier.[3]

Even today the bonds between the musicians and their patrons remain strong. Just the other day the father of the musician Bundu, who has performed in many parts of India and the world, passed away. Now Bundu's family has been living for many years now in the Langa colony in Jodhpur, and as such, it has lost direct contact with its jajmān. Nonetheless, the formal relationship remains, and Bundu was able to get a substantial amount of money from his patrons for the death ceremony of his father. This is a perfectly normal procedure of financial support that continues even to this day, and the musicians cannot afford to ignore it.

On the other hand, it could be asked what the patrons stand to gain from continuing this tradition. And their response is very simple: 'These musicians carry the weight of our genealogy on their heads.' Through this geneaology, the families of the patrons are given cognizance and respect in society at large, and the musicians contribute to their status in a significant way.

'Divorcing' Patrons

Significantly, the services performed by professional caste groups can be suspended when the workers in question *divorce* their patrons. The word literally used in such circumstances is '*talāq*'. I can give you a very definite example, when such a 'divorce' took place resulting in a great deal of difficulty for the patrons. Around 150 years ago, the Dāyamā Brahman community was highly dependent on the nāis, or barber community that was serving them. When a dispute arose between the two parties, the nāis promptly decided to boycott their patrons because they had other Hindu communities to fall back on. Not only did this result in the obvious inconveniences for the Dāyamā Brahman community; the greater problem related to the fact that nāis also provided a number of important functions—for example, they were used as messengers for marriages in the Dāyamā Brahman community; they were also responsible for washing all the utensils for various ceremonies of this community; and, more critically, they were entrusted to carry the fire to the cremation ground for death rituals. When other barbers refused to work for the Dāyamā Brahman community, they had no other option but to employ Muslim barbers in their households. Needless to say, this decision challenged a number of caste taboos.

From this example, it becomes clear that if a relationship is disturbed, then occupational caste groups have the power to stop essential services. If carpenters, or cobblers, or washermen stop doing their jobs, then society faces a problem primarily at physical and economic levels. However, when musicians 'divorce' their patrons, the consequences can be more critical. Musicians dissatisfied with their patrons have many ways of registering their protest.[4] First of all, they can stop reciting the panegyric verses (*shubhrāj*) in honour of their patron's families. If this sign of protest does not result in any reconciliation with the patron, they can then proceed to bury their turbans under the sand outside their patron's house. If this fails to have any effect, the musicians can then proceed to bury the strings of their musical instruments in front of their patron's house. And if that doesn't yield any results, they can resort to the final humiliation of making an effigy (*lolaṛ*) of their patron, which they tie to a donkey's tail, while beating it in full view of the entire neighborhood. After completing this ritual of *lolaṛ bāndhnā* (literally, 'tying on an effigy'), no Langa or Manganiyar musician will ever again contribute musically to any of the ceremonies of their patron's household.

Needless to say, this creates enormous social problems for the patrons, who find it difficult to get their sons and daughters married. There is also the risk of being ostracized by the community at large. In addition, patrons run the risk of being subjected to highly abusive poems composed in couplets called *bhūnd*, by which the musicians formally sever their ties with the families. Needless to say, no patron is comfortable about being censured in this way, because the entire legacy and future of his family are at stake. By asserting the power of retaliation through ritualized practices and threats, therefore, the musicians are capable of prevailing on their patrons and asserting their hereditary rights.[5]

Codes of Patronage

Despite the difficulties that can occasionally surface between musicians and patrons, the reality is that their relationship continues to be very strong and is sustained through mutually understood codes. One term that needs to be kept in mind is *dhaṇi*. Suppose I am a Manganiyar, and I am singing for your family and I am attached to it, then you are my dhaṇi. You will be obliged to pay me when the occasions arise—marriage, death, or whatever—and I, thereby, have a right in your family. Now, regarding the distribution of rights within the Manganiyar families, it is something like this. If I have two sons and I am attached to fifty families, then my sons will divide the rights equally—twenty-five families for each son. So patrons are divided like property, which means the system enables all members of the Manganiyar family to sustain themselves economically. When the patron's sons form their own households after getting married, then they, too, are obliged to continue supporting the musicians associated with their family. In this way, the number of families attached to a particular musician increases over the course of time.

There is another type of jajmāni that is known as *siroli* jajmāni. This means that as a Manganiyar, for example, I can go to any house and the patron castes will have to pay me, but this system works on a first-come-first-paid basis.

Even if some individuals in a Langa or Manganiyar family cannot sing, this doesn't mean that they can't have patrons. If any musical service is needed in the patron's house, they will invite those musicians who can sing to provide the necessary services. The non-practising musicians will have to be paid what is called *nēg*—a fixed amount, regardless of the fact that they can't sing. Those who do sing will be provided with *inām*, or money in the form of a gift. Briefly, this is how the jajmāni system operates through specific attachments and understandings between musicians and patron families, not only for Langas and Manganiyars, but for Ḍholis, Ḍhāḍhis, and other musician groups as well.

The performing arts situation is a little different. Here entire villages are divided among the artists. So if I as a performing artist am attached to five villages, and I have two sons, then they will have to divide their share of the villages equally—two and a half villages for each son. When the individual members of the performer's family increase in number, there is a problem. Each performance group of acrobats (naṭs), for instance, is likely to include five to ten people, if not more. So it becomes more difficult for actors and acrobats to sustain themselves outside of the jajmāni system, because they are dependent on entire villages rather than on individual families. And villages don't grow as easily as families. Likewise, the bahurupiā or itinerant mime artists who impersonate mythical gods and goddesses, are also attached to villages, which have their own internal organization for contributing to the costs of each performance.

Categorizing Musicians and Patrons

It is important to keep in mind that there are two types of Langas, one who is identified as Sārangiā Langa, and the other as Surṇāiā Langa. The former plays the sārangi (bowed stringed instrument) and sings, while the latter plays aerophonic instruments like the *surṇāi* (a kind of *shehnai*), the *murli* (gourd-pipe), the *satārā* (double-flute), but does not sing. In fact, this convention is a taboo that cannot be broken, even though Surṇāiā Langas can sing for their personal pleasure. The jajmāns of these Langas are Mehar Muslims, and not Sindhi Sipahi, who patronize the Sārangiā Langas. Significantly, these two groups of Langas do not intermarry, thereby keeping their specific patronage links intact.

Interestingly, the songs sung in the Sindhi Sipahi households incorporate Hindu themes and images. So if a male child is born in a Sindhi Sipahi home, he can be referred to as Krishna, with all the accompanying references to Mathura and Gokul. Only in the last ten years or so are these songs beginning to disappear through the growing Islamization of the community. Likewise, the Manganiyars, for instance, are Sunni Muslims, but most of them sing for Hindu jajmāns. Indeed, so closely do their identify with their patrons, that at one time their repertoire of songs related to Hindu customs, religious figures and themes. The Hindu patrons could come from different caste groups, ranging from upper-caste Rajputs to other caste groups like tailors, carpenters, and even low-caste Bhāmbhi families, though some of these low-caste patrons are not always acknowledged by the Manganiyars.

Among Manganiyars there are also two groups—one which sings exclusively for Hindu families, and the other which sings for both

Hindu and Muslim families. However, unlike the Langas, the Manganiyars intermarry. But they continue to be differentiated according to the instruments they play. Those who sing for Hindu families play the kamāychā, while those who sing for both Hindu and Muslim families play the *jāḍi ki sārangi*. While these two-stringed instruments resemble each other very closely in terms of their size, pegs, strings, their tuning systems are different. From these two instruments have emerged two distinct musical styles. (For more technical details on the production of these styles in relation to instruments, *rāga* and *tāla* structures, see Appendices A, B, C.)

Contexts of Songs

Regardless of these styles, the different groups of Manganiyars are expected to play music at all the important ceremonies in their patrons' homes relating to childbirth, marriage, and death. When a child is born in one of their patron's homes, the Manganiyars sing songs wishing the child a long life, apart from honouring all the members of the family on the auspicious occasion. Depending on the size of the family, the song extends to numerous stanzas, each stanza honouring a single relative. *Gīt baṛā yā got?* (Which is bigger, the song or the family?')—this is a popular saying for such songs.

The marriage ceremonies have even more songs that are prescribed for specific rituals—apart from general songs in praise of the bridegroom (*bannā*) and the bride (*banni*), there are songs that describe every stage in the marriage ceremony. From the *ghoṛi* which is sung while the bridegroom is proceeding to the bride's place on horseback, to the *bidāi* which is sung when the bride leaves her own home, there are songs for all the rites and ceremonies of the marriage—for instance, the *pīṭhi* songs (sung during the massage of the bride and groom with pīṭhi paste, which is made up of turmeric and oil); the *mehendi* songs (sung while henna is applied to the hands of the bride), interspersed with bawdy songs (*gāḷi*) where the two sides of the family tease each other. So, at every stage of the marriage, which can extend over weeks, there are songs that accompany the rituals.[6]

While their presence is mandatory for all the rituals, the musicians sing their wide repertoire of songs without any particular audience in mind. More often than not they are taken for granted, singing in one corner of the marriage site. However, a more formal interaction with the musicians is arranged in special musical sessions called *kacheri* (or *rihāṇ*), where the skills of the musicians are more virtuosically displayed to discriminating listeners.[7]

Interspersing this soiree are highly sophisticated musical games such as the *kānkari* ('pebble'), in which the bridegroom's party has to locate a hidden object according to the directional hints provided by specific rāgas played on instruments. There is no vocalization for these musical numbers, except at the very end of the search in order to identify the object itself. Otherwise there is a repertoire of at least eight rāgas which designate eight different directions (north, north-east, south-west, etc); these are supplemented by two more rāgas indicating 'up' and 'down', and one more rāga that designates a change in direction. Needless to say, the intricate knowledge of music demanded in this game requires the presence of at least one musical connoisseur in the bridegroom's party, failing which it could be subject to ridicule.

Multiple Caste Names

As far as caste is concerned, the Manganiyars are mainly found in Jodhpur, Jaisalmer, and Barmer districts, and in very few villages in Bikaner. They are also found in Sind, Pakistan, and the southern district of Jalor, where they call themselves Mirāsi. Actually, Mirāsi is the honorific term that refers to all Muslim professional singers. Even Manganiyars can be respectfully addressed as Mirāsi, though the word Manganiyar literally means 'one who begs' (originating from the verb *māngnā*, 'to beg'). Today however it does not have such a servile connotation, and refers simply to a particular group of musicians.

Now caste-wise, what is the situation generally? Suppose somebody asks me in Delhi, 'Who are you'? Then I will say: 'I am a Jain'. But if somebody wants to know a little more about me, he may ask: 'What Jain'? Then I will say, 'Shwetāmbar Jain.' Then he could continue to ask, 'What Shwetāmbar Jain?' Then I will say, 'Murti Pujak Shwetāmbar Jain.' Then only, at this point in the dialogue, will he ask, 'What is your caste?' Then I will say, 'Oswāl Dugar.'

It should be clear by now that the naming of caste is a complex matter. In what context is the question of caste raised in the first place? And for what purposes do we identify ourselves within the boundaries of a particular caste? For the most part, people resort to general categories: every Langa born in a particular family will call himself or herself Langa, and every Manganiyar will do likewise. If Muslim singers are generically categorized as Mirāsi, Hindu singers tend to go by the name of Ḍholi.[8] Though there is a Ḍholi caste, it is important to keep in mind that there are Ḍholis affiliated to a number of other castes—so you have Gujar Ḍholis, Bania Ḍholis, Patel Ḍholis and so on. These individual groups do not intermarry. In Sind, the general term for musicians will be Fakir, but only some musicians will be addressed as such. Likewise, if a Manganiyar is addressed in a general forum, he will identify himself as 'Muslim.' But when the question of identity is pursued, 'What Muslim?', then he will say, 'Manganiyar.'

Social Structure

Now, at one level, the Manganiyars are an endogamous group in so far as they marry only among themselves. But there are almost seventy to eighty sub-castes within the Manganiyars, like Dhola, Babar, Jīṇā, Solanki, and so on. The important point is that marriages cannot take place within the same sub-caste. So a Dhola cannot marry another Dhola, a Jīṇā cannot marry a Jīṇā, but a Dhola can marry a Jīṇā. This is the restriction, which we find in Hindu communities as well. What we discovered from our research, covering almost 2,000 families, is that most of the marriages among the Manganiyars have taken place within a radius of sixty-five miles. The reason for this is that the community is very compact with a relatively small population. In one particular village, you will find only one sub-caste living together. So if there are ten families living in a village, all of them will be Dholas, or Jīṇās, or Babars.

But there are exceptions. Supposing in a village of Jīṇās there is one Dhola, then he could either be a *pāvṇā* or *jamāi*, the son-in-law whose connection could go back to an earlier generation. Or he could be identified as *bhāṇo*, or *beṭi kā laḍkā*, the daughter's son, the daughter having married into another sub-caste living somewhere else. These are the only exceptions, but by and large, the norm is 'one sub-caste for each village.' This would apply to other caste groups as well—among the Jāṭs, you can come across entire villages where all the families are Bidiasar; all Chāraṇs living in the village of Narva are Lalas, and so on. As a Dugar, if I lived in any village, then all the people living there would be Dugar.

Let us focus now on the internal social organizations in the rural areas of Rajasthan.[9] These exist independently of the panchayat (or panch, as it is known at a more familiar level), which consists of the elected representatives of the people, who are authorized to make decisions relating to land titles, houses, roads, schools, buildings, clinics, and so on. Then there are the government authorities represented by the collector, the sub-division officer, the *tahsīldār*, *paṭwārī* (registrar of revenue and land accounts), who have their own legally sanctioned power to assert their authority in specific ways. In contrast, there are local community and caste organizations, which can extend to twelve geographically continguous villages, like the *chokhlā* or *khatmebhāi*, and at times to as many as eighty-four villages, like the *chorāsi*. There are also male kinship groups like the *birādarī* and larger community groups determined primarily by area like the *nyat*.

It is important to keep in mind that all these local organizations are authorities in their own right. You can't cross their paṭh, especially when it comes to issues relating to customary practices. Keep in mind that they have the power to inflict punishment, both capital and physical, on those members in the community who transgress community values and norms. At one level, these disciplinary procedures can be considered illegal, because they exist independently, and are often counter to the laws of the country. Nonetheless, they continue to be inflicted whenever there are disputes concerning property or marriage or adoption. These local community leaders may not be appointed by the state, but they wield power in their own right. Their members are often wealthy and play a key role in the economy of the region.

The internal caste organizations have all kinds of functions relating to marriage, death, and to other social and ritual occasions. Whether you are dealing with Muslims or Hindus, you will invariably encounter a cluster of at least twelve villages, which form a unit. Among the Muslims, this cluster is called khatmebhāi, while among the Hindus, it is known as chokhlā. Now, what we found is that these clusters of villages play a very important role for all death-related rituals and arrangements. Whenever there is a death in the family, these villages have the right to be informed first, as well as to be involved in the arrangements for the death ceremony, and so on. The chokhlā/khatmebhāi also plays an important role in matters concerning property disputes and other family-related matters. If, for any reason, the dispute in question cannot be resolved at this level, then the matter is taken up by the chorāsi.

Apart from the human resources, we have also been able to derive much information from the chokhlā/khatmebhāi on water, land, ecology, and the crops to be found in each village. For example, we are able to ask specific questions on land like, 'In your village what kind of land do you have—*thaḷi*, *dhāṭ* or *tharḍā*? What plants grow there? How do you build your houses? What type of drinking water sources do you rely on?' What we have discovered through our experience over the years is that the information derived from these sources is never wrong. Time and again I have been struck by the accuracy of the information.

Customs

When we turn to the local customs of the Langas and the Manganiyars, we notice their syncretic nature. Even though these communities were converted to Islam at some point in time, in all probability during the late medieval period, when many other artisan communities like potters, weavers, and carpenters got converted, they continue to uphold Hindu social customs. Their women, for instance, wear *chuṛa* (bangles)—earlier, these were made of ivory and coconut, and they would be broken when the women were widowed. For marriage (*niqāh*), the brides continue to wear white for the brief ceremony, but are colourfully attired for all the celebrations surrounding the marriage. The wedding procession, the *toran* (wooden emblem) decorating the entrance to the bridegroom's house, the codes of festivity, the music: all these signs reveal a syncretic culture in which Hindu and Muslim elements have been embraced.

When I first entered this field in the late 1950s, all the marriages among the Muslim musical communities that I encountered were performed not by the *moulvi* (priest), but rather, by a non-initiated priest known as *sai*. Today all the marriages are performed by moulvis, and in the remotest villages as well. In Barnawa village, there are almost 150 Langa families living together. When I went to this village in 1956, there were only twenty to twenty-five families. I remember how I was once introduced to one Jaman Khan who had been to the masjid of Navtala for Eid. Now Navtala is barely twenty kilometres away from Barnawa. In Barnawa there was no masjid at that time, so any person who travelled twenty kilometres to do namāz in Navtala was considered almost as great as a person going for Haj. Of course, all this has changed now with the growth of transportation and the increasing economic stability of the Langas and Manganiyars.

A few rituals like the death-feast, which is known as *osar* among the Langas, and as *dhām* among the Manganiyars, still continue to be practised, though not too frequently. In my lifetime I have only participated in two such osar ceremonies of the Langas.[10] Actually, it is not entirely accurate to refer to these ceremonies as funerary feasts. They have nothing to do with lamentation or condolences. Rather, they are more like investiture ceremonies in which the successor to the particular member of the family who has passed away—and in whose honour the osar is being conducted—is duly commemorated.

Now, in the osar that I last attended, an enormous amount of money was spent on feeding the entire community. This is typical of a ceremony whose scale depends on the number of meals that are served during its course. In addition to being fed, thousands of people will be presented with food items such as ghee, wheat, and guṛ (jaggery). Who is responsible for sponsoring the osar? A patron affiliated to the concerned family, without whose guarantee of support the osar will not be permitted by the elders in the community. At every step of the way the community is involved in the organization of the feast, including the preparation of food: will it be cooked in pure ghee or vegetable oil? Will food preparations like *lāpsi* and *kaṛhi* be served? Who will cook the food? At what times will the different servings take place? And so on.

Through the details that I have mentioned above, I think it should be clear that the lives of communities like the Langas and Manganiyars are strongly determined by any number of indigenous social structures and customs. From choices relating to marriage determined by kinship groups like the birādarī, to death-related issues controlled by the chokhlā and khatmebhāi, to property disputes negotiated by the panch and the chorāsi, to investiture ceremonies conducted during feasts like osar and dhām, these communities are subject to collective decision-making processes at every step of the way through their own organizations. All matters relating to birth, marriage, property, inheritance and death have their own specific modes of negotiation.

Listening to Komalda work through the intricate nomenclature of the internal social organizations of the Langas and Manganiyars was not easy. There were many confusions, overlapping categories, and dead-ends in the vocabulary—and perhaps, not least, in my own listening process. It didn't help to be presented with different versions of the same terms and categories collated by colleagues in the field, who have collaborated with Komalda over the years.[11] *And yet, my update on these terms did not always match with their documentation.*

Despite this difficulty, which I think is inevitable in any kind of oral sociology, the contextualization of the musicians' lives within the minutiae of their caste organizations is what makes Komalda's understanding of their music so much more profound. It could be argued, of course, that there are no direct equations between social organization and musicality. For that matter, there is no literal correspondence between social reality and music, despite the strenuous attempts made in certain ethnomusicological circles to affirm that 'music is *culture and what musicians do* is *society.'*[12] *Without upholding these essentialisms, one can acknowledge that the lives of the musicians and the music they play are necessarily mediated by their internalization of particular social laws and modes of communication. These in turn affect the group dynamics, improvisational skills, mnemonic resources, and transmission of their musical traditions. It is this last issue—transmission—to which Komalda turns his attention now.*

Transmission

The musical skills of traditional musicians like the Langas and the Manganiyars are still transmitted exclusively on the basis of hereditary links within particular families. This raises critical questions about the future of these musical traditions in the absence of new recruiting practices. Before elaborating on the specificities of this situation, let us broaden our perspective briefly to consider how other professional caste groups like carpenters, cobblers, tailors, weavers, and ironsmiths are dealing with the processes of recruitment and transference of jobs in a changing world. Do the old caste restrictions still apply?

To repeat what I said earlier, all caste groups function like polytechnics; they provide the know-how of particular skills and crafts. As long as society does not provide alternative vocational training centres, the caste organizations will continue to remain important to society at large.[13] It is necessary to keep in mind that the artisans trained in these groups are self-employed for the most part and are no burden to society. Those who are particularly skilled are now earning a good living. In Jodhpur you can't get a carpenter today for less than Rs 150–200 per day; even a *mistri* will not be available for much less. So the skills acquired through hereditary caste groups continue to be economically viable.

Earlier, it was harder for artisans and craftsmen to abandon their particular skills because of social bonds and loyalties to particular groups, but today we are seeing many changes. Generally, the shift is from low to high rather than high to low. In other words, it is unlikely that any person belonging to an upper-caste professional group would want to become a leather-worker. However, in the last fifty to sixty years, a lot of new people are entering old professions—like the *darzi* (tailor), for instance. Today when a tailor identifies himself not merely as darzi, but as *sui darzi*, then we know that he has inherited this profession from his family. The fact is that many other people from other caste-groups have taken to tailoring for a livelihood. In carpentry as well, we find recruits, but generally from caste groups lower than the carpenter. In fact, there are many Manganiyars today who work as carpenters, and very good ones too.

With ironsmithry, the situation is somewhat different. In the traditional sectors, there are no recruits from the other castes to this profession. The work is hard and demanding. But a wide cross-section of workers from different caste backgrounds is now working in iron-related small industries, lathe-work, and car repair shops. Traditional nomadic groups like the Gaḍolia Luhār, whom I have mentioned earlier in the section on 'Nomadism' in the second chapter, have not lost their relevance, as they continue to provide iron-related technical services in the rural areas. Today they are particularly known for their firing skills at the forge and in making implements for carpenters, brass and copper workers, goldsmiths, silversmiths, and other artisans. They are also masters at joining raw iron and steel grade iron for the production of tools with a wide range of uses.

While in the rural areas the Gaḍolia Luhār community continues to live a nomadic existence, large sections of this caste group have now settled in urban areas where small-scale iron industries are predominant. In the Rāvan-kā-chabutrā area in Jodhpur, for instance, you will find many of them near repair shops and iron workshops, as well as the railway warehouses. Almost all the tools used in small-scale technical industries are made by the Gaḍolia Luhār. Stone workers using the *ṭānkī* (chisel) and other tools also need the services of these craftsmen to sharpen their implements. There are at least twenty to thirty different types of ṭānkī that are used for different purposes; their blades and edges have to be constantly sharpened in order to be effective. It becomes obvious, therefore, that the community has not lost its relevance. If somebody wants to achieve the expertise found in Gaḍolia Luhār workmanship, he is free to do so, but in that case, he will also have to accept the Gaḍolia Luhār as his teachers.

The same situation does not apply to the musical traditions represented by the Langas and Manganiyars, who have no system of transmitting their musical knowledge to any person outside of their social context. Now, if we look into the classical tradition of Indian music, we encounter different *gharānās* like the Kirānā, the Jaipur, the Seniā, the Gwalior, and so on. These gharānās are musical schools with very distinct styles and modes of transmitting traditions. But among the Langas and Manganiyars, the transmitting processes are entirely different. Their transmissions are of a kind where nothing is taught, and yet something is learned.

By contrast, if you take any gharānā, for example, there are specific ways in which students are trained to continue the tradition. There is no such teaching structure among the Langas and Manganiyars. We have video documentation, for instance, covering six consecutive years in the training of a Manganiyar student, from his tenth to his sixteenth year. So we have some record of how he learned and from whom he learned. But would we be in a position to say that such-and-such person *taught* him? The answer is 'no'.

I will give you another example. There are two major sārangi players among the folk musicians of Rajasthan today—the Langa musician, Mehra, who plays the sindhi sārangi, and the Manganiyar musician, Lakha, who plays the jāḍi ki sārangi. Though their instruments are not essentially different, their musical styles are highly individualized. I once brought these two musicians together, in order to select musical material from the Kālbeliā song collection. Now, if Mehra and Lakha are asked to re-play the songs of the Kālbeliā on their instruments, they can do so, because the sārangi is a full instrument. But when they are asked to adhere strictly to the rhythmic patterns of the Kālbeliās, without resorting to their own rhythms, then they find it difficult to 'break' their traditions. It is very hard to crack the shells of these Langa and Manganiyar traditions. I would say that the cross-fertilization of different rhythmic patterns across musical traditions is not an easy task, and therefore, the possibilities of transmission from one tradition to another are restricted.

Yes, one can borrow songs across musical groups. Today, for instance, a large number of the popular songs sung by the Langas and Manganiyars in public forums come from the Kālbeliā repertoire, which are sung primarily by women. Significantly, the Kālbeliās themselves never sing any song that originates with the Langas or Manganiyars, though they have no problem in taking back their compositions with some stylistic changes. So there is some give-and-take across groups, at the level of individual songs. One can even learn Manganiyar music, it's no problem, but one will have to be prepared for a very different learning procedure for the simple reason that there is no teacher. Lakha is an excellent sārangi player, I tell you. Even Pandit Ram Narayan and Ustad Sultan Khan, they all agree that he is a great player. But is he a teacher? The answer is 'no'.

Once we gave him a student—Samsu, from the Langa community—who was very small at that time. He wouldn't learn and Lakha had no method of initiating the child into the learning process. He was not ready to go back to his own childhood and remember how he had learned the sārangi. As an expert, all he wanted to do was to play his instrument in front of the child, and naturally Samsu was not able to follow him. Then Lakha would beat him, verbally abuse him, not give him food. For almost one year Samsu got a scholarship from the Sangeet Natak Akademi and he learned nothing, nor was Lakha able to do anything.

Obviously, the guru-shishya paramparā does not exist here as in the classical tradition, where there is a method (*tarīqā*), which has to be followed, with hours and hours of practice (*riyāz*). But in the folk musical traditions, not just in Rajasthan but in the world at large, you learn but you are never taught. It is like your own mother-tongue, which you imbibe without anyone teaching you. When a child is even three years old, it has a vocabulary of hundreds of words. The child doesn't know who taught him these words, nor does society know who taught him the rules of grammar. The same situation holds true in folk music.

So in order to learn these traditions, you have to accept that they are not structured in the classical sense. And yet, there are surprises. Remember, I was talking about Samsu. After he failed to learn from Lakha, I was very angry with him. After all, we were responsible for the grant that he had received. For almost four years I didn't have any contact with the boy. I didn't select him for any programme. But once, what happened was that I needed a sārangi player for a concert, and only Samsu was available. So I said, all right, I'm angry with him, he didn't do what I wanted, but let him come and play. He came and played and I was stunned, because he was playing in the Lakha style. His bowing, his fingering, everything was like Lakha. What had happened? From Lakha's point of view—and indeed, from my point of view—he was not learning. But today, if you listen to him alongside Mehra and Lakha, you will see that he has the style of Lakha and not of Mehra. So these are some of the insights that I have learned in dealing with the process of transmission.

This example is typical of Komalda's 'method' of inscribing the unpredictable within his seemingly detached, omniscient discourse.

He can hold forth on what appears to be an immutable principle—in this particular case, the non-availability of teaching methods among traditional musicians—and then, at the very end, he can come up with contradictory evidence. Let us now deepen Komalda's perspective on musicians by contextualizing it not merely within their indigenous contexts, but in relation to their larger national, international, and global affiliations. In the next chapter of this book, there is a different kind of contemporaneity relating to folk music that I wish to prioritize, and there is no better way of doing this than to actually trace the relationship between Komalda and the musicians in a more historical framework.

11

FROM THE LOCAL TO THE GLOBAL

Rajasthani folk music in performance

The penultimate chapter of this book extends the material covered in the last chapter on the social background of Rajasthani traditional performers and musicians. Here we focus on the more personal dynamics between Komalda and the musicians from the time he first met them in the late 1950s to their subsequent tours both within India and abroad. Inevitably, this terrain enables us to reflect on the larger politics of national culture, the international festival circuit, and the inevitable globalization of folk culture, which raises tricky and difficult questions. We begin the chapter with a brief retrospective of Komalda's interactions with traditional musicians, primarily from the Langa and Manganiyar communities, in Rajasthan itself.

THE NATIONAL CONTEXT

It was around 1953 that I first began to look around for folk musicians. At that time I was co-editing a monthly literary journal called *Prerna* (Inspiration) in Rajasthani, with my friend Vijay Dan [Detha]. We wanted to publish one folk song in each issue, every month. What mattered to us at that time was not the musical quality of the song, but its poetic content. Of course, there were many collections of folk songs that had already been published by then, but we wanted to collect new songs. So, with this in mind, we got in touch with four Langas—Noor Mohammed, Alauddin, Sumar Khan, and Kammu Khan—who were professional musicians, but working as labourers for grain merchants in the area surrounding Jalori Gate ki Bari in Jodhpur. When we got to know that they could sing, we organized some sessions with them—I still remember that we paid them four annas each for each session.[1] The Langas would dictate the words of their songs to us, and we would then transcribe a selection of these songs and publish their edited versions in issues of *Prerna*.

So, it was through this literary interest that I first came into contact with folk musicians. At first the Langas were quite apprehensive about us, but gradually we won their confidence and our relationship grew. I started going with Noor Mohammed to his village of Barnawa, and it was through such meetings that our association and understanding of each other deepened. Around 1956, I remember being approached by the officers of the All India Radio in Jaipur, who wanted me to recommend musicians for their inauguration ceremony. It was then that I introduced the Langas as singers in a public forum. From that point on, I became specifically interested in their music, which I began to research in greater detail for a special issue of folk songs (1958), co-edited by Vijay Dan and myself for a new quarterly magazine called *Parampara*. The research deepened as I joined the Jodhpur office of the Sangeet Natak Akademi in December 1958 as its first Secretary. By 1960 we started recording folk songs at the Akademi, but our annual budget for the entire office was a mere Rs 50,000, and this included all the salaries and maintenance costs. So there was very little that we could do.

You must keep in mind that when I joined the Sangeet Natak Akademi I hadn't yet come into contact with the Manganiyars. In fact, I didn't even know of their existence. Then, one day, while walking to the Akademi office from my house, I saw a man on the street, holding a kamāychā in his hand. I had never seen such an instrument before. So I requested him to come over to our office. Though he sang very well, he refused to be recorded and ran away.

The second time I saw a Manganiyar on the street, he was carrying a harmonium. This was Ramjan Hammu, who became a good friend and worker in our team. Initially, he too refused to be recorded. I asked him, 'Why?' And he said that there were two problems: one, as a Manganiyar, he was supposed to sing exclusively for his jajmāns—if other people heard him sing, then he would risk losing their patronage. Secondly, he felt that the 'electricity' (his word for 'microphone') would steal his voice away if I tried to record it, and if his voice were stolen, then he wouldn't be able to sing any more. I found that all Manganiyars with whom I came into contact at this time had a very real fear of the microphone.

My first successful recording session with the Manganiyars took place in 1962, in Jaisalmer, in the company of the director of the National School of Drama in New Delhi, Ebrahim Alkazi. Through a particular Manganiyar, who worked as a peon in the collector's office, we managed to mobilize the participation of more than fifty musicians. At that time, Jaisalmer was no tourist paradise; it had just one ramshackle dharamshālā near the railway station. Yet we managed to hold a workshop for almost seven to eight days, listening to the musicians and even recording their songs. Of course, we first had to win their trust by recording our own voices on the tape-recorder and playing them back, thereby reassuring them that their voices wouldn't be stolen away. Once their fears were removed, we began to talk more freely. I still remember that Chhuga, the father of Gazi, who is now very well known on the international circuit as a khaṛtāl player, participated in this workshop. Gazi himself participated much later in the first musical camp that we held in Borunda in 1986, organized by the Rupayan Sansthan. He had lost his father by that time. Over the years we have organized many such camps, and I am now in touch with the third generation of many of the musicians whom I first encountered in Jaisalmer.

Looking back on my relationship with the folk musicians, I would say that the entire process has been very demanding. When I first started to work with them for particular concerts and presentations, I found that their repertoire was very loosely structured. I had to work hard to identify specific compositions, their intrinsic musical values, melodic lines, improvisational possibilities, and their impact on a wide spectrum of listeners unfamiliar with the Rajasthani folk tradition. In the early days, we used to have long all-night sessions, which were held either in my house or in the villages of the musicians. When my son Prashant got married in Jodhpur, almost seventy to eighty musicians assembled in my house for almost fifteen days. Day and night, we heard music. I used the celebrations surrounding my son's wedding to initiate an informal learning process for all of us.

Later, during the camps organized in Borunda, we began to address musical questions more systematically. These camps became the training grounds for young musicians. With the guidance of senior musicians, we raised a number of questions such as: 'How do you check that the strings on your instrument are correctly tuned? And that the bridge is in place? What type of strings are you using? What is their measurement? Can you standardize your strings?' And so on. From these technical questions, we then began to explore more subtle issues relating to performance: 'What musical composition are you playing? What are its expressive possibilities? When you play the instrument and sing at the same time, how does this differ from when you accompany someone else singing?' To these questions, we never expected answers in an academic sense. Our approach was always to get the performers to 'do it, and see what happens.'

Interventions

Let me now reflect on some of the challenges presented by folk music in relation to other nationally-recognized musical traditions. When you first hear folk music, the immediate feeling is that it's very close to classical music. But if you listen more attentively, you will find that it's far removed from the discipline of classical traditions. This illusion of proximity to classical music presents one of the biggest risks for folk musicians. At one level, the music of the Langas and the Manganiyars can be viewed as an embryonic form of classical music. But the question then arises: Why did it remain at this stage? I have constantly reminded the folk musicians that they should in no way attempt to imitate classical or semi-classical styles. These are not easily resisted. For example, if four or five singers get together, it's very easy for them to lapse into a *qawwali*-like singing mode. But what they don't understand is that qawwali has its own set of rules, and what the folk musicians land up doing sounds like poor imitations of this tradition. So, to all the folk performers with whom I have worked over the years, I have never failed to emphasize: 'Protect yourselves by developing your own style, within your own musical tradition. There are a lot of spaces here to be explored and improved on. So don't disregard them.'

There is another problem presented by the very nature of the instruments played by folk performers. Earlier, if these instruments had to be played solo, with no accompaniment, the musicians would not have been able to sustain a piece for more than two to three minutes. Because, when all is said and done, folk musical instruments are, essentially, accompanying instruments. Only a few of these instruments have the potential to be used in solo performances. One of my interventions has been to explore this potential with individual musicians on the kamāychā, the sārangi, the satārā, and so on. Though I am not a musician myself, I have intervened by listening to different musicians side by side, and by getting them to listen to each other. If Karim and Mehra are playing different renditions of the same piece, I will point out ten different things being done by Karim that Mehra isn't doing, and *vice versa*. Then I will challenge them: 'Can you do this as well?' Through this process I have begun to understand the improvisational possibilities of different musicians, and also the limits of improvisation that can be sustained on particular instruments.

Yet another challenge for folk music in the larger national context has been the modern conditions and contexts of performance. How do we sustain the interest of an audience in the enclosed space of a proscenium theatre auditorium for one-and-a-half hours? And how do we meet—and stretch—the expectations of the sponsors? Today there are many so-called 'cultural programmes' being organized all over India, by the West Zone Cultural Centre, tourist departments, radio stations, and so on. Invariably, I ask the sponsors of these programmes: 'What exactly do you mean when you say that you're organizing a 'folk' programme'? But, at the same time, I question the folk musicians themselves: 'Instead of playing the same thing over and over again, do you ever question *what* you're playing? Can you work within your own form to stretch its possibilities, and actually *do* something instead of merely repeating what you already know?'

Today, the musicians know that I take their music very seriously, and if I tell them anything they will definitely respond to my views. We have built up our trust over the years, and this enables me to speak to them freely, and to criticize them if necessary. I wouldn't say that they see me as a guru. Perhaps, initially, I had some feeling of superiority in relation to them, but over the last twenty to twenty-five years, I have realized how much I learn from them. Indeed, I owe my understanding of Rajasthani folk music entirely to them. I can't point to any one person who was my teacher, but, collectively, I would say that the folk musicians have been my gurus. Now they realize that I mean well for them, even if I stop them from doing certain things, or if I accuse them of negligence or absence of responsibility or indiscipline, or whatever.

One of the consequences of organizing musical groups as I have over the years is that it has enabled me to bring together Langas and Manganiyars from different villages, who earlier might never have played together. In this kind of situation, one has to be open to stylistic differences. While the Langas tend to sing on a high pitch, for instance, their diction tends to be clearer than that of the Manganiyars, whose strength lies in melodic improvisation. Then also there are differences that emerge out of their use of particular instruments. The Langas, for instance, had no tradition of playing the ḍholak (drum) until twenty or so years ago, so their skill in drumming is as yet rudimentary. Despite the commonalities in the social backgrounds of the Langas and Manganiyars—both groups sing for initiation ceremonies, and for births and marriages in the families of their patrons—one has to deal with fundamental tonal differences in the production of their voices. *Sur ke jo lagāv hai, woh dono mein pharak hai* (There's a difference in the very thrust of their notes). One reason for this has to do with the varying pitch produced by the instruments—while the sindhi sārangi has steel strings as well as two gut strings, the kamāychā's strings are made of gut only. Gut strings cannot be tuned very high, while steel strings cannot be tuned very low. Inevitably, the two instruments cannot be evenly matched. Only if the kamāychā (played by the Manganiyars) is tuned on *pa*, and the sindhi sārangi (played by the Langas) is tuned on *sa*, then only can the two instruments be played together.

This difference in pitch between the instruments, however, has been put to very good use in the shaping of new musical compositions. It has provided us with two systems of musical codes, which, once understood and grasped, can be adapted freely. Apart from these differences in singing styles, one should point out that the basic vocabularies of the Manganiyar and Langa traditions are fundamentally similar. This is what enables us to bring them together in performance.

A few decisive factors underlying Komalda's representation of Rajasthani music within the larger national context need to be highlighted here:

1. His impetus to search for Rajasthani folk musicians came out of a literary interest. In this regard, it is sometimes forgotten that Komalda was both a student and teacher of Hindi literature in his early years. As a Left-leaning intellectual and short-lived member of the Communist Party of India,[2] *he was keenly aware of the social realist literature promoted by organizations like the Progressive Writers' Association. As I have discussed in some of my earlier writings,*[3] *the 'folk' was a deeply contested category in such Left forums, where it was simultaneously affirmed as a resource in propagating anti-imperialist and anti-fascist themes, but also subtly denigrated for its feudal links and modes of patronage. With Komalda's interaction with the Langa performers in the late 1950s, it is possible to see a very different trajectory of 'folk culture' in the making, which I would characterize as context-sensitive and inventive within a framework of conservation, as opposed to the more decontextualized 'use' of folk traditions in urban performance structures.*

2. Komalda's success in facilitating the national recognition of folk performers cannot be separated from his own affiliations to national institutions like the All India Radio and the Sangeet Natak Akademi. The Akademi had organized the First Drama Seminar in New Delhi in 1956, where one of the most heated subjects of discussion focused on the future of 'folk theatre' and the dubious prerogative of urban practitioners to intervene in social and aesthetic matters relating to 'the folk'. It is interesting in this regard to note the brief reference in Komalda's retrospective to the presence of Ebrahim Alkazi at the meeting of traditional musicians in Jaisalmer. In the First Drama Seminar, Alkazi (who had not yet been appointed as the Director of the National School of Drama) had taken a strong stand against the urban use and 'improvement' of folk forms, which I have discussed in an earlier essay.[4] *The point is that by the time Komalda was beginning to interact with folk musicians, there was already an intellectual context surrounding both the necessity of 'reviving'/re-inventing folk culture, as well as of keeping it free from urban contamination.*

3. Perhaps the most moving aspect of Komalda's interaction with folk musicians is that, despite his official links with national institutions, it was sustained at a very personal and amateur level. Whether it involved transcribing a folk song for a local journal (part of the 'little magazine' movement that thrived throughout post-Independence India) or visiting the homes of traditional musicians, the 'interventions' were very modest but significant. Today, in certain elite developmental circles, it is almost chic to claim the friendship of traditional artisans and performers from the most downtrodden sections of society. However, if one had to contextualize the difficulties in crossing caste barriers at a social level in Rajasthan of the 1950s, then this relationship that Komalda established with the Langas and Manganiyars, and which he has sustained over three generations in certain families, cannot be brushed aside as mere professionalism. Let us now contextualize this relationship within the larger context of the internationalization of folk performers.

THE INTERNATIONAL CONTEXT

By 1956 I had started coming in contact with many researchers and impresarios of folk music from foreign countries. The first breakthrough was with Deben Bhattacharya, a Bengali living in Paris who had collected, recorded and created numerous programmes around folk music from Hungary, Czechoslovakia, Russia, Africa and Brazil. In 1962 he had collaborated with the BBC on a film devoted to Pabuji ki paṛ, at a time when I knew very little about this form or the performers involved in it. After that we had a chain of scholars beginning with Geneviève Dournon from the Musée de l'Homme, who first came to Rajasthan in the early 1970s to record a wide range of Rajasthani folk singing traditions. This was a great opportunity for us to tour practically all the regions of Rajasthan.

Earlier, I had been travelling on the very meagre funds provided by the Sangeet Natak Akademi, but they were so limited that it was difficult to sustain any kind of research. At times there was no money to travel, even by bus or train, to a distant region, in order to deepen our understanding of a particular instrument. Most of the time, we walked from place to place. I remember how we used to walk almost fifty to sixty kilometres on a single day to track down an instrument, or to follow up on what we had heard about it. But with the funding available for Geneviève's project, it became possible for us to hire a vehicle and travel long distances, often staying overnight in small towns. We could even pay people for their information and songs, and we must have collected seventy or more hours of recorded music, which are still in our archives today on spool tapes.

Gradually, I came in touch with other folklorists and ethnomusicologists, who brought not only their own expertise to our research, but a highly sophisticated technology of recording and documentation. These researchers were of enormous help in providing us with basic equipment for our own recording purposes. By this time, I had already left the Sangeet Natak Akademi to devote my attention full-time to Rupayan Sansthan, an institute for the study of Rajasthani folklore which was based in the village of Borunda, that I had co-founded with Vijay Dan as early as 1960.

One thing needs to be kept in mind: Even though we were not very well established in our early years, we always insisted on certain conditions when we collaborated with foreign researchers on any project. One, we made it clear that we needed to have a copy of whatever had been recorded during any field-trip. This extended to prints of all photographs and photocopies of all notes. Two, if for any reason we needed access to the original material, this would be made available to us. Against these rights of access to the research material, we waived our own professional fees. So, in this sense, we worked for 'free'.

There were other benefits that developed through our growing contacts with foreign scholars. Today there's no problem in travelling abroad, but earlier, this was very difficult. For a start, there was no money to even think about foreign trips. So, when researchers like Geneviève [Dournon] tried to mobilize an interest in Rajasthani folk music by organizing performances in France, this enabled us to widen our links of Rajasthani folk culture within the larger field of ethnomusicology and 'world music'. Our first major international exposure was in Paris, in November 1980, where I still remember how by the third or fourth day of the performances at the concert hall of the Musée Guimet, there was a long queue of people lining up to get into the hall. Over the years, this became a regular feature of almost all our performances, which invariably play to full houses. After our Paris 'debut', we performed at least twice at the Edinburgh Festival through the support received by Jean Jenkins. These early programmes had a number of items—songs by the Langas and the Manganiyars, a short section of Terātāli, even excerpts from Pabuji ki paṛ.

This first phase of our international exposure was made possible only because of the direct involvement of our foreign research collaborators. The second phase, from the mid-1980s to the early 1990s, was organized by the Festivals of India under the administration of the Indian Council for Cultural Relations (ICCR).

At the Festival of India, in Russia, there were almost eighty musicians, performers, and puppeteers from Rajasthan. I still remember how the theatre staff and management of the former Soviet theatres would regard us with some condescension. I always got the impression that they didn't take us seriously, and that they thought we were a funny lot of people wearing peculiar clothes. Also, Russian theatres are massive—they have huge stages in which our folk musicians would get totally lost. It was almost impossible to see them on the stage. So the first thing that we had to do was to limit the performance space, and for that we needed the close cooperation of the Russian theatre personnel, who were not particularly forthcoming. Invariably, there would be difficulties in communication, but as soon as we would begin the sound-check for the microphones, and the musicians would start singing and tuning their instruments, we would feel a total transformation in the attitude of the technicians. Now they would be ready to do almost anything for us.

Like this, we have had different experiences in different places. I should point out that our programmes have been held in the world's most prestigious theatres, such as Lincoln Centre, Carnegie Hall and the Kennedy Centre in the United States, the Royal Festival Hall in London, the Paris Opera in France, the Kremlin in Russia, and so on. And almost everywhere we've played to full houses and standing ovations.

Let me tell you a funny story. When we performed in Carnegie Hall in New York City, we found that we had been given a slot of one hour and fifteen minutes, the first half of the programme. In the second half, after the interval, Nikhil Banerjee and Zakir Husain would perform on the sitar and tabla. When I got to hear about this arrangement, I was initially very cross with the organizers. I told them that they should have informed me about the overall programme, because now the audience would be coming to hear Nikhil and Zakir, and not Rajasthani folk musicians. I felt that we were being used as 'fillers'.

So I was not happy about the situation, but there was nothing that I could do about it. I got all the musicians together and said, 'This is the situation. Now let's try to explore something by which we will be able to match these great wizards of the country. What should we do?' I reminded them of the practice in Indian classical music where it's customary for the audience to give *tāla* (i.e. to beat out the rhythm with their own hands, either by clapping or tapping the hand on the thigh, and so on). Even if an audience doesn't have a very good knowledge of the *tāla* system, they invariably make an attempt to participate. I then told the musicians that we should select those songs in which the audience can identify two beats, but the third beat should be off [i.e. delayed, not in its expected place]. In other words, the audience should be made to feel somewhat uncomfortable that they cannot quite fix the beat of the song. With this in mind, I selected a number of songs—tricky and difficult songs—and we started the programme.

Now, the person who organized that programme, one Mr Roberts, had made it very clear to me, 'You have only one hour and fifteen minutes for your programme, not a minute more, because we have to pay Carnegie Hall for each extra minute of the programme. So please stick to your time.' After the first two or three songs—I was sitting on the stage with the musicians giving a little introduction to each song—I noticed that Zakir and Nikhil were both standing in the wings and gesturing to me, '*Kar kyā rahe ho, yaar*?' (What are you doing?) After one hour and fifteen minutes, we stopped, on schedule. But I could sense the energy in the hall, and I knew that it would not be easy for us to leave. The clapping just went on and on. Roberts was backstage. I asked him, 'What do you want us to do?' He said, 'I can't help it, go back on stage.' So we went back, *namaste kiyā*, but the clapping didn't stop. People were standing on chairs in Carnegie Hall. So I told the musicians, 'Sing just one more song, no more.' But they continued to sing for another forty-five minutes, standing up, with no microphones beyond the general amplification on the stage.

When I returned backstage, Nikhil and Zakir told me, 'You've made our lives very difficult.' Nikhil would have to start with the *ālāp* after the interval for their rāga, but the mood in the audience had been completely transformed. So this is one situation which gives you some idea of the kind of response we've received on the international stage.

I can't deny that there was an undercurrent of pride and subtle one-upmanship that came through in Komalda's rendering of this story. Not for the first time in listening to him talk about Rajasthani folk music did I pick up very clear signs that, for him, it is a very distinct musical heritage that has to be sharply differentiated from the classical tradition. And yet, in the Carnegie Hall performance, it is also clear that he wants to demonstrate the folk tradition's capacity to outwit the classical 'wizards' (as he often describes maestros) through experiments in 'tāla'.

I bring these points up to inflect the traditionalist assumption that the so-called 'desi' (folk) and 'margi' (classical) traditions are coterminous, linked through complementarity rather than differentiation, and ultimately subsumed within a larger metaphysical framework of 'interconnectedness'.[5] *As always, Komalda does not enter theoretical debates directly, but if you listen to him closely on this particular debate, there can be no doubt that he believes very strongly in the autonomy of folk musical traditions and their resistance to being assimilated within a classical canon. In fact, the process of cross-fertilization across folk musical traditions themselves is an extremely complex endeavour. 'You can't crack their shells': this phrase by Komalda recurred a number of times in our conversations. It was both illuminating and humbling for me to hear the most recognized authority on Rajasthani folk music acknowledge that he had not yet been able to fully grasp the specificities of individual traditions, which are not easily 'translatable'.*

Let us now return to the internationalist scenario of Rajasthani folk music with Komalda reflecting on its most recent development, followed by a brief description of his encounter with the French equestrian theatre Zingaro. A phenomenon in the international festival circuit, Zingaro represents a kind of 'total theatre', involving horses, equestrians, musicians, drummers, and spectacle. Komalda's involvement in this global theatrical phenomenon is worth exploring.

Now we have entered the third phase of our travel, which has been sponsored primarily by independent producers on the international festival circuit. In Europe, particularly in Germany, you will find that almost every municipality has some kind of festival that is funded by the government with additional resources from the private sector. Some festivals function more independently, with no governmental affiliation at all. What generally happens is that these producers try to organize ten to fifteen programmes in neighbouring cities and towns, so that the expenses for the tour can be shared by different organizations. With these independent producers, we find greater scope in negotiating the terms of our interaction in terms of payment, scheduling of programmes, and we also find more personalized attention in relation to matters like food, cooking arrangements, transportation, and so on.

And yet, there are problems with these producers. For a start, they tend to sponsor only those programmes that can draw large audiences—in other words, the music selected has to be popular and not make too many demands on the attention of the foreign audiences. In addition, I find that there are new demands involved in the selection of the artists themselves. Earlier, for instance, I would be approached to form a group with funding for, say, ten to fifteen musicians. And on that basis, I would make my own selection of the performers and their repertoire. Today, it is more common for independent producers to make their own selection of the performers and the repertoire—a selection that is generally made during their quick trips to India.

The problem is that they insist that the same musicians should go for all the programmes, so that they can be 'sold'. These international sponsors have even started naming groups. In relation to folk cultural practice this creates problems, because most folk artists function within larger contexts of their own tradition and community; they are not individual stars. But according to the demands of the international cultural market, it helps to have brand names in one form or the other.

The Zingaro Connection

One of our most serious and sustained interactions with an international group has been with Zingaro, the internationally renowned equestrian theatre directed by the French director Bartabas. Bartabas first got in touch with us through Roshan Khazandar, who had come in contact with the Rajasthani musicians while they were performing at the Festival of India in Paris. Actually, it was Roshan's wife, Françoise, who had suggested to Bartabas that he should think of using Rajasthani folk singers for his forthcoming production *Chimère* (1994). Earlier, Bartabas had worked with Georgian folk musicians for one of his productions. Françoise followed up on this interest by getting in touch with my brother Keshav, who had become Secretary of the Sangeet Natak Akademi, and it was not long before Bartabas and Françoise came to Rajasthan for the selection of the musicians. I think we must have invited about 150 musicians, and out of those, ten were selected to participate in Bartabas's *Chimère* for one year.

Work had already started on this production so far as the horses were concerned. Bartabas had also done a lot of research on Indian equestrian traditions—he was aware of the ritual uses of horses, their decorations, and other details connected with the cultural dimensions of horse-rearing. The only problem was that Bartabas wanted these ten musicians to stay away from India for as long as a year. His argument was that once the musicians were acclimatized to the programme, and most of all to the horses, then it would be difficult to change them. Horses have their own rhythms and sense of time; there are very specific things that they can—and cannot—do. All their movements have to be meticulously rehearsed. I understood Bartabas's position, but I also realized that if the musicians were away for as long as a year that they would be cut off from their patrons, and separated from what they were doing in India to earn a living. I felt that this separation from home would pose some difficulties. So, finally, it was decided that they would perform for three to four months, and then come back to India for a month at Zingaro's expense, and then return to complete their contract.

However, when the first ten musicians returned from France, I realized that it was necessary to change the artists. And the reason for this had to do with the large payments that the musicians were receiving. I felt strongly that this privilege should not be monopolized by a coterie of singers, and that others should have a chance as well. But Bartabas resisted my position very strongly, and stressed once again, 'You've got to understand that we're working with horses, and once we have prepared the musicians from this point of view, then if you change anything, we have to start the rehearsals all over again, which is very stressful.' Then I reassured him that I would personally supervise the training of the new group of musicians, and finally he agreed. In the course of the production's run, I was able to involve around thirty-five musicians in the show. For example, a few that Bartabas had selected the first time round eventually backed out from going for the entire year. However, when the first lot of musicians came back with a lot of money, then these musicians who had earlier said 'no' now wanted to go. In a way it worked out well, because the production that was supposed to continue for a year, was on the road for three consecutive years. It was a big hit.

Listening to Komalda talk about his seemingly unqualified success in the field of international performance leaves me with mixed feelings. My own field as a cultural theorist has been the politics of interculturalism, on which I have written over the years focusing on issues relating to the ethics of cross-cultural exchange, the decontextualization of performance traditions, cultural tourism, and so on.[6] *On the national front as well, I have polemicized in numerous articles the reductionism and commodification of indigenous performance traditions, both from the folk and tribal sectors, in the larger construction of 'festival culture'. I have taken issue with the ways in which traditional performances have been packaged and transported to First World metropolitan centres, with very little thought given to 'foreign-returned' performers within their own social context of deprivation and neglect. Needless to say, underlying all these critiques, is a confrontation of how the agencies of the State are increasingly in collusion with marketing forces in the age of globalization.*

While acknowledging that this is contested territory, there is also growing evidence and corroboration among scholars, practitioners, and critics worldwide on the difficulties and rip-offs faced by non-Western practitioners in the international festival circuit. Against this background, Komalda's seemingly uncomplicated 'success story' surrounding the internationalization of Rajasthani folk music needs some unpacking.

If I were doing a conventional critique of intercultural practice here, it wouldn't be too difficult to analyse the equestrian spectacle of Zingaro, for example, within a well-established repertoire of orientalist tropes [see note for further elaboration].[7] *However, I also recognize that the participation of traditional folk musicians on the international stage, singing their own repertoire, cannot be equated with those 'intercultural' experiments in which the techniques and skills of traditional performers have been adapted and 're-invented' within Eurocentrist frameworks of representation. It should be noted in this regard that Komalda has never favoured any kind of 'fusion' experimentation between Rajasthani folk music and musicians representing 'world music' or 'New Age' music. The focus has always been on representing the traditional repertoire, without making an undue fuss about its 'purity' or 'authenticity'.*

These basic facts need to be kept in mind to acknowledge the minimal difficulties that Komalda seems to have encountered both conceptually and aesthetically in dealing with foreign programmes. He remains in control over the repertoire, and to a large extent, the selection of the musicians. In this regard, his decision to challenge

Bartabas's professional demand for a fixed group of musicians on a one-year contract is to be commended, because it indicates how he never loses sight of the local conditions of the musicians and the social ecology of their community life. In all his seemingly small interventions, Komalda's role has been judicious, but has it been free of difficulties and contradictions?

Hardly. In the following section, I will change my strategy of interrogating the politics of international performance by adopting a dialogic mode. I realize that there are many complex issues that need to be drawn out of Komalda in relation to specific challenges posed by internationalism. So, instead of listening to him in sections, and then providing a commentary, which is what I have been doing so far in this book, I will now intervene and conceptualize problems along the way as they emerge in and through critical dialogue.

Problematizing Internationalism

Komalda, let me enter the discussion at this point. You're obviously concerned, as you mentioned while describing your Zingaro experience, that when musicians from underprivileged groups like the Langas and Manganiyars go abroad and earn a lot of money, there are possible tensions that can emerge through such trips. These musicians are not just being separated from their families, but from their patrons as well. So their traditional source of livelihood can be seriously affected. But tell me, how do you actually deal with the discrepancies of money, of those foreign-returned musicians who've acquired new wealth, and of those who stay behind and continue to survive on a pittance. After all, the moment you internationalize the folk, you're dealing with another economy.

Yes, on the one hand, there is the question of economy, but on the other hand, the important thing is that, when you select a musician, his other colleagues should be clear that you're not trying to favour him. It's on the basis of his quality and capability as a musician that he gets selected. I would say that this is one area in which I have never been questioned by any of the musicians. No one can claim that I have favoured any one particular musician over the others. When they assemble in my house before any programme, I tell them very clearly, 'All right, you play the kamāychā, can you play me such-and-such piece? And if you cannot play the things that I'm requesting, then how can I help you? You have to learn these pieces, work hard at them, and only then will you be able to say why I don't want to select you. It's through your expertise alone that you get selected. So, if your playing is good, then there should be no problem, but if you cannot play your instrument properly, or you don't know how to tune it, then how can I help you? I am sending you to a foreign country where people are aware of these basic things. In India, if you go for any tourist programme, nobody will ask if your kamāychā or ḍholak is properly tuned or not— they don't know left from right. But when you come to me for any foreign programme, then I have to check everything.'

In this way, I talk to the musicians and reason with them. And nobody in all these years has ever accused me of favouritism. Besides, I've never worked in an institutional framework, in the sense that I've never directed any one particular group of musicians on a permanent basis. It would have been very easy for me to select twenty top musicians and identify them as Rupayan Sansthan artists, and go on representing these twenty performers for all shows. But I've never done anything like this, and the musicians know that I won't do such a thing. For each programme we assemble a new group of singers and musicians, who don't have to be rigorously rehearsed. Whatever the musicions do comes naturally from their own context, and we merely select the items for each programme and give it a particular structure.

I'm interested to know more about how folk musicians adapt to living conditions in foreign countries, as in Europe. After all, they don't just play music in these countries—they live there, at times for weeks and even months on end. For example, it seems that on the Zingaro tour that the Rajasthani musicians insisted on cooking for themselves. As Brigitte (Bartabas's wife) put it in one of our conversations, 'They never touched our food.' Perhaps, some of them tried French bread, maybe some vegetables, but by and large, they cooked and ate their own meals. Now this strikes me as being rather important. Could you reflect on some of the perceptions of the musicians to foreign cultures when they travel abroad?

In terms of food, they will never eat anything that they have not seen or eaten before. They will not even experiment at any level. In this regard, I'm reminded of my grandchildren, Tosh and Tejal, who are ready to eat something different only if they have seen it on television. Otherwise, they are not likely to eat anything that they can't identify. The musicians are no different. In the 1980s, when we first went to Europe, they never raised the issue of halal, even though they are all Muslim. But later, there were rumblings in the group. After that I said, 'All right, I'm taking a group to Germany. Those of you who insist on halal, I will not be able to take you with me. I want you to eat well when you're abroad, and if you don't accept their food, there will be a problem.' At that time nobody raised any questions. But now they all insist on halal, which is difficult to locate, even though it is available. Of course, one doesn't know whether it's truly halal or not, but that is what is believed.

So, definitely, food has always posed a problem. Living indoors in hotels and apartments and keeping the rooms clean has posed another problem. In the early days, before they got used to travelling, their rooms would invariably be in a mess. I would have to enter each room and tell the musicians how to use the wash basins and toilets, going into details not only of flushing the toilet after use, but of cleaning the bowl regularly. Sometimes they listened to what I was saying, and at other times, they continued doing their own thing.

But a few things have struck me as being quite extraordinary. We travel constantly on our tours, maybe twenty kilometres or more every day, from Paris to small towns, and so on. Yet, despite this constant travel and long distances, I find that the musicians never lose their way. The routes are like maps drawn in their minds. So we fall back on the musicians for directions when we get lost. They have extremely sharp observations of landmarks on the road, and can remember any route without any problem.

Another remarkable thing is how, after one or two trips abroad, they have become very keenly aware of foreign currencies. So, what's happening to the pound, the euro, the yen, the moment they check into the hotel from the airport—within an hour or so, you can be sure that they know the value of the foreign currency in relation to the Indian rupee. Exchange rates pose no problems whatsoever. Most of the time, I had have to depend on them for making my own monetary calculations. Economically, they are very canny.

But when all is said and done, it's very hard to penetrate their social shell, not unlike their music, which is also hard to crack. While listening to them play a particular piece, I can tell them, 'Why don't you try this out? You can do this as well,' and maybe, in my presence, they will do what I say, but there's no guarantee that they will repeat what I, or someone else, may have suggested. To get through to them in the first phase of our interaction was very difficult. They relate to their music on their own terms. But one thing should be pointed out here—whenever or wherever they perform, even if there is a very renowned musician in the audience, they never lose their confidence.

No stage nerves?

I tell you, nothing. Whether they are singing in their village or in the Paris Opera House or in the Kremlin, it makes no difference to them whatsoever. Nothing seems to change for them; they are not tense about the performance or anything like that. They just do what they have to do in the best manner possible. And they always shine when they have an audience. So strong is their performance instinct that the moment they start singing, they are able to identify four or five or six people in the theatre who seem particularly receptive to their music. And from that moment onwards, their eyes are always fixed on these individuals in the audience, whose response they elicit in very perceptible ways. As the performance proceeds, the musicians never fail to capture the spirit of the entire audience through their interaction.

Tell me, is there anything like a warm-up before the musicians go on stage?

No. However, I've noticed that they've begun to do certain things that they never did earlier on. On entering the stage they will now touch the ground, and before starting the programme, they will greet everybody accompanying them, and then formally greet the audience, before beginning to sing. This kind of etiquette they have developed for themselves over the years, and to my mind, it looks a bit awkward.

They never did these things earlier?

No, never. They've picked these things up from watching classical musicians, and dancers in particular, who have elaborate rituals. I would say that this trend began around the 1980s.

What about costume? I know it's important to you that they look dignified.

Nowadays, it has become difficult to insist on the dress of the younger men, who tend to wear trousers and shirt, or sometimes a suit, or kurta pyjama. But the older members of the group continue to wear their traditional clothes—the same clothes that they wear in everyday life, except that they would be more carefully washed and ironed. That's the only difference. I used to tell the musicians quite candidly that in order to 'sell' them [i.e. their performances], they needed to wear their own clothes, because that gave them more 'character'. But today the younger boys, they wear what they want . . . The behavioural patterns have changed; earlier, they behaved like ordinary Manganiyars, now they have become *kalākārs* (artists).

How have the folk musicians learned to deal with technology? As you yourself have indicated, when you first started your research in the 1960s, they were afraid to be recorded. So a tremendous shift seems to have taken place in their attitude.

They have no problems whatsoever with the microphone today. Nor are they camera conscious. In fact, they like to be photographed. They are not tense about these situations, but perfectly relaxed.

Let me now lead to a somewhat harder question: How much do the musicians 'take in' of a foreign place? I'm not just thinking about their concerts as such, where they seem to have no problem in striking a rapport with the audience. I'm thinking about the larger social interactions abroad. How do these interactions affect them when they get back home?

What I've observed over the years is that when I first used to go their villages and stay with them, they cared very little about matters relating to hygiene, whether this involved drinking water, or blankets or quilts or pillows. Their living conditions were filthy. It was hard for me to sleep in their homes in those days. But now I find that they are very conscious about hygienic matters, perhaps not always for themselves, but certainly for their guests. So in more recent years, when I have gone to their places, I have been struck by how clean and neat everything is. So, at this level, there has been some change in their social customs and attitudes.

In music, I wouldn't say that there have been significant changes. What they tend to do these days is to focus on things that are playful, and which do not present any particular musical challenge to them. Today we find them singing songs where they want the entire audience to clap together. They can go on clapping like this for hours on end. They have come to realize that the text of these songs doesn't really matter.

Has the text suffered in the process of all the international exposure of the folk singers?

Yes. We have lost many nuances from the text of the songs. The musicians have also come to realize that improvisations go down very well with their audience. So today they are beginning to develop all kinds of clichés. Even after ten minutes of a song, you will find these clichés appearing. But the musicians feel that they get appreciated because of these clichés. So, at one level, it could be said that they are becoming slaves of these clichés. And that is not a good way to render music.

Intimate Controversies

I would like to shift the discussion into a somewhat difficult area that is not generally discussed in academic work on the performing arts—the breakdown in human relationships among performers. In one of our earlier conversations, you mentioned that a rather serious feud is taking place between the families of two musicians whom you have worked with. Could we address this feud without mentioning the real names of the parties involved? What strikes me is that these musicians, who could be fighting together in real life, can also sit together on the same stage and create beautiful music. How does this happen?

You are right, when they sing there is no problem. You could never once feel that Abdul and Bashir—[all names addressed in this section have been changed][8]—are incapable of sitting together in real life because of the family feud that divides them. Bashir's daughter was betrothed at a very young age to the son of Ismail, the elder brother of Abdul's father-in-law. So there is no direct conflict between Abdul and Bashir as such—the feud exists because of larger family connections. Now, it so happened that Ismail's son turned out to be mentally retarded in his teenage years, so naturally Bashir wanted to withdraw from the earlier promise that his daughter would be married to him. But, in withdrawing from this pact, he was also disobeying community rules. In this situation, Abdul has no other option but to oppose Bashir, because his own in-law's family is directly involved. To make matters even more complicated, Bashir has now arranged the marriage of his daughter in another family, and this has increased the rift between his family and that of Abdul. They cannot even sit together and eat from the same plate.

Are they living in the same village?

No, in separate villages, but the entire communities of these villages are now involved in the feud. Once it became clear that Ismail's son could not be married to the girl, since she had already been married off to someone else, then Ismail's community began to put pressure on Bashir to find an appropriate girl for Ismail's retarded son. So, Bashir then arranged for one of his relatives to give her daughter to this boy in marriage, and in exchange he would reimburse all marriage expenses. Now, this girl is only ten years old, and the boy is around twenty-one years old, and still mentally retarded. The question is: should this woman give her daughter in marriage to this boy? This is a very hard situation.

Indeed, on hearing about this feud, one is almost thrust back into another time.

But this is the scenario in the rural areas of Rajasthan today. There are all kinds of stories in the newspapers today. In one such story, a Bishnoi girl was actually married, not just betrothed, when she was only one year old. Then, later on, her father decided to get his daughter married to another person. When this marriage took place, the family of the former bridegroom kidnapped this girl and kept her in custody in Ahmedabad for many months, raping her and abusing her in all kinds of ways. Finally, when the police rescued her, she was found to be pregnant. An abortion was forcibly done on this girl, and now she has gone back to her father's place. Now, the basic problem, as I see it, is that she was married at the age of one, and for her father to subscribe to this can only be regarded as one of the greatest sins. Such incidents are not uncommon in the rural areas of Rajasthan. What is worse is that they are endorsed by communities at large.

Coming back to the world of performance, how do we deal with these warring factions, when people in everyday life are not capable of sharing the same space? Would Abdul and Bashir talk to each other during the tour? Did you notice any changes in their attitudes to each other?

There was very little communication between them. Sometimes no participation at all in common activities. But the feud continues. For example, I would very much like to send Baharul, who is Bashir's younger brother, along with Ismail for a programme. But Ismail is not ready to accept Baharul, even though they are brothers-in-law in real life. If I send Baharul for the programme, then Ismail will drop out. Baharul, on the other hand, doesn't mind accompanying Ismail, but there's a stalemate.

All of this sounds very complicated. It seems to me that even when the folk musicians get internationalized, after getting their passports, and visas, and tickets, in order to perform in different international forums and festivals, and even while acknowledging that certain things do change in their lives when they return home—for example, you mentioned their more hygienic living conditions—the point is that certain things don't seem to change at all.

Exactly. Their lives remain deeply rooted in the family. They are so deeply rooted, I cannot begin to tell you. I would regard most Langas and Manganiyars as hen-pecked husbands. It is their wives who govern them. They cannot govern their wives. And the relationship with their children is so acute and so intimate, it's impossible to think of any change in that bond. It's so firmly intact.

So, then, what does 'internationalization' really mean in this very local context? If we get past the obvious mechanics of travel and foreign trips, in what ways has this exposure to the outer world shifted the consciousness of the musicians?

I tell you their shell remains so strong that it's still very hard to penetrate.

Interaction with Kanjar women

All the musicians we talked about are male. What has been your experience with female performers from Rajasthan on the international circuit?

The most challenging encounter has been with the dancers from the Kanjar community. At one time they were identified as criminal tribes, which are now regarded as 'de-notified' tribes.[9] I didn't know very much about them till I saw them dance for the first time in the Kota region. In the early days, the tradition was for unmarried Kanjar girls to gather together in a particular place in the village, whereupon different villagers would select a girl to dance for a particular night in their particular village. An advance of one rupee would be given to an older woman chaperone accompanying the girl, and later that night, the girl would show up at the respective village along with a drummer, who invariably came from the sweeper's caste. Then this woman would dance through the night, from 8 p.m. onwards, and on the main street of the village itself, with the entire community assembled to watch her, men on one side, women on the other. Fathers, mothers, wives, children—the entire village would be assembled on the street.

The primary dance for which the Kanjar women are best known

is the *chakri*, which as its very name suggests, is built around circular movements. The dancers wear traditional ghāgrās, which weigh anything between fifteeen to twenty kilogrammes. As I mentioned earlier, the solo dancer is accompanied by a drummer, who beats any number of fast and tricky rhythms on his ḍholak, to which the dancer is expected to respond, changing her movement every time he changes the beat. The very sharp sounds of the beat are accentuated by the *chāṭi* (bamboo sticks) attached to the fingers of the drummer. Now that these dancers have become very popular, their own husbands demand to be included as professional drummers in their programmes. Earlier also, only unmarried girls could dance in public; this is no longer the case.

If you had to ask me what this dance most closely resembles,[10] I would say the *mujrā*, that kind of erotic dance tradition associated with Kathak, where the female dancer entertains her predominantly male audience with suggestive gestures and sexual interplay with individual spectators. We had a direct exposure to this kind of mujrā outside my own house in Jodhpur, in the *chowk* (square), where I had invited some hundred people to watch the dance. One of the women in the group, Shyama, who was very robust and forthright in her ways, asked me very directly: 'Do you want me to dance as we do in the village? Will your people mind?' And I reassured her that nobody would mind and that she should dance exactly as she wanted to. Well, there came a moment in the performance, when she sidled up to a very senior and respected old man, and started to caress him. I think she was just about to sit on his lap when he ran out of the performance area, with Shyama following him in hot pursuit.

This sounds a bit like a traditional form of cabaret. How did you adapt the context of this dance tradition for the professional stage?

Well, around the time that I first saw the Kanjar dancers in Kota—it must have been in the mid-1980s—the ICCR wanted me to select a varied group of Rajasthani artists for a trip to Russia, and they wanted me to include at least one dance tradition. I made it clear to them that the only dance that I was interested in would have to be performed by traditional communities—I was not interested in any kind of choreography of 'folk' dances learned by women in the urban areas. I suggested that Terātāli could be one of the forms represented, and the other could be the kind of street dance that I had recently seen in Kota.

Needless to say, I was aware of the difficulties involved—for a start, how was it possible to make a 'group dance' out of these solo performances? Secondly, I realized that the Kanjar dancers do not dance for formal audiences, but for street people. Third, it was unlikely that they would be familiar with the elementary rules of entrances and exits, not to mention the other conventions of urban, proscenium theatres. It was obvious that we needed to rehearse with them before they could go to Russia. The ICCR agreed to my conditions of rehearsal and I arranged for a few Kanjar women to come to Jodhpur and work on their dance for about fifteen days. In order to provide some kind of a structure to their dance, I got my own daughter Uttara involved, to learn their basic steps, but more importantly, to time the entry and the exit of the dancers.

Was the challenge in dealing with them primarily technical?

No, as a matter of fact they adapted to the performative conditions very well. But there were other problems in terms of social interaction. I tell you these Kanjar girls are very sharp and beautiful. They can get anything out of a man—his wallet, his watch, anything—but dare a man so much as touch her, and he's likely to be very sorry. Apart from squeezing anything out of those whom they befriend on false pretexts, these women are also very foul-mouthed. So it's best to be cautious in their company.

Let's not forget that they were branded till quite recently as a criminal tribe. When they danced in Russia—it's interesting to keep in mind that their first 'urban' audience was not in India but in Russia—they were paid, like all the other artists, a mere five roubles per day for their per diem allowance. It had practically no value at that time. Of course, they could have bought a number of things in Russia itself, which were very cheap. But the Kanjar women refused to do so. And their reasons were very telling. They said that whenever they buy anything new and keep it in their homes, the police invariably confiscate these items as stolen goods.[11] Even a *kambal* (blanket) would not be safe from their greed. So the women demanded that I should give them money—not roubles because this would be of no use to them, but rupees. Then I had to organize with the other musicians that they should buy the roubles from the women and pay them in Indian currency.

Today, however, the situation has changed and the Kanjar women are performing all over the world. The good thing is that they are no longer involved in criminal activity of any kind, though that slur on their community continues to exist. Now there is a very real possibility for their development at large.

Shafi's Death

Finally, getting back to some of the more difficult moments in your encounters with traditional musicians, would you care to share that very tragic incident involving the musician Shafi? What exactly happened?

Shafi was part of a later group that participated in the Zingaro tour in Europe. In Belgium, he had teamed up with Multan as his room-mate because they came from neighbouring villages. Since Shafi was very young, Multan could afford to boss him around. So while Multan took a nap, Shafi would cook and attend to the other chores. Before going to the performance one night, it appears that they had used the gas stove, but it had not been shut properly. After their performance, which finished around 9.30 p.m., Shafi rushed back to his quarters to prepare dinner. Multan was following him. It appears that as soon as Shafi opened the door to his room, he switched on the light, and there was an electric spark, followed by an explosion. The room was full of gas and he was severely burned. Multan was also injured in the explosion, but Shafi died after being treated for almost a week at the NATO hospital in Brussels, one of the most highly-equipped hospitals in the world for all kinds of burn injuries.

One of the members in the group brought back Shafi's body to India. He was accompanied by the manager of the Zingaro company. The body had been very well preserved. The hard part—the very hard part— was to break the news to the family, which I had to do. For a few days after the accident, Shafi continued to live. So during that time, I had informed them that an accident had taken place, nothing more. The NATO hospital staff did their best to save Shafi's life, but he couldn't survive. When the report came, elaborating on the details of his death, it said that though Shafi was only twenty-two years old, his inner, biological system was that of a man over fifty. On the surface, he looked so healthy and strong, but his body was obviously a lot weaker than we had thought. Understandably, the group was terribly shocked at first, but the show went on. The other musicians didn't need any persuasion in this matter.

I've noticed among my contacts with groups like the Langas and Manganiyars that they don't respond to death, as we do, like a tragedy or trauma. They seem to accept it a lot more readily. This was true of Shafi's family when the body was brought back to the village. Nor did they expect anything from us. But here one has to mention the extraordinary care and generosity of the Zingaro company. To this day, Shafi's wife is supported by the company on a regular basis—not only has a substantial amount of money been sanctioned for her, but there continues to be a personal contact between Shafi's family and Bartabas and his wife Brigitte. In my own way, I have helped to sustain this relationship and keep the families in touch with each other.

It's hard to enter the narrative at this point, but after narrating Shafi's death, Komalda is silent for a while and it's obvious that we've come to the end of our session. As I see it, this very poignant episode indicates the many levels at which intercultural exchanges can be deepened through any number of obstacles—in this particular case, the death of a young performer. If this inflection of 'friendship' in the larger contested terrain of intercultural practice seems sentimental, let me add a story from Komalda's biography that, sadly, got erased during one of our recording sessions. If I fall back here on my own memory of his recollection of this story, I trust that some of it will come alive in my description.

During one of his trips to the United States with the musicians, there was a break in the schedule of the tour, and the entire company including Komalda were all put up in an unlikely 'dharamshālā': an old folk's home. This accommodation was justified on the grounds that it was temporary and inexpensive. Undeniably, it must have been strange not only for the Rajasthani musicians to be living in such a place, but for the old Americans, many of them frail and disabled, to see these tall, bearded and mustachioed men, dressed in kurtas, dhotis and colourful turbans, sharing their space. Obviously, neither the musicians nor the old folk shared the same language, so there was no possibility of communication beyond a few greetings, and inevitably, little gestures of support—like the musicians picking up bags for the old people, or opening the doors for them. When the time came for the musicians to leave, they decided that they would sing for their hosts in an improvised concert. What followed was something 'unprecedented' in Komalda's experience.

Barely a few songs into the concert, held informally in the living room of the old folks' home, Komalda recalls—and I recall him telling me this with great intensity, sadness, and wonder—that there was a peculiar kind of whimpering that began to be heard among the old people. Gradually, this became crying, and eventually, sobbing. It was not possible either to ignore this reaction or to continue with the songs. The musicians stopped singing and of their own accord the old people got up from their seats, went forward to the musicians and embraced them, one by one. 'It was something unbelievable', as Komalda recalled it.

This is how I recall the story being told to me. While the emotionalism accompanying such intercultural encounters may seem maudlin, the immediacy of non-verbal communication should not be underestimated. This does not mean that non-verbalism itself cannot be falsely mystified or used as a camouflage to evade a confrontation of more critical issues. Keeping this in mind, I would like to turn my attention now to increasingly 'verbalized' issues in the complicated rhetoric surrounding intellectual property rights, without which no discussion of folk culture in the age of globalization would be complete.

12
MARKETING THE 'FOLK'

It would be incomplete to end this book without some critical dialogue on the actual marketing of the 'folk' in the age of mechanical and electronic reproduction. Earlier, in the section dealing with the patronage of traditional musicians, we had referred to the 'jajmāns' (patrons) as the 'property' of the musicians. This property, which is scrupulously shared on the basis of customary laws and rules, continues to be valued today. Even as it faces new pressures with the gradual urbanization of 'nuclear' families, the traditional system of patronage remains comprehensible both to the musicians and to a large percentage of their patrons as well.

Today, however, there are new 'patrons' in the making through the availability of new modes of musical reproduction. With the widespread use of new technologies, primarily the cassette recorder, CDs, and the video, folk artists are becoming increasingly more 'mediatized'. Whether their songs and stories are recorded by archives, or sold on locally produced cassettes, the point is that there are new markets opening for folk culture. To what extent this culture remains 'folk' within the larger negotiations of mass culture, elicits mixed responses.

On the one hand, postmodern advocates of public culture like Arjun Appadurai (1994) would stress that the new modes of mechanical reproduction are perhaps not 'as new as they might first appear'.[1] *Indeed, folk texts and performances have 'hybridized' in all kinds of ways over the years through 'intertextual' interactions with other modes of representation. On the other hand, there is a very perceptible caution at work in Stuart Blackburn and A.K. Ramanujan's (1986) emphasis that mechanical reproduction 'stands diametrically opposed to the variation that animates folklore.'*[2] *Here there is a sharp divide between 'folklore' and 'popular culture', which is 'commercially produced, in a standardized form, for mass consumption, with an emphasis on individual authorship.'*[3]

Clearly, there are blurred lines in these seemingly incontrovertible distinctions which I attempt to tease out in my dialogue with Komalda. While focusing on two primary areas of debate—intellectual property rights and the cassette industry—I should prepare the reader for some interpenetration in these areas of inquiry.

Intellectual Property Rights

When did you first become aware of intellectual property rights in the work that you've been doing over the years?

Initially, when we started to collect material, we knew nothing about it—neither intellectual property rights nor copyright. However, when we would record musicians, and pay them for the recording, we gradually began to collect receipts from them. We went on like this without thinking about what would happen to our recorded material. In our minds we were clear that this material was meant for research purposes, it was an in-house kind of thing; from the point of view of copyright there was no problem.

But then, when people began to request copies of our recorded material, problems emerged. Someone would request us to copy the songs of Gavri Bai or Allah Jilahi Bai because they happened to like them, or else, some scholar needed an extract from an oral epic that we had recorded. There were all kinds of requests. Some of them came from other institutions like the offices of the Sangeet Natak Akademi in Jodhpur and Delhi. So there was growing pressure on us to provide copies of our recordings. Initially, we complied—we asked no questions because we ourselves functioned with no rules whatsoever in this regard. But gradually, we began to lay down conditions—if you wish to have a copy of this recording, we would tell our applicants, then you have to pay the artist whose performance has been recorded.

Is there any such thing as a concept of 'rights' that exists within the world of the folk musicians?

I would say that some of the professional ones are beginning to become aware of them, but I wouldn't say that they are as conscious about recording and distribution 'rights' as artists in the film industry or classical musicians. However, as their material gets disseminated, at times through their own compositions, on radio and television programmes, and increasingly, on cassettes and CDs, many people are now beginning to actually think about where these things are originating—where has this song come from? Who has rights on it? Or no rights? These questions are beginning to emerge.

Would the musicians have any concept of 'property' in relation to their songs?

No. For the most part, I would say as far as folk musicians are concerned that they are still not aware of what 'copyright' means. And if they don't know what this means, then naturally the concept of 'property' does not arise. But let us shift the focus of 'rights' from the musicians to those among us who collect their recordings in our archives. Here I think we have to acknowledge a grey area—grey, in the sense that once we have recorded particular musicians and paid for their services, do we have a right to disseminate their songs in the market? A lot of things have happened in the last thirty years in relation to the understanding of intellectual property rights—the situation is becoming tighter and tighter from the legal point of view. Earlier, the situation was that the person who recorded the material assumed that he owned the copyright, and not the performer.

This was some kind of an implicit copyright, wasn't it? It was rarely substantiated by any legal document, nothing was signed.

Exactly. Earlier, if I wanted to give any sample from my archive to anybody for commercial purposes, then it was taken for granted that I had a right to do so. After all, if I recorded someone, then I automatically owned that recording. But now, that is no longer the case. If a performer has not surrendered his or her rights to you, then, legally, you cannot use that recording without his or her permission.

Why don't we map the different stages as to how you arrived at this principle of recording rights and distribution?

As I said, we started off by paying the musicians and collecting receipts from them, assuming that we could do what we wanted with their material. That was the first stage. Then I think it was around 1979 that we had our first real encounter with the world of intellectual property rights. A French organization called Radio Diffusion wanted to broadcast selections from a live recording of folk songs from different parts of Rajasthan.[4] For the first time, we began to question how the material was going to be *used*. Though at that time we had little technical knowledge about copyright laws, we were nonetheless cautious in our negotiations with the radio company. We wanted to know if they would be paying for one broadcast alone or for multiple broadcasts of the same songs. The company wanted blanket rights on all the music recorded. Then I remember insisting that if they take these rights, then they needed to pay the musicians accordingly.

What made you aware about the situation at this point, Komalda? Why did you become more vigilant in 1979?

You see, even before this incident I had been associated with a recording project conducted by the ethnomusicologist Geneviève Dournon for the Musée de l'Homme. Out of these recordings had emerged long-playing records later re-issued on CDs like *Flutes of Rajasthan* and *Musical Instruments of the World*.[5] Since the Musée de l'Homme is not a production company, they handed over their selections to other recording companies who marketed the records. They never wrote to me about these deals, but when we would go to France for our concerts, we were presented with these records which we happily received as gifts. At no point did the issue of intellectual property rights come to mind. However, the turning point came when these records sold in very large numbers. [The CD compilation of

Musical Instruments of the World sold 16,000 copies, while the CD *Flutes of Rajasthan* sold 6,000 copies, surpassing the average number of 1,500–5,000 copies of most musical recordings brought out by the Musée de l'Homme.][6]

Let's get the time frame a little clear. It was in the early 1970s that you had accompanied Geneviève Dournon on her trip to Rajasthan which was sponsored by the Musée de l'Homme. The musicians were paid fees for their contribution. It was during this time that you assisted in what was then the most comprehensive recording of Rajasthani folk music to date.

That is right. And a copy of these recordings remains with us in the archives of Rupayan Sansthan. That was our agreement in the early days with all the foreign researchers whom we assisted—in exchange for our work, Rupayan Sansthan would receive a copy of the research and all recording materials. And Geneviève complied with our request by sending us copies of all our recordings and photographs as well.

But beyond that there was nothing?

As far as anything written is concerned, there was nothing. We received no honorarium or royalties from the sales of the records/CDs; nor did we expect anything because we had not entered into any official contract. The real problem arose when an American insurance company got in touch with the Musée de l'Homme to seek television commercial rights for a one-minute excerpt from a piece called *Naṛ*, which had been included in *Musical Instruments of the World*. [See note for fuller elaboration of the technicalities underlying this deal].[7]

So the music travelled from Rajasthan to France to the US.

We didn't know anything about this sitting here in Jodhpur, but somehow or the other, the problem surfaced when this American company got interested in using this music for its own purposes. After some initial complications, the entire matter was negotiated between this insurance company and the Musée de l'Homme, and between them it was decided that a sum of US $30,000 would be paid as a licensing fee for a one-minute use from the *Naṛ* piece. Half of this amount was sanctioned to me, not personally, but to Rupayan Sansthan to be used for the larger development of Rajasthani folk music, in order to serve the tradition and the people from which this music had emerged.

And what about the remaining money?

That was taken by the Musée de l'Homme. Here again we had to deal with another problem. Geneviève felt that since she was largely responsible for implementing the project that she should be given some part of the money. So she approached the Musée de l'Homme, and they agreed to pay her $2,000, which she felt was too little.[8] So then she wrote to me in this matter, and I said, 'All right, all of this money is out of the blue anyway, whatever you decide, we will agree to it. Send us whatever money you think is appropriate.' But then I had to face another problem--since the money was not coming to me personally, but to Rupayan Sansthan, which is a duly registered institution, and moreover, since this money was being given explicitly for the larger development of Rajasthani folk music, was it possible for Rupayan Sansthan to grant money to Geneviève as an individual?

Obviously, the question raises legal problems.

Yes. I had to write to Geneviève and ask her how we should address the situation. Could she be included in the money being given for the development of Rajasthani folk music? Clearly this was not possible. So finally, after three years or so, the money eventually came to us at Rupayan Sansthan. It goes without saying that in the meantime we had become a lot more aware of the ramifications of copyright in our work, not just in relation to research, but also to our international concerts in France, Britain, America, and elsewhere.

In the earlier days, would you allow people to record you, or were you even aware that people could have been recording you without your permission?

In the earlier days, we were only too happy to be recorded. But gradually, as we started to travel to a lot of places, we began to be a little more alert. On the home front, we also began to question whether we had the right to give copies of any piece of music without the permission of the artists concerned. Today it has become increasingly clear to all archives and research organizations that written permission is needed from all parties concerned before anything can be copied and distributed.[9]

While it is necessary to become more vigilant about performance rights, what are the implications of this vigilance in relation to the values of folklore? After all, in folklore, where some notion of 'community' is central to almost any cultural practice, how do you deal with concepts of 'authorship', 'individuality', 'excellence' which are so strongly inscribed, yet debated, in matters concerning intellectual property rights. Where you do feel this entire debate is going?

Copyright as a word is very specific. It does not relate to the utilization of general things which are available in any given society. But if X musician sings a song, then that exact copy cannot be reproduced by anybody else. So, if Gazi has sung a seven-minute song on one of the tapes produced by Rupayan Sansthan, then if anybody copies these seven minutes and uses this piece for anything else without the rights being acquired, then this is an infringement of copyright. However, the fact that Gazi has sung a song belonging to the Manganiyar folk tradition does not by itself imply an infringement of rights for the simple reason that this tradition is not copyrighted. Nor can Gazi claim copyright on the basis of the song in this traditional repertoire. What he can claim is his rights on a particular rendition of a song that he has recorded at a specific place and time.

Can the song that he sang be regarded as his own composition?

No. The song which he has sung belongs to his particular society and tradition. But since he sang it, he has a right on the physical copy [i.e. the exact recording] of that song.

But if somebody else had to sing the same song, that's not an infringement of copyright.

Not at all. It doesn't belong to any one individual.

But if a recording company took Gazi's song and did something with it for a television commercial or for any other purpose, then that poses a problem.

Exactly. Copyright does not imply blanket rights on any one particular composition. It is the individual who rendered the song who can claim a right on his or her rendition. In this context, we keep telling our musicians to be more alert—don't get yourself recorded so easily, know why you are being recorded, for what purpose, by whom. Some of them are beginning to be aware of the implications involved, particularly the professional musicians who tour on the performance circuit.

So far we have been assuming some kind of unequal exchange between musicians and artists from the so-called 'traditional' and 'folk' sector and their urban clientele and consumers. But how does the issue of acknowledgement get negotiated within the context of folk musicians? For example, you once told me that you didn't want the Langas and Manganiyars to sing a particular song by the Kālbeliā women for a particular period of time. What was the reason for this? So that they could stake their own claim on that song?

I remember introducing the Langas and Manganiyars to recordings of Kālbeliā songs, with one specific instruction, that they should not sing these songs professionally in their stage appearances. One particular song that I stopped them from singing at any concert or radio station is called *Dudhaliā Bannā*, a very catchy marriage song celebrating the smooth and fair appearance of the bridegroom—the title of the song suggests that he is as fresh as milk. I wanted the Kālbeliās alone to sing this song because they were not very well known at that time. Later I said that everyone had the right to sing it, by which time it had become one of the most popular Rajasthani songs all over India.

So at one level you could say that I was concerned that the Kālbeliā women should be identified with their compositions. But the reality is that most of the popular songs by the Langas and Manganiyars or other professional groups actually come from the Kālbeliā source.

Whenever these groups sing the Kālbeliā songs, they insert their own musical material and make the necessary changes.

Do they acknowledge the Kālbeliā source?

Whenever they need to, they do. But if they are not asked, then it will be assumed that it's a Langa or Manganiyar song. Not that anybody is likely to ask them that question.

How do the Kālbeliā women feel about this?

Oh, they feel very happy that their song is being sung. Sometimes they even adopt the musicality of the Langas and Manganiyars into their own songs.

So they adopt the Manganiyar version of the Kālbeliā song—there's a wonderful irony here, isn't there, a creative give-and-take? Don't you feel at some level that the entire controversy around copyright and intellectual property has messed up this kind of creative exchange, and all the generosity and sharing that goes with it?

No, I don't think so. Even if there are hundreds of Manganiyars and Langas singing in everyday life, there is still the issue of recording that needs to be confronted. That poses other problems.

You're right, if we didn't have the means of mechanical reproduction, a song would not be recorded or copied or disseminated, and the problem of violating rights would not arise. It could be argued in this regard that the very idea of copyright is alien in a predominantly oral, pre-modern culture, but with the advent of new technologies like digital recording, sampling, dubbing, and mixing, there are new problems.

Let me give you an example. A cultural organization (which I shall call X) was staging a ballet on a Bhakti saint-composer. They invited me to provide some material relating to her compositions. So I sent them some excerpts from our collection at Rupayan Sansthan. Out of these compositions a renowned classical singer, whom I shall call Aparna [name changed] for the purpose of this discussion, composed the music for the ballet for which she received a certain amount of money. The organization X did not produce any cassette of this ballet for commercial purposes. But when Aparna sang her own compositions from this ballet for a cassette, the issue of copyright came up. At this point X sued her on the grounds that since she had already been paid for her compositions, she had no right to make any additional profit on it. Now, X would like me to give them in writing that I have provided the necessary material, which I refuse to do because I don't want to be involved in this kind of controversy. However, when I met Aparna on one occasion, I did tell her that it would have been nice if she could have given credit to the group of traditional singers from which the recording of the songs had been made. With her acknowledgement, this particular tradition of singing could have received some more recognition. It's not the money that matters.

What exactly did she do with the songs? Did she repeat them with the same melodic and rhythmic structure, or did she create new compositions?

She created new compositions.

So it's obviously 'her' work, but nonetheless, there is a matter of etiquette involved here. I think we're opening the delicate issue of acknowledgement.

Acknowledgement is a very important matter, especially when we are dealing with a particular social group that needs to be identified and recognized. Only by acknowledging such groups can we create a healthy tradition in our given society. It becomes all the more necessary to provide strength to such unacknowledged traditions at a time when folklore is considered to be 'dying', and many people lament our so-called 'dying forms'.

Not only is the archive one of the primary repositories of 'dying forms', it could be one of the biggest players in the complex debate surrounding intellectual property rights. Today, archives are being marketed and sold. Scholars and researchers have rights to certain archives, while others are out of bounds for them. Archives have become new power centres, as knowledge becomes increasingly more patented and commodified. I'd like to share a story in this regard.

Some years ago I was at a seminar in Berlin dealing with the politics of intercultural exchange. One of the participants was an aboriginal cultural activist from Australia who was showing us a series of slides depicting aboriginal cultural artefacts. At one point, I asked her for a clarification of one of these objects. She shrugged her shoulders, and said: 'I don't know anything about it. I've never seen it with my own eyes. I've never held it in my hands. I'm not even sure how to pronounce its name. But I saw it in a catalogue printed by the curators of a national museum, and I requested them to send me a slide of the object for which I sent them a fee. Actually, what I'm showing you is a slide of a slide from the archives library.' From this example, it became clear to me how much power is concentrated in the archive—it has almost become the chief arbitrator of the rights of folk and indigenous artists to access their own culture. How do you view the role of the archive in the context of Rajasthani folklore?

I would link the problem of the archive to the assumption that no folkloric material from any tradition can be claimed by any individual. Only a community has the right to claim this material as its own. In Australia, from where you draw your example, there are very complex situations in which land rights, for example, of a particular community have been linked to specific songs and artefacts. These songs and artefacts then begin to acquire legal significance. I remember one controversy surrounding an aboriginal image that was originally printed on an Australian banknote. It appears that this image was excerpted from an aboriginal painting without due acknowledgement. On the basis of claiming this painting as part of their ancestral heritage, a group of aboriginal activists succeeded in getting the image removed from the note, apart from claiming compensation.[10]

Now while this kind of controversy surrounding the violation of cultural rights is going on in Australia, there are other issues that are beginning to emerge in relation to the manufacture of textiles and graphics drawing on traditional designs and iconography.

What do you think are the pitfalls of community rights? We tend to assume that the 'entire' community should decide what needs to be done in a particular controversy. But in actuality, we know that communities are not organic phenomena but social constructions. In almost any community, there are hierarchies, conflicting egos of leaders and spokespersons, who cannot be assumed to represent the rights of 'the community' at large. They have their own vested interests in controlling the assets of the community. So how do we deal with this problem?

We need to identify those people who are working in the field who can be regarded as working for the larger good of the community. There are also a number of institutions that are committed to the development of particular disciplines like the performing arts, folklore, handicrafts, textile design. While subsidizing these institutions, a number of conditions need to be laid down so as to guarantee a genuine utilization of the resources. For example, before the amount of $15,000 could be sanctioned to Rupayan Sansthan by the Musée de l'Homme, I had to spell out how the money was going to be used for the creation of a corpus fund by which our research activities in Rajasthani folklore could be subsidized. We also had to submit our constitution, and it was only on the basis of such evidence, that the money was finally released. Basically, I believe that funding should go to any institution which can ensure that the money will be used for the purpose prescribed.

The Cassette Industry

From these comments relating generally to the issue of copyright and intellectual property rights, Komalda moves on to examine the relationship of these issues to the growth of the cassette industry. An all-India phenomenon, this massively lucrative and seemingly grass-roots industry opens up critical issues relating to positive developments such as 'decentralization, diversification, autonomy, dissent, and freedom'. However, its 'negative features' associated with the mass media persist, notably 'manipulation, deculturation, monopolization and homogenization'.[11] *Without using the language of communications theory, Komalda provides concrete evidence of the very tricky negotiations at work in the 'cassetization' of Rajasthani folk music.*

Once again, my strategy in this section has been to draw out the conceptual and theoretical problems through dialogue, while attaching notes at specific junctures in the text to highlight the more technical dimensions of the analysis.

* * *

Komalda, in an earlier conversation, you had told me a disturbing story of a very popular folk singer, Methi,[12] whose hit songs have been played in almost every public place imaginable, all over Rajasthan. She's a craze wherever she's heard in Rajasthan, particularly in the rural areas. And yet, you mention that she gets a pittance of Rs 1,500 for each recording. This opens up the problematic area of the cassette industry. Could we talk about it?

Everybody tends to assume that folk songs are anonymous, and therefore, no one has any rights over a particular song. Who composed the melody of the song, who wrote the lyrics, all these facts tend to be ignored. On the one hand, there is some truth in the anonymity of many folk compositions, but it is equally true that folk musicians go on composing new things, both at textual and musical levels. And the people who belong to a particular region are in a position to recognize a contemporary composition.

Take the *Nimbuḍā* song composed by Gazi Khan of Harwa village. Everyone from this area knows that this was an original composition by Gazi. Gradually, it became very popular and now millions of people in Rajasthan sing it and dance to it. Now, this song was used in the popular Hindi film *Hum dil de chuke sanam*. This is a very different situation from, say, reproducing traditional folk songs like *Ghoomar* or *Gorbandh*, which have been sung many times in a variety of cassettes. Whether these songs are sung 'authentically' or not, the point is that they have not infringed on anyone's rights. But when *Nimbuḍā* got reproduced in the film, then a lot of us felt that something was seriously wrong. This situation made us more critically aware of the 'new composers' among traditional folk musicians—composers like Bhungar Khan and Ramzan Khan whose names are invariably acknowledged by other folk singers. So, it is obvious that some kind of 'authorship' is at work here, and that these composers have rights on their particular compositions.

Now, to take a broader look at the cassette industry, I'm not sure how it works in all parts of India, but I know a little about Rajasthan. When this phenomenon first emerged,[13] I realized that it was important to recognize the specific types of cassettes that were emerging from the sub-regions of Rajasthan. So, for instance, if anything came from the Alwar region, it was sold only in Alwar. If I wanted a copy of this cassette in Jodhpur, it was not available.

Was it a matter of poor distribution?

At one level, yes, but nobody was interested in it.

Because it was too specific to the Alwar region?

No, the cassette didn't have any reach. Even today the situation hasn't changed. The cassettes produced in Jodhpur you will not find in Udaipur, or Kota, or Jaipur, or Alwar. Whatever comes from Sirohi remains confined to Sirohi. Now, from an archival point of view, when we first encountered this phenomenon, we felt the need to collect these cassettes because they were very deeply rooted in the cultural life of these sub-regions, apart from being linked to specific performers from these regions. We began to do research on how these performers get recorded, where they get recorded, who puts in the money, and who are the technicians involved. Needless to say, in any marketing or business enterprise, one has to survive commercially. So what are the routes of distribution? What are the marketing circuits? These were some of our questions.

While studying the recording conditions, we need to keep in mind that all folk music generally involves groups of singers and instrumentalists. These groups are generally paid Rs 1,500 for a one-hour recording. At the moment, there are six recording studios in Jodhpur, which work round the clock. If a singing group happens to be much in demand, they can get a maximum of Rs 5,000 for a one-hour recording, but that's the upper limit. In exchange for this payment, the producers of the cassette secure total blanket rights from the musicians, who are told in plain terms that they cannot sing the same songs for any other producer.

So far as the quality of the recording is concerned, it's a one-shot deal. Within one hour, whatever is good or bad is recorded, regardless of technical problems, repetitions, memory lapses, whatever. No additional work is ever done on these recordings. Quality-wise, they are sometimes worse than the ones we make on field-trips. Once the session has been recorded, multiple copies of the tapes are duplicated at an average rate of Rs 1.25. The manufacturer makes cassettes available for Rs 14 and Rs 18. Needless to say, the tape which is sold for Rs 14 in the market is of very bad quality and rarely lasts a number of times. The Rs 18 cassette on the T-Series is surprisingly sturdy.

Now, who are the people purchasing these cassettes? Truck drivers all over Rajasthan, they enjoy these cassettes. Taxi drivers serving tourist agencies, they play these cassettes day and night, to keep themselves awake. Wherever you find groups of labourers working on a construction site, you can be sure that they will invest in a tape recorder and the tapes will go on playing while they work. *Dhabas* and *pān* (betel-nut) shops are major haunts for travellers and local residents, who enjoy the latest hits on cassettes blaring from these sites. Likewise, marriage parties use these cassettes. The reason why they are so popular in the local market is that the people recognize the singers from their own regions. While the initial number of cassettes produced for any tape is around 1,200 copies, this number generally rises depending on the demand, and some particularly phenomenal hits have been known to sell thousands of copies.

How has this cassette industry affected folk music in musical terms?

When we think of folk songs musically, there are two things that essentially matter: the text and the melody. Very often we find cassettes where the melodies of old folk songs have been retained, while the text has been changed, if not entirely substituted by a new text. So what we encounter here is a parody of the melody, not a parody of the text.

Who makes these changes, and who decides that the text should be altered?

The marketing people determine these changes. For some reason, they may want to insert new texts into old songs—for example, the numerous *bidāi* songs in the folk repertoire, which bid farewell to the bride. The producers want to create new idioms for these familiar situations, so they approach local poets to compose new lyrics. These poets are paid anything from Rs 200–500 for their efforts. Other changes include getting a song from one particular folk group sung by another group. So the cassette producers will ask a group of Ḍholi women singers to sing songs from the Langa repertoire. Yet another change involves the infusion of sexual overtones in the new compositions, on which I will have more to say. These elements are becoming mandatory—they just have to be there, unlike earlier folk songs whose obscenity was very clearly contextualized.

One important area that has been tapped by the cassette industry is devotional music, including the bhajans of Mirabai, Kabir, Gorakhnath, and many other bhakti saints, whose compositions are sung in numerous rātijāgā and jāgraṇ ceremonies all over Rajasthan. You can hear these bhajans blaring from many shrines in the rural areas, from early in the morning to late at night. There's a large market for these songs particularly during the melās held in the name of some god or goddess. For example, almost two million pilgrims attend the Ramdeoṛa fair every year in honour of Ramdev—you will find thousands of cassettes dealing with Ramdev, Mirabai, Kabir, Rupānde ri bel, and other related material, which are sold in cassette shops located on the melā grounds.

Yet another source of material for the cassette industry is the epic story (*kathā*) and ballad tradition. There are dozens of cassettes dealing with Pabuji, Dev Narayan—some of these epics are recorded in several parts. Apart from this traditional material, we have cassettes containing new stories and narratives from a diversity of regions.

So, would you say that Rajasthani folk culture has grown through the cassette industry?

At the moment, it would seem so.[14] People are beginning to identify with these things in a big way. Now, so far as the market is concerned, this poses its own problems. There is, for instance, the problem of piracy. When musicians are called for a marriage party, the host can ask them to come in the morning before the ceremony begins and sing for him personally. During this time, he records two to three hours of their songs. Then he sells these very songs to local producers. I have come across a number of cassettes that have been made in these circumstances in western Rajasthan. That's one trend.[15]

Another trend that I've observed applies to tourists, who record local musicians and then make cassettes out of these recordings when they get back home. So the problem of piracy doesn't exist only in India—it's happening outside as well.

Tourism is a big industry in Rajasthan, and not surprisingly, the state has been visually rendered in any number of 'spectacular' and 'panoramic' ways on the media. Along with audio cassettes, have you come across any cases of video piracy? After all, it's no big deal to record any traditional performance on video.

I do not know of any specific instances relating to video piracy, but you do see many Rajasthani traditional performances on television commercials, for example, both nationally and internationally—for example, the Langas and Manganiyars singing with khaṛtāls, Jogis dancing like gypsies, and so on. Sometimes for a few seconds, you catch a glimpse of a double-flute, and hear a snatch of music from a Rajasathan-sounding instrument. It's hard to say how much of this has been paid for.

Forget the commercial sector on television. There are many questions that need to be asked about video recordings of performances organized by institutions like the Sangeet Natak Akademi and the Zonal Cultural Centres in India. Sometimes, city cable television units record these performances and air them on their channels. But no money is given to the musicians concerned. They are paid only for their 'live' performance by the organization in question, nothing else. The city cable units are getting a free programme at their expense.

Aren't we seeing a critical shift here, from 'exchange value' to 'market value' in the very production and reception of folk songs? Shouldn't we question what exactly is being 'exchanged'? Surely when traditional musicians sing for themselves or for each other or for their 'jajmāns', it's a very different context from when they sing in a recording studio for the purpose of making a cassette, which will then be sold in the market. The relationships within these contexts are not the same.

One could, for instance, argue that a process of 'democratizing' folk music is at work in freeing it from its feudal sources of patronage.[16] *But, on the other hand, you have argued that the 'jajmān' system has been absolutely essential for the very survival of these folk musical traditions. Apart from the shift in patronage, aren't we also seeing some more fundamental shift in the very belief-systems underlying folk songs? Wouldn't a mere cassette recording of a ritual or religious ceremony divest it of its significance?*

At one level, yes, but there again, you can see it differently. For example, all those devotional songs that are sung in the shrines of gods and goddesses, or at religious fairs, may not be known to the present generation, who may nonetheless continue to believe in these shrines and have some respect for their religious traditions. So when these young people attend the fairs, and buy cassettes of devotional music, which they then play back in their own homes during their household ceremonies, it fulfils a need. I can't tell you how many people have approached me, for instance, to bring out cassettes dealing with marriage songs. This kind of cassette could sell so easily, because many women no longer remember these songs in their entirety, or else they have forgotten the words. In these circumstances, the cassette fulfills a need.

So the cassette helps to restore cultural memory.

Yes. Sometimes it is possible to invite professional singers to sing through the night. This is one way out. But at other times, even if you are willing to pay a substantial amount, they may not be available. The other problem is if that if a family comes from an upper-caste group, there is some reluctance to invite singers from the lower castes to sing for the rātijāgā. So that poses another kind of problem. With the playing of the cassette through the night, a social need for a group of people in a particular community is fulfilled.

Today when you go to Kolkata or Mumbai for any marriage ceremony, you are bound to hear Ustad Bismillah Khan's *shehnai*. Now, he never played that music with this particular marriage in mind. But his cassette comes in useful for many other marriage ceremonies in Jodhpur or Jaipur or Bhilwara, where you hear the shehnai blaring from morning till night.

But isn't it very different to have a cassette blaring for eight hours on end and to hear live musicians singing for the same amount of time? Isn't the cassette getting rid of the live performance?

Yes, this has been a worldwide phenomenon.

At the same time, don't the Manganiyars and Langas continue to be invited to all kinds of ceremonies? Their business as such has not suffered.

For all the widespread use of cassettes, the live contact of music still continues to matter, and the Langas and Manganiyars continue to be invited to sing at different marriages.[17] Sometimes they are paid very well, at other times, poorly. But today they are singing for all communities—Malis, Rajputs, Oswāls, anybody. They no longer sing exclusively for the ceremonies in their jajmān's home.

There's yet another aspect that needs to be considered here— the dimension of interactive pleasure that one gets through listening to any live performance. I would like to believe that any live performance is capable of giving us more joy and energy than listening to a cassette.

This is particularly true of those occasions where people want to dance to live music. Today there are many compositions in pop music, for example, the ones featuring Daler Mehndi, that are composed specifically with dance in mind. The tracks in these cassettes are of ten to twelve minute duration. They are played for all kinds of social occasions, not just in marriage parties but in school functions as well. People dance to them.

So what are the implications of pop music, or the pop renditions of folk songs, for folk music itself? Is folk music likely to suffer on account of these new experiments?

Suffer or not suffer, one can't say, but one has to keep in mind the trends of the market and the availability of traditional material for different kinds of use. At one level, when you think of a phenomenon like *bhangra* pop, you could argue that its roots continue to remain in bhangra. But the time will come when it will no longer be 'folk', it will become entirely 'pop'.[18] However, in the meantime, it is possible that folk music itself would move on to other things, which could be even more creative, and which could again be adapted for commercial purposes. New forms are likely to emerge which are not 'pop', not least because folk musicians are not likely to match the acoustic backing and orchestration of special effects in pop songs.[19] In effect, the 'live' performance of the folk musicians will continue in new forms. Keep in mind that even Daler Mehndi gets more money out of his live performances than from his recorded material.

Do you see something emerging that could be called Rajasthani folk pop?

We see two trends. One is film music, which is not exactly pop—this phenomenon derives a lot of material from the folk melodies of Rajasthan. The text may not be used, but the borrowing of folk melodies is very obvious. So, through the mediation of cinema, we are addressing a much larger area of popular culture.

The other trend is the growing popularity of other kinds of obscene songs, which draw heavily on the folk repertoire. Not only are the melodies and lyrics of these songs appropriated, they also draw on familiar social customs and practices conducted during marriage ceremonies, like riddles, for instance. These songs play with double meanings, puns, and sexual innuendo.

But isn't that inventive, in so far as there is no direct transference between the folk song and the new composition? Rather, there seems to be an elaboration and improvisation of a particular genre—in this case, the riddle. It's not a straight 'lift'.

The problem is that the end result of this arbitrary selection from a folk source lands up becoming obscene. Now, obscenity is not what the riddling songs were intended for in the folk context: they have to be seen in the larger context of sanctifying the consummation of marriage. The problem is that when you extract only one element from a folk tradition, and see it from a specific angularity, you lose out on the larger meaning.[20]

No respect for context: what do you think can be done about this? If a folk song gets transformed into a popular Hindi film song, do you feel there should be any acknowledgement of the source?

Certainly, if the folk song in question is the creation of a particular individual, then there are financial implications involved in addition to the treatment of the song. When the film composer claims, 'It is my song', we have to ask, 'Is this true?'

Has there ever been a challenge in this regard? You brought up Gazi's song . . .

Yes, *Nimbuḍā*. Composed in a rural area of Rajasthan, it became popular among folk singers, and then got picked up by the film industry. And now, all over the country, in Tamil Nadu and West Bengal, people recognize it as a song from the film. But from where did the film get the song? Today the film song is copyrighted, so ironically, if Gazi had to sing his own song, he could be infringing this copyright.

This a classic irony. What other kinds of problems have you experienced with documenting folk culture?

Recently an independent film-maker came to see me from Canada. He said that he didn't have any money but he wanted to do a film on the Manganiyars. He wanted to work with the musician Sakar and observe how he lives with his family and transmits his musical tradition. The film-maker emphasized that since he would be spending his own money on the project, he wouldn't be able to pay the musicians. So I told him: You've come all the way from Canada to India, and then you will return to Canada—for this you spend money. You come from Delhi to Jodhpur—you spend money. For your stay, your food, everything, you spend money. Why do you think that it's not necessary to pay anything to the performers? Surely you don't tell the airline company—I'm doing good work with the Manganiyars, so give me a free ticket. In the hotel, you ask how much the room costs, and you pay the bill without asking any questions. When you develop your film in the laboratory back home, you pay for the editing, the sound, the dubbing, and so on. In all these expenses, there's just one group that gets left out of any financial consideration—the musicians.

The film-maker said: 'You're right, but this is my situation.' So I told him, 'All right, do it, make your film, but on one commitment. If you are able to sell it to any television channel in Canada, America, Britain, Europe, or wherever, from whatever you receive, make sure that you compensate the musicians. Maybe you will not be able to pay them today. But if you stand to gain anything from your work, then share it with them. However, if it remains with you as your personal property and you don't find any outlet for the film, then you don't need to pay them.'

I encounter such situations all the time. Next month, two French journalists are coming to Rajasthan. They want to cover the lives of the Jogis through still photography. Once again, nothing is likely to be paid to the subjects involved. When journalists take photographs, I generally request them to give me a copy. Invariably, they hesitate to give it without protecting their rights over it. But the people whom they have photographed have no rights whatsoever. The problem is that folk musicians and artists from the downtrodden sectors of society are ready to give their services free because they believe that through these photographs and images, they will get to be known worldwide. That sort of situation exists in the Third World.

At one level, of course, it could be argued that the independent film-makers and photographers that I have alluded to *cannot* pay the musicians because they themselves don't have the money. If they had to pay extra money to the musicians, then it would be even more difficult for them to get their work done.

It's a fact that not everyone coming from abroad is rich.

And usually those artists who are involved in this kind of activity are not rich. Moreover, they are not operators. They are genuinely interested in pursuing a particular project. So we have to accept that.

But to reiterate what you said, it's only ethical that if the film-maker you mentioned does succeed in selling his film that he is obliged to give a token fee to the musicians, without whom there would have been no film in the first place. This future reimbursement, however, can only work on trust. There are certain things that can only work on the basis of this one-to-one understanding. We need to work with that and accept its possibilities.

The point is not simply to reimburse the individual Manganiyar musician who sang the song for you—whether he gets benefited or not is not the entire question. Are the second and third generations of this Manganiyar musician likely to benefit from the recognition given to him? The kind of recognition that we are addressing here has a generational value. It's not individual authorship that is in question here. We're talking about generations of folk artists and the future of their tradition.

AFTERWORD

As we come to the end of this book, with Komalda affirming the future of the traditions upheld by communities like the Langas and the Manganiyars, it is necessary to speculate on how this 'future' can be sustained by folklore research institutes like Rupayan Sansthan. Co-founded by Komalda and Vijay Dan Detha as early as 1960 in the village of Borunda, this institute, now based in Jodhpur and funded by the Ford Foundation, has been around long enough to prove itself. And yet, if one had to critically retrospect on Komalda's active fieldwork in Rajasthan during these years, one would be compelled to acknowledge that it has been driven by a passion for 'local knowledge' with scant regard for the demands of institutionalization.

Indeed, it could be argued that it is precisely Komalda's innate resistance to institutionalizing his practice that has enabled him to be recognized as this extraordinarily vibrant, though somewhat uncategorizable 'folklorist'. Would we want him to be anything else? Here we face a paradox: On the one hand, we value him precisely for his endearingly personal and non-academic approach to his field, but on the other hand, we have no other choice but to acknowledge that he has become a one-man institution.

This phenomenon is not unusual in the cultural history of post-Independence India, where there have been many such 'institutions' inextricably linked with the personalities and individual visions of particular luminaries. Inevitably, in the absence of long-term, collective, consensual decision-making processes, there is nothing to fall back on to sustain—and question—the legacies of these individuals. Komalda is not unaware of this problem. Introspecting on his own predicament, he once put it to me with a combination of regret and resignation, 'It should have happened, but it didn't.' Komalda was referring here to the necessary systematization of people's knowledge systems, collected during his research, without which it is not possible, at a concrete level, to think about the present, leave alone the future of any folklore institute.

Opposing this position, a predictable anti-modernist/anti-Enlightenment argument could be that 'folklore doesn't need institutions for its survival—after all, it belongs to "the people", and they will sustain it with their own inventions and changes. The institutionalization of people's belief-systems is just another conversion of knowledge into the discourse of power.'

For all its determinism, this Foucauldian line of argument cannot be written off. Indeed, is there any guarantee that the existing 'successful' institutions of folklore in India are doing anything meaningful for the sustenance of people's knowledge-systems? Arguably self-serving and ensconced within their own power structures, sustained precariously by an abject dependency on foreign funding, it is questionable if the 'knowledge' preserved in these institutions is being channelized back to the traditional communities from which it has been drawn. Here one is not merely addressing the protocol of acknowledgement in research, but more pragmatically, the various levels of material and developmental assistance, so necessary for the survival both of the communities concerned and the making of their art, which are inextricably linked.

In this regard, one should mention the very creative and practical intervention of the Rupayan Sansthan in embarking on a massive project—the construction of 100 sindhi sārangis and 100 kamāychās for free distribution to young Langa and Manganiyar musicians. Inevitably, this project, which is Komalda's brainchild, emerged out of a very acute problem—the gradual disintegration of the old instruments in the field, with no infrastructure for their replacement. After failed attempts to interact with a few master craftsmen in the field, notably Ridmal Khan Langa, whose instruments tended to land up in museums rather than in the hands of musicians, Komalda sought a different route.

Drawing on the expertise of one Dhananjay Kumar, who runs a modern well-equipped carpentry shop in Jodhpur, he initiated a dialogue in close collaboration with traditional musicians, who gave detailed advice on every aspect of their instruments—the wood, the pegs, the strings, the holes, the placement of the bridge. With the generous financial support of the National Folklore Support Centre (of which Komalda is the Chairman), supplemented by a grant from the Sangeet Natak Akademi, it was possible to commission the actual construction of new instruments. Subtly 're-invented', with traditional principles reinforced by new, more durable materials, the instruments gained a new lease of life. Today they are being used in live performances by a new generation of musicians.

This is a good example to my mind of the kind of intracultural dialogue that is so necessary within regional cultural contexts, where individuals cutting across class, caste, and profession can work together for the larger sustenance of traditional practices, without which they can have no viable future. It becomes clear that the making and distribution of these new instruments could possibly be one of Komalda's most long-lasting contributions to the field of Rajasthani music. Indeed, he is more likely to be remembered as a musical adviser and interventionist in the field rather than as an administrator of a folklore research institute.

Without belabouring the point, I would acknowledge that while writing this book was pleasurable and insightful, particularly in the warm person-to-person contact I had with Komalda, it was also a bit of a nightmare at times because I had no way of accounting for what he was saying. While this unverifiability can be ascribed to the very nature of any oral discourse, it would be wrong to deny the accountability of 'orality' through other sources of evidence. This evidence may not be academically processed (like the critical notes that I've appended to this book), but it could take the form of jottings, scribbles in diaries, memorabilia, souvenirs, itineraries, recorded anecdotes, tapes, and so on. All these materials are hypothetically 'extant' in the archives of Rupayan Sansthan. But are they readily accessible? I learned very fast in the early stages of listening to

Komalda that whenever he made remarks like, 'Oh, I've got a list of 130 categories of grass written down somewhere', that you would never find this list in the totally disorganized archival material of his institute.

On a more positive note, however, I learned to accept this chaos as a critical deterrent to the transformation of knowledge into discourse. In retrospect, I am even oddly grateful that it existed because it taught me not to take this transformation for granted. I trust that some of the struggle underlying this transformation has been inscribed in the larger narrative of the book, and that it will inform the research of other interlocutors, not only in the field of Rajasthan, but in the larger speculative realms of oral history. If in the introduction to this book, I had indicated some of the problems involved in the process of transcription, here let me share some of the intimate lessons that I've learned in the course of writing the book.

For a start, I would say that even as the local knowledge of people's belief-systems, mediated by an observer like Komalda, is not always verifiable at oral levels, it can be supplemented by other written and theoretical interventions in the field. In this regard, I have come to grips with the truism that orality and critical theory can, and indeed, need to complement each other's 'truths'. The contingency of the spoken word can challenge the much-fetishized rigor of theory, while the precision demanded of theory can regulate in turn the volatile flow of the human voice. Both oral and written histories, counterpointed, though not necessarily brought into harmony, are necessary for a more inflected representation of local knowledge.

In writing this book, I also learned not to be afraid of my own ignorance, but to seek ways of addressing and pushing its limits. Here I could not have found a kinder and more generous guide than Komalda, who never once made me feel that I had no business picking his brains on a particular issue, when I was no authority in the field. Today, having written the book, I should acknowledge that it would be much more difficult to raise the kind of 'obvious' questions that I did in the course of researching it. It is not that I know more at this point in time, but I have simply become more self-reflexive of the limits within which Komalda's knowledge of a particular field operates.

This brings me to the value of limits and to the recognition that knowledge is essentially imperfect. The purveyors of knowledge rarely claim omnisicence or total clarity, even though it would seem that their 'words of wisdom' cover 'everything under the sun'. What I learned in the course of listening to Komalda, is not what he knows or doesn't know, but rather, what remains to be known in a particular field. In this crucial sense of incompletion, knowledge remains provisional.

There is also the illusion of time to contend with here—while listening to Komalda, it was very easy for me to forget time, but as he himself cautioned me more than once, 'What I'm saying now may not hold in the next fifty years.' What he failed to add is that this *existing* provisional knowledge on a particular subject—and knowledge is always in the present, even though it may be dealing with the past—does not cease to be significant for being mutable.

Finally, in the age of globalization, knowledge has often been juxtaposed against the ubiquity and surfeit of information. All too often information is valorized as the intellectual capital of 'our times', knowledge itself being reduced to some kind of archaism. There is a danger here of assuming that knowledge is a pre-modern/non-modern avocation, which gains respectability only when it is patented and reduced to a commodity.

Perhaps there are other modes and routes of retrieving knowledge through what Gayatri Chakravorty Spivak so tellingly describes as the search for 'ecological sanity' in 'our global predicament'.[1] Without romanticizing the 'living culture' of tribal peoples, notably 'denotified' tribes, who were (relatively) 'left alone' by the dominant power structures in colonial and pre-colonial times, is it possible to use some 'residues' of this culture to 'fight the dominant, which has irreducibly changed us'?[2] Though Spivak raises this somewhat utopian question, she is too much of a realist not to acknowledge that this 'living culture' is 'as much on the run, as ungraspable, as anyone else's'—in short, it is not a source of quasi-religious, eternal belief-systems, uncontaminated by time and history. Rather, through its very vulnerability, it offers possible ways of 'learning to learn' some forgotten lessons of ecological sanity and resilience.

While listening to Komalda talk intimately about the very humble, yet startling insights of knowledge that continue to animate the lives of nomadic communities—the Kālbeliā, the Kuchbandiā, the Gaḍolia Luhār, among other groups—I have learned that these communities cannot be arbitrarily subsumed in a 'narrative'. The so-called 'narrative of community', which has been set against the modernity of the nation-state, is essentially a theoretical manoeuvre in the communitarian-secularist debate.[3] In actuality, communities are far more diverse, complex, mutable, and contradictory than the existing communitarian theory in contemporary India suggests. Apart from undermining specific areas of people's knowledge, this theory, it could be argued, is insufficiently informed of the multiple negotiations of and resistances to modernity at ground levels. What is needed, therefore, is a more empirically researched 'history from below', which can yet ignite a renewed subalternity in which the subaltern is not absented (and then, theoretically justified for being so).

I had wanted to end this book on a lyrical note, and instead, I find myself engaging with these critical questions. At one level, I cannot deny that they work against the thoroughly non-polemical demeanour and discourse of my subject. But, at another level, I do find it fascinating that while Komalda himself eschews controversial positions on almost any issue, his work raises very complex questions relating to the politics of representing the 'folk', the future of subalternity, intellectual property rights, the limits of institutionalization, and so on. While my inscriptions of these debates have been minimal in the course of the narrative, I trust that they have resonated for the reader and that they have succeeded at some level in demystifying Komalda's knowledge.

Let me acknowledge that demystifying any phenomenon is not meant to undermine its significance, but rather, to take it more seriously instead of being seduced by its charisma. Nothing could be more unfair, to my mind, than to reduce Komalda to that 'wise old man from Jodhpur' with which I began this book in a conscious pastiche of folkloric hagiography. Komalda's life of the mind is far too rich and steeped in the minutiae of local traditions to be so falsely romanticized. More critically, in the very incompletion of his relentless search for the multiple and interconnected dimensions of knowledge, the body of his research raises more questions than answers. Its limitations are as significant as its achievement. And for all these reasons, I have a simple plea on which to end this book: While honouring him and taking his insights into even deeper and more intractable areas of knowledge, let us not reduce Komalda to folklore.

NOTES

Introduction

1. A.K. Ramanujan, 'Is There an Indian Way of Thinking?: An Informal Essay,' *The Collected Essays of A.K. Ramanujan*, (ed.), Vinay Dharwadker, 1999, pp. 34–51.
2. See Chapter 12 on 'Marketing the "Folk"', pp. 267–277, for an extended discussion of this controversy within the larger context of intellectual property rights.
3. The 'narrative of community' has been theorized by Partha Chatterjee in a series of publications— *The Nation and its Fragments* (1994), 'Beyond the Nation? Or Within?' (1997), 'Community in the East' (1998), 'On Civil and Political Society in Post-Colonial Democracy' (2001). A far less inflected advocacy of 'community' in relation to traditional sources of knowledge, has been provided by Ashis Nandy, who specifically takes an anti-secularist stance in his influential essay 'The Politics of Secularism and the Recovery of Religious Tolerance'. First published in *Alternatives* XIII in 1988, this essay continues to be reprinted along with 'An Anti-Secularist Manifesto' with scant respect for the numerous critiques that it has elicited in the intervening years.
4. A particularly strong critique of Nandy's (1988) valorization of 'pluralism' and 'tolerance' in traditional sources of knowledge can be read in Achin Vanaik's chapter on 'Communalism, Hindutva, Anti-Secularists: The Conceptual Battleground,' *Communalism Contested: Religion, Modernity and Secularization*, 1997, pp.162–9.
5. Among the increasingly textured readings of secularism provided by

numerous interlocutors in the field, notably Rajeev Bhargava (1998) and Akeel Bilgrami (1997), one still encounters strident affirmations of 'die-hard secularism' in essays such as Meera Nanda's 'Breaking the Spell of Dharma: Case for Indian Enlightenment' (2001).

6. Though Homi Bhabha is credited with the invention of 'vernacular cosmopolitanism', there are many variants and complements to this construct, notably Sheldon Pollock's (1998) historicization of the 'cosmopolitan vernacular'.
7. See Chapter 11, 'From the Local to the Global: Rajasthani Folk Music in Performance,' pp. 243–257, for more details relating to the global travel of traditional musicians and its impact on their lives.
8. For a contextualization of this principle, read Geertz's seminal reading of 'thick description' in the first chapter of *The Interpretation of Cultures*, 1973, pp. 3–30.
9. Tellingly, the strongest examples of 'rewriting' history have been sparked by the violence of communalism, in seminal studies by Pandey 1991 and Butalia 1998. Amin 1995 and Dube 1998 also provide rich and layered examples of oral history intersecting—and in the process, questioning—the seeming authenticity of archival resources.

   Within the specific context of Rajasthan, the study by Ann Grodzins Gold and Bhoju Ram Gujar entitled *In the Time of Trees and Sorrows: Nature, Power and Memory in Rajasthan* (2002) offers a particularly dense and reflexive ethnography on subaltern community life. Recently published in India even as this book goes to press, I will limit my comment to saying that the very structure of the narrative in which Gold represents Gujar, without Gujar talking back to Gold, mirrors the dilemma of subaltern representation. Since Gujar does not share the theoretical language of the book, as his one brief statement in formal Hindi (translated by Gold) indicates only too clearly, in whose voice is the co-author represented? For all its postmodern polyvocality, the actual framing of this study raises critical questions regarding the relationship of collaboration and co-authorship within the larger dynamics of 'dominance' and 'hegemony'.
10. See Chapters 5–9 in my books *Theatre and the World: Performance and the Politics of Culture* (1993) and Chapter 3 in *The Politics of Cultural Practice: Thinking Through Theatre in an Age of Globalization* (2000a) for a fuller elaboration on my interaction as director and dramaturge with 'other' languages.
11. Peter J. Claus, *Essays in Performance Analysis* (2001), p. 4. 'Performance' is linked here to two distinct philosophies of language upheld by J.R. Austin and Paul Grice, as well as to the sociology of Erving Goffman.

12. Helen Myers, 'Theory and Method: Fieldwork,' *Ethnomusicology: An Introduction*, (1992), p. 23.
13. Stuart H. Blackburn, 'Performance Markers in an Indian Story Type,' *Another Harmony: New Essays on the Folklore of India* (1986), p. 168.
14. In the voluminous literature on the subject, in explicating the distinctions between 'inscription', 'transcription', and 'description', James Clifford's 'Notes on (Field)notes' (1990) remains a model of clarity and eloquence.
15. I am thinking in particular of Peter J. Claus and Frank Korom whose widely used textbook *Indian Folklore and Folkloristics* (1990) argues strenuously for the symbiotic use of these two terms and their practices. While the 'folklore' in question is marked 'Indian', 'folkloristics' remains problematically unmarked in its international affiliations. Perhaps, it would be more accurate to read Claus and Korom's advocacy of 'folkloristics', specifically within the 'Third World' context of India, as one particular enunciation of the priorities and imperatives of folklore studies in American academia today. The critical issue of *framing* entire disciplines of study for 'other' cultures, supplemented by the larger politics of international funding, is in question here.
16. Clifford 1990, p. 58.
17. Ibid.
18. Talal Asad, 'The Concept of Cultural Translation in British Social Anthropology,' *Writing Culture: The Poetics and Politics of Ethnography* (eds. James Clifford and George E. Marcus), 1986. Cited in Clifford (1990), p. 58.
19. See Bharucha (2000a), pp. 68–71.
20. See Clifford (1990), p. 62, for a sharp reading of Clifford Geertz's 'subtle fusion of native and ethnographic subjectivities in a common interpretive project'.
21. 'Another Harmony' is the title of one of the most important contributions to the study of folklore in India, co-edited by Stuart H. Blackburn and A.K. Ramanujan (1986). Ironically, it could be argued that 'harmony' does not really exist as a concept in Indian musical traditions, both classical and folk. And, therefore, Blackburn and Ramanujan's conceptual foregrounding of the term is somewhat unproblematized in the way it elides 'harmony' with 'autonomy' and the 'counterpoint' of folk traditions in relation to the classical tradition. Where, one could ask, is the role of dissonance in this reading of 'harmony'? And why should it be 'another' harmony, ostensibly duplicating the harmony assumed by classical traditions, which is itself questionable?

1. The Past in the Present

1. Another variant of this story and the discussion surrounding it can be read in Komalda's address to the participants in a workshop on documenting folklore, organized by the National Folklore Support Centre, in Jaisalmer, February 2001. Published in *Folklife*, Vol. 1, Issue 5, April 2001, pp. 51–2.
2. 'Who Needs Folklore?,' *The Collected Essays of A.K. Ramanujan*, 1999, pp. 538–48.
3. Quoted by A.K. Ramanujan in 'Who Needs Folklore?,' (*ibid.*), p.539. Elaborating on Narayana Rao's position, Ramanujan states that while Vedic pundits are learned in Sanskrit 'grammar, syntax, logic and poetics', their 'literacy' is 'imbued in their bodies', in so far as their mode of acquiring and transmitting knowledge is entirely 'oral.' A learned man is referred to as '*kanṭhastha*', one whose knowledge is contained in his throat.
4. A.K. Ramanujan, 'Who Needs Folklore?,' (*ibid.*), p. 540.
5. While '*sarg*' and '*pratisarg*' refer to the primary and secondary stages of creation, '*kalpa*' refers to the longest period of time, consisting of 4320 million years. Each *kalpa* is made up of 14 *manvantaras*, the age initiated by Manu or primeval man. It is in the reign of the seventh Manu that the Great Flood (*pralaya*) occurs—this event serves as a time marker to separate the period of the Manus from that of the Kshatriya kings that follow.

   For an authoritarive contextualization of these terms within readings of cosmological and historical time, read Romila Thapar's *Time as a Metaphor of History: Early India* (1996), and 'Genealogy as a Source of Social History' from her earlier book *Ancient Indian Social History: Some Interpretations* (1978).
6. Like the story of *Chiḍa-Chiḍi* described earlier in the essay, the story being discussed in the remaining section of this chapter was also narrated in an abbreviated version in the seminar at Jaisalmer, February 2001. See *Folklife* (*ibid.*), pp. 49–50, for a somewhat more cursory rendition of the story from the one presented in this chapter.
7. In 'Social Mobility in Ancient India,' *Ancient Indian Social History* (1978), Romila Thapar mentions how the earliest dynasties recorded in the *Puranas* were classified into two categories—the *Suryavanshi* (Sun-Family) and the *Chandravanshi* (Moon-Family)—both of them tracing their ancestry to the hermaphrodite son of Manu, the primeval man. 'Apart from the symbolic significance of this myth,' she adds that, it became the mythical 'prototype of all rulers seeking

Kshatriya genealogies' (pp. 132–33). The Rajput royal families of Rajasthan were no exception.

2. Land

1. See my critical essay 'Politician's Grin, Not the Buddha's Smile' (1998a) for a fuller account of my position on the nuclear tests in Pokaran, Rajasthan, on 11 and 13 May 1998.
2. The present state of Rajasthan (identified as Rajputana in pre-independence India), was constituted under the States Reorganisation Act, 1956. From the documentation provided in the 'People of India' series on *Rajasthan*, 1998, we learn how the state came into existence through seven stages, incorporating the systematic merging of former Princely States. The states of Bikaner, Jaipur, Jaisalmer, and Jodhpur, for instance, merged with Rajasthan in 1949.

   Today, after the truncation of Madhya Pradesh through the formation of the new state of Chhattisgarh, Rajasthan is the largest state of India, with 32 districts, and as many as 7,292 gram panchayats (village assemblies).
3. For a more technical overview on the intricate connections between globalization and the seed industry, and their specific impact on cotton farmers in India, read 'Globalisation and Threat to Seed Security: Case of Transgenic Cotton Trials in India,' by Vandana Shiva, Ashok Emani, and Afsar H. Jafri (1999). For an authoritative overview on environmental problems in the context of social ecology and equity, read Gadgil and Guha 2000.
4. Arjun Appadurai, Frank J. Korom, and Margaret A. Mills, 'Introduction', *Gender, Genre, and Power in South Asian Expressive Traditions*, 1994, p. 4.

3. Water

1. P. Sainath, *Everybody Loves a Good Drought*, New Delhi: Penguin Books India, 1997.
2. In most of his published writings, Komalda has translated '*jāgraṇ*' as 'night-wake'. This is somewhat misleading because jāgraṇs have no specific funerary or death-related associations. They can be held for any number of reasons—for example, the construction of a house, the building of a well, or the appeasement of a spirit. While the participants in the jāgraṇ 'stay awake' through the night, the 'night-wake' has other connotations of a vigil, in which a dead body

is preserved and displayed for the family and community before being buried.

3. For more details on *nāḍis*, read M.A.Khan's extended abstract on 'Revival and Modernisation of Traditional Water Management Systems in Western Rajasthan,' *Keynote Papers and Extended Papers* (hereafter PPST), presented in the Second Congress on Traditional Sciences and Technologies in India, Madras 1995, section 11, p. 8.
4. On the *ṭānkā* system of water harvesting, read M.A. Khan (*ibid.*).
5. For an elaborate reading on *dān* in the larger context of gift-exchange, read Romila Thapar's essay '*Dāna* and *Dakshinā* as Exchange,' *Ancient Indian Social History: Some Interpretations*, 1978, pp. 105–121.
6. Nirmal Sengupta, 'Traditional Water Management Systems—Primitive or Precious?,' PPST, 1995, section 11, p. 3.
7. See A.S. Kolarkar's comprehensive account of the 'Khaḍīn: A Sound Traditional Method of Runoff Farming in Indian Desert,' *Keynote Papers and Extended Papers* (hereafter PPST), presented in the First Congress on Traditional Sciences and Technologies in India, Bombay, Nov.-Dec. 1993, section 7, pp. 2–6.
8. The indigenous knowledge-systems of people were acknowledged even by the British colonial army engineers in charge of irrigation schemes. Nirmal Sengupta in his essay on 'Traditional Water Management Systems' (*ibid.*) quotes Sir Arthur Cotton in this regard praising the intelligence of 'native engineers' (pp. 11.3–11.4). For a broader perspective on irrigation, read M.S. Vani's 'Traditional Irrigation Systems: Law and Policy,' PPST, 1993, section 7, pp. 44–49.
9. Sujeet Sarkar in 'Three Normal Years in a Hundred,' *Humanscape*, June 2001, p. 12, elaborates on how 'the small and marginalized sections of society' have failed to benefit from the Canal.
10. Milind Bokil, 'Drought in Rajasthan: In Search of a Perspective,' *Economic and Political Weekly*, 25 November 2000, pp. 4171–5.
11. Amartya Sen, *Poverty and Famines: An Essay on Entitlement and Deprivation* (1981).
12. From Milind Bokil (2000), p. 4174, we learn that the animal population in Rajasthan has gone up from 4,77,73,208 (1992) to 5,43,48,901 in (1997).
13. Rāni Bhaṭiyāṇi is discussed later in the book in the context of sati and her patronage of the Manganiyar musicians. See Chapter 6, pp. 142–144.
14. Prahlad Singh Shekhawat, 'Traditional System of Water Harvesting and Development in Arid Rajasthan,' PPST, 1993, section 7, p. 60.
15. For more on the Girdawari report as a 'tool to delay matters' in relation

to drought relief, read Bokil (2000), p. 4171. It appears that in 1999–2000, 'the drought situation had become apparent in September itself but drought was declared on 10 January 2000 and relief work was started in April 2000' (p. 4172).

16. At present, there are two wage employment schemes organized by the Rajasthan government—the 'Ashwasit Rojgar Yojana' (ARY—Assured Employment Scheme), and the Jawahar Rojgar Yojana (JRY)—which have been amalgamated into the Swarna Jayanti Rojgar Yojana (SRJY). Despite these impressive sounding schemes, their budgets are meagre, and have even been cut because the bureaucrats have not been able to use the allotted funds on time. See Bokil (2000), p. 4173.
17. I am grateful to Vijay Dan Detha for contributing these dohās and to Ira Sisodia for translating them with additional inputs by Shubha Chaudhuri and Manohar Lalas. In his essay 'Musicians for the People: The Mānganiyārs of Western Rajasthan,' (1994), p. 228, Komalda defines the dohā as a couplet—'an independent verse form of the *mātrik* (moraic) variety. Mātrik meters are quantitative, based on total moraic count of short syllables [one *mātrā*] and long syllables [two *mātrās*] rather than feet . . . The dohā, of which there are many varieties, has 24 mātrās in each line, with a caesura after the thirteenth [mātrā] and different rhyming possibilities.'

4. Oral Epics

1. In refuting the possibility of musical instruments migrating of their own volition from one region to another, Komalda is obviously working against the notion of the 'autotelic', which is an important phenomenon in folklore. With his characteristic lucidity, A.K. Ramanujan (1999) describes this quality as the capacity of folklore items to 'travel by themselves without any actual movement of populations. A proverb, a riddle, a joke, a story, a remedy, or a recipe travels every time it is told.' (p. 536). Significantly, while the transmission of music would seem to be less mediated by 'language', Komalda never assumes the easy accessibility of folk music across borders. Rather, he tends to emphasize the regional specificities and styles of folk musical traditions, which are not readily transmitted outside their indigenous contexts. As for folk musical instruments, they do not travel in an autotelic mode, but rather, are carried by specific communities on their migratory routes.
2. For a meticulous transcription and analysis of the *Dev Narayan* epic, read Miller (1994).

3. A fuller description of the rāvanhatthā has been provided by John D. Smith (with inputs by Jean Jenkins) in one of his numerous endnotes to *The Epic of Pabuji* (1991) p. 41.
4. Stuart H. Blackburn, 'Patterns of Development for Indian Oral Epics,' *Oral Epics in India* (1989), pp. 17–8.
5. Ibid., p. 5.
6. Alf Hiltebeitel, *Rethinking India's Oral and Classical Epics: Draupadi among Rajputs, Muslims, and Dalits* (1999), p. 22.
7. Ibid.
8. Drawing on common principles of 'grafting' and 'accumulating' motifs, Stuart Blackburn (1989) posits two patterns of development for oral epics. Pattern 1 goes through three stages of 'death and deification', 'supernatural birth', and 'pan-Indian identity', while Pattern 2 eliminates the first stage of 'death and deification', while retaining the second and third stages. Pattern 1 applies largely to 'martial' and 'sacrifical' epics, while Pattern 2 is almost exclusively linked to 'romantic' epics. To these two patterns, Blackburn incorporates the ritual and entertainment priorities of the actual performance contexts of oral epics. Ritual and entertainment are not 'mutually exclusive' categories, but shifting priorities on the same continuum.

   Bringing these intricate variables together, Blackburn states that the crucial factor is the 'death motif'. 'If [this] motif is present, the hero is deified, the context is ritualistic, and the tradition follows Pattern 1.' (p. 21) This is the case with *Pabuji*, even though it is a 'regional' and not a 'local' tradition, where the 'death motif' is strongest. As oral epics spread outwards at 'supra-regional' levels, 'the human origins of the hero are further obscured, historical and geographical specificity fade, ritual dimensions weaken, and the hero/god may be fully absorbed into a transcendent figure such as Krishna or Rama' (p. 26).

   While Blackburn's models are intricately worked out, they raise many empirical and theoretical questions, as we shall examine later in this chapter.
9. All additions and corrections to Komalda's narrative are taken from John D. Smith's (1991) succinct summary of the 'Pabuji' story, pp. 9–12, supplemented by details from his transcription of the epic text.
10. The dispute revolves around a hare hunted by Būṛo, Pabu's elder brother. The wounded hare runs into the court of Saragde Khīchī, Jindrāv Khīchī's father, who refuses to part with the hare when Būṛo demands that it be returned to him. Instead, Saragde insults Būṛo by saying that he can take the headless body of the hare, but nothing else. Provoked, Būṛo elicits Pabu's support in waging war against the Khīchīs.

11. John Smith (1991) argues that an 'inflation of history' has been used to justify the anachronistic inclusion of Gogo Chauhāṇ in the Pabu story. For more details on his somewhat strenuous attempt to problematize Gogo Chauhāṇ's allegedly historical links with Mahmud of Ghazni (c. eleventh century), see his section on 'Pabuji the man', p. 74.
12. Guru Gorakhnath is yet another anchronistic character in Pabuji. As described in John Smith's transcription of the epic (1991), the guru initiates Harmal Devāsi as his disciple by splitting his ears and inserting earrings into them. From the ears come 'spurts of milk' rather than 'torrents of blood' (p. 346). Pleased by the authenticity of his disciple's devotion, the guru gives Harmal a pair of sandals (by which he is able to walk across the seas on his way to Lanka); a begging-bowl, which, when turned upside down and then the right way up, ensures him a meal; and a drinking-gourd in which the poisonous milk offered to him by the Rabāris of Lanka fails to be filled.
13. After the final cataclysmic battle when the palanquin descends to take Pabu to heaven, there is in most renditions of the epic a symbolic scene in which Deval is shown separating three streams of blood represented by the Rabāri, Bhil, and Rajput warriors who have died in the battle. At this critical juncture, Pabu stops Deval from separating the blood by saying, 'O goddess let this blood mingle. These [warriors] have died in my service, they are my own warriors...If their blood remains separate, then (in future) Bhils will not protect Rajputs and Rajputs will not protect Bhīls, and nobody in the world will recognize Pabuji.' (Smith 1991: p. 451).
14. While John Smith (1991) is less equivocal than Komalda in identifying *Pabuji's* characters as *avatārs* from the *Ramayana*—there is 'unfinished business' that has to be contended with here, as he puts it sharply—he makes an important qualification: 'It is not necessarily safe even to assume that the stories of the Sanskrit epics are known to performers of oral epics; as an example, the only version of the *Mahabharata* current in Rajasthani oral performance today is so different from the Sanskrit version that it is barely recognizable. Some performers of the Pabuji epic, moreover, do not know the name of Vishnu' (quoted in *Oral Epics in India* ,1989, p. 9).

    This emphatic clarification, however, does beg the question *why* the connections between *Pabuji* and the *Ramayana* should be so deeply internalized, as John Smith seems to assume in his commentary on the performance.
15. In 'Epics and Ideologies: Six Telugu Folk Epics', *Another Harmony:*

New Essays on the Folklore of India (1986), Velcheru Narayana Rao provides a succinct summary of the *Kāṭamarāju Kathā*, an epic narrative revolving around the cattle herder-caste of the Yādavs, also known as Gollās. From Rao's summary, we learn that the protagonist Kāṭamarāju 'owns a large herd of cattle and enters into an agreement with Nallasiddhi, a king of the Chola dynasty: in return for all the male calves, the king will let Kāṭamarāju's cattle graze on Nalasiddhi's land. The actual words of the contract are these: "All the grass that is born out of the water is yours, and all the male calves that are born from the cattle are ours." When a drought afflicts the area and there is not enough grass for the cattle, Kāṭamarāju takes his contract literally and grazes his cattle on the rice crop, since it is also a kind of grass which grows from water. The result is a disastrous battle, resulting in the tragic death of many Yadava heroes' (pp. 136–7).

16. Alf Hiltebeitel, *Rethinking India's Oral and Classical Epics* (1999), p. 19.
17. Ibid., p. 43.
18. The background on the *bhomiyā* and his mythification has been covered in detail in Komalda's 'The Shrine: An Expression of Social Needs', *Gods of the Byways: Wayside Shrines of Rajasthan, Madhya Pradesh and Gujarat* (1982), pp. 14–6.
19. Komal Kothari, 'Performers, Gods, and Heroes in the Oral Epics of Rajasthan', *Oral Epics in India* (1989), p. 113.
20. The question of history is not resolved in John Smith's (1991) scholarly attempt to trace linkages between existing oral renditions of the *Pabuji* epic and the written account presented in Muhato Nainasi's seventeenth-century *Khyata* (Chronicle), which Smith claims with 'near-certainty' was 'oral in origin' (pp. 72–3). Addressing this sceptical, yet relentless search for 'a presumed historical original and an unembellished prior text' for *Pabuji*, Alf Hiltebeitel claims that it is fundamentally flawed in its 'rationalized and historicized hermeneutic' (Hiltebeitel 1999: p. 94). The problem deepens for Hiltebeitel when this 'prior text' of *Pabuji* is assumed to have been permeated with the myth of the bhomiyā itself.

    Underlying Hiltebeitel's disagreement is a larger unease with the 'bottom up' approach to studying oral epic traditions, as exemplified by Stuart Blackburn (1989). In this approach, there is an all too organic development built into a particular 'death event', which 'leads to deification, to worship, to a cult, and eventually to a narrative which is ritually performed to invoke the spirits of the dead' (Blackburn 1989:

23). Tellingly, in the course of developing this thesis, Blackburn quotes one of Komalda's many arresting phrases—'generative point'—to justify how the 'death event' precipitates 'stories in local traditions'. It would be a mistake, however, to assume on the basis of such clues that Komalda shares the 'bottom up' theoretical approach to explaining epic narratives in relation to death and deification practices. As his statement in the following sentences of the paragraph makes clear, the relationship between death, ritual, and performance in *Pabuji* remains 'unclear'.

21. Komal Kothari, 'Performers, Gods, and Heroes in the Oral Epics of Rajasthan' (1989), p. 110.
22. From John Smith's (1991) detailed reading of the pictures in the *paṛ*, we learn how chronological sequences in the *Pabuji* narrative are visually represented far apart from each other. So there is a disjunction between temporality and spatiality. For example, Pabu's encounters with Mirza Khan and Gogo Chauhāṇ follow in immediate succession in the epic, but the two locations to which they are linked—Patan and Pushkar, respectively—are 'separated by many feet' (pp. 56–7).
23. With microanalytical logic, John Smith (1991) points out how in the scene where Kelam and her female companions swing in the garden, there is no iconographic representation of the gardener as such. So the bhopā merely 'points to the nearest male figure', an attendant in Pabu's court. 'Iconographically,' as Smith explains, 'this man cannot be a gardener (gardeners do not carry fans); in terms of scenic organization he cannot have anything to do with the girls in the garden (he has his back to them); but for a second or two he nonetheless becomes the gardener' (p. 64).
24. Even though Komalda emphasizes that the paṛ is a mobile temple, he does not elaborate on its ritual dimensions. John Smith (1991: 67) emphasizes that since the paṛ is regarded as a 'sacred object', it cannot be discarded without appropriate rituals.
25. In John Smith's (1991) book, Pabuji's bard-priests (*bhopās*), whom Smith refers to as *bhopos* (following Rajasthani usage), are identified as belonging to the Nāyak caste. This caste, according to Smith, is 'listed (regrettably enough, under the abusive synonym *Thorī*) as one of the scheduled castes of Rajasthan—the Nāyaks occupy a very low rank in the social hierarchy' (p. 6). Elsewhere, in the glossary, Smith acknowledges that Bhil is 'sometimes used to refer to members of the Nāyak caste' (p. 503), but this is not how he identifies Parbu Bhopo in the book.
26. John D. Smith, *The Epic of Pabuji* (1991), pp. 38–9.

5. Folk Gods and Goddesses

1. In 'The *Kathā* of Sakat: Two Tellings', *Another Harmony: New Essays on the Folklore of India* (1986), Susan Wadley describes kathās as 'myths whose primary function is to instruct devotees in the proper ritual forms (including correct mental attitudes). This purpose of the kathās is evident in their structure: given an initial situation of human—or other—unhappiness (such as poverty), the gods reward faith with mercy and service with boons which lead ultimately to happiness' (p. 200).
2. Much of the material covered in this section on 'shrines' has been addressed by Komalda in one of his more descriptive pieces of writing—'The Shrine: An Expression of Social Needs' (1982), pp. 5–31. The fluid translation by Uma Anand is counterpointed by the vivid photography of Vivek Anand.
3. The figure of the bhomiyā has already been discussed in the last chapter with reference to Pabuji.
4. See Komalda's essay on 'The Shrine' (1982), pp. 23–4, for more details. In the worship of Ghas [Grass] Bhairon, it appears that '[a] big unhewn stone is placed on a triangular cart with very small wheels. Before the rains set in, the villagers gather together and try to drag the cart with the stone, Bhairon, around the whole settlement' (p. 24). If the cart moves smoothly, the monsoon can be expected to be good. However, if it gets stuck, then there is a strong possibility of drought.
5. Ann Grodzins Gold, in her essay '*Jātrā*, *Yātrā* and Pressing Down Pebbles: Pilgrimage within and beyond Rajasthan' (1994), makes a sharp distinction between *jātrā* and *yātrā*. While the Rajasthani jātrā implies a trip to 'the countless shrines dedicated to "goddesses-and-gods" (*devidevatā*) most often of local origin and fame', the more formal Sanskrit and Hindi usage of yātrā indicates a pilgrimage to one of the established *tīrthas* ('crossing place'), such as Prayag or Gaya or Hardwar (p. 82). Inevitably, the deities of jātrās are 'lesser gods and goddesses', who are invoked specifically to fulfil particular needs and vows, while the 'bigger' gods and goddesses offer possibilities of *darshan* (vision), thereby facilitating the ritual obligations of the yātrīs (pilgrims) in relation to *punya* (merit), *dharma* (moral duty), and occasionally, *moksha* (release) (*ibid.*).

   Significantly, when I brought up the jātrī/yātrī distinction, Komalda simply brushed it aside as some kind of academic overstatement, and continued to use yātrī for the rest of the discussion.

6. See 'A Joker in the Deck: The Many Faces of a Rajasthani *Bahurupiyā*', *The Idea of Rajasthan*, Vol. 1 (1994) by John Emigh and Ulrike Emigh, for a fuller exposition on the subject.
7. Even as I urged Komalda to give more details about the different aromas of incense, I realized that I was picking his brains for facts that he didn't know. I would suggest to the frustrated reader also searching for more definitive facts in his discourse that it might be more useful not to view Komalda as a repository of encyclopedic information. Rather, he is better read within the context of the limits of his knowledge—a local knowledge, which is by no means omniscient, but partial, tentative, and yet, insightful.
8. In 'The Shrine' (1982), Komalda provides more details on the Gaṭodji shrine, which is 'considered to be of great importance because it is from here that the stone tablets of Gogāji, represented in the form of a snake, are blessed, before being set up for worship.'
   Komalda also adds that 'Gaṭodji icons are not given to persons of low caste, who can be served at the Gogā shrines if they come as *yātrīs* (pilgrims), [but] they cannot, on their own, set up a shrine with their own *bhopā*' (p. 18).
9. Sudhir Kakar's *Shamans, Mystics and Doctors: A Psychological Inquiry into India and its Healing Traditions* (1982) remains a groundbreaking book in its combination of highly empathetic and vividly descriptive encounters with grassroot *vaids* (doctors), seers, tantriks, mediums, and shamans, within an analytical Indian framework that questions the limits of psychoanalysis itself.
10. A good example of this mode of research would be Ann Grodzin Gold's *Fruitful Journeys: The Ways of Rajasthani Pilgrims* (1989), which almost fetishizes the immediacy of 'being there' with detailed descriptions of rites, ceremonies, pilgrimages, trances, and funerals. Viewed in close-up as it were, these descriptions are scrupulously distanced through an almost copy-book demonstration of anthropological expertise and accountability.
11. It should be kept in mind that Komalda has not spent very much time with his family in Jodhpur. This became very clear to me on talking to his younger son, Kuldeep, who is now largely responsible for the administration of Rupayan Sansthan. As he and his older brother Prashant were growing up in Jodhpur, Komalda was based for the most part in Borunda, where Rupayan Sansthan was first instituted.
12. In Fruitful Journeys (1989), Ann Gold provides some useful discriminations: '[I]f a person dies before his marriage, and the spirit lingers, it will manifest as a *pattar*' (p. 64). The 'Rajasthani equivalent

of Hindi and Sanskrit *pitr* ['father', 'forefathers', 'ancestors'], the *pattar* are not merely "predecessors" of a particular family lineage, but more specifically, they are 'unmarried children—virgins and therefore categorically without progeny' (p. 65). Moreover, a *pattar* cannot be installed in an icon without its wishes being consulted (p. 69). These facts are also substantiated in Komalda's discourse though he does not invoke the Sanskrit affiliations of *pattar*, whom he refers to as *pitar*.

13. Ann Gold (1989) offers a different terminology here for the first wife's spirit—*agali* ('the one who came first', 'the preceding one'), p. 68. These are regional variations of the widespread local phenomena of deified spirits.
14. *Sati* will be examined in the next chapter. See note 1 of Chapter 6 for an explication of the different meanings of *sati*. Here Komalda is talking about the '*kuldevi*' or family goddess, who is worshipped within the confines of a particular household.
15. See Chapter 6 for fuller elaboration on the different marxist/feminist and communitarian readings of *sati*.
16. Drawing on local resources, Ann Gold (1989: pp. 64–5) suggests that the original meaning of *jhunjhar* as a heroic warrior who dies in battle (*junjh*; *yuddh*), and whose spirit has not found release, can no longer be taken literally in the contemporary world where there are 'no wars'. Gold also adds that the word *jhunjhar* is used for different caste groups not associated with martial communities like the Rajputs. Washermen can also be *jhunjhars*, and the term even applies to some women.
17. Komalda's description of the rituals and rites surrounding death is obviously contextualized within the framework of his own Oswāl Jain *Bania* community. For a more detailed description of 'dying, cremation and [the] immediate aftermath' in a more brahmanic context, read the different stages documented by Ann Gold (1989), pp.80–92.

6. Sati

1. There are at least three broad definitions of '*sati*' as a 'good wife, an immolated widow [who burns herself on her husband's funeral pyre], or the goddess principle of '*shakti*' [energy]', which the feminist analysts Sudesh Vaid and Kumkum Sangari work against in their rigorous analysis of 'Institutions, Beliefs, Ideologies: Widow Immolation in Contemporary Rajasthan' (1991), pp. WS2-WS18.

   The 'anglicization of the Sanskrit word *sati*' as '*suttee*' draws on the actual practice of widow-burning, whereby the 'virtuous woman' (*sati*) and 'faithful wife' (*pativratā*) can be linked, at a doctrinal level, to traditional texts like the *Dharmashastras*. As Sally J. Sutherland elaborates on this context in 'Suttee, Sati, and Sahagamana: An epic Misunderstanding?' (1994), there are traditional terms like '*sahagamana*' and '*anumarana*', both of which describe the action of a woman who 'chooses' to immolate herself following the death of her husband. While in *sahagamana*, the woman burns herself on the same pyre as her husband, *anumarana* refers to the burning of the woman on a separate pyre at a different time (p. 1596). Sutherland acknowledges that the incorporation of these highly idealized traditional terms into daily life practices remains 'largely unknown' (*ibid.*).

2. Till the early 1990s, there have been at least 40 instances of widow immolation in Uttar Pradesh, Madhya Pradesh, and Maharashtra, with at least 28 cases reported in Rajasthan itself (Vaid and Sangari, 1991, p. WS16.) The most highly politicized of recent sati incidents revolved around Roop Kanwar who was immolated in Deorala on 4 Sept. 1987.
3. For an extensive bibliography on *sati*, read the special issue on the subject brought out by *Seminar*, no. 342, New Delhi , February 1988.
4. Sudesh Vaid and Kumkum Sangari (1991, p, WS3) consciously differentiate the 'primary violence' of 'widow immolation' from those 'structures of belief and ideology which gain consent for widow immolation' through the 'religious aura' of the word 'sati'.
5. This polarization of traditional belief systems against modernity has been most strongly identified with the numerous writings of Ashis Nandy on the subject. While his early essay on 'Sati: A Nineteenth-Century Tale of Women, Violence and Protest' (1980) was tempered by his acknowledgement of the ambivalences underlying Rammohun Roy's anti-sati campaign, the same cannot be said for his later journalistic interventions on the subject following Roop Kanwar's immolation. Articles like 'The Sociology of Sati' (1987) and 'The Human Factor' (1988) have played up the dubious agenda of cultural authenticity in Nandy's now familiar diatribe against secularism and the modernity of the nation-state.
6. I am greatly indebted to Shubha Chaudhuri for clarifying many details of the Rāni Bhaṭiyāṇi story, which did not correspond to the somewhat confused version that I received from Komalda.
7. Vaid and Sangari (1991), p. WS-3.
8. At one point in their analysis, Vaid and Sangari (1991) describe a *jhānki* (sequential tableaux) celebrating the life and death of Narayani Devi, where in one particular scene, [t]he figure of a woman holding her husband's head in her lap, bobs up and down burning in red crepe paper flames—worked by a hidden mechanical device and a fan. As the figure

subsides into the flames, a goddess arises behind her with a *trishul* [trident] in one hand and a *chakra* (halo) around her head' (p. WS-11). It is at this point that the authors document a peasant woman exclaiming, '*[D]ekho, sat kaise hotā hai*' (See, this is how *sat* happens).'

Instead of dealing with this specific response, Vaid and Sangari promptly go on to assert the obfuscation of the material fact of widow immolation in symbols like the *trishul* and concepts like *shakti*. But this obfuscation, I would argue, is obvious—what is not so obvious is the faith of the peasant woman in *sat*, which is reinforced rather than displaced by the mechanics of technical gimmickry. To unravel the constituents of that faith, one needs to acknowledge the role of enigma in shaping unacknowledged subjectivities, which I have briefly addressed in my comment on a similar situation depicted in Anand Patwardhan's documentary *Father, Son and Holy War* (see chapter on Patwardhan in my book *In the Name of the Secular: Contemporary Cultural Activism in India*, 1998b, p. 157).

9. At this point in the discussion, Komalda made a tangential comment in relation to 'the Mother Theresa phenomenon.' 'For Mother Theresa to be declared a saint,' as Komalda emphasized, 'it is essential that her life and work should subscribe to the laws of beatification. This means that after her death she must be able to perform certain miracles, or else, she has to mediate people's problems, in order for the Pope to have sufficient evidence of her sainthood.'

   Despite their obvious differences in context, the beatification process of the saint and the deification process of the sati would seem to have some parallels. Where the comparison breaks down, of course, is in the authorizing agencies which are legitimized to declare the authenticity of beatification and deification, respectively.

10. At a physiological level, *sat* manifests itself through *tej* or 'inner heat'. In most reports of sati, as carefully delineated by Vaid and Sangari (1991), the body of the woman is said to emit such 'heat' that it is said to *burn* the hands of the people trying to touch her. The other common trope in descriptions of sati concerns the self-ignition of the pyre on which the sati sits with her husband's head in her lap. Needless to say, such affirmations coexist with eye-witness reports testifying that the pyre was actually lit with a match by a family member. The 'truth' of the miraculous dimensions of sati and its blatant subterfuge are embedded in each other's discourses.

11. From 'Trial by Fire: A Report on Roop Kanwar's death' (1987), prepared by the Women and Media Committee of the Bombay Union of Journalists, it appears that 'when preparations for Roop Kanwar's

immolation began, she ran and hid but was dragged back; she was surrounded by armed guards on the way to the funeral, and her struggle to escape when the pyre was lit was prevented by these guards as well as by the logs and coconuts piled on her' (Reported in Vaid and Sangari 1991, p. WS-6).

Even Ashis Nandy, in his arguably less affirmative reading of sati in his early essay (1980) is compelled to acknowledge that widows at the end of the eighteenth century 'were being drugged, tied to the bodies of their dead husbands, and forced down with bamboo sticks on the burning pyres' (p. 4).

12. On the mediatization of the Jai Santoshi Ma phenomenon, read Veena Das's (1985) essay on 'The Mythological Film and its Framework of Meaning: Analysis of *Jai Santoshi Ma*'.
13. Vaid and Sangari (1991, pp. WS9–WS10) for a thorough reading of the Rāni Sati phenomenon, which is controlled by a temple trust of the Shekhāwaṭi Agarwal community drawing on members largely based in Mumbai and Kolkata. Till 1991, this trust had supervised the building of 105 Rāni Sati temples by coordinating 'a formidable network of donors within the trading-manufacturing community' (p. WS-10).
14. The rātijāgā (literally, 'night-awake') ceremony will be discussed in the next chapter in the context of women's songs. What is interesting to point out here is that the sati songs are sung by women in the early part of the rātijāgā ceremony, while the more erotic songs (to be addressed in the next chapter) are heard in the latter half of the night.
15. Kavita, Shobha, Shobhita and Sharda, 'Rural Women Speak', *Seminar*, no. 342, Feburary 1988, pp. 40–4.
16. The most subversive and powerful reading of the *ḍāyan*, among other marginalized women in the rural and tribal cultures of India, has been provided by Mahasweta Devi in numerous stories. She is particularly adept at deconstructing the ironies of pretence, as, for instance, in *Rudāli*, where women pretend to mourn for the dead while earning their living as professional lamenters.

7. Women's Songs

1. I have not attempted to use western musical notation to document these songs. From an earlier attempt—see notation of Manipuri folk songs in my book *The Theatre of Kanhailal: Pebet and Memoirs of Africa* (1992)—I realize that this becomes a totally redundant, if not misleading

exercise, in the absence of a musicological analysis documenting the limitations of the process.

2. In his essay 'Musicians for the People: The Māngaṇiyārs of Western Rajasthan' (1994), pp. 218–9, Komalda states that while the Manganiyar women sang in groups in separate places from the Manganiyar men during wedding ceremonies held in their patrons' homes, the subject matter of their songs corresponded. Manganiyar women also participated in the rātijāgā sessions held in their patrons' homes.
3. Komalda develops this point in relation to tribal renderings of oral epics, particularly the Ramayana. He contrasts, for instance, the strength of the Bhil Sita with the Brahman paradigm of the *pativratā* (devoted wife): 'Among the Bhils, monogamy is not a virtue. Premarital sex is not prohibited and there is no social stigma attached to it' (Kothari 1989, p. 115). Likewise, in the Garāsiā version of the Ramayana, Rama begins to weep after Sita has been abducted, provoking his brother Lakshmana to say, 'Why are you weeping for that woman? I will get as many Sitas as you want!' (*ibid.*, p. 116).
4. I am grateful to Ira Sisodia for her transcription and reading of the *Badhāwo* song, and the comments relating to its actual performance during wedding ceremonies.
5. I am aware that these comments can be critiqued for being too 'literary', and that the song has not been situated within a performative context. Unfortunately, since such a context did not present itself, I had no other option but to draw on a reading of the Rajasthani transcription and English translation of the song, which have been rendered by Ira Sisodia, Shubha Chaudhuri, and Manohar Lalas.
6. Ira Sisodia contributed to these notes from her own experience of rātijāgā ceremonies. I particularly appreciated the candour of her comments relating to the soporific nature of these songs—what tends to sizzle with sexual innuendo in reading the songs is obviously not representative of how the songs are actually rendered and received. 'We're half-asleep by the time these songs are sung in some incoherent way. No one really bothers about them,' as she told me. And yet, as a translator, these songs were a revelation to her in their bold exposition of startlingly complex—and contemporary—social situations.
7. The song was originally published in *Gāi Gāi Re Samand Talāv* (Songs on the Embankment of the Lake), Jodhpur: Rajasthan Sangeet Natak Akademi, n.d. This is one among numerous publications brought out by Sri Vijay Dan Detha, Rajasthan's foremost fiction writer and collector of proverbs, among other verbal genres of Rajasthani folk culture.

8. Shrimati Mohini Devi's transcription of *Jetal De* has been included in her compilation of songs entitled *Gīt Ratnamālā*. Printed by Ram Dutta Ojha, the third edition of this booklet (from which we draw the text of the song) was published in 1982.
9. This somewhat confusing reference to the 'backrest' suggests that the maid is lying in bed supporting Jagpati with her arm around him.
10. 'Stories have their own stories to tell,' as the acknowledged master of meta-folklore A.K.Ramanujan was fond of telling his students and colleagues. Not only are there stories within stories, there are stories about stories. This meta-folkloric dimension can be applied to other genres—there are jokes about jokes, proverbs about proverbs (see Ramanujan 1999, p. 470). One could add rātijāgā songs about rātijāgā events.

8. Terātāli

1. A definitive reading of the Kāmaḍ community that takes into account not just its origins, but its mutations of identity, is provided by Dominique-Sila Khan in 'The Kāmaḍ of Rajasthan—Priests of a Forgotten Tradition' (hererafter TKR), *Journal of the Royal Asiatic Society*, Third Series, Volume 6, Part 1, April 1996, pp. 29–56.
2. See Khan, TKR (1996), pp. 54–6, for a broader context on the banning of Terātāli. It appears that when the Kāmaḍ were included among the 'scheduled castes' in post-Independence India along with their untouchable patrons like the Meghwāl, Baḷāi, and Bhāmbhi, they tried to dissociate themselves from their own originary affiliations with these low castes. Instead, they sought a more elevated heritage for themselves by linking themselves with the upper castes, and by abandoning their 'unclean' habits and adopting vegetarianism. The banning of Terātāli has to be seen within this context of the Kāmaḍ *bhekh panchayat* (assembly of ascetics) bowdlerizing its own low-caste cultural affiliations, while continuing to claim its ritual authority as priests of the Ramdev cult of worship.
3. Komalda's reading of these objects is functionalist rather than symbolic. Although I tried to open the discussion to other possibilites of reading these objects—for example, the phallic associations of the sword and the more subtle fertility-related ritual associations of the pot of water—he did not pursue the matter. A 'thick description' of Terātāli would need to relate its very contained sensuality and incremental rhythmic energy to the use of the body as an instrument.

4. This is not entirely true as Khan points out (see TKR, p. 54), because today the Kāmaḍ have to compete with other middle and upper caste devotees of Ramdev, who prefer to entrust the organization of all ceremonies to members of 'cleaner' groups, such as the Kumhār (potters), Nāi (barbers), and members of the Nāth or Dasnāmi sect. This growing upper-caste hegemony is particularly apparent when new temples are created in Ramdev's honour.
5. The primary source of information relating to Ramdev's obscure life is contained in numerous bhajans and ballads composed by his 'model devotee' Harji Bhaṭṭi, notably the composition entitled *Ramdevji ro bīyavlo* (Ramdev's wedding). However, as Dominique-Sila Khan (1996) points out, even though Harji Bhaṭṭi is often considered a contemporary of Ramdev in the hagiography surrounding the saint, he is more likely to have lived in the eighteenth century (TKR, p. 47).
6. Dominique-Sila Khan, *Conversions and Shifting Identities: Ramdev Pīr and the Ismailis in Rajasthan* (hereafter CSI), 1997, p. 68. As Komalda points out, this is an elusive category—at once linked to an autonomous ritual activity, but also hyphenated with *jāgraṇ* (*jamā-jāgraṇ*). Increasingly, through the process of re-Hinduization, the word *jamā* is being replaced by the more Hindu-sounding '*jāgraṇ*', not unlike *samadhi* which seems to be replacing the more traditional and accurate description of Ramdev's grave in Ramdeoṛa as a *dargah* (CSI, p. 165).
7. An alternative reading of the facts is presented by Khan (1997) in the more 'current, Hinduized version of the [Mallināth-Rupānde] legend'. In this version, Rupānde is 'a poor Rajput girl [who] marries the ruler of Mallani. He does not know that, in her native village, she has an untouchable *dharam-bhāi* (adoptive brother), Dhāru Megh, a Meghwāl. The latter had invited her a few times to participate in satsangs (devotional sessions) organized by his Rajput guru Ugam Si' (CSI, p. 86). Significantly, in Komalda's version it is Dhāru who is represented as the guru, and not Ugam Si, who is not even mentioned.
8. See Khan 1996, TKR, pp. 35–6, for a more extended discussion of the material covered in this paragraph.
9. Khan 1997, CSI, pp. 67.
10. Khan 1996, TKR, p. 30.
11. Krishna grants Ajmal two sons, the younger of which is Krishna's own incarnation. According to one version of the legendary story, the child is not born naturally, but appears miraculously sleeping alongside his brother in the same cradle. See Khan 1997, CSI, p. 65.
12. Khan 1996, TKR, p. 38.

13. Khan 1997, CSI, pp. 128–9. It is important to keep in mind that Ramdev and his spiritual predecessors had prohibited idol worship. Indeed, one of the central sites of worship in a Ramdev shrine is the *dhuni*, or sacred hearth, remants of which are still visible in small shrines like Pānch Pipli. Today, all prayers and rituals in the Pānch Pipli shrine are conducted in a newly erected temple in the precincts of the shrine, where there is an icon of Ramdev seated on his horse. The dhuni has been abandoned, but offerings continue to be made at an adjoining *mazār* (gravestone), which includes syncretic signs associated with the worship of Ramdev, including the *pagliyā* (stone footprints) and minuscule rag horses (votive offerings made out of cloth).
14. Drawing on ethnographic research on the tribes and castes of Punjab, Khan calls attention to the initiation rituals of the Lalbegi Bhangis of Punjab. Though it is not possible to clarify that this ritual was similar to the one indicated (but not disclosed) by the sweeper from Borunda, it is worth describing for the concreteness of its detail:

    > On a rectangular pit is put a *chārpāi*, and beneath it, the candidate is seated in the pit, while the Chuhras [a broad caste category including, it seems, Bhangis, scavengers and Chamars, leatherworkers] sit on the *chārpāi*. Each bathes in turn, clearing his nose and spitting, so that all the water etc., falls on to the man in the pit. He is then allowed to come out and is seated on the *chārpāi*. After this all the Chuhras wash his body and eat with him.
    >
    > (Quoted in Khan 1997, CSI, p. 155)

15. The facts in the next paragraph are drawn from Khan (1997), CSI, p. 132–3.
16. With characteristic rigor, Khan (1997) makes cogent inter-ritual observations revolving around *pāyal*: 'In common Hindu rituals *charanāmrit* refers to the water or sacred liquid with which a divine image or the feet of a guru have been washed. Here the water of the *kuṇḍa* [pot] is also called pāyal. The pāyal ceremony of the *dasā panth* incidentally recalls a Sikh custom which consists in drinking the water where the ordinary devotees have washed their feet before entering a *gurudwara*: like the various types of *amrit* used for their initiation, this water is referred to as *pāhul*' (CSI, p. 133).
17. Read Mayaram 1996 for an authoritative reading of how 'liminal' religious identities got congealed during the colonial rule of India within larger monolithic categories like 'Hindu' and 'Muslim', reinforced by

the census reports of the British. To reiterate Sudipta Kaviraj's famous description of this crisis, Indian communities lost their 'fuzziness' as they were 'enumerated'.

9. Puppetry

1. For a more scholarly sifting of facts and historical evidence, read Nazir Ali Jairazbhoy's unpublished monograph 'Kaṭhputli Puppetry of Rajasthan: Microcosm in a Little Tradition', n.d., available at the ARCE library, Gurgaon, New Delhi.
2. The historical evidence would seem to suggest that the Mughal emperor in question here is Shah Jahan rather than Aurangzeb.
3. This dialogue is included in Komalda's notes on 'Traditional Kaṭhputli Marionette Play from Rajasthan,' written specifically for the Festival of India, France, 1985, p.3.
4. Komalda's methodology in exploring the social identity of the performers is very different from the academic research process of scholars on 'material culture' like Henry Glassie (2001). From his lecture on 'Performance theory and the documentary act,' delivered at the folklore workshop in Jaisalmer, February 2001, it becomes clear that Glassie *individuates* the process of research by focussing, albeit hypothetically, on one particular puppeteer, Kherati Ram Bhaṭṭ, 'master puppeteer' of Jaisalmer, not another *kaṭhputliwalla*. 'Quality' is obviously an important criterion for Glassie's social research.

   From considerations of puppet as 'text', to explorations of 'space' in which the puppet is located, to an examination of the 'social arrangements that surround the text in the place', Glassie insists on a 'complete biography of Kherati Ram Bhaṭṭ'—not just 'a few facts, but an autobiography that will permit rich interpretation.' Unsparing in his documentary zeal, Glassie spells out his priorities: '*We have to know the interior of Kherati Ram's skull if we are going to understand that puppet.*' (My emphases, see *Folklife*, Vol. 1, Issue 5, April 2001, p. 46).

   Contrast this approach to Komalda's informal 'method' of research, which is perfectly content to observe and document 'a few facts', without getting into problematic issues relating to 'autobiography'. Indeed, one needs to question what 'autobiography' as a genre signifies in the first place within the world of folk artists.
5. Since the material being discussed here is sensitive for its derogatory associations relating to particular individuals in a community, I have

followed Komalda's instruction in not identifying either his informant or the village in question. The comments relating to the dual identity of the Ḍākot, however, are an invaluable input to the discussion.

10. Professional Caste Musicians

1. The key theorist of the 'narrative of community' within the framework of subaltern studies is Partha Chatterjee, who has numerous writings on the subject (1994, 1997, 1998, 2001).
2. This material is covered in Komalda's article 'Musicians for the People: The Manganiyars of Western Rajasthan' (1994), p. 206.
3. It would seem that the crisis in the patronage system of the Raj Damāmis, a sub-group of the Ḍholi musicians, was far more critical. In 'Musicians for the People', (*ibid.*), p. 210, Komalda specifies that this group of musicians attached to Rajput jāgirdārs and royal families lost their patrons when the jāgirdāri system was abolished in the post-Independence period. Many of these musicians had no other option but to seek employment in 'urban brass bands'.
4. The details in this paragraph have been elaborated in 'Musicians for the People' (1994), p. 207.
5. In 'Musicians for the People' (1994), pp. 207–8, Komalda highlight a particularly violent form of protest by the Chāraṇs (bards) asserting irreconcilable differences with their patrons. At such moments of crisis, 'a Chāraṇ would take a big knife and gradually cut off first his fingers, and then other parts of the body, until he eventually died' (p. 207). This protest through suicide called *tāga* had terrible implications for the patrons, who were assumed to be cursed by the Chāraṇ's self-immolation.
6. There are more song categories provided in 'Musicians for the People' (1994), pp. 218–9—*kāmaṇ* ('song to ward off the evil that could befall the couple'); *pherā* ('song sung during the seven rounds around the sacred [nuptial] fire'); *māyaro* ('song sung when the bride or groom's maternal uncle gives gifts to his sister'), *chānvari* ('songs about the temporary canopy [*chānvari*] under which the wedding ceremony takes place').
7. For more details on the *kacheri* and the *kānkari* musical game, read 'Musicians for the People' (1994), pp. 219–21.
8. 'The name Ḍholi ("player of ḍhol") is obviously derived from the double-headed membranophone, *ḍhol*, which is the characteristic instrument of the Ḍholis of Western Rajasthan' (Jairazbhoy, 'Music in Western Rajasthan: Stability and Change 1977: 63). Whether or not the [Muslim] Manganiyars may have been Ḍholis at one point in time,

on the basis of a certain resemblance in their clan names (*ibid.*: 65), is speculative. What is clear is the very low status of the Ḍholi community who, till quite recently, found it difficult to be buried or cremated within the precincts of their own villages. Komalda had a specific experience in this regard with a Ḍholi family living in Borunda, who had to seek the assistance of Rupayan Sansthan in getting their dead father cremated in the village. To this day Ḍholis can be shunned by the most downtrodden of leather-working communities like the Bhāmbhi.

9. For a detailed analysis of these organizations, read Komalda's co-authored text with Daniel Neuman and Shubha Chaudhuri, *Bards, Ballads and Boundaries: An Ethnographic Atlas of Music in West Rajasthan* (forthcoming). I should add that this authoritative work has been in the making for many years, and yet, Komalda never once brought it up during our discussion. It wasn't as if he was trying to hide anything from me, but as he put it candidly when I raised the issue, 'It's a completely different project from the one we are working on.' More scholarly, I would add, replete with statistics, ethnomusicological data, and social categories. This valuable contribution to the field can be meaningfully read, to my mind, in counterpoint with Komalda's oral history presented in this book.
10. Consult *Bards, Ballads and Boundaries: An Ethnographic Atlas of Music in West Rajasthan* for more background on the *osar* and *dhām*.
11. I am grateful in this regard to Shubha Chaudhuri for numerous clarifications of nomenclature. When our facts did not tally, even though Komalda was the common source of information in many cases, I realized it was best to edit the confusions in his text as far as possible, and to include what was accountable with many of Shubha's suggestions.
12. John Merriam arrived at this position in 1975, after upholding more conventional anthropological views that ethnomusicology is 'the study of music in culture' (1960), which he later modified to 'the study of music as culture' (1973). For a succinct contextualization of these mutations within the larger struggle to define the field of ethnomusicology, read the first chapter of Helen Myers's edition of *Ethnomusicology: An Introduction* (1992), p. 8.
13. Komalda complicates this view in one of his very few ideological interventions—an unusually critical reading of a 1990 reprint of *The Castes of Marwar* (1894), a Census Report authored by Munshi Hardayal Singh, the Superintendent of the Census Operations in Jodhpur State. Komalda makes a number of valid points here which are worth itemizing:

a. The disjunction between the author's description of his study of people's 'ways, manners, and customs' as an 'amusing task' in opposition to the colonial administration's use of his material for political purposes. (p. ii)
b. The strenuous attempt to identify 'authentic' Rajputs for recruitment in the army. (p. iii)
c. The inclusion of Muslim communities like Musalman Rajput, Desi Musalman, Kaim Khanis, and Sindhis within the category of 'Rajput', which would indicate the prevalent *caste* identifications of Muslims in the late nineteenth century. (p. v)
d. The insufficient acknowledgement of those low-caste communities providing Brahmanical services to other low castes, notably for the maintenance of genealogies. (p. vii)
e. The homogenization of categories relating to occupations like pottery—the category of Kumhār, for instance, does not take into account the Jatiya Kumhār who are weavers; the Khetaṛ Kumhār who are agriculturists; and the Mātaṛ Kumhār who specialize in making pots with clay. (p. ix)

These are extremely detailed points, but tellingly, Komalda's critique of the Census Report does not lead to a critique of caste as such. After raising rhetorical questions, 'Has modern scientific and technological development loosened the strong roots of [the] caste structure? Has [the] new education policy been able to make inroads into the citadel of caste organization?', Komalda settles for equanimity in a highly generalized conclusion: 'We are neither colonialists nor missionaries. Only a thorough cognizance of all the different aspects of the caste system can help us to find a way to transform its more unpalatable features without losing some of its benefits' (pp. xii-xiii).

It is worth indicating that these comments were made in 1990, amidst turbulent controversies and violence surrounding reservations and quotas for 'backward' and low-caste communities recommended by the Mandal Commission, on which Komalda doesn't mention a word.

11. From the Local to the Global: Rajasthani Folk Music in Performance

1. Even if we are dealing with the early 1950s, this amount of money does seem extremely meagre. I questioned Komalda about this, hinting that perhaps he needed to qualify the amount involved, but he was rather

sanguine about the fact. That's what was paid to the folk performers: four annas per song.

2. When I questioned Komalda about this seemingly significant detail in his biography, he brushed it aside as not being very important. But from what I could make of his off-hand comments on the subject, it seems that he was expelled by the Communist Party of India (CPI) on at least three grounds. One, the Party authorities based in Calcutta wanted him to get involved in the trade union movement, while he enjoyed sneaking off to Santiniketan on the weekends to converse with progressive art luminaries such as Nandalal Bose and Ramkinkar Baij. Two, he was not fluent in Bengali which would have been needed for his interaction with labourers—indeed, at that time Komalda was teaching Hindi literature in a local college in Calcutta. Three, as Komalda mentioned, not without a wry sense of humour, 'The Bengalis have a love-hate relationship with Marwaris.' Identified as a 'Marwari', whose father had held an important government position during the Raj, Komalda was not above board so far as his political credentials were concerned. Having stated these points, I should also add that Komalda did not reveal any particular bitterness about this unfortunate encounter with the Party. Indeed, he has been deeply respected and loved by many friends on the Left.
3. See section on 'Inventing the Folk' in 'Notes on the invention of tradition', *Theatre and the World*, 1993, pp. 197–200, and section on 'Appropriating the Folk' in the section on 'The Indian People's Theatre Association (IPTA)' in *In the Name of the Secular*, 1998b, pp. 42–51.
4. Rustom Bharucha, 'Notes on the invention of Traditon,' *Theatre and the World*, 1993, p. 200.
5. 'Interconnectedness' is a leitmotif that runs through the learned writings of Kapila Vatsyayan on classical Indian dance and its connections with literature, the visual arts, and philosophy. In a recent interview (*Folklife* 2001, pp.56–7), she defended her position with characteristic robustness by asserting 'the integral relationship of man and nature and environment', along with the principle of 'mutation' which generates a 'consciousness' that 'the gross can become subtle, the unrefined can become refined.' Affirming the reciprocity of '*mārg*' (the classical) and '*desi*' (the folk), Vatsyayan strongly contested the assumption that the singing traditions of the Langas and Manganiyars are not 'related' to the so-called classical canon, even though she acknowledged that 'distinctions' need to be made in their uses of *rāga* and *tāla*. (p. 57).

   I should add that while Komalda 'inter-connects' any number of knowledge-systems relating to water, land, livestock, agriculture, oral epics, myth, and so on, his grounding of 'interconnectedness' in material culture is different from Vatsyayan's more textual and ideational mapping of India's diverse cultural traditions. It goes without saying that while Vatasyayan's encyclopedic, arguably 'Himalayan', perspective, encompasses the relatively unproblematized category of 'India', Komalda's periphery of knowledge remains strongly located within 'Rajasthan', a category that he himself acknowledges is limited in dealing with knowledge at local levels.

6. *Theatre and the World* (1993), *The Politics of Cultural Practice* (2000a), *Consumed in Singapore: The Intercultural Spectacle of 'Lear'* (2000b) are some of my publications in the field of interculturalism. They cover a wide ground, ranging from my early critique of the Eurocentrist dimensions of intercultural exchange in the late 1970s to the more recent experiments in inter-Asian cultural spectacle.
7. Some perspective on Bartabas's equestrian theatre is necessary here for those readers unfamiliar with its performative context. I will focus my remarks on a production that I have seen— *Tryptik*, which was massively popular at the Avignon Festival in 2001. In this circus-like spectacle, the primary 'non-Western' input in the first part of the production was *kalarippayattu*, the martial arts tradition from Kerala. At one level, one could take issue with Bartabas's inadequate understanding of the inner kinetic rhythms of *kalarippayattu* in relation to Stravinsky's *Rite of Spring*—indeed, one could legitimately question whether Stravinsky was not a total imposition on this martial tradition. However, the real problem for me had to do with the semantics of the 'Indian' bodies on display. On the one hand, they were exalted in their 'instinctive' and 'organic' physical connection with horses, but on the other hand, they were primitivized. In one sequence, for instance, the loin-clad, mud-smeared martial artists were dragged on the floor while holding on to the tails of the horses.

   While I have only seen *Chimère* on video, which makes it difficult for me to make any sustained comparison with *Triptyk*, it did strike me as being a more muted and subtle work. Here the 'non-Western' input was both visible and audible through the presence of the Rajasthani musicians, who did not intervene in the *mise en scène* for the most part beyond providing the music, the traditional repertoire of Langa and Manganiyar songs. In this sense, it could be argued that the musicians were minimally 'exoticized', but 'exotic' they undeniably were as they sat with great dignity in a three-tiered tableau with a white-bearded seer-like musician positioned right at the top of the pyramid.

8. The issue of confidentiality is crucial here, but I do not see how one can avoid dealing with critical issues like family feuds. All too often, I would argue, 'the folk' are infantilized, reduced to repositories of wholesomeness and innocence. It is almost as if they are immune to the problems of our times, or else, they tend to be seen as victims of these essentially 'modern' problems. This is clearly not the case, as the family feud presented in this section demonstrates, revealing the non-negotiable patriarchy of traditional communities.
9. The so-called 'criminal tribes', who were branded under the colonial Criminal Tribes Act of 1871, were 'de-notified' in 1952 on the somewhat illusory grounds that all citizens of India had fundamental rights under the Constitution. Today, they are called 'de-notified tribes'. However, as Milind Bokil points out in his informative article 'De-notified and Nomadic Tribes: A Perspective' (2002), these tribes are also called 'nomadic tribes' because many of them do not have a fixed residence, and are consequently denied land rights and house titles.

   While Bokil's research draws primarily on de-notified tribes in Maharashtra, it is interesting to note the large number of subaltern entertainers who continue to be linked with these tribal groups. Dancers, acrobats, tumblers, jugglers, wrestlers, snake-charmers, monkey trainers, bear exhibitors are among some of the performers associated with 'de-notified tribes.' (p. 151) Contrary to Bokil's belief that the advent of television has killed the interest in these traditional forms of entertainment, the meteoric rise of the Kanjar dancers in the performance circuit provides at least one strong counter to such bleak predictions.
10. On seeing videos of the Kanjar women performing the *chakri*, I was initially reminded of the stunning dancer Gulabo, who is very popular on the festival circuit. Komalda, however, was emphatic that the dance of the Kanjar women had nothing to do with the kind of dance that Gulabo has 'created'. As he explained it to me: 'Gulabo dances, you might say, in the "Jogi style". Keep in mind, however, that this style has been inspired by the popular Hindi film *Nāgin*, rather than by any tradition. Even the black ghāgrā worn by Gulabo is inspired by Rekha's outfit in the film. The Kanjar dances are far more powerful—these dancers can dance for six to eight hours non-stop. They have a very different energy and stamina.'

    I should add that this position on Gulabo's 'invention of tradition' via the Rekha-inspired exotica of *Nāgin*, was strongly denied by one of my Kālbeliā informants, who claimed that this dance was very much part of his '*paramparā*' [his word]. The question does arise, however, why this dance was not seen in public for so long, unlike the dances of the Kanjar women, which have always had local audiences. Today 'the Jogi dance', or the dance of the Kālbeliā women, is a fixture in any tourist programme of Rajasthan.

11. Even though the Criminal Tribes Act of 1871 was revoked in 1952, when 'criminal tribes' got 'de-notified', it was replaced by the Habitual Offenders Act, which is supposed to target individuals and not communities. But, as Milind Bokil (2002) points out, old habits die hard, and the police continue to brand and stigmatize entire communities of de-notified tribes, thereby perpetuating the older colonial prejudice against criminal tribes. (p. 150). Women from de-notified tribes are particularly vulnerable to the 'exploitation' of the police, not least because their own men are often 'either absconding or are locked in police custody' (p. 152).

12. Marketing the 'Folk'

1. Arjun Appadurai, 'Afterword', *Gender, Genre and Power in South Asian Expressive Traditions* (1994), p. 473.
2. Stuart H. Blackburn and A.K.Ramanujan, 'Introduction', *Another Harmony: New Essays on the Folklore of India* (1986), p. 24. In a terminology and perspective that seem far removed from the valorization of electronic modes of folklore today, Blackburn and Ramanujan would regard even older technologies like the radio and cinema as 'removed' from folklore. As they spell out their position, 'The technology of their production and distribution widens the gap between carrier and audience, so that they cannot be *spoken aloud* by one person to others' (my emphasis, p. 25). 'Immediacy', it would seem, is the distinguishing characteristic of folklore, whose oral and written narratives remain '*human* products' which circulate within '*personal* networks' (my emphases, p. 26). Within such early modernist priorities, premised on the fundamental opposition between the 'oral-written' and the 'printed' word, it is obvious that there is no place within Blackburn and Ramanujan's discourse for a personalization of virtual communication or the production of new electronic 'communities'.
3. Blackburn and Ramanujan (1986), p. 24.
4. This project was supposed to be tied up with a short film on the folk music of Rajasthan to be directed by none other than Satyajit Ray. Unfortunately, on account of bureaucratic complications relating to shooting the film on the border of India—a problem that Ray refused

to intervene in by getting in touch with the appropriate government departments—the film project fell through. The recording session with the musicians, however, continued, as originally planned.

5. In the total chaos of his disorganized papers and notes—a nightmare for any researcher—it was providential that Komalda managed to unearth Hugo Zemp's brilliant and authoritative article 'The/An Ethnomusicologist and the Record Business,' *Yearbook for Traditional Music*, Vol. 28, 1996. This is the source for all technical information relating to the controversy that follows. If I had relied on Komalda's memory here, I would have been in serious trouble.

   From Zemp's documentation, we learn that *Musical Instruments of the World* and *Flutes of Rajasthan* were first issued by the French National Centre for Scientific Research (CNRS) and the Musée de l'Homme in 1978 and 1977 respectively; they were later reissued as CDs in 1990 and 1989.
6. Zemp (1996), p. 55.
7. From Hugo Zemp's account, which reads like a detective story, we learn that in January 1996 he received a telephone call from the lawyer of a 'highly respected' American insurance company [The Prudential], requesting rights to use one minute of music from the Rajasthani recording of *Naṛ* for a television commercial. This request was promptly turned down on the grounds that the Museum did not sell its intellectual and cultural research for commercial purposes. Two weeks later, a videocassette arrived with the commercial itself, which showed 'a [white] man in the snow with the music of the *Naṛ* flute from the Rajasthan desert in the background.' A sum of US $15,000 was offered as a licensing fee. The lawyer also mentioned in a fax that he had contacted Geneviève Dournon, who was in favour of entering into an agreement with the insurance company.

   After a brainstorming, Zemp and his colleagues decided that they should not pursue the matter because it could only set up an unfortunate precedent for the commercial exploitation of their essentially scholarly and archival work. The very next day, before this message could be communicated to the insurance company, Zemp received yet another offer from the insurance company for US $30,000. But in true capitalist fashion, a decision had to be made on the matter within 24 hours!

   'Are the ethics different for $30,000 than for $15,000?', as Zemp puts it pithily. Finally, he decided that there were 'two good reasons' to accept the money—half could be used to support Rupayan Sansthan, and the other half could help to finance a CD project of Zemp's own institute, for which funding had fallen through. However, he was also clear in his mind that neither the collector nor the present employees of the institute were entitled to any money from the licensing fee. (See Zemp 1996, pp. 49–50) This ethical provision, however, was not agreeable to Geneviève Dournon—see endnote 8 for the subsequent complication in this intellectual property drama.

8. Dournon believed that the $30,000 should be split in three parts—'$10,000 for the record company, $10,000 for Rajasthan, and $10,000 for her' (Zemp 1996: 51). The only problem was that when she had recorded this music, she had implicitly accepted the protocol of the institution to which she was affiliated that 'after the first payment, the collector renounces successive royalties on behalf of the Société Française d'Ethnomusicologie for helping young researchers in fieldwork' (p. 50). No longer a young researcher herself, Dournon believed that she deserved her share of the fee because without her 'unpaid' assistance, Rajasthani folk music could not have been internationalized. Besides, her 'harmonious' collaboration with Komal Kothari and continued good relations with the musicians were exemplary, and therefore, there was no reason to assume that they would object to her getting a fair share of the money. This assumption, as Komalda elaborates in his text, posed a problem, because the money given to Rupayan Sansthan carried its own weight of responsibilities.
9. Consult Anthony Seeger's essay on 'Ethnomusicologists, Archives, Professional Organizations, and the Shifting Ethics of Intellectual Property' (1996) for the different technicalities relating to these interrelated subjects. For specific reference to folkloristics, read Lauri Honko's 'Copyright and folklore,' *FF Network*, no. 21, March 2001.
10. For a broader perspective on the very contentious intellectual property rights disputes in Australia, revolving around the cultural rights of indigenous peoples, read the excellent legal perspective provided by Terri Janke in her report *Our Culture: Our Future*. This text is available online at www.icip.lawnet.com.au
11. These terms are provided by Peter Manuel in his comprehensive study of *Cassette Culture: Popular Music and Technology in North India*, 1993, p. 3.
12. Sadly, even as this book goes to press, I learn that Methi was killed in a roadside fight in her village in which she had attempted to save her son from being attacked by her female co-singer, her husband, and their son. Earlier in 2002, Methi was widowed and had allegedly developed a relationship with her co-singer's husband. Alcoholism and growing monetary problems contributed to the build-up of tensions

leading to the fight, in which Methi was allegedly stabbed to death. One of the most prolific composers of Rajasthani folk music in the local cassette industry, Methi was beginning to receive the recognition that she so richly deserved. Her untimely and tragic death affirms the harsh realities of survival among subaltern performers in India that demands sustained attention among cultural and social activists.

13. According to Manuel (1993), cassettes began to have 'some impact' by 1980 through the initiative of local entrepeneurs like Jodhpur's Chhanvarlal Gahlot and Nandu Records, which 'began recording local performers and selling individual tapes (for around fifty rupees) to shopkeepers who could duplicate copies for customers. By 1985 an active regional cassette industry had emerged [in Rajasthan], consisting primarily of small provincial producers' (Manuel 1993, p. 183).
14. This contradicts Manuel's (1993) somewhat too categorical statement that, 'Komal Kothari has been one of several folklorists concerned that the spread of the mass media may homogenize and thereby impoverish the present rich diversity of regional folklore traditions' (p. 185). As it becomes clear from his comments, Komalda has a more complex perspective on the phenomenon.
15. This form of piracy is 'bootlegging', which, as Manuel (1993) elaborates with considerable detail, is 'most desirable in the case of oral-tradition, improvised genres where each performance is a unique event' (p. 79). From his own experience as a student of Hindustani music, Manuel claims that this form of piracy was most prevalent in the 1970s during classical music concerts where live programmes were recorded surreptitiously on cassette recorders. By the late 1970s some bootleg tapes of *ghazals* were marketed in India and Pakistan, while the business around the folk-music genre of *birahā* was particularly strong in Benares and the surrounding Bhojpuri area. (Manuel 1993, pp. 79–80).

    Other forms of piracy studied by Manuel (and indicated sketchily by Komalda) are 'dubbing' whereby different songs from various soundtracks are duplicated onto a single cassette for a fee; and the more widespread 'mass duplication' and sale of copies of extant commercial recordings, at times with the complicity of the recording company itself. (See Manuel 1993, pp. 81–2 for an extended discussion).
16. Manuel (1993) takes the process of 'democratization' even further by considering the impact of recorded religious rituals and recitations on cassette. For instance, weddings and death ceremonies can be performed today in low-caste Hindu households without the presence of an officiating Brahman priest.

17. Based on a 'personal communication' from Komalda, Peter Manuel acknowledges the seemingly paradoxical fact that 'whether despite or because of the vogue of Rajasthani kathā tapes, live renditions of kathās by professional singers at Rajasthan temple jāgraṇs seem to be held more often now than at any time in living memory' (1993: 128–9). On the basis of such evidence, Manuel concludes that the cassette phenomenon and the performance of live jāgraṇs and kathās would seem to be 'mutually reinforcing, rather than competitive' (p. 129).
18. This would seem to be the case with *bhangra pop* and other derivatives of folk music in diasporic cultures, where the 'origins' of these musical sources are of far less concern than their treatment within contemporary musical cultures.
19. In one of his many attempts to balance the dominant critique of the mass media, Manuel succumbs to a peculiar construction at one point in his discussion of folk music: 'If the peasant from an isolated hamlet becomes disenchanted with the crude and unpretentious folk music of his area, he may also apply the higher technical standards of the professional music he hears on the radio to *improving* his own traditions' (My emphasis, 1993: 8). Apart from the dubious criteria underlying 'improvement', the more concrete question to be asked is *how* a peasant can 'improve' his folk music tradition without access to an altered technology.
20. The discriminations between traditional 'obscenity' and contemporary 'vulgarity' are hard to define, and yet, as the Punjabi star vocalist Gurdas Mann told Peter Manuel in an interview, distinctions need to be made between '*masala*' and 'decadent *masala*, *masala* mixed with manure' (Manuel 1993: 174).

Afterword

1. Gayatri Chakravorty Spivak, 'Cultural Talks in the Hot Peace: Revisiting the "Global Village"' (1998), p. 341.
2. Ibid.
3. While the most forceful theorization around the 'narrative of community' has been provided by Partha Chatterjee (1994, 1997, 1998, 2001), there is a decisively new emphasis in his theory on 'political society', which is no longer annexed to non-modern, non-urban, quasi-religious traditional communties. Rather, 'the community' that concerns Chatterjee today is an amorphous categorization of non-party political formations, including the unemployed, destitute, and marginalized sections of the population. Denied basic civic rights, this 'community'

explores unprecedented means to deepen its struggle for democracy outside the norms of the state.

While Chatterjee's re-reading of community deepens even as it remains resolutely anti-modernist, Ashis Nandy's anti-secularist upholding of the 'religious tolerance' and 'plurality' of traditional communties continues to be uninflected and politically regressive. In contrast, Veena Das's (1996) refusal to sanitize communities within the nostalgia of an 'innate moral order' enables her to highlight the violence of communities—a violence that resists the negotiation of individual rights, particularly by women seeking to critique or reject communitarian norms.

APPENDICES

These appendices on folk music instruments, the rāga concept, and the rhythmic traditions of the Manganiyars have been excerpted from Komalda's essay 'Musicians for the People: The Māṅganiyārs of West Rajasthan', The Idea of Rajasthan, Vol. 1, *eds. Karine Schomer, Joan L. Erdman, Deryck O. Lodrick, Lloyd I. Rudolph. New Delhi: Manohar Publishers and American Institute of Indian Studies, 1994, pp. 205–37.*

Appendix A

Instruments of the Manganiyars

All Manganiyar musicians must have two essential sets of instruments. The first consists of ḍhol and thāḷi. The ḍhol is a large, two-headed cylindrical drum. The thāḷi, which always accompanies the ḍhol, is a small circular instrument made of bell metal. Ḍhol and thāḷi are considered auspicious, and are required for all ceremonial occasions. Thus Manganiyars will lead a family procession playing ḍhol and thāḷi, and all ceremonies must begin with the beat of these two instruments. The second set of auspicious instruments consists of the surṇāi (a form of oboe), accompanied rhythmically by ḍhol, ḍholak or nagāṛā. The ḍholak is a barrel-shaped wooden drum, both heads of which are covered with parchment; it is smaller than the ḍhol, and both sides are played with the hands. The nagāṛā consists of two kettle-drums, one large and one small, and is played with two long, thin sticks.

The ḍhol is a simple rhythm instrument and does not require much practice. The player suspends the ḍhol from his neck and usually plays in a standing position. The right side, considered female (*mādā*), is played with the finger and palms of the hand, and produces a high pitch. The left side, considered male (*nar*), provides the bass tone and is played with a small stick that is thick and curved. Usually, an assistant joins in on the male side of the drum with two thin bamboo sticks. Some Manganiyar ḍhol players use sticks for both sides, one small and thick, the other with a sharp point. They play at a very fast tempo, and when the parchment vibrates loudly, a sudden stroke with the pointed stick causes a sharp, cracking sound. This is a feat that only a few drummers can execute.

Several different rhythmic patterns are played on the ḍhol. *Gāgar* and *maṭki* (or *maṭku*) are played for particular women's dances, *chakkar* for men's sword dances. The rhythm for wedding processions is known as *banḍoli*. *Tājiyā* or *tābut* is played during the processions of the Muslim Muhurram festival, and *kaṭak* when getting ready for combat. Two very powerful rhythms are *sati* and *vāru*. Sati is played when a widow performs the rite of sati, and *vāru* to announce a calamity and call people to gather together. In rural areas, *vāru* has tremendous sanctity and is played only at times of crisis. No one is allowed to play it just for pleasure, and if someone does, there is heavy punishment. These different rhythmic patterns are all understood by village people, and they respond to them readily.

While Manganiyars play ḍhol, thāli and surṇāi for ceremonial occasions, their true musical virtuosity lies in the kamāychā and the *pyāledār sārangi*. The kamāychā is a bowed string instrument played to accompany vocal singing. Two types of kamāychā players are found among the Manganiyars. One only accompanies himself as he sings, while the other accompanies another singer or plays the instrument solo. The difference between the two is noticeable. The singer-instrumentalist does not play the vocal melodies, but plays instead a repetitive *chala* (pattern of notes), with rhythmic bowing stresses on certain beats. When the second type of kamāychā player accompanies a vocalist, he follows every nuance of the melody. When he plays solo, he uses techniques that are purely instrumental, improvising on the melody in many different ways. The pyāledār sārangi is a variant of the sindhi sārangi played by the Langas. The two instruments differ in the arrangement and tuning of their strings, as well as in the method of fingering.

Other string instruments played by the Manganiyars are the *srīmanḍal* (a trapezoid box polychord), the *jagtārā* (a drone instrument with a single or double open string), and the *chautāro* (a drone instrument with five strings). Nowadays, there are only two old men left who play the srīmanḍal. The reason for this is that for an entire generation, the children of men who learned the srīmanḍal died, a coincidence that frightened people away from this instrument.

The jagtārā provides not only the drone but also the basic rhythmic pattern, as its playing technique involves a strong right-to-left stroke. It is usually played by those Manganiyar musicians who are adept at religious, devotional and Sufi songs. The chautāro is also known as *bīno* or *tanduro*.

Chautāro actually means 'four strings', but the instrument has five strings. The name probably comes from the tuning pattern, in which two strings are tuned in unison and are therefore counted as one. This instrument is connected with religious and devotional songs, and with certain epics and ballads. The compositions sung with it have to do with Ramdev, the popular regional deity worshipped by low-caste groups from Rajasthan, Madhya Pradesh, Gujarat, Haryana and Punjab. The chautāro is always played to accompany group singing, and supplemented rhythmically with ḍholak, manjirā and khaṛtāl.

Among the wind instruments played by the Manganiyars is the surṇāi, a double-reed instrument. It is considered auspicious, and is always accompanied by ḍholak. Another wind instrument is the *murali*, a double-reed gourd-pipe. Though elsewhere murali is the name used for the transverse flute, in the desert region it has come to refer specifically to the gourd-pipe. It has been adopted by the Manganiyars and Langas from the Jogis, a nomad group. The Jogis call the instrument *pungi* or *bīn*. There are three types of murali, each with a different pitch. The lowest-pitched murali is called *āgor*; its tonic is suitable for the singing voices of older women. The medium-pitched murali, pitched at a level suitable for the voices of young girls, is known as *mānsuri*. The third type, known as *ṭānki*, is pitched very high and cannot be used to accompany any vocal music. The Manganiyars and Langas mostly use the ṭānki, though the āgor may be used to accompany *āḍā gīt*.

The final wind instrument used by the Manganiyars is the *ghaṛā*, a clay pot whose belly is supported by both hands and kept high over the head so that the musician can blow into it forcefully. It produces a deep sound and rhythmic beat. It is used for devotional music, and is usually accompanied by the chautāro. The ghaṛā is played by ordinary people as well as by Manganiyar professionals, but in [a] seated position rather than standing.

Appendix B
Rāgas in Manganiyar Music

In classical music, rendering a composition in a certain rāga involves two distinct melodic sections. *Sthāi* (the refrain section) moves in the lower middle octaves, *antarā* (the verse or stanza section) in the middle and upper octave. Very few songs in the Manganiyar tradition follow this pattern. Most of their compositions are limited to a range of one and a half octaves at the most, and there is no sectioning into sthāi and antarā. *Bandish* (melodic form) as known in the classical tradition is absent from their music. Many songs consist of a single melodic line repeated over and over to accommodate a developing poetic theme. But within this limited compositional framework, there are many places where improvisation or additional melodic material can be added by a good musician . . .

The Manganiyar's repertoire of rāgas differs from that of North Indian classical music. Some rāga names—Kalyan, Jog, Paraf, Sindhi Bhairavi, Bilawal, Todi, Salang (Sarang)— resemble those of certain classical rāgas. However, with the exception of Sindhi Bhairavi, these rāgas do not have the same characteristics as the classical rāgas.

Some rāgas of regional origin (Sorath, Des, Māru, Pahāḍi) are shared by both traditions. They are, however, rāgas which play a minor role in classical music, where they are used only for the *chhotā khayāl* genre or the semi-classical genres of *thumri*, *ghazal*, *dādra* and bhajan. There are a few true classical rāgas in the Manganiyar repertoire, such as Asa and Dhani, but they are rarely performed. Finally, there are rāga names (Suhab, Sāmeri, Birvās, Mānjh, Khamāychi) which are not found in the classical tradition at all. Some of these rāgas exist in the classical tradition, but are known there by other names. Khamāychi, for instance, also known as Khamaji, is the Khamāj of classical music. It is sung by the Manganiyars when they lead a wedding procession or welcome guests. Several rāgas of the Manganiyars (Rāṇo, Sasvi, Sindhi Bhairavi, Mānjh, Kohiyari) are of Sindhi origin.

Entirely absent from the Manganiyar repertoire is rāga Mand, a popular rāga of folk origin that has become incorporated into the classical North Indian repertoire. This is especially surprising in view of the fact that the Jaisalmer region may have been this rāga's place of origin. Mand is known in Rajasthan, but is associated with the Hindu Ḍholi singers rather than with the Manganiyars.

In classical Indian music, rāgas are defined by at least ten elements, the most important of which are the sequence of ascending and descending notes (*aroha-avaroha*), notes defined as consonant or dissonant (*samvādi-vivādi*), characteristic repetitions of certain notes (*pakaṛ*), and characteristic end phrases (*nyās*). In rendering their rāgas, the Manganiyars observe these rules, but they do not have a theoretical understanding of notes and intervals. Though they use the seven-note scale of classical music, at the conceptual level they recognize only two notes: *dādar* (the tonic, corresponding to classical *sa*), and *āgor* (the fourth, or sometimes the fifth, corresponding to classical *ma* or *pa*). All other notes are explained by numbers. The situation is similar to that of beginning students of classical music, who may have mastered some compositions, but do not understand the theory of music.

Appendix C

Rhythmic Patterns in Manganiyar Music

There are two main rhythmic patterns in Manganiyar music: *kalvāṛā* (a rhythm of 8 beats or *mātrās*) and *tintār* (a rhythm of 7 beats or mātrās). In classical music, the corresponding patterns would be *kaharvā* (8 beats) and *chāchar*, *rupak* or *addhā dīpchandi* (all 7 beats). Some Manganiyars use *jhaptāl* (a 10-beat pattern) or *dīpchandi* (a 14-beat pattern), though only with certain compositions. *Dādrā*, the 6-beat rhythmic pattern of classical music, is well known to the Manganiyar musicians, but they have very few compositions in it.

Manganiyars use rhythmic patterns as the basis for extremely elaborate improvisation. Excellent percussion accompaniment (on the ḍholak) is always very important for a successful performance. A good percussionist is expected to follow all the rhythmic nuances of the lead vocalist or instrumentalist, while at the same time maintaining the fixed rhythmic pattern.

Though many of the terms [cited above] are the same as those in the classical tradition, there is a major difference. The rhythmic patterns of classical music, called *tāl*, are consistently cyclical, with the point at which the melodic composition and rhythmic accompaniment come together (*sam*) occurring with absolute, repetitive regularity. In addition, different sections of the *tāl* are defined as *khāli* (empty) or *bhari* (full), depending on whether the leading beats are light or heavy; these marked beats serve to further establish the rhythmic cycle. Thus *tīntal*, the most common classical tāl, consists of 16 beats divided into sections of 4 each. The first, second and fourth sections are designated as bhari, the third as khāli; when the khāli sound is heard, sam is always 9 beats away.

In the rhythmic patterns of the Manganiyars, there is also a point at which instrumentalist/vocalist and percussionist meet on a common stress. This point is referred to as *muddā* or *gur*. However, the point of convergence is not based on the principle of a regularly returning sam. If classical tāls are cyclical, the movement of Manganiyar rhythmic patterns can best be described as spiral.

The rhythmic patterns of Manganiyar music are not defined by the percussion accompaniment alone, but by an interplay between these rhythms and those created by the verbal text. It is the words and phrases of the refrain or first line (referred to as *mukhaṛā*) that dictate the rhythmic accompaniment by creating a certain pattern of stresses. Though not all songs sung by the Manganiyars have this *mukhaṛā* feature, all their *moṭa gīt* [big song] compositions do. The mukhaṛā and the spiral pattern of rhythmic stresses created by it are a distinguishing feature of Manganiyar music. By contrast, the community folk songs of the general population (especially women's folk songs) have a single, steady beat and a rhythmic movement that is straightforward and linear.

BIBLIOGRAPHY

Amin, Shahid. *Event, Metaphor, Memory: Chauri Chaura 1922–1992*. New Delhi: Oxford University Press, 1995.

Appadurai, Arjun, Frank J. Korom, Margaret A. Mills. 'Introduction,' *Gender, Genre and Power in South Asian Expressive Traditions*. Delhi: Motilal Banarsidas Publishers, 1994.

Appadurai, Arjun. 'Afterword,' *Gender, Genre and Power in South Asian Expressive Traditions*, *op. cit*., 1994.

Asad, Talal. 'The Concept of Cultural Translation in British Social Anthropology', *Writing Culture: The Poetics and Politics of Ethnography*, (eds.) James Clifford and George Marcus. Berkeley: University of California Press, 1986.

Bhargava, Rajeev. 'What is Secularism For?,' *Secularism and its Critics*, New Delhi: Oxford University Press, 1998.

Bharucha, Rustom. *The Theatre of Kanhailal: 'Pebet' and 'Memoirs of Africa'*, Calcutta: Seagull Books, 1992.

——. *Theatre and the World: Performance and the Politics of Cult* London and New York: Routledge, 1993.

——. 'Politician's Grin, Not the Buddha's Smile,' *Economic and* *Weekly*, 4 July 1998 (1998a).

——. *In the Name of the Secular: Contemporary Cultural Activ* New Delhi: Oxford University Press, 1998 (1998b).

——. *The Politics of Cultural Practice: Thinking Through* *of Globalization*, London: The Athlone Press and H of Wesleyan Press, 2000 (2000a).

____. *Consumed in Singapore: The Intercultural Spectacle of 'Lear'*, Singapore: CAS and Pagesetters, 2000 (2000b).

Bilgrami, Akeel. 'Secular Liberalism and Moral Psychology of Identity,' *Economic and Political Weekly*, 4 October 1997.

Blackburn, Stuart H. 'Performance Markers in an Indian Story-Type,' *Another Harmony: New Essays on the Folklore of India*, (eds.) Stuart H. Blackburn and A.K. Ramanujan. New Delhi: Oxford University Press, 1986.

____. 'Patterns of Development for Indian Oral Epics,' *Oral Epics in India*, (eds.) Stuart H. Blackburn, Peter J. Claus, Joyce B. Flueckiger and Susan S. Wadley. Berkeley: University of California Press, 1989.

Blackburn, Stuart H. and Joyce Burkhalter Flueckiger. 'Introduction,' *Oral Epics in India*, *op. cit.*, 1989.

Blackburn, Stuart H. and A.K. Ramanujan. 'Introduction,' *Another Harmony: New Essays on the Folklore of India*, *op. cit.*, 1986.

Bokil, Milind. 'Drought in Rajasthan: In Search of a Perspective,' *Economic and Political Weekly*, 25 November 2000.

____. 'De-notified and Nomadic Tribes: A Perspective,' *Economic and Political Weekly*, 12 January 2002.

Butalia, Urvashi. *The Other Side of Silence: Voices from the Partition of India*. New Delhi: Penguin Books India, 1998.

Chatterjee, Partha. *The Nation and its Fragments*. New Delhi: Oxford University Press, 1994.

____. 'Beyond the Nation? Or Within?,' *Economic and Political Weekly*, January 1997.

____. 'Community in the East,' *Economic and Political Weekly*, 7 February 1998.

____. 'On Civil and Political Society in Post-Colonial Democracy,' *Civil Society*, (eds.) Sudipta Kaviraj and Sunil Khilnani. Cambridge: Cambridge University Press, 2001.

Claus, Peter J. *Essays in Performance Analysis*, Prasaranga, Kuvempu University, Karnataka, 2001.

Claus, Peter J. and Frank J. Korom. *Indian Folklore and Folkloristics*, Udupi: Regional Regional Resources Centre, 1990.

ford, James. 'Notes on (Field)notes,' *Fieldnotes: The Makings of nthropology*, (ed.) Roger Sanjek. Ithaca: Cornell University Press, 1990.

ena. 'Mythological Film and its Framework of Meaning: Analysis of *ntoshi Ma*,' *Women and Culture*, (eds.) Kumkum Sangari and Sudesh Research Centre for Women's Studies, SNDT University, 1985.

al Events: An Anthropological Perspective in Contemporary w Delhi: Oxford University Press, 1996.

Devi, Mohini Smt. *Gīt Ratnamālā*. Scrapbook of songs printed by Ram Dutta Ojha, third edition, 1982.

Detha, Vijay Dan. *Gāi Gāi Re Samand Talāv* (Songs on the Embankment of the Lake). Jodhpur: Rajasthan Sangeet Nataka Akademi, n.d.

Dube, Saurabh. *Untouchable Pasts: Religion, Identity and Power Among a Central Indian Community, 1780–1950*. Albany: State University of New York Press, 1998.

Emigh, John with Ulrike Emigh. 'A Joker in the Deck: The Many Faces of a Rajasthani Bahurupiya,' *The Idea of Rajasthan: Explorations in Regional Identity*, Vol. 1, *Constructions*, (eds.) Karine Schomer, Joan L. Erdman, Deryck O. Lodrick, Lloyd I. Rudolph. Delhi: Manohar and American Institute of Indian Studies, 1994.

Folklife. 'The Advent of Asian Century in Folklore,' Jaisalmer Workshop Special, National Folklore Support Centre, Vol. 1, Issue 5, April 2001.

Gadgil, Madhav and Ramachandra Guha. *The Use and Abuse of Nature*. New Delhi: Oxford University Press, 2000.

Geertz, Clifford. *The Interpretation of Cultures*. New York: Basic Books, 1973.

Gold, Ann Grodzins. *Fruitful Journeys: The Ways of Rajasthani Pilgrims*. Delhi: Oxford University Press, 1989.

——. '*Jatra*, *Yatra* and Pressing Down Pebbles: Pilgrimage Within and Beyond Rajasthan,' *The Idea of Rajasthan: Explorations in Regional Identity*, *op. cit.*, 1994.

—— and Bhoju Ram Gujar. *In the Time of Trees and Sorrows: Nature, Power, and Memory in Rajasthan*. Durham: Duke University Press, 2002.

Glassie, Henry. 'Performance Theory and the Documentary Act,' *Folklife*, Vol.1, Issue 5, April 2001.

Hiltebeitel, Alf. *Rethinking India's Oral and Classical Epics: Draupadi among Rajputs, Muslims, and Dalits*. Chicago and London: The University of Chicago Press, 1999.

Honko, Lauri. 'Copyright and folklore,' *FF Network for the Folklore Fellows*, no. 21, March 2001.

Jairazbhoy, Nazir A. 'Music in Western Rajasthan: Stability and Change,' *Yearbook of the International Folk Music Council*, Vol. 9, 1977.

——. 'Kaṭhputli Puppetry of Rajasthan: Microcosm in a Little Tradition,' unpublished monograph, Delhi: ARCE Library, n.d.

Kakar, Sudhir. *Shamans, Mystics and Doctors: A Psychological Inquiry into India and its Healing Traditions*. New Delhi: Oxford University Press, 1982.

Kavita, Shobha, Shobhita and Sharda. 'Rural Women Speak,' *Seminar*, Special Issue on Sati, no. 342, 1988.

Khan, Dominique-Sila. 'The Kāmaḍ of Rajasthan—Priests of a Forgotten

Tradition,' *Journal of the Royal Asiatic Society*, Third Series, Vol. 6, Part 1, April 1996.

____. *Conversions and Shifting Identities: Ramdev Pīr and the Ismailis in Rajasthan*. New Delhi: Manohar and Centre de Sciences Humaines, 1997.

Khan, M.A. 'Revival and Modernisation of Traditional Water Management Systems in Western Rajasthan,' extended abstract, Second Congress on Traditional Sciences and Technologies in India, Madras, 1995, section 11, pp. 8–9.

Kolarkar, A.S. 'Khaḍīn: A Sound Traditional Method of Runoff Farming in Indian Desert,' paper presented in First Congress on Traditional Sciences and Technologies in India, Bombay, 1993, section 7, pp. 2–6.

Kosambi, Damodar Dharmanand. *An Introduction to the Study of Indian History*. Bombay: Popular Prakashan, 1956.

Kothari, Komal. *Monograph on Langas: A Folk Musician Caste of Rajasthan*, Borunda: Rupayan Sansthan, 1972.

____. 'The Shrine: An Expression of Social Needs,' *Gods of the Byways: Wayside Shrines of Rajasthan, Madhya Pradesh and Gujarat*, trans. Uma Anand, Museum of Modern Art, Oxford, 1982.

____. 'Performers, Gods, and Heroes in the Oral Epics of Rajasthan,' *Oral Epics in India*, *op. cit.*, 1989.

____. 'Introduction: A View on Castes of Marwar,' *The Castes of Marwar* (Census Report of 1891) by Munshi Hardyal Singh. Jodhpur: Books Treasure, 1990.

____. 'Musicians for the People: The Māngaṇiyārs of Western Rajasthan,' *The Idea of Rajasthan*, Vol. 1, *op. cit.*, 1994.

Manuel, Peter. *Cassette Culture: Popular Music and Technology in North India*. Chicago and London: The University of Chicago Press, 1993.

Mayaram, Shail. *Resisting Regimes: Mythology among the Meos*. New Delhi: Oxford University Press, 1996.

Miller, Joseph C. *The Twenty Four Brothers and Lord Devnarayan: the Story and Performance of a Folk Epic,'* Vols. 1–6, Ph.D dissertation, University of Pennsylvania, 1994.

Myers, Helen. 'Ethnomusicology,' *Ethnomusicology: An Introduction*. London: Macmillan, 1992.

Nanda, Meera. 'Breaking the Spell of Dharma: Case for Indian Enlightenment,' *Economic and Political Weekly*, July 2001.

Nandy, Ashis. 'Sati: A Nineteenth-Century Tale of Women, Violence and Protest,' *At the Edge of Psychology*. New Delhi: Oxford University Press, 1980.

____. 'The Politics of Secularism and the Recovery of Religious Tolerance,' first published in *Alternatives*, Vol. XIII, 1988, later reprinted in *Time*

Warps: The Insistent Politics of Silent and Evasive Pasts. Delhi: Permanent Black, 2002.

____. 'The Human Factor,' *The Illustrated Weekly of India*, 17 January 1988.

____. 'The Sociology of Sati,' *Indian Express*, 5 October 1987.

Pandey, Gyanendra. 'In Defence of the Fragment: Writing about Hindu-Muslim Riots in India Today,' *Economic and Political Weekly*, Annual Number, March 1991.

Pollock, Sheldon. 'The Cosmopolitan Vernacular,' *Journal of Asian Studies*, Vol. 57, no. 1, 1998.

Ramanujan, A.K. *The Collected Essays of A.K.Ramanujan*, (ed.) Vinay Dharwadker. New Delhi: Oxford University Press, 1999.

____. *Folktales of India*. New York: Pantheon, 1991.

Rao, Velcheru Narayana. 'Epics and Ideologies: Six Telugu Folk Epics,' *Another Harmony: New Essays on the Folklore of India*, *op. cit.*, 1986.

Sainath, P. *Everyboy Loves a Good Drought*. New Delhi: Penguin Books India, 1997.

Sarkar, Sujeet. 'Three normal years in a hundred,' *Humanscape*, June 2001.

Seeger, Anthony. 'Ethnomusicologists, Archives, Professional Organizations, and the Shifting Ethics of Intellectual Property,' *Yearbook for Traditional Music*, Vol. 28, 1996.

Seminar. Special issue on Sati, no. 342. New Delhi: February 1988.

Sen, Amartya. *Poverty and Famine: An Essay on Entitlement and Deprivation*. Oxford University Press, 1981.

Sengupta, Nirmal. 'Traditional Water Management Systems—Primitive or Precious?,' paper presented at the First Congress on Traditional Sciences and Technologies in India, Bombay, 1993, section 11, pp. 2–8.

Shekhawat, Prahlad Singh. 'Traditional System of Water Harvesting and Development in Arid Rajasthan', paper presented at the First Congress on Traditional Sciences and Technologies in India, Bombay, 1993, section 7, pp. 60–4.

Shiva, Vandana and Ashok Emani and Afsar H. Jafri. 'Globalisation and Threat to Seed Security: Case of Transgenic Cotton Trials in India,' *Economic and Political Weekly*, March 6–13, 1999.

Singh, K.S. *People of India: Rajasthan*, Vol. XXXVIII, Part One. Mumbai: Popular Prakashan, 1998.

Smith, John D. *The Epic of Pabuji: A Study, Transcription, and Translation*. Cambridge: Cambridge University Press, 1991.

Spivak, Gayatri Chakravorty. 'Cultural Talks in the Hot Peace: Revisiting the "Global Village"', *Cosmopolitics: Thinking and Feeling Beyond the Nation*, (eds.) Bruce Robbins and Pheng Cheah. Minneapolis: University of Minnesota Press, 1998.

Sutherland, Sally J. 'Suttee, Sati, and Sahagamana: An Epic Misunderstanding?,' *Economic and Political Weekly*, 25 June 1994.

Thapar, Romila. *Ancient Indian Social History: Some Interpretations.* Hyderabad: Orient Longman, 1978.

——. *Time as a Metaphor of History: Early India.* New Delhi: Oxford India Paperbacks, 1996.

Vaid, Sudesh and Kumkum Sangari. 'Institutions, Beliefs, Ideologies: Widow Immolation in Contemporary Rajasthan,' *Economic and Political Weekly*, 27 April 1991.

Vanaik, Achin. *Communalism Contested: Religion, Modernity and Secularization.* New Delhi: Vistaar Publications, 1997.

Vani, M.S. 'Traditional Irrigation Systems: Law and Policy,' paper presented at the First Congress on Traditional Sciences and Technologies in India, Bombay, 1993, section 7, pp. 44–49.

Vatsyayan, Kapila. 'Reflections: Interview with M.D.Muthukumaraswamy and Venu,' *Folklife, op.cit.*, 2001.

Wadley, Susan. 'The *Kathā* of Sakat: Two Tellings,' *Another Harmony: New Essays on the Folklore of India, op. cit.*, 1986.

Women and Media Committee of the Bombay Union of Journalists. 'Trial by Fire: A Report on Roop Kanwar's death,' 1987.

Zemp, Hugo. 'The/An Ethnomusicologist and the Record Business,' *Yearbook for Traditional Music*, Vol. 28, 1996.

GLOSSARY

ākhā : whole grain which can be ground to flour and cooked as *roṭi* or *chapāti*, as opposed to *chokhā*.

ākṛā : type of plant in the desert.

adak : healthy looking plant that grows out of man-made seed with no reproductive capacity.

āgor : catchment area for any open water body.

ajmā : *ajwain*, a spice.

akāl : drought, famine.

alaukik : the otherworldly, supernatural.

algojā : a double-flute providing a drone effect, played with fingers on both flutes simultaneously.

anāwari : calculation of yield of crop during drought year based on division of sixteen annas to a rupee.

ān : sacred grassland where cattle can graze but where the grass cannot be cut.

arthāv : the explanatory part of any oral narrative declaimed in prose, which counterpoints the *gāv* or the sung part.

arthi : bier.

asinchit : non-irrigated.

āzān : Islamic call to prayer.

bahurupiā : itinerant impersonators who mime gods and goddesses in elaborate costume, and mimic the idiosyncrasies of human characters.

bēr : agricultural land where rain water flows without cutting into the soil.

bājrā : pearl millet.
barsālo : songs related to the rainy season.
bāvaḍi : step-well.
bāwan vīr : fifty-two male malignant spirits under the command of Mahavīr Hanumān.
Behtarā : literally 72, the plague infested drought year of 1915, which, as calculated by Indian (Vikram Samvat) calendar, is 1972.
bel : a poetic composition that is longer than a ballad and shorter than an epic; also the name of a related metre in Rajasthani.
badhāwo : ceremonial welcome song.
bhains : female buffalo.
bhainsā : male buffalo.
bhajan : generic term for devotional song.
Bhil : a category associated primarily with tribals living in the hilly regions of south-west Rajasthan, also associated with low-caste groups in the desert zone. The term has a wider range of reference incorporating tribal communities in Gujarat and Madhya Pradesh.
bhomiyā : a folk hero who sacrifices his life for the protection of cows.
bhūnd : abusive and insulting verses used against patrons.
bhopā : a category including shaman-priests presiding over shrines, also used for the epic narrators of Pabuji and Dev Narayan.
chabutrā : platform.
chakri : a women's dance form with circular movements, performed by the Kanjar women from Kota region.
chal-sampati : moveable property.
chanā : gram.
changḍi : small frame-drum.
chauki : term used for '*thān*' (shrine) on an active day of worship.
Chhabbīsā : literally 26, the drought year of 1869, which, as calculated by Indian (Vikram Samvat) calendar, is 1926.
chhand : metre in poetic composition.
Chhappannā : literally 56, the drought year of 1899, which, as calculated by Indian (Vikram Samvat) calendar, is 1956.

chitā	:	funeral pyre.
chokhā	:	any rice-like grain that is boiled with total absorption of water, as opposed to *ākhā*.
chokhlā	:	a cluster of twelve contiguous villages ritually activated during death among Hindu caste groups.
chorāsi	:	a group of seven *chokhlās* constituting eighty-four villages, which are activated during disputes among local communities.
chowk	:	courtyard.
chuṛēl	:	a malignant spirit of a dead woman possessing another human being.
chuṛiyān	:	bangles.
dān	:	charity through gifts, alms, donations.
ḍākan	:	a living woman perceived as a witch with an evil eye.
Damāmi	:	a professional musician caste.
dēr	:	an expanse of land where rain water collects in a depression and dries within some time, used for winter crop without irrigation.
ḍāyan	:	another name of *ḍākan*.
devi-devatā	:	goddesses and gods.
Dev Nārāyaṇ	:	a legendary folk deity worshipped by the Gujar and other cow and sheep-herding communities; the subject of a long epic narrative named after him.
dhām	:	open platform shrine on which the icon is placed; the term *dhām* is used for that period of time when a large number of pilgrims are attracted to a particular shrine following a miracle or supernatural event.
dhaniā	:	coriander.
dharamshālā	:	inn; generally free or very cheap lodgings run by religious orders and caste organizations in pilgrimage sites.
dhāṭ	:	ethno-geographic region of the desert.
ḍhol	:	a large cylindrical drum struck with the hand on the right side and beaten with a stick on the left.
ḍholak	:	a barrel-shaped double-headed drum played with hands on both sides.
Ḍholi	:	a professional musician caste; the term is used more generally to refer to musicians from other caste grups.
dhorā	:	sand-dune.
dohā	:	couplet.

dūdhiā : milky.
gērmumkin kasht : non-cultivable land.
gāḷi : literally 'abuse'; a song sung in jest at wedding ceremonies, generally directed against the in-laws.
gandh : aroma, smell from incense.
gāv : the sung part of any oral narrative.
gehun : wheat.
ghāgrā : full-length skirt.
gharānā : school representing a distinct musical style.
ghāṭ : crushed grain.
ghaṭṭi : stone-mill rotated by the hand.
ghuṛlā : literally horse, the vehicle of a deity that manifests itself when the *bhopā* goes into trance.
gobar : cow dung.
gochar : grassland used as grazing grounds for cattle.
gotra : lineage based on kinship ties between particular groups, initially restricted to Brahman communities.
gūgri : boiled whole grain that can be sweetened or made spicy and eaten as a complete meal.
guṛ : jaggery.
gwālā : milkman.
hār : necklace.
hazuriā : assistant or ritual attendat of all activities conducted in the shrine.
hunkārio : respondent to any oral epic narrative.
imli : tamarind.
jāt : caste; the word has etymological connections with 'birth' and 'origin' linked through the hereditary ties of family, profession, and community.
jāgraṇ : an all-right singing session of devotional songs.
jajmān : patron.
jalkāl : drought condition resulting from the absence of water.
jamā : an open or secret congregation of the faithful gathered together for an all-night religious ceremony.
janglāyat : forest land.
jantar : a two-gourd stringed instrument with frets used for Dev Nārāyaṇ epic performances.
jātrī : a pilgrim who visits local and small shrines and temples for the fulfillment of specific needs.

jawār	:	sorghum.
jīrā	:	cumin.
jīv	:	life.
jhalrā	:	well of large circumference with water oozing from the side walls.
jhaṛū	:	broom.
jhunjhār	:	the spirit of someone who dies a violent death, also used for the icon representing the spirit.
joganiā vīr	:	sixty-four female evil spirits under the control of Mahavīr Hanumān.
Jogi	:	a generic term for nomadic groups associated with the Nāth sect.
jogiā sārangi	:	bowed stringed instrument used by Jogi community.
jyot	:	sacred flame.
jyotishi	:	astrologer.
kāl	:	time.
kacheri	:	musical assembly.
kaḍā	:	thick bangle.
kaṛhi	:	a light curry made of gram flour and buttermilk.
kaḍuva kāvā	:	first meal from the in-law's or neighbor's house after coming home from the cremation.
kafan	:	shroud.
kāgaz-miṭṭi	:	*papier-mâché*
kāi	:	algae, green fungus.
Kālbeliā	:	a nomadic Jogi group providing technical services.
kamāychā	:	bowed stringed instrument with round belly played by the Manganiyars.
kānchli	:	bodice, blouse.
kānkaṛi	:	musical riddle-game played during marriage ceremonies with stringed instruments, involving both parties of the bride and the bridegroom.
kaṭhputli	:	stringed wooden puppet.
kāvaḍ	:	a small wooden shrine in the shape of a cupboard.
kendra	:	a two-gourd stringed instrument without frets played with plectrum for drone and rhythm.
keri	:	raw mango.
khaḍin	:	indigenous irrigation system in desert area.
khālsā	:	villages from which the king collects the revenue directly.
kharif	:	summer crop.

khaṛtāl	:	wooden clappers.
khatmebhāi	:	a group of twelve villages ritually activated during death among Muslim castes
khīch	:	grain pounded and cooked with water.
khur	:	cleft in animal's hooves.
koṭwāl	:	literally a police official, the term is also used for the ritual attendant of a shrine.
koylā	:	coal.
kunḍ	:	square pool surrounded by steps on four sides.
kunḍa	:	open-mouthed clay pot.
kuri	:	natural seed used as cereal.
Langā	:	endogamous Muslim musician caste group.
līd	:	horse and donkey dung.
lilā	:	divine play.
lolaṛ	:	effigy made to insult patron.
māch	:	North Indian operatic folk dance-drama.
mākhaṇ	:	butter
makkā	:	maize.
malichā	:	natural weed used as cereal which grows in wheat fields.
Māngaṇiyār	:	endogamous Muslim musician caste group.
manjirā	:	cymbals.
mashak	:	bag-pipe.
masjid	:	mosque.
māṭā	:	pot-drum played for performance of *Pābūjī* epic.
mehndi	:	henna.
mīngṇā	:	camel dung.
mīngṇi	:	goat dung.
melā	:	religious fair.
mēṭ	:	clay.
moriyā	:	peacock.
moṭh	:	brown lentil.
moulvi	:	Muslim priest.
mujrā	:	literally 'salutation', a dance form with erotic overtones performed by professional women dancers for men.
Mukhbānchā Bhāṭ	:	oral genealogist.
mumkin kāsht	:	cultivable land.
murti	:	icon.
nāḍi	:	man-made pond.
nāi	:	barber.

nēg	:	ceremonial payment
nath	:	nose ring.
nauṭanki	:	North Indian form of operatic folk dance-drama.
Nāyak	:	a low-caste community identified with the performance of the *Pābūjī* epic.
nīl	:	indigo.
nyāt	:	community determined over a large geographical area.
oḷakh	:	invocational songs sung in honour of gods and goddesses at their shrines.
oran	:	sacred grove.
osar	:	an elaborate death ritual feast of the Langā community.
Pābūjī	:	a legendary folk deity worshipped by diverse pastoral groups in Rajasthan; the subject of an epic sung and performed by *bhopās* (epic narrators).
panchatatva	:	the five elements.
panth	:	sect.
paramparā	:	tradition.
paṛ	:	painted scroll used in performances of *Pābūjī* and *Dev Nārāyaṇ*.
pāṭavi	:	primogeniture inheritance.
pāṭh	:	religious text.
pāwā joḍi	:	double flute, one functioning as drone while the other plays the melody.
phul	:	literally, 'flowers'; bone remains of the cremated body.
pitar	:	male member of a family who dies prematurely without children, and who manifests himself as a spirit.
pitrāni	:	the spirit of the first wife who dies and later manifests herself in the family; she has to be appeased or else she becomes malignant.
pothibānchā bhāṭ	:	a genealogist who maintains written records.
prasād	:	sacred food, offering to the gods which is distributed after being blessed.
pujāri	:	priest.
pungi	:	single-reed aerophonic instrument.
punya	:	merit.
rāb	:	grain flour blended with buttermilk and cooked.
rābi	:	winter crop.

rātijāgā	:	an all-night singing session held within family households for birth, marriage, and death ceremonies.
Rāikā	:	a pastoral nomadic community herding camel or sheep.
rāvanhatthā	:	bowed stringed instrument used for the singing of *Pābūjī* epic.
rekhaṇ	:	a locust.
sānḍ	:	she-camel.
sāgar ke kuey	:	a well with a small diameter and deep water source linked to an aqueduct.
sākaliā	:	a technique of playing cymbals in the Terātāli dance form.
sākh	:	literally 'branch', Rajasthani term for sub-caste.
santhāra	:	voluntary denial of food and water leading to death, practised primarily by the Jains.
sar	:	type of area where rain water collects and can be drained; used for winter crop without irrigation.
sarson	:	mustard.
sīr	:	well with underground running water source.
sevan	:	rich grass with high nutritional value growing in arid regions.
sivāychak	:	fallow land made available by government bodies to diverse parties.
sinchit	:	irrigated.
sindhi sārangi	:	a bowed stringed instrument with hour-glass shaped belly played primarily by the Langā musicians.
siyāri	:	a type of *ḍākan* or witch, who can look into the past and has a limited power to foretell the future.
sūnṭh	:	dried ginger.
stuti	:	invocatory prayer.
subedār	:	military official from the ranks.
surṇāi	:	a double-reed aerophonic instrument.
talāq	:	literally 'divorce', used figuratively to cut ties with patrons.
tambuḍi	:	small tent, diminutive of '*tambu*', tent.
tandurā	:	a five-stringed drone instrument played with a plectrum.
ṭānkā	:	water-harvesting tank
terātāli	:	a dance form performed by the women from the Kāmaḍ community with cymbals attached to their bodies.

thardā	:	ethno-geographic region in the desert.
thān	:	platform on which the icon is placed in an outdoor shrine.
Thōri	:	a pejorative term for the Nāyak community.
toran	:	a wooden emblem hung above the main entrance of the bride's house to be touched with the sword by the bridegroom during the wedding ceremony.
trikāl	:	drought condition resulting from the absence of three elements—water, fodder and grain.
ugarne wāli	:	woman who leads a group song.
vāni	:	sacred grove where no tree can be cut.
vāru ḍhol	:	a particular rhythmic beat played on the *ḍhol* during states of emergency and war.
vesh	:	disguise, as used in the impersonation of gods and goddesses and other human characters in *bahurupiā* performances.
vrat kathā	:	stories told by women during their ritual fast (*vrat*).
yātrī	:	a pilgrim who visits established *tīrthas* or pilgrim sites for salvation, merit and self-renewal.

INDEX